PEOPLE OF CHACO

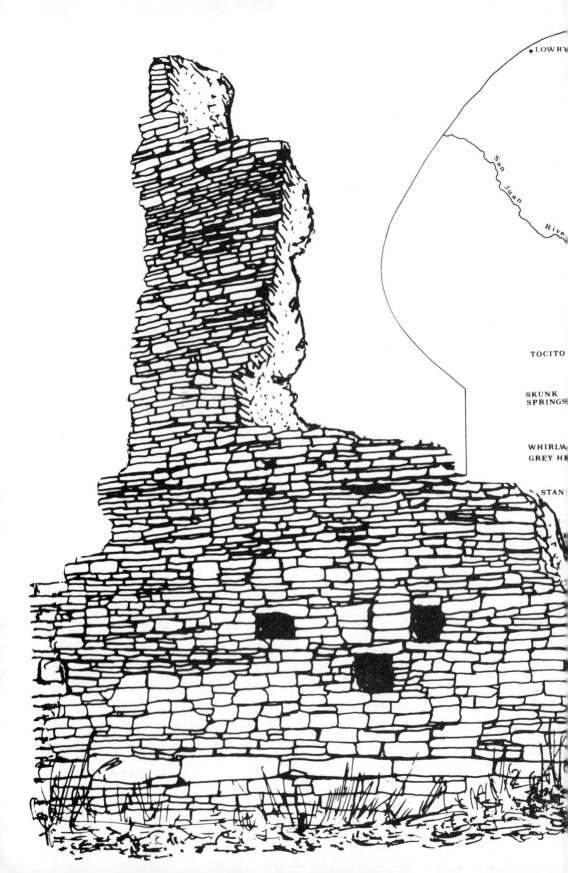

● LOWRY

San Juan River

TOCITO

SKUNK
SPRINGS

WHIRLW
GREY HI

STAN

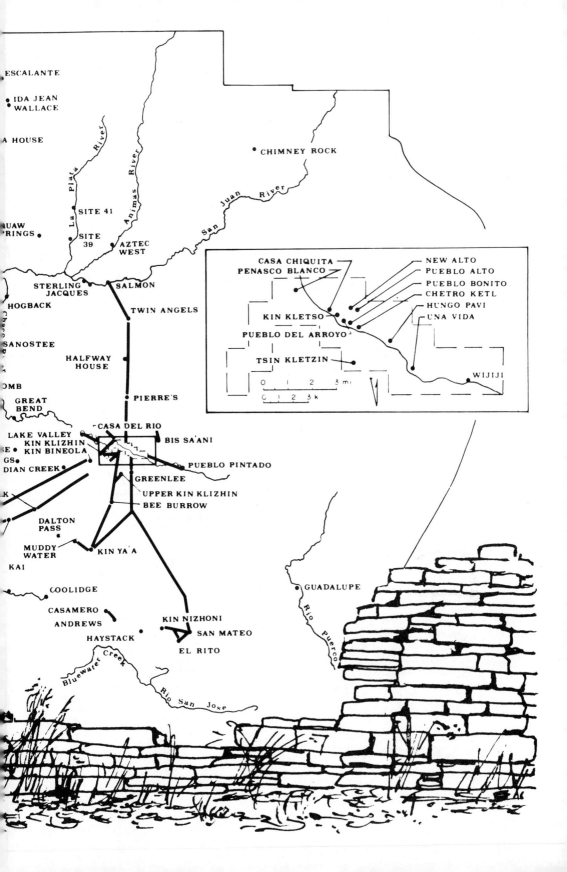

ESCALANTE

IDA JEAN
WALLACE

A HOUSE

CHIMNEY ROCK

SITE 41

QUAW
RINGS

SITE
39

AZTEC
WEST

STERLING
JACQUES

SALMON

HOGBACK

TWIN ANGELS

SANOSTEE

HALFWAY
HOUSE

OMB

PIERRE'S

GREAT
BEND

CASA DEL RIO

LAKE VALLEY
KIN KLIZHIN
KIN BINEOLA

BIS SA'ANI

GS

DIAN CREEK

PUEBLO PINTADO

GREENLEE

UPPER KIN KLIZHIN

BEE BURROW

DALTON
PASS

MUDDY
WATER

KIN YA'A

KAI

COOLIDGE

GUADALUPE

CASAMERO

ANDREWS

KIN NIZHONI

HAYSTACK

SAN MATEO

EL RITO

Bluewater Creek

Rio San Jose

La Plata River

Animas River

San Juan River

Chaco River

Rio Puerco

CASA CHIQUITA
PENASCO BLANCO

NEW ALTO
PUEBLO ALTO
PUEBLO BONITO
CHETRO KETL
HUNGO PAVI
UNA VIDA

KIN KLETSO

PUEBLO DEL ARROYO

TSIN KLETZIN

WIJIJI

0   1   2   3 mi
0   1   2   3 k

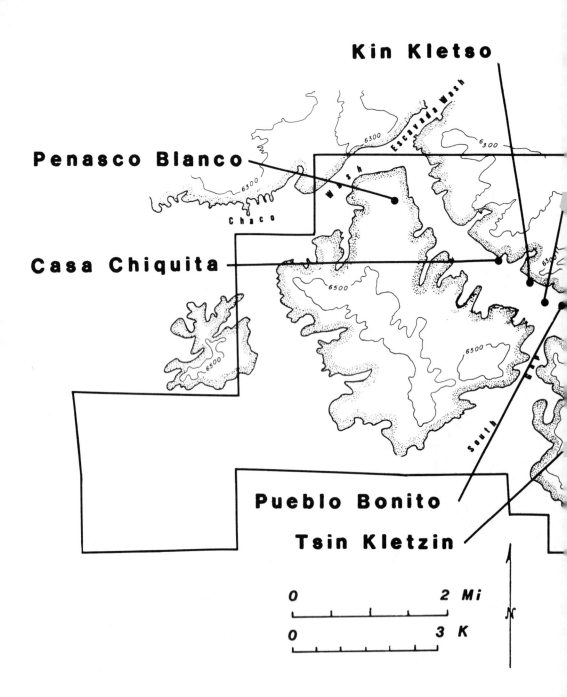

Kin Kletso

Penasco Blanco

Casa Chiquita

Pueblo Bonito

Tsin Kletzin

6300

6300

6300

6500

6500

6500

Chaco

Escavada Wash

Wash

South

0   2 Mi

0   3 K

N

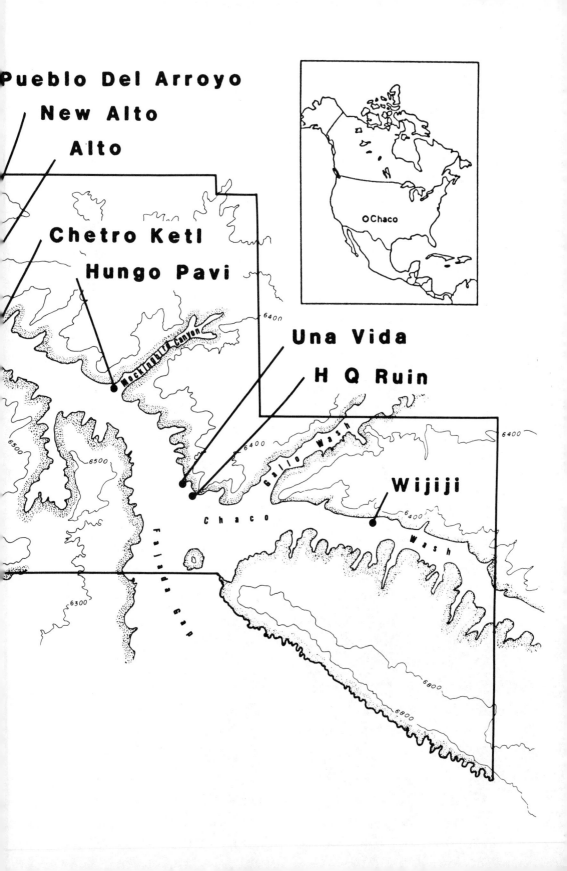

Pueblo Del Arroyo
New Alto
Alto

Chetro Ketl
Hungo Pavi

Una Vida
H Q Ruin

Wijiji

Mockingbird Canyon

Chaco

Gallo Wash

Wash

Fajada Gap

O Chaco

6400
6500
6500
6400
6400
6400
6300
6800
6800

PEOPLE OF CHACO

A Canyon and Its Culture

Updated and Expanded

KENDRICK FRAZIER

W. W. NORTON & COMPANY · *New York London*

Manufacturing by The Maple-Vail Book Manufacturing Group
Book design by Jacques Chazaud
Production manager: Amanda Morrison

ISBN 0-393-31825-7 (pbk.)

W. W. Norton & Company, Inc.
500 Fifth Avenue, New York, N.Y. 10110
www.wwnorton.com

W. W. Norton & Company Ltd.
Castle House, 75/76 Wells Street, London W1T 3QT

1 2 3 4 5 6 7 8 9 0

Dedicated to the People of Chaco,
past and present:

the Ancient Ones who created this unique
prehistoric culture and the cities of stone that
so touch our imagination,

the Pueblo Indians of today,
who continue to live a life of harmony with nature
and whose ancestors include the Chacoans,

and the archaeologists who probe and illuminate
the mysteries of Chaco,

with respect and admiration.

Contents

Preface to the 2005 Edition 7
Prologue: The Ancient Way 13

1. The Lieutenant and the Cowboy *23*
2. Judd and the Geo Excavations *43*
3. The Secrets of Time *63*
4. The Chaco Project *85*
5. Canals and Irrigation *95*
6. Roadways and Signal Towers *105*
7. The Outliers *128*
8. Population, Burials, and the Mexican Connection *153*
9. The Chaco Phenomenon *171*
10. The Sky-Watchers of Chaco *188*
11. Destinies and Destinations *203*
12. Chaco in the Twenty-First Century *213*
13. The Quest Continues *228*
14. Cosmography, Meridian, and Violence *259*
15. The Chaco Synthesis Project *283*

APPENDIX. Chaco Place Names *307*
SELECTED BIBLIOGRAPHY *309*
INDEX *319*

Preface to the 2005 Edition

This is a major expansion and update over previous editions. What was one new chapter in the 1999 edition has become four new chapters in this 2005 edition. Such a considerable undertaking wasn't my original intention, but I found that the extraordinary amount of new archaeological work in the past few years concerning Chaco demanded it.

In those new chapters (12 to 15) I describe new studies by Tom Windes and Dabney Ford examining how the Chacoans cut, processed, finished, and transported the wood to create their impressive structures; studies by two different scientific groups, the most recent by Steve Durand, using modern chemical evidence to identify the locations of the distant forests that supplied that wood; a fascinating study by John Stein, Richard Friedman, and Dabney Ford combining classic archaeological analysis with modern geographic information systems and the global positioning system to reenvision and precisely "reconstruct" the Chacoans' iconic Pueblo Bonito in its different construction phases over two-plus centuries. I try to summarize a new book-length reevaluation of the central place of Pueblo Bonito in the Chacoan world. I've described what some now call the Chacoan "cityscape," a dense array of smaller structures that once lined the canyon, housed most of its population, and brought a sense of life to the otherwise monumental majesty of the major Chacoan "great houses." I've added a section on cosmographic expression to do some justice to the remarkable work of Anna Sofaer and her Solstice Project on cosmographic orientations and interrelationships of many of the major Chacoan structures. I've delved deeper into the touchy question of violence in the prehistoric Southwest, Chaco included, and tried to provide a bit of a balanced assessment. Along the way I've encountered fascinating ideas, such as the possibility that Pueblo Bonito may have had just one "master architect" or that all of Chaco may have had two elite rulers.

And then there is the Chaco Synthesis Project. The core of this book begins with the Chaco Project of the 1970s and 1980s, the largest archaeological field project ever carried out in Chaco Canyon. It is fitting that, with this new edition, it ends with the Chaco Synthesis Project (1998–2005), now nearing completion, an ambitious effort to assimilate and synthesize all that was learned in the Chaco Project. If the Chaco Project was classic field archaeology, the Chaco Synthesis Project represents another way good science works. Virtually all the Chacoan archaeologist "old hands" (whatever their age) came together with fresh new voices in a variety of forums to discuss, rethink, reexamine, and reassess everything we learned, or thought we learned, about Chaco in the past three decades. The output of this project, led by Steve Lekson, has already been prodigious—entire special issues of archaeological journals, book-length conference proceedings, and a massive final synthesis volume nearly complete. Their goal has been to provide insight and understanding into the substantial fascinations, complexities, and mysteries of Chacoan culture. How broad was its extent? How was it organized? How powerful was it and how was that power exercised? It has been my task, and my pleasure, to in effect eavesdrop on the results of their reassessments and try to provide, for you, a synthesis of their synthesis, some kind of readable summary that does justice to their effort. Chapter 15 is my attempt at that.

Just as Chaco Project Director Jim Judge in the 1980s threw open to me the then still mostly unpublished results of the Chaco Project, Steve Lekson has done the same for me now with the Chaco Synthesis Project. In a commendable commitment to communicating the results of Chacoan research to the public, he generously allowed me access to the draft final synthesis volume so that I might provide you the latest information and insights. He didn't need to do that, but I am grateful that he did. He has also been generous in countless other ways, and this new edition could not have been accomplished without his help. Tom Windes continues his prolific and brilliant work into countless fascinating aspects of Chacoan life, and he too has once again been open with his help and support. He graciously invited me on one of his field trips outside the canyon. Other archaeologists likewise helped tremendously: John Kantner, Stephen Durand, Jill Neitzel, Richard Friedman, and John Stein, plus astronomer McKim Malville, to name a few. It was a great pleasure to renew my intellectual friendship with Anna Sofaer.

My early trips with her and my family up to the extraordinary Fajada Butte solstice marker in the late 1970s started a chain of events that led to this book. Her continuing passion for demonstrating expressions of the Chacoans' cosmology in the design, orientations, and placement of their structures knows, I am happy to say, no end. A delightful informal, impromptu meeting with key archaeological staff at the Chaco Culture National Historical Park visitor center in early January 2004 helped me get this new edition under way. I am grateful for their encouragement and enthusiasm. They were Stephanie Dubois, superintendent; Bradley Shattuck, chief of natural resources; Russ Bodnar, chief of interpretation; Dabney Ford, archaeologist; and Roger Moore, vanishing treasures archaeologist. Curator Wendy Bustard gave me an impromptu tour of the National Park Service's Chaco Culture National Historical Park Museum Collection on the University of New Mexico campus. David A. Phillips, Jr., curator of archaeology at UNM's Maxwell Museum of Anthropology, showed me the museum's collection of Chacoan pottery and artifacts and took me on a tour of the new Hibben Center, next to the museum, where both the NPS and UNM Chaco collections will be housed. At W. W. Norton, Ed Barber, who got me started on *People of Chaco* so many years ago, again has been instrumental, and I am grateful for his appreciation of this book and his continual commitment to keep it as up to date as seems humanly possible. Amy Cherry and Lucinda Bartley have guided the updated manuscript and made valuable suggestions for improvements. Thanks to many Chaco researchers for new graphics and photos, and to photographer friends Randy Montoya and Susanne Page for several fine new photos of theirs. I am grateful to many other friends and colleagues (especially at Sandia National Laboratories, New Mexicans for Science and Reason, the Skeptical Inquirer, and the Center for Inquiry) for encouragement and support. And to my family, which, like this book, has expanded over several editions, and especially Ruth, who again has been with me every step of the way.

—Kendrick Frazier
January 2005

PEOPLE OF CHACO

Pueblo del Arroyo at sunset. Photo by author.

PROLOGUE
The Ancient Way

We know them by their works, these ancient people of the rock. All across the plateaus of the Four Corners region of the southwestern United States we find their "ruins," our curiously inadequate word for the tangible remains of culture. Their long-deserted villages of stone engender both sadness and awe. We cannot contemplate the remnants of their structures without seeking to understand the essence of their lives. We feel our mind's vision drifting back into the mists of prehistory. Back a thousand years, when culture flowered here.

These are the people the archaeologists call the Anasazi, the ancient ones, the ancestors of the Pueblo Indians, whose scattered villages dot the valleys and mesas of northwestern New Mexico and northeastern Arizona today. We might better call them by the Hopi word *Hisatsinom* or the Zuni word *Enote.*

More than likely they considered themselves, whatever was the sound in their language, *the People,* for their life and their land was their world. They were builders, these people, and although the signs of their habitation are nearly everywhere across the vast Four Corners region, three sites of concentrated civilization command most attention: Mesa Verde in Colorado, Kayenta in Arizona, and Chaco Canyon in New Mexico.

We will be concerned particularly with the Chacoans here. But before turning to see what made the people of Chaco different in some special ways, let's explore what they had in common with their other Anasazi or Hisatsinom brothers.

We view cultures, present and past, through the filter of our own perceptions. Some view the daily life of the Anasazi as unmitigatedly harsh, a constant struggle against the vicissitudes of the semi-arid climate and marginal growing conditions. Others, while not denying the difficulties, emphasize the sense of community that gave structure and support so the people could cope with everyday problems.

Take these words, from archaeologist Neil M. Judd writing in the 1920s on his view of everyday life in Pueblo Bonito, the largest of all structures in Chaco Canyon: "Life in prehistoric Bonito was surprisingly modern. It was both strenuous and complex; yet it remained simple. . . . The daily struggle for existence was paramount then as now, and each inhabitant of the village, old and young alike, necessarily contributed his share to the support of the community as a whole."

Anasazi life and culture in the Four Corners region has been fairly well delineated. The people lived in houses made of stone. Sometimes these structures were tucked into depressions high up into the sides of canyons, as with the cliff-dwellers of Mesa Verde. At other places, the homes were on mesa tops or along the sandy bottoms of shallow canyons, as we see at Chaco. Sometimes the walls of these houses were held together with mortar, sometimes not. The inside walls were often smoothly plastered. The roofs were supported by huge beams across which smaller wood strips and branches were laid and fastened securely to form a snug ceiling.

The ancient ones were patient and expert farmers. They had to be to eke out subsistence crops in marginal conditions. They intensively cultivated corn, beans, and squash in nearby garden plots. They used as their main farming implements wooden digging sticks and hoe-shovel combinations consisting of a forked stick to which was lashed a flat rock. Vegetables were the staples of their diet, but they also ate rabbit and occasionally larger game such as deer. They ground their corn into meal on smoothed-out grinding stones, or *metates.*

They had bows and arrows, and carrying sacks and sleeping pads made of yucca fiber. Their sandals were plaited with split leaves of the yucca, or they were woven from its tough fibers. They made exquisite pottery in much the same manner their predecessors of centuries before had made baskets: they created a bowl or jar by building up layers of long ropes of, in this case, clay. Then they pinched together and smoothed out the sides and polished them with a stone. Using yucca fibers as their brushes, they painted their pottery in characteristic styles and designs that enable archaeologists, those modern-day sleuths, to classify cultures in time and place.

It is not hard to imagine one of these ancient villages—the adults going about their tasks, the children playing or learning at their side. We can almost smell the rabbit stew cooking in the earthen pot and the aroma of corn roasting over the coals of the cookfire; we can almost see the freshmade paper-thin *piki* bread—all this in anticipation of the day's-end meal after the men have returned from attending to the fields or building a new village structure.

Without a written history, we can only speculate about key elements of their lives. Yet the traditions of their descendants may serve as some guide to ancient customs. A statement by the Hopi Indians about their land and matrilineal system perhaps contains truth about the ancient ways as well. This document was signed by 123 clan and village leaders from all three Hopi mesas and addressed to "the Washington chiefs" in 1894:

"The family, the dwelling house and the field are inseparable, because the woman is the heart of these, and they rest with her. Among us the family traces its kin from the mother, hence all its possessions are hers. The man builds the house but the woman is the owner, because she repairs and preserves it; the man cultivates the field, but he renders its harvest into the woman's keeping, because upon her it rests to prepare the food, and the surplus of stores for barter depends upon her thrift.

"A man plants the fields of his wife, and the fields assigned to the children she bears, and informally he calls them his, although in fact they are not. Even of the field which he inherits from his mother, its harvest he may dispose of at will, but the field itself he may not. . . . Our fields and houses always remain with our mother's family. . . . Our fields are numerous but small, and several belonging to the same family may be close together or they may be miles apart, because arable localities are not continuous."

The document also refers to the exigencies of nature they face, as their ancient ancestors had before them:

"In the Spring and early Summer there usually comes from the Southwest a succession of gales, oftentimes strong enough to blow away the sandy soil from the face of some of our fields, and to expose the underlying clay, which is hard, and sour, and barren; as the sand is the only fertile land, when it moves, the planters must follow it, and other fields must be provided in place of those which have been devastated."

Sometimes these events require limited changes in land holding, all "effected by mutual discussion and concession among the elders, and among all the thinking men and women of the family groups interested." Under this system of holding and method of planting "we provide ourselves with food in abundance. . . ."

In many ways their lives and concerns *were* much as ours: the needs of food, clothing, and shelter occupied their attention. Yet something is missing here. The spiritual view of the ancient ones, if their Pueblo Indian successors are a reasonable guide, gave their culture its essential structure and governed their daily activities. Religion permeated every aspect of life; indeed it was inseparable from life itself. Chaco Canyon's buildings are marked by abundant, giant kivas, the underground ceremonial chambers that serve as centers of all ritual observances. In many respects these kivas resemble those in today's Hopi villages on the mesas of northeastern Arizona or those the nineteen Pueblo tribes of New Mexico use throughout the year for ceremonial functions.

Ritual and ceremony provide meaning and solidity to life where otherwise there would be only environmental uncertainty. They emphasize place, purpose, and unity where otherwise there would be lack of identity and cultural fragmentation. Indian cultures, particularly the Pueblo cultures, are rich in their many layered world view, a richness that eludes much of modern society. We have no reason to believe their Anasazi or Hisatsinom ancestors devoted less attention to essential spiritual matters.

In just one room of just one structure, Chetro Ketl, in Chaco Canyon, archaeologists found more than 200 ritual artifacts, mostly painted and carved wooden figures: birds (parrots, turkey heads, blackbirds), horns, hoops, discs, prayersticks, lightning lattices, and plume circles. On many of them the brightly colored paints—green, brown, black, yellow, white, red, and blue—decorating these eleventh-century ritual articles still shine bright and clear.

Archaeologist R. Gwinn Vivian in a report a few years ago on these discoveries recalled that work: "It has been about 30 years but I can recall the hurried preparations we made following a telephone call from my father [archaeologist R. Gordon Vivian] asking that we go to Chaco to help him excavate and record what he thought could be an important collection of painted wooden artifacts from a room in Chetro Ketl. November weather in Chaco can be pleasant, and in 1947 we were fortunate in having a number of warm days while we worked in Room 93. . . . As each item was discovered it was cleaned, plotted on a gridded plan of the room, and then removed. . . . The complexity and superb preservation of the artifacts helped to stimulate our interest through long hours of cramped work. . . . When we had finished it was clear that the artifacts represented the most complete collection of painted wooden artifacts ever recovered from an Anasazi site."

Vivian and his collaborators believe these particular ritual artifacts do suggest certain means for religious expression. The colorful and intricate wooden figures were components of "elaborate paraphernalia" developed for processions, dances, and other public rites "to achieve more dramatic effect." In this view, they were used not so much for secretive and limited esoteric rites but for public dramatizations on roads, within the great kivas, and in town plazas.

Whether secret or public, ceremony and ritual shape Pueblo life today, and almost certainly did so as well among their ancient ancestors at Chaco and elsewhere.

From infancy onward, Pueblo children are brought up among a caring family and community. They are imbued with a sense of sharing and participation in all the culture's values, of a communal identification with the clan, tribe, land, and natural world. I don't doubt, for instance, that the children of the ancient ones, at Chaco Canyon and elsewhere, were prayerfully presented to the sun a certain number of days after their birth.

Ethnologist Mathilde Stevenson has described this beautiful and solemn ceremony among the Zuni people: "... On the morning of the tenth day the child is taken from its bed of sand, ... and upon the left arm of the paternal grandmother is carried for the first time into the presence of the rising sun. To the breast of the child the grandmother carrying it presses the ear of corn which lay by its side during the ten days; to her left the mother of the infant walks, carrying in her left hand the ear of corn which lay at her side. Both women sprinkle a line of sacred meal, emblematic of the straight road which the child must follow to win the favor of its gods. Thus the first object which the child is made to behold at the very dawn of its existence is the sun, the great object of their worship."

The prayer spoken while presenting the infant to the sun goes like this [in part]:

> *Now this is the day.*
> *Our child,*
> *Into the daylight*
> *You will go out standing.*
> *Preparing for your day,*
> *We have passed our days. . . .*
>
> *Now this day,*
> *Our fathers, Dawn priests,*
> *Have come out standing to their sacred place,*
> *Our sun father,*
> *Having come out standing to his sacred place,*
> *Our child, it is your day.*
>
> *This day,*
> *The flesh of the white corn, prayer meal,*
> *To our sun father*
> *This prayer meal we offer.*
>
> *May your road be fulfilled.*
> *Reaching to the road of your sun father,*
> *When the road is fulfilled,*
> *In your thoughts may we live,*
>
> *May we be the ones whom your thoughts embrace,*
> *For this, on this day*

The Hopi mesa-top village of Walpi in northeastern Arizona. Hopi man stands at kiva entrance in foreground. This scene, taken in the early part of the twentieth century, looks much the same today. Charles Martin © National Geographic Society.

> *To our sun father,*
> *We offer prayer meal.*
> *To this end:*
> *May you help us all to finish our roads.*

Is this poignant ceremony still carried out among the Pueblos today? Yes indeed. In the present, the family members carefully watch the predawn light on the twentieth day after the baby's birth to judge the proper time to begin the baby-naming ceremony. At the appropriate moment female representatives of the father's clan wash the baby's head and give it its name. Both child and mother are blessed. The paternal grandmother, accompanied by the mother, carries the child outdoors, a trail of blessed corn meal marking their path. And then the baby, who has been kept indoors away from the sun and away from the community since birth, is held up to the just-rising sun. The father's mother prays for the baby's welfare and long life and recites the baby's names. The act introduces the baby to the world and requests permission of the sun, the symbolic father of all Hopis, to raise the child.

The course to a life lived in the Hopi Way has now been properly entered into. This is only the first of many transition rituals marking the path toward full adult status in Hopi society. Other Pueblo tribes have similar ceremonies to launch their children on the proper path of life. Their ancient ancestors, it seems almost certain, did too.

The Pueblo concept of orientation in space, that is, of Sacred Space, likewise has antecedents among the people of Chaco and the other Hisatsinom. The coordinate system for Hopi Sacred Space, for instance, is defined by the four seasonal extremes of the sun's position on the horizon—northeast, southeast, southwest, and northwest. Joining these four horizontal directions are the two vertical directions, above and below. The *sipapu,* the covered hole on the floor of each underground kiva, symbolizes the origin of this coordinate system. This hole represents the primeval sipapu through which members of the clans first symbolically emerged from the underworld, a powerful symbol of the Pueblo people's sense of unity with nature. Many of the kivas at Chaco Canyon, like those in today's pueblos, have sipapus.

The six directions provide an absolute orientation that fixes Hopi Sacred Space—although each kiva has its own sipapu and therefore its own center of Sacred Space. The Hopi concept of space has a beguiling multiplicity that ordinary space lacks. The six directions permeate every phase of Hopi thinking and life. They bolster the implicit concept that one's village is the center of the universe.

Associated with each of the directions are all manner of other things. The bear, the color blue, and the bluebird are associated with the southwest, for example; the mountain lion, yellow, and the oriole, with the northwest. So the six directions provide the Hopi and other Pueblo tribes with a system of orientation in space and define relationships with numerous deities and many aspects of the natural world. The Zunis also organize much of the world according to the six directions: not only clans, but kivas, societies, priesthoods, corn, animals, seasons, and colors. Pueblo Indian thought is linked inseparably with sky and land.

Did the ancient Chacoans likewise consider their canyon the center of the universe? We have no way of knowing, but I think it is likely they did. Did they consider themselves an integral part of nature, not something separate from nature? Again, it is very likely. The concept pervades all Pueblo thought today; its roots are deep in culture and time. Thus this Tewa prayer (the Tewas consist of five Pueblo tribes along the Rio Grande in northern New Mexico) celebrates this unity with nature:

> *My words are tied in one*
> *With the great mountains,*
> *With the great rocks,*
> *With the great trees,*
> *In one with my body*
> *And my heart.*

Do you all help me
With supernatural power,
And you, Day!
And you, Night!
All of you see me,
One with this world!

The chief of the Bluebird clan at the Hopi Second Mesa village of Shongo-povi once succinctly expressed this identity of land and spiritual life: "The Hopi land is the Hopi religion. The Hopi religion is bound up in the Hopi land." As I recently heard a former Hopi leader say: "We consider ourselves a part of the natural environment."

This is true of the other Pueblos too. For the Zunis, for instance, all aspects of nature, man included, belong to one great system of related life.

Pueblo ritual and ceremony—and I feel certain this was true of their ancient ancestors as well—have at their heart the necessity to live in harmony with the world. This necessity is shaped by dependence upon the elements, particularly summer rains and winter snows. It is often said that all Pueblo dances have as an essential purpose the invocation of rain, and that is true. In agrarian societies which are so close to the margin of existence, moisture holds an importance diffi-cult for others to appreciate.

The climate of Chaco Canyon during the rise of the Chacoan culture was generally the same as it is now. Rainfall was modest but not nonexistent, eight or nine inches a year, though unpredictable from year-to-year. And the peak decades of splendor of the civilization were accompanied by years of above-average rainfall. These patterns may have shaped Chacoan culture in important ways, as we will see later.

The Pueblo people appeal for winter snowfall as well as for rain. This chant from the San Ildefonso pueblo in northern New Mexico is especially beautiful:

Hasten clouds
from the four world quarters;

Come snow in plenty, that water
may be abundant when summer comes;

Come ice, cover the fields, that the planting
may yield abundance,

Let all hearts be glad.

Just about a hundred miles west of San Ildefonso lies Chaco Canyon, and we can easily envision the people of Chaco offering similar invocations to the clouds of winter and summer.

Yet the ceremonial life of the Pueblos and certainly their ancestors before them is far more than an appeal to favorable natural elements, as important as that may be. Ritual structures all life. This inseparable entwinement is almost impossible for outsiders ever fully to appreciate, and probably no non-Indian ever really can.

We can see and listen, study, admire. We can sit for hours during the middle of the night in a crowded underground rectangular kiva at the Hopi villages of Walpi and Kykotsmovi, and be entranced as a succession of spectacularly cos-tumed kachinas dance in the intricate *Powamu* (Bean Dance) ceremony. Nearly awestruck, we can watch the ancient Snake Dance at Shipaulovi, with a myriad of unanswered—perhaps unanswerable—questions dancing in our minds. We can observe the annual ceremony where the ogre woman *Soyoko* climbs up the mesa at dawn and, accompanied by all sorts of other fearsome ogre kachinas, goes to the home of each child to punish bad behavior and therefore reinforce good. We can watch the social dances and laugh along with the Hopis at the sometimes outrageous antics of the clown kachinas during otherwise solemn plaza ceremonies. At the Zuni pueblo, we can observe the dramatic all-night win-ter Shalako ceremony that includes the seven giant Shalako spirits. We can watch hundreds of squash- or turquoise-painted men and black-dressed women in the frequent corn dances at Jemez, Santo Domingo, or the other Rio Grande pueb-los, and we can partake of the extraordinary culinary feasts they offer to family and visitors alike. We can learn that the deeply religious Hopi initiation ceremony *Wuwuchim* involves, among other rituals, a lengthy recitation by the priest, an oral history of tribal events and migrations extending all the way back to the times of the ancient ones.

We can observe and learn something of these things, and feel enriched for having shared in them, but we can never fully understand their inner meaning to the Pueblo people. And perhaps that is the way it should be.

Thus all aspects of Pueblo Indian culture carry meaning and purpose for their people that help sustain life and tradition. To be privileged to witness some part of them is to admire the beauty of the flower without necessarily understand-ing all of its inner molecular workings. With the Pueblo people, our task is to appreciate all we can of their culture, and yet to know that unfathomed layers of cultural richness remain hidden from our view.

I hope that when we explore the ruins of Chaco Canyon we see more than deserted stone buildings and barren surroundings, more than potsherds, artifacts, and archaeologists' diagrams. Think not of ruins and dead cultures but of life and continuity. The extraordinary cultures of a millennium past may have left stone walls and dust, but the people who succeeded them have built their own societies that continue and build upon many of the ancient cultural ways. Look to today's Pueblo people, and you will see the dwellings of Chaco Canyon come alive.

1. The Lieutenant and the Cowboy

At seven in the morning of August 26, 1849, an expedition of 500 U.S. Army troops and Indian guides out of Fort Marcy in Santa Fe, New Mexico, broke camp along Torreon Arroyo and headed northwest. They were beginning the tenth day of a military reconnaissance mission into Navajo country.

In their company was James Hervey Simpson, a thirty-six-year-old first lieutenant in the Corps of Topographical Engineers. The expedition, headed by Lt. Colonel John M. Washington, commander of the Ninth Military Department, Santa Fe, had as its primary mission "to make a movement against the Navajo Indians," who had lately been troublesome to new settlements along the Rio Grande. Lieutenant Simpson was charged with "making such a survey of the country as the movements of the troops will permit."

Until three months earlier when he had escorted a wagon train of emigrants from Fort Smith, Arkansas, to Santa Fe, Simpson had never been west of the Mississippi River. In fact, his duty immediately preceding the Fort Smith assignment was supervision of construction of a lighthouse near Monroe, Michigan. A

Aerial view of Chaco Canyon, looking east. In foreground are Pueblo Bonito (left) and Pueblo del Arroyo (right). Photo by Paul Logsdon.

23

native of New Jersey and a graduate of West Point, Simpson had served in Maine, Virginia, and South Carolina. Since his transfer to the Engineers, he had helped make harbor improvements along the east shore of Lake Erie, build roads near the Florida Everglades, and survey the northwestern lakes in Michigan.

He was an intellectually curious and somewhat bookish man. These qualities were balanced by ample quantities of energy and endurance. Fortunately for us he was also a methodical man, and he kept a narrative journal of the expedition. It is to it, resurrected a century later from the dust of a Senate executive document of the time by Frank McNitt, that we owe our detailed knowledge of the expedition's discovery of the ruins of Chaco Canyon.

The expedition's first week of travels had taken them southwest to Santo Domingo Pueblo, along the banks of the Rio Grande, and then northwest to Jemez Pueblo, where they had strengthened their force with additional troops, Indian guides and scouts, and fifty-four Pueblo Indian mounted militia volunteers.

Now they were in the midst of high country, "more prairielike and rolling" than the "broken country made up of low swelling hills, isolated cones and mesa heights, sprinkled with pine and cedar of a scrub growth" they had passed through on the day before. The Jemez mountains were visible off in the distance behind them to the east. To the south, some twenty miles away, "lay an extensive range of mountains of a mesa and ridgy character."

The arroyo they had camped at that night contained a small amount of water filled with clay, "as scanty in quantity as unpalatable to the taste." A few cotton-woods skirted the arroyo. Grass wasn't abundant. "The pasturage about camp," wrote Simpson, "is but tolerable."

The weather, however, was excellent, "beautiful, clear, and pleasant," if quite cold at night.

As they left camp and set course for the northwest along a "generally ascending" route, they passed a fifty-foot-high mound of twisted lava rock "exhibiting very strikingly the gradual effect of igneous action upon matter in proportion to its proximity to the source of heat." A mile and a half further he noted a locality where coal cropped out of the soil. Nearby in a shallow basin "we found some beautiful specimens of petrified wood—in two instances the trunks of the trees still standing erect and *in situ.*" Simpson wondered if this meant that in some previous time the country had held timber. To him the landscape seemed appallingly barren.

They continued their march a few miles more and passed over the Continental Divide. "Seven miles from our last camp, we reached the highest point of the land dividing the tributaries of the Gulf of Mexico from those of the Pacific." Here the Divide is not along a high mountain back as it is farther to the north in Colorado but along a low rise. The elevation here is about 6,800 feet.

"The highest point of land just referred to reached, we commenced gradually descending its western slope—three miles more bringing us to the Rio

Landscape on the way toward Chaco Canyon. Lt. Simpson passed near this very point. He marveled at the towering butte, Cabezon Peak, at right: ". . . I thought I had never seen anything more beautiful, and at the same time grand." Photo by author.

Chaco, a tributary of the Rio San Juan; and five miles more to a point whence could be seen in the distance, on a slight elevation, a conspicuous ruin. . . ."

The Indians and Mexicans with them had various names for the ruin. Simpson chose for it the one offered by Carravahal, the expedition's Mexican guide: "Pueblo Pintado." Pueblo Pintado means "painted village." Carravahal was a native of San Ysidro, south of Jemez, and he was thoroughly familiar with the land from the Rio Grande west to Canyon de Chelly in western Arizona. Carravahal, said Simpson, "probably knows more about it than anyone else." Despite Simpson's deference to Carravahal, the guide of course could not have known the name used by the ruin's original, long-vanished inhabitants. McNitt, Simpson's modern editor and annotator, suggests that Simpson possibly found "Pintado" more pleasant to the ear and more appropriate than the four other names offered by the Mexican and Indian guides: in English, Montezuma's Pueblo, Red Pueblo, Great Pueblo, and Pueblo of Rats.

Pueblo Pintado, the first Chacoan ruin encountered by Lieutenant Simpson's expedition, as painted by expedition artist Richard Kern. Library, The Academy of Natural Sciences, Philadelphia.

One guide, Hosta, the civil governor of Jemez Pueblo, told Simpson that Pueblo Pintado was built by Montezuma and his people when they were on their way from the north toward the Valley of Mexico. This was to remain a popular legend for a considerable time, until a research tool of the next century would effectively demolish it. As McNitt points out, tree-ring dates of the major ruins in and around Chaco Canyon gives dates around A.D. 1000. Montezuma I ruled from 1440–69 and his grandson Montezuma II from 1503 till his death in 1520.

Simpson and the expedition found a spring of good water along their path and, having marched 21.45 miles for the day, encamped. Their campsite was about a mile from the ruins.

After a bite to eat, Simpson and his two assistants, the brothers Edward and Richard Kern, artists, topographers, and cartographers, set off to examine the ruins of Pueblo Pintado.

Since this is the easternmost of the great Chaco ruins (separated by about ten miles from the rest) and this is the first known written account of them, Simpson's description bears recounting in his own words:

"We found them to more than answer our expectations. Forming one structure, and built of tabular pieces of hard, fine-grained compact gray sandstone (a material entirely unknown in the present architecture of New Mexico), to which the atmosphere has imparted a reddish tinge, the layers or beds being not thicker than three inches, and sometimes as thin as one-fourth of an inch, it discovers in the masonry a combination of science and art which can only be referred to a higher stage of civilization and refinement than is discoverable in the works of Mexicans or Pueblos of the present day. Indeed, so beautifully diminutive and true are the details of the structure as to cause it, at a little distance to have all the appearance of a magnificent piece of mosaic work."

Simpson, the Army career man who missed the lush landscapes of his native New Jersey, had finally found something amidst all the barrenness that stimulated his sense of aesthetics. Perhaps his own experience in civil engineering contributed to his appreciation of the fine but unusual building methods he beheld. His descriptions are quite detailed.

"In the outer face of the building there are no signs of mortar, the intervals between the beds being chinked with stones of the minutest thinness. The filling and backing are done in rubble masonry, the mortar presenting no indications of the presence of lime. The thickness of the main wall at base is within an inch or two of three feet; higher up, it is less—diminishing every story by retreating jogs on the inside, from bottom to top. Its elevation at its present highest point is between twenty-five and thirty feet, the series of floor beams indicating that there must have been originally three stories."

Simpson counted the number of "apartments" (fifty-four on the ground floor), examined the "very small" doorways (some as small as 2½ by 2½ feet, others a foot taller), and measured the exterior ground plan (about 403 feet including the court).

He found that the system of floor beams consisted of unhewn beams, six inches in diameter, laid transversely from wall to wall, overlain longitudinally by a

Pueblo Pintado as it looks today. Photo by author.

number of smaller ones, about three inches in diameter. He speculated that most probably these had then been covered with brush, bark, or slabs, with a layer of mud mortar over that. "The beams," he remarked, "show no signs of the saw or axe; on the contrary, they appear to have been hacked off by means of some very imperfect implement." (Those implements, we now know, were stone axes.)

"At different points about the premises were three circular apartments sunk in the ground, the walls being of masonry. These apartments the Pueblo Indians call estuffas [kivas], or places where the people held their political and religious meetings."

The ruins were on a small knoll above the surrounding plain, two or three hundred yards from the Rio Chaco. Simpson saw no growth of wood usable for the room beams "visible within the circuit of a mile" but did find that the stones used for the walls apparently came from a quarry "just back of our camp."

Simpson and the Kerns weren't able to finish their examination of the ruins of Pueblo Pintado before day's end, so they returned early the next morning, even though the troops had begun moving westward without them. Their curiosity had been piqued.

"On digging about the base of the exterior wall we find that for at least two feet (the depth our time would permit us to go), the same kind of masonry obtains below as above, except that it appears more compact." They could find no signs of "the genuine arch" in the structure. The lintels of the doors and windows generally consisted either of a number of pieces of wood laid horizontally side by side or of a single stone slab. Occasionally he found a series of small stones "so placed horizontally upon each other, whilst presenting the form of a sharp angle, in vertical longitudinal section, they would support the weight of the fabric above."

They found fragments of pottery scattered all around, "the colors showing taste in their selection and in the style of their arrangement, and being still quite bright."

That was it for Pueblo Pintado.

"We would gladly, had time permitted, have remained longer to dig among the rubbish of the past; but the troops having already got some miles in advance of us, we were reluctantly obliged to quit."

Simpson and the Kerns moved on to the northwest. Two miles of travel brought them to the beginnings of Chaco Canyon (or as they referred to it, the Cañon de Chaco), which they entered by following the main (north) branch of the Chaco Wash.

The canyon was about two hundred yards wide. Simpson wrote that sandstone rocks "massive above, stratified below, constitute its enclosing walls." They began to see numerous small deserted stone and masonry habitations "excavated in the rocks." One area was littered with a number of "very large sandstone

Wijiji, the easternmost ruin in Chaco Canyon, as drawn by Richard Kern.

boulders" that had fallen from above, the volume of some "probably as much as fifteen thousand cubic feet." On some of the boulders they found "a number of hieroglyphics."

Thirteen miles from the previous night's camp they came to another old ruin. Carravahal called it Pueblo Weje-gi. (The modern spelling is Wijiji.) Like Pueblo Pintado it was built of very thin tabular pieces of compact sandstone. Its circumference, including the court, was nearly 700 feet. Judging from what was distinguishable, Simpson estimated its number of apartments on the ground floor at ninety-nine. The 25-foot-high exterior wall appeared once to have been higher, based on the great mass of rubble below.

Simpson says nothing more of Wijiji, except to remark upon the excellent view from it. "The view from these ruins, both up and down the canon, is fine. Rocks piled upon rocks present themselves on either side and in such order as to give the idea of two parallel architectural facades, converging at either extremity at a remote distance."

Farther to the west they came upon another outstanding natural feature. "Another and more splendid view burst upon us as we turned an angle of the canon, just before reaching camp. The chief object in the landscape was Mesa Fachada, a circular mound with tableau top, rising abruptly midway in the canon to a height of from three hundred to four hundred feet." The modern name for this isolated sandstone feature is Fajada Butte. We will hear more about it later.

Winter view of Fajada Butte, with ruins of Una Vida in right foreground. Richard Kern painted this same scene in 1849. Photo by author.

This view sent Simpson into a rare moment of attempted lyricism: "The combination of this striking and beautiful object with the clear sky beyond, against which it was relieved, in connexion with lesser mounds at its base, the serried tents of the command, the busy scene of moving men and animals in the vicinity, and the curling smoke from the camp fires, which made up a picture which it has been seldom my lot to witness."

They had traveled 14.86 miles that day between their camp at Pueblo Pintado and their strikingly situated site in Chaco Canyon east of Fajada. (Yes, Simpson gives the mileage figures in hundredths!) Again, despite the dramatic topography, Simpson's overall impression was of barrenness. "Scrub cedars, very thinly scattered, were to be seen on the heights. . . . Some patches of good gramma grass could occasionally be seen along the Rio Chaco. The country, as usual, on account, doubtless, of constant drought, presented one wide expanse of barren waste."

The soil, he said, "has given indications of containing all the earthly elements of fertility, but the refreshing shower has been wanting to make it productive."

As for the Chaco Wash, he found its clay-colored flow meager. "The Rio Chaco, near our camp, has a width of eight feet and a depth of one and half." (This was the rainy season, although the expedition hadn't run into rain yet. Eighteen inches is a generous amount of flow for the wash today, except for immediately after rains; a good part of the year it is devoid of water altogether.)

The next morning the troops planned a route that would take them out of the canyon and then back again before nightfall. Simpson, having heard reports of "some more ruins of an interesting character," obtained Colonel Washington's permission to proceed down the canyon and visit them. He took with him Richard Kern, the guide Carravahal, and seven mounted Mexicans as escort.

The first they reached was Pueblo Una Vida (Carravahal's name again). Simpson found it to be 994 feet around. Like the others it was built of very fine-grained tabular sandstone. The highest wall was only about 15 feet and two stories were clearly apparent, "but the mass of debris at the base of the walls certainly shows that there must originally have been more." They detected the remains of four circular kivas.

A mile farther down the canyon they encountered the ruins of Hungo Pavi, 872 feet around. They counted seventy-two rooms on the ground floor. There

Hungo Pavi, as Kern envisioned it must have appeared when occupied.
Library, The Academy of Natural Sciences, Philadelphia.

was but one circular kiva, placed in the north portion of the building, midway from either extremity.

The main walls towered up to thirty feet and were two and three-quarters feet thick at the base. The ends of the floor beams were still visible. They showed plainly that there had been a vertical series of four floors. And the great amount of debris around the base hinted that there may have been even more. The floor beams, which were round, were eleven inches in diameter. The windows were as small as twelve by thirteen inches. Both floor beams and windows, Simpson noted, were "arranged horizontally with great precision and regularity."

One and three-quarters miles farther down the canyon loomed another extensive structure in ruins. Carravahal called it Pueblo Chettro Kettle (usually now spelled Chetro Ketl), and he said that meant the Rain Pueblo. Its name remains unexplained to this day. (McNitt points out that some architectural features of the pueblo suggest influences imported to Chaco from Mexico or Central America, but he adds, "If such influences there were, they go too deep into prehistory to account for Carravahal's foreign-sounding Chetro Ketl.")

Chetro Ketl was thirteen hundred feet around. The masonry was the same as at the other pueblos. Simpson could detect four stories. He noticed that originally there had been a series of windows (four and a half by three and a half feet) in the first story, but they were now walled up. There must have been 124 rooms on the first floor. He found six circular kivas. They were deeper than any he had seen. One showed certainly two stories, and possibly three.

One room in the northwest corner of Chetro Ketl was almost perfectly preserved. "The stone walls still have their plaster upon them, in a tolerable state of preservation. . . . The ceiling showed two main beams, laid transversely; on these, longitudinally, were a number of smaller ones in juxtaposition, the ends being tied together by a species of wooden fibre, and the interstices chinked in with small stones; on these again, transversely, in close contact, was a kind of lathing of the odor and appearance of cedar—all in a good state of preservation. Depending from the beams were several short pieces of rope, a specimen of which I got. . . . A large quantity of pottery lay strewed about the ruins."

Several hundred yards farther down the canyon, the Simpson party came upon yet another large pueblo. This one was to become the most famous of all the ancient Chacoan ruins. Its name, Simpson was told, was Pueblo Bonito (Beautiful Village). Simpson found that this pueblo, "though not so beautiful in the arrangement of the details of its masonry as Pueblo Pintado, is yet superior to it in point of preservation."

Its perimeter was thirteen hundred feet. It clearly had had at least four stories of apartments. Simpson counted the number of rooms on the ground floor as 139, not including apartments indistinguishable in the east portion of the pueblo. That he figured would increase the number to 200. Assuming four full stories of this size, he estimated the maximum number of rooms in the original pueblo at

Pueblo Bonito ("Beautiful Village") at the time of the Chacoans, as drawn by Richard Kern.

800. Yet he realized that some of the upper stories may well have been set back in "a retreating terrace form on the court side" and reduced the estimate to 641.

He counted the number of kivas at four (we now know there are at least thirty-two) and said the largest was sixty feet in diameter (the actual figure is fifty-two feet). Simpson said that this largest of the two Great Kivas at Pueblo Bonito showed two stories and a present depth of twelve feet. "All of these estuffas are, as in the case of the others I have seen, cylindrical in shape and nicely walled up with thin tabular stone."

Some of the rooms were in excellent shape. Simpson remarked upon that as well as the exquisite masonry work: "Among the ruins are several rooms in a very good state of preservation—one of them (near the northwest corner of the north range) being walled up with alternate beds of large and small stones, the regularity of the combination producing a very pleasing effect."

The ceiling also pleased his aesthetic sense. "The ceiling of this room is also more tasteful than any we have seen—the transverse beams being smaller and more numerous, and the longitudinal pieces which rest upon them only about an inch in diameter and beautifully regular. These latter have somewhat the appearance of barked willow."

The room had a doorway at each end and one at the side; each led into adjacent apartments. Light entered through a window on the north side.

Simpson's pleasure at this room caused his group to leave their mark here. When more than a quarter century later, in 1875, the explorer-photographer William Henry Jackson visited Chaco Canyon, he described finding this: "In . . . a

The exquisite masonry at the Chacoan pueblos has impressed all visitors, beginning with Lt. Simpson. This wall is at Pueblo Bonito. Courtesy H. M. Willis.

T-shaped doorway at Pueblo del Arroyo. Photo by author.

small room in the outer tier of the north side . . . we found the names of Lieutenant Simpson, Mr. R.H. Kern, and one or two others, with the date, August 27 [28], 1849, scratched into the soft plastering which covered the walls, the impression appearing plainly as if done but a few days previously."

Simpson and his group came across the ruins of Pueblo del Arroyo a few hundred yards farther down the canyon, but they had run out of time and couldn't examine them. Apart from estimating the perimeter at about one thousand feet, he said no more of them except to express his reluctance to leave. The expedition's troops were "doubtless many miles in advance of us." (In fact Simpson's small group failed to catch up with the command by nightfall and had to stay the night in the open without provisions or bedding.)

But they weren't through observing. On their way out of the canyon, they came across another large ruin that exhibited some important differences from the rest. Simpson's remarks again are worth repeating: "All the ruins we have seen today, up to this point, have been on the north side of the cañon and within a few feet of its escarpment wall. . . . Two miles further down the cañon, but on its left or south bank, we came to another pueblo in ruins, called by the guide Pueblo de Penasca Blanca, the circuit of which I ascertained to be approximately one thousand seven hundred feet. This is the largest pueblo in plan we have seen, and differs from others in the arrangement of the stones composing its walls. The walls of the other pueblos were all of one uniform character in the several beds composing it; but in this there is a regular alternation of large and small stones, the effect of which is both unique and beautiful."

He noted that the large stones, about a foot in length and half a foot in thickness, form a single bed. Alternating with these were three or four beds of very small stones each about an inch thick. This beautiful stonework archaeologists of Chaco have since termed Superior Type III banded masonry. It is quite striking, but Simpson was wrong in saying it was unique to Penasco Blanco (the modern spelling of the name). It is found also in Wijiji, Chetro Ketl, and Bonito.

The general plan of Penasco Blanco also differed from the others, "approximating the form of a circle." Simpson later pondered at some length what they had seen and decided that the inner apartments must have originally existed in a terrace form, the "best conduce to light and ventilation for the interior range of apartments."

Simpson and his party passed the last ruins of Chaco at 5 P.M. and headed west. They beheld a fine view of the Chuska Mountains, some forty miles to the west. Also they could see "the waters of the Chaco, glittering under the rays of an opposite and declining sun, coursing their way as far as they could be seen towards them."

By the time they bedded down for the night, thirteen miles away from Chaco Canyon, "our saddles serving as pillows," the whole distance they had traveled during the day "was about twenty-three miles," said Simpson. "Considering the

Penasco Blanco differs from other Chacoan ruins in its approximate circular shape. Chaco Center, NPS.

amount of labor we accomplished at the ruins, we look upon our day's work as being considerable." Indeed.

We move now from the first recorded descriptions to the first archaeological explorations of Chaco Canyon. Here we meet one of the most remarkable men of Southwestern archaeology, the rancher turned ardent archaeologist, Richard Wetherill. The time is 1895. The place, the Wetherill ranch at Mancos, Colorado. Mancos is north and a bit east of Mesa Verde in the southwestern corner of the state. Already Wetherill and his brothers are famed as the discoverers (on December 18, 1888) and first explorers of the spectacular cliff dwellings of the deep canyons of Mesa Verde. It was Richard who gave the major ruins of Mesa Verde their names: Cliff Palace, Spruce Tree House, Square Tower House.

Wetherill was an energetic and indefatigable explorer of the canyons and ruins of the Four Corners area. Frank McNitt, Wetherill's able biographer, records an anecdote told years later by the Southwestern archaeologist Alfred Kidder: "A number of years ago, Jesse Nusbaum and I were exploring cliff dwellings on the west side of Mesa Verde. We saw one that was high up on the canyon wall opposite us, and decided to look into it. But it was a terribly hard climb—up a sheer wall and across a narrow ledge, with a long drop below. But we finally made it. With great elation over our discovery and the successful climb, we peered down through an opening in the rocks at our ruin. And right there before our eyes was an upended slab of stone. On it we read these words: 'What fools these mortals be. R. Wetherill.' "

One late summer day in 1895, a Quaker family of traveling musicians from Burdett, Kansas, the S.L. Palmers, arrived in Mancos to see the now famous Mesa Verde ruins and meet the Wetherills.

Around the campfire one night, the Palmers asked about vague reports of ancient ruins called Pueblo Bonito in northwestern New Mexico. A decade before, they said, they had visited Albuquerque and the towns along the Rio Grande but could find no one who could tell them exactly where these great villages of the Chaco were. Richard Wetherill had heard rumors of them too. Before the evening was out, the decision was made: His brothers could handle the ranch duties this winter; he would take the Palmers to Chaco Canyon.

On a cold October morning they left, outfitted with supplies for two months. Six days they traveled generally southward. Eventually their Navajo guide led them down an arroyo and suddenly there they were in the broad expanse of Chaco Canyon.

The first ruin they beheld, off to the west, was the silhouetted form of Penasco Blanco. Turning left they soon came upon Pueblo Bonito, the object of their journey. Wetherill scampered about the ruins, the late-afternoon light lending softly golden illumination. He was transfixed. These great pueblos exceeded his greatest expectations. The anticipation of exploring the remains of this lost civilization excited him as never before.

They stayed about a month. Wetherill examined the entire canyon and did some digging, but he realized this was just the beginning. Around the middle of November they journeyed eastward to Jemez, Santa Fe, and the muddy streets of Albuquerque, where Wetherill sent off a letter to a man he knew could help, Talbot Hyde.

The Hyde brothers, Fred and Talbot, were youthful heirs to a New York soap company fortune in New York. Richard had met them several years before, and they had begun an association to do archaeological work in the Southwest, named (by Richard) the Hyde Exploring Expedition. The brothers in effect financed Wetherill's archaeological explorations. Already a season of work at Grand Gulch, a tortuous fifty-mile-long canyon in Utah filled with cliff houses and burial places, had been completed.

But now Wetherill's mind was on Chaco Canyon. His letter of December 1, 1895, to Talbot Hyde touted the possibilities. He told how he had just returned from a visit to the ruins of New Mexico, those of Chaco Canyon "being the greatest" and "almost unknown." "I was successful after a few days search in finding relics in quantity—the ruins there are enormous—there are 11 of the large Pueblos or houses containing from one hundred to 500 rooms each and numerous small ones. ... Grass and water is plenty—wood is scarce. A wagon can be driven to the Ruins in 5 or six days from our Ranch." He told Hyde he would send him his voluminous notes of the trip and a detailed map of prospective sites.

Thus began the Hyde Exploring Expedition's interest in the great ruins of

Richard Wetherill (right), George Pepper (next to him), and other members of the Hyde Exploring Expedition search for turquoise beads in dirt taken from a room in Pueblo Bonito. Library Services Department, American Museum of Natural History.

Chaco Canyon. Wetherill's letters persuaded Talbot Hyde to devote the next summer's archaeological work not to Marsh Pass in northeastern Arizona as originally planned but to Pueblo Bonito in Chaco Canyon. Talbot asked Professor Frederic Ward Putnam, curator of anthropology at the American Museum of Natural History as well as curator of the Peabody Museum at Harvard, to direct the expedition. Putnam's schedule prevented him from taking an active part. He sent instead George Hubbard Pepper, a twenty-three-year-old student with no experience in the Southwest or out of the classroom.

Wetherill gathered the supplies and outfitted the wagon for the trip, Pepper joined them in Mancos, and one spring day they began the overland journey south to Chaco Canyon. Pepper methodically recorded the distance, 149.4 miles. Upon their arrival, Wetherill appropriated three rooms in Pueblo Bonito for their use, one as a storeroom, one as a photographic darkroom, and one for the food supplies. One of these three rooms was still smoothly plastered, and Wetherill noted that on the wall was enscribed the name of Lieutenant James H. Simpson and the date of August 27, 1849.

Wetherill hired Navajos to do the digging, and he closely supervised every phase of the effort. The work proceeded well, although everyone was soon wondering why so few burial sites were unearthed. July brought both visitors and the seasonal rains. The visitors, especially Dr. Jacob L. Wortman of the American Museum, were welcome. The rains made a mess of things.

This early excavation work concentrated on the old north-central section of the pueblo. Eighteen rooms and one large kiva had been cleared. Wetherill helped Pepper exhaustively measure every aspect of the work. They measured exactly every feature of every room, compiling a complete record of size and relationships. They photographed each room in detail.

Late in August, they struck a huge deposit of pottery, one of the largest ever found in the Southwest. Carefully uncovering a tiny room close to a large kiva in the north-central area over a two-day period, they found 114 cylindrical jars, 22 bowls, and 21 sandstone jar covers. A dozen turquoise pendants were among them.

In the first of two connecting rooms adjacent to this cache, they found something even more interesting: a sealed burial cache. The bones of the skeleton had been scattered by water seepage, but with the bones was a quiver of eighty-one arrows, a bird effigy, its tail inlaid with turquoise and shells, and some three hundred staffs of wood.

Frog carved in jet and found by Hyde expedition in Pueblo Bonito. *Library Services Department, American Museum of Natural History.*

Examples of pottery from Pueblo Bonito. American Museum of Natural History.

The second room held greater treasure. There were fourteen skeletons, two of them relatively undisturbed. One of these men must have enjoyed a high station in life. Around his wrists and ankles he wore huge bands of turquoise beads and pendants. Around his neck and his abdomen he wore two pendants containing more than four thousand pieces of turquoise. There were also stone effigies of frogs and tadpoles and a cylindrical basket with a solid mosaic of turquoise on its exterior. Richard found it to be surprisingly heavy. Inside were 2,150 turquoise beads, 152 small turquoise pendants, 22 large turquoise pendants, and 3,317 shell beads and small pendants.

Thirty-seven rooms had been cleared when the season's work concluded on September 24. A collection of artifacts that would fill an entire railroad freight car had been sent to Durango for transportation to the American Museum of Natural History in New York.

Richard Wetherill and Marietta Palmer, the daughter of the S.L. Palmers, the family of curious musicians whose interest had first brought him to Chaco, were married late that year. They made their summer home in Chaco, first in a wall tent. Then in July 1898 they moved permanently into a rectangular structure built almost adjacent to Pueblo Bonito's westernmost wall. Its roof timbers were ancient beams borrowed from the ceilings of Pueblo Bonito. (This would antagonize archaeologists later.) The Wetherill brothers, in association with the Hydes,

had earlier established a trading post in the west end of the erected structure. Navajos came from throughout the region to sell newly made blankets, as well as sheep, goats, mules, wool, and pelts, and the store did a relatively booming business. Most of the modest profits went toward the archaeological work, and all evidence indicates that Richard was fair in his dealings with the Navajo.

The Hyde Exploring Expedition's work at Pueblo Bonito continued over four seasons, from 1896 through 1899. Professor Putnam finally came out to Chaco for the first time in 1899 to see the excavations and review the project's accomplishments. One hundred ninety rooms at Pueblo Bonito had been excavated. An unparalleled collection of artifacts had been collected and shipped to the American Museum of Natural History. The cost to the Hydes had been fairly low, about $25,000. The excavation was the major archaeological effort of its kind in the Southwest until the twentieth century. Although modern archaeological approaches directed toward understanding cultural behavior would not be developed for many more decades, the Wetherill-spurred Hyde project had amassed a valuable and detailed record of Chacoan material culture.

Yet not everyone was pleased. Certain critics, some of them not personally familiar with the project, feared that the excavation of the Chacoan sites constituted vandalism for personal gain. An investigation was launched, reports written, and affidavits filed. Wetherill and the Hydes vehemently denied the accusations.

But Federal officials in Washington, acting at least partly on misinformation and on statements made without documentation, shut the Hyde Exploring Expedition down. Richard Wetherill, the discoverer and explorer of more ancient ruins in the Southwest than any other man, was enjoined from doing any further excavations at Chaco Canyon. But a positive outgrowth of the critics' effort was passage of the Antiquities Act of 1906 to preserve the nation's ancient ruins and the signing of legislation by President Theodore Roosevelt in 1907 creating Chaco Canyon National Monument.

As for Richard Wetherill, at 6 P.M. on June 22, 1910, in a sudden and still inexplicable act, he was ambushed while herding some stray cows in the shadows of a bend about half a mile west of Pueblo Bonito. A Navajo Indian named Chischilling-begay fired a .33 caliber Winchester three times. The first shot missed, the second tore through Wetherill's hand and into his chest. The third, while Wetherill lay sprawled on the ground, ripped into the right side of his head. Richard Wetherill, pioneer explorer of Pueblo Bonito, died in the dust of Chaco Canyon.

Richard Wetherill's gravestone west of Pueblo Bonito. *Photo by author.*

2. Judd and the Geo Excavations

Pueblo Bonito and the other ruins at Chaco Canyon reposed in relative silence over the next decade. National Monument status the canyon may have had, but visitors were few and no systematic archaeological quests probed stone or soil.

The place had all but been forgotten. The General Land Office reported that only a dozen parties visited the ruins in 1915. A hundred people came in 1916. A National Park Service flyer published in 1917 did little to encourage the less than hearty: "The reservation can only be reached by team, mountain hack, and camping outfit from Farmington, New Mexico, and from Gallup or Thoreau. . . . The trip . . . will consume from two to three days on the road each way."

This obscurity was soon to end. Chaco Canyon was about to come under its most concentrated scientific attention yet. And this time a large segment of the general public would hear about it.

Key figures in the scientific and public renaissance of interest in the ruins at Chaco were archaeologist Neil M. Judd and a well-known sponsoring group, the National Geographic Society.

In 1921 Judd was the thirty-four-year-old curator of American archaeology at the new U.S. National Museum (Smithsonian Institution). Already he had compiled an impressive record of archaeological work and discovery. In 1909, just graduated from the University of Utah with a degree in archaeology, he had participated in the expedition that discovered Rainbow Bridge in Arizona. Judd would always consider that discovery a highlight of his life.

Judd had joined the staff of the Smithsonian in 1911 while the National Museum was still being readied for its public opening. In 1915 he had supervised the California-Pacific Exposition's reproduction of the stone monuments of an ancient Mayan religious site in Quirigua, Guatemala. And two years later he had directed a Department of Interior expedition to restore Betatakin, a terraced cliff-dwelling in northeastern Arizona.

In April 1920 the National Geographic Society's research committee decided to send an archaeological reconnaissance group to Chaco Canyon to determine whether a detailed examination of a Chaco Canyon ruin should be undertaken. The Society arranged to have the Smithsonian give Judd a three-month leave of absence to direct the reconnaissance. Judd made the trip and was intrigued by what he found. From the very first he found Pueblo Bonito to be extraordinary—that it covered three acres of ground in the shape of a D, stood four stories in height, and contained "fully eight hundred rooms." As he later wrote in one of a series of articles for the National Geographic: "No other apartment house of comparable size was known in America or in the Old World until the Spanish Flats were erected in 1882 at 59th Street and Seventh Avenue, New York City."

In November of 1920, Judd formally recommended a comprehensive study of Pueblo Bonito and its neighbor immediately to the west, Pueblo del Arroyo. The research committee accepted his proposal, and plans were drawn up for a five-year program of investigation. It invited Judd to organize and direct the project. He considered it an honor. The Smithsonian granted him a four-month leave of absence each summer to make it possible. The Interior Department granted the necessary permits, and the National Geographic Society arranged to donate all the cultural material collected to the American public as represented by the U.S. National Museum.

So it was that in early May 1921 Judd and his first season's party arrived in Chaco Canyon. Eventually they set up a series of huge tents (which were several weeks late in arriving) on the canyon floor a hundred yards or so directly south of Pueblo Bonito, dug a well in the nearby arroyo, erected an elevated water tank to which the camp's water was pumped, and went to work. The June issue of National Geographic announced the new expedition. The unbylined article's subtitle gave the summary: "Ruins of Chaco Canyon, New Mexico, Nature-Made Treasure-Chest of Aboriginal American History, to be Excavated and Studied; Work Begins This Month."

"This expedition hopes to discover the historic secrets of a region which was one of the most densely populated areas in North America before Columbus came, a region where prehistoric peoples lived in vast communal dwellings whose ruins are ranked second to none of ancient times in point of architecture,

and whose customs, ceremonies, and name have been engulfed in . . . obliv-
ion. . . ."

It said the report of the previous summer's reconnaissance party "bristled
with . . . interesting scientific problems." Through the expedition's findings the
Society "expects to reveal to its members a shrine of hidden history of their own
country." It pointed out that the expedition included agriculturists and geologists
as well as archaeologists. They "hope to patch from a crazy-quilt of half-sub-
merged ruins a complete picture of the lives, customs, and culture of these early
Americans."

A photograph of Judd in the article, taken with the governor of Santa Clara
Pueblo in New Mexico during the previous year's reconnaissance expedition,
shows a serious-looking man of at least medium height with short-clipped dark
hair, strong, almost-handsome features, and a determined look.

**Neil Judd with Santiago Naranjo, governor of Santa Clara
Pueblo.** *Charles Martin, © National Geographic Society.*

The big problem that first spring and summer was the sandstorms. They were an almost daily torment, even after the midsummer rains began. Dust and sand were everywhere. No corner of their camp was safe from intrusion. "It was a weird sight indeed," Judd recalled, "to see a cloud of flour-like sand rolling over a distant cliff and up the canyon on the very heels of a saturating shower. Nothing escaped this dust; it found a way beneath watch crystals, into locked trunks, and, worst of all, into food served by an incomparable cook."

The sand had *really* been a problem during the first few weeks, before their tardy tents had arrived. "Sand showered down on piles of equipment like a fog of pumice thrown out by that greatest spewer of all, old Katmai." (Mount Katmai, the Alaskan volcano, was the Mount St. Helens of this era. It had exploded in 1912, darkening the daytime sky to blackness for hundreds of miles around—Kodiak, Alaska, had sixty hours of total darkness—and dropping thick layers of ash on land, sea, and ships.) For partial protection from the scourges of sand, they dragged the camp's stove to an abandoned dugout "fresh with the unmistakable odor of Navaho goats." The storms eventually diminished, but "the smell and taste of them remained to the very end."

The summer rains were less of a chronic irritant than the sandstorms, but they were still a nuisance. One Sunday afternoon, when on exploration duty, the expedition's automobile, a black Model-T with "National Geographic Society" painted on its driver's side door, got bogged down in the mud and soggy sand of Chaco Wash, "the Chaco Canyon quicksands." There it remained stuck, the water over its floorboards. An Indian runner was sent for help. The car was eventually rescued, but only through the six-hour exertion of ten men, a team of horses, and a truck.

Judd hired Zuni and Navajo workmen. He had been warned that he was asking for trouble to expect men of these two totally different and historically antagonistic Indian cultures to work together, but no problems developed. In fact, he found that the Zunis were frequently welcome guests in the homes of the Navajo in the surrounding area, and the Navajos "were invariably present" during the Sunday night dances the Zunis put on in front of the weekly camp bonfire.

At this time in the Southwest the best archaeological tool to suggest the degree of development at any one site was pottery. The pottery of the later Pueblo cultures, wherever found, was distinctively different from the pottery of earlier Pueblo people, wherever it was found. Potsherds were therefore valuable evidence of, as Judd put it, "both material culture and passing time." It was believed that the tossed-out fragments of broken pottery from the trash dumps of Bonito would provide a stratigraphic record of cultural change—older fragments at the bottom, newer types near the top.

As soon as they organized their camp, they turned their attention to the Bonito dump. There were two conspicuous rubbish piles just beyond its south edge.

They dug a trench into the larger one, expecting to find a neat vertical cross-section revealing major changes in the villagers' material culture during the many generations of occupation of Pueblo Bonito. No such luck. "The results of that first test," said Judd, "proved amazing." They were confronted with a mystery: fragments of pottery known through experience to be of earlier design and manufacture were found to be above fragments known to be later. "Greatly perplexed, we cut a second section—and with the same result. Something was wrong!"

Later trenches showed the same result. Four years would elapse before Judd solved this mystery. That's when they discovered the floor of a huge kiva, more than fifty feet in diameter, beneath the West Court. Its construction had required expanding into a vast accumulation of older Bonitian rubbish. The builders of this phase of Pueblo Bonito had carried this excavated rubbish outside the newly enlarged village and dumped it on top of the trash mound already rising there. There the rubble remained in "inverted" order, a perplexing challenge to its archaeologist excavators some eight hundred years in the future.

Judd and his pottery experts, Frank H.H. Roberts, Jr., and Monroe Amsdem, did find an undisturbed remnant of the old trash pile. The sequence of pottery types they found preserved there in that thirteen-foot-deep trench served as the foundation for the project's analysis of Pueblo Bonito ceramics. They would help establish a detailed chronology of pottery and culture at Pueblo Bonito.

After encountering the mystery of the inverted trash dump, Judd's expedition turned their attention to the excavation of Pueblo Bonito itself.

George Pepper, the scientific director of the earlier excavations at Bonito by Richard Wetherill and the Hyde Exploring Expedition, unfortunately had not found time to write the final report he had hoped to prepare about that work. (He would die in 1924 before ever doing so.) In its stead, publication of his rough field notes was authorized in the fall of 1920. They became available to Judd, Pepper's close friend for the past few years, in page-proof form late in May 1921. Judd realized they would be of limited usefulness to one not intimately familiar with Bonito, and he noted sympathetically that they "are often confused and incomplete, as are my own." Nevertheless they were very useful to Judd. "The text, and a number of prints from Pepper negatives . . . enabled us at the outset to identify the rooms Pepper had excavated and thus avoid any possible duplication of effort."

In a lively article about this first season's archaeological work the next spring for *National Geographic* (he was an uncommonly clear and interesting writer by today's standards of archaeological prose), Judd enthusiastically described some of the pleasures:

"This work of exploration, this digging into deep rooms, this ferreting out, of hidden facts, has its difficulties and its rewards.

"The chief recompense is the satisfaction one derives from adding a few sentences to the world's history, in contributing even a short paragraph to the story of human progress. There is an immeasurable joy in starting work on a

Southeast section of Pueblo Bonito showing rooms excavated by Judd's 1921 expedition. Tents of the expedition's partially razed camp are at upper right.
O. C. Havens, © National Geographic Society.

gigantic rock pile—the accumulation of fallen walls and centuries of wind-blown sand—and finding, after a few hours' labor, a whole series of ancient dwellings unfolding itself."

As for problems, he noted that the difficulties of excavation increase in proportion to depth, "and the uninitiated can scarcely realize the problem of clearing deep rooms beneath interlocked and, often, insecure walls."

One of the most important results of their first season's work, Judd felt, was identification of distinct types of masonry used in the construction of Pueblo Bonito. He initially identified three types but later expanded the classification to four. The first and crudest was found in the oldest sections of the pueblo, in its north and northwest sections. This aged settlement of irregular outline formed the nucleus of the newer and much larger community that would become the "modern" Pueblo Bonito. Roughly broken off pieces of sandstone the full width of the wall were laid into abundant quantities of mud.

In the other three varieties of masonry, the interior of the wall was rubble faced with a much more elegant stone veneer. In the second type, intermediate in age, the facing consisted of blocks of sandstone smoothed on their outer face only and chinked all around with small flat chips of sandstone. The third and fourth types were both later masonry. In the third type, the veneer consisted of even horizontal rows of matched large blocks alternating with bands of smaller, inch-thick tablets of sandstone. In the fourth type, the veneer was made of tabular slabs of sandstone almost all of the same thickness laid with a minimum of mud plaster between them.

The quality of the masonry wasn't all that was noteworthy about the later dwellings at Bonito. They had an almost measured regularity, neatly squared corners, and ceiling timbers selected with discrimination, and cut and peeled while green.

From all this Judd concluded that "irresistible influences" were at work affecting the masonry craft at different times. "But whether these influences represent merely local developments or culture phases introduced by newcomers is a problem we have yet to resolve."

The continual building and rebuilding evident at Pueblo Bonito, often the newer sections cannibalizing materials from the older ones, kept things interesting for the archaeological sleuths at Bonito. "Whenever one of the old Bonitians got the new idea," Judd wrote, "he set about its realization, even if this meant destruction of the house he had erected with infinite labor. Beneath a large majority of the 40-odd rooms excavated during the summer of 1921 we found the razed walls of still older houses."

This passage is typical of Judd in a way I find interesting. In his descriptions of the work at Bonito he never had any qualms about populating the rooms and courtyards with people—the "Bonitians" he called them. He obviously considered that one goal of the expedition's work was to help bring to life the ancient culture of Chaco. His writings reveal an interest in the people as people and a talent for communicating the intriguing discoveries about Chacoan culture to a wider public. Not for him merely the dry recitation of archaeological detail. He spoke of the desirability of coaxing meaning out of every stone and pottery fragment, "to breathe new life into these cold, inanimate objects."

Even his two major professional reports on the work at Chaco, nearly 800 pages of material in two books published decades later by the Smithsonian Institution, have lengthy sections on living conditions, means of subsistence, dress and adornment, household tools, hunting weapons, and so on. His approach and thinking, although firmly founded on painstaking archaeological detail, never seemed to lose sight of the culture they were attempting to elucidate. He didn't

Women at Pueblo Bonito grind corn into flour on large troughed stone, the metate, with smaller, loaf-shaped stone, the mano. Drawing by Jerry Livingston, National Park Service.

forget the general amidst all the specifics. And he didn't shy from well-informed speculation and extrapolation.

Take these passages on family life and living conditions, for example:

"Family life in Pueblo Bonito probably differed very little from that which [ethnologist-photographer Victor] Mindeleff saw among the western Pueblos in the final quarter of the nineteenth century. Descent was unquestionably matrilineal, as it still is; the mother, rather than the father, was head of the household. Married daughters, with their husbands and children, continued to live in the maternal home. All shared the same living quarters, the same hearth and kitchen utensils. Meals were eaten twice a day from food bowls placed directly upon the floor; fingers served in lieu of forks. Blankets and pelts were folded as sets by day and spread upon the floor at night."

He suggested that Bonitian homes as a rule consisted of a general living room and one or more rooms for storage. The three successive types of masonry "each of a quality to awaken presentday admiration" was "invariably hidden under a thin coat of plaster." The lower part of the interior walls were often whitened or washed with a contrasting clay or set apart by a single white band. For whitewash, the people had used a soft, muddy-looking sandstone. Judd and his colleagues found several worked pieces of such sandstone. They did an experiment and learned that it readily disintegrates in water "and produces a grayish pigment identical in all outward appearances with that employed by the ancients."

The Bonitians also had clothes racks. "Anticipating the modern Zuni practice, our Bonitians sometimes built in, at time of construction, single poles for suspension of surplus blankets and wearing apparel. These poles invariably crossed the lesser dimension of the room." There was also evidence of sundry shelves, cupboards, and wall pegs.

Furniture presented a problem. "In all the rooms of Pueblo Bonito we found but one piece of furniture—a stool made from a section of pine log." But Judd reminds us that in 1883 neither the Hopi nor Zuni considered chairs and tables necessary house furnishings.

Beds, to judge from remnants found with burials, were "one or two thin rush mats, nothing more." For bed coverings they had daytime cotton garments, turkey-feather robes, and tanned hides.

"Housewives pursued their daily tasks out of doors when possible—making pottery, preparing food, tending babies, etc.—on the terraced rooftops or in the courtyard below. Naked children romped, like happy puppies, all over the place." Some out-of-the way corners of the courtyards had shelters of cottonwood boughs to provide shade for summertime comfort. The project found two such arbors.

The Bonitian farmers, Judd felt certain, located their fields in the paths of rainwater running off higher land or in areas where low earth dams helped impound some of the water. As he noted, this "floodwater" method of irrigation is still widely practiced by Southwestern tribes, especially the Navajo of Judd's time in the vicinity of Chaco.

The people of Pueblo Bonito, and Chaco Canyon generally, made highly distinctive black-on-white pottery. Judd appreciated it for its breathless aesthetic appeal as much as for its scientific value. Pottery had been elevated "to the high plane of a fine art," he said. "Nowhere else in all the United States are earthenware vessels of ancient times found which surpass those of Chaco Canyon in beauty of form and decoration."

Once again he found himself thinking of the patient Chacoan craftsman (in this case craftswoman) at work. "The tracing of thin black lines over highly pol-

Three scrapers found in Pueblo Bonito made of bone, each beautifully inlaid with turquoise, jet, and shell.
Drawing by Jerry Livingston, National Park Service.

ished white surfaces, in patterns rarely if ever exactly duplicated, gave obvious joy to the Bonitian housewife." Without immense pride in her own handiwork such wonderful masterpieces could never be created. "The pottery of Pueblo Bonito stands at the very apex of ceramic achievement among the prehistoric peoples of our country."

Judd was also in awe of some of the jewelry unearthed in Pueblo Bonito. Even years later his enthusiasm over the discovery of one particularly elegant piece did not wane.

It was found quite by chance. They were working in Room 320, a small interior room on the west side of Pueblo Bonito. Baskets, pots, and disarticulated skeletons had been found so far, and Judd had joined two Zuni men working there. The floor had been half cleared. As they prepared to remove a couple of baskets from below the east door, Judd had a sudden impulse to turn once more to the north end. The floor had already been swept with handbrooms. Nevertheless Judd stroked his hand trowel into the dirt, once, twice. The second stroke turned up several beads. Using an awl and a brush, a few moments later, he turned up a carefully coiled turquoise necklace. With it were two pairs of "marvelously blue" earrings.

"I cannot adequately describe the thrill of that discovery," he wrote. "A casual scrape of a trowel across the ash-strewn floor, a stroke as mechanical as a thousand other strokes made every day, exposed the long-hidden treasure." It seemed to him that the necklace had been deliberately hidden, coiled and placed in a hollow between two pieces of flagstone and then covered with mud and ashes.

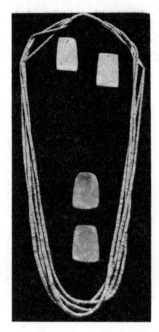

The extraordinary four-strand turquoise necklace and earrings Judd discovered in Room 320 of Pueblo Bonito. The necklace contains 2,500 handmade turquoise disks. Anthony B. Stewart, © National Geographic Society.

Bird carved from turquoise and found in Pueblo Bonito.
From Judd, Smithsonian Institution.

Word of the discovery spread like electricity. In minutes every Indian work-man and every one of Judd's assistants was hanging over the wall above, "look-ing down on the spectacular find." The original material on which the turquoise beads had been threaded remained in only faint traces. The expedition's camp of men had no needle fine enough to pass through the beads, so they requisitioned a lesser string from a workman's tenor banjo. In this way they were able to remove the turquoise disks in their proper sequence. The beads were arranged in four strings, and these had been tied together. The strands were about fourteen inches long. Judd marveled at the effort and skill that had gone into making this prehistoric jewel. It contained 2,500 beads, each painstakingly made individually by rubbing small disks of turquoise against sandstone and drilling each piece separately. The four ear pendants of oblong polished turquoise were each between one and two inches in length and a little more than one inch wide. The necklace was later restored as nearly as may be to its original condition and, along with the pendants, displayed in the Hall of Explorers at the National Geo-graphic Society's building in Washington.

"If another complete turquoise necklace has ever been discovered in a Pueblo ruin," said Judd in his scientific report three decades later, "I fail to find published record of it. Ours is therefore treasured for its rarity as well as its own inherent beauty."

Turquoise was a treasured possession in those days, just as it is among today's Southwestern Indians, both Pueblo and Navajo. The abundance of it at Bonito, Judd felt, would in itself have made Chaco Canyon widely known. Trade relationships seemed inevitable. He envisioned vendors of parrots arriving from Vera Cruz and dealers in seashells making the perilous journey on foot from the Pacific Coast.

Judd felt certain the archaeological evidence pointed to Pueblo Bonito being the product of two distinct groups of people. He called them the Old Bonitians and the Late Bonitians. In his view the Old Bonitians were the founders of the pueblo. The Late Bonitians were invited immigrants and the primary developers of Bonito. It seemed as though the two peoples jointly occupied the pueblo for a hundred years or more. "Yet the houses they built and lived in, the tools they made and used, differ so much that physical, linguistic, and mental differences between the two may be presumed." He felt the Late Bonitians were aggressive and had taken over the leadership immediately upon their arrival. The Old Bonitians, he believed, were ultraconservative, clinging to their old habits and ways. It was the Late Bonitians, in this view, who created the Classic Chaco culture, "most advanced in all the Southwest." For example, it was they, he said, who were responsible for all parts of the pueblo faced with the sophisticated masonry of Types 2, 3, and 4. The Old Bonitians used the rough-hewn Type 1. He thought of the Old Bonitians as intellectually dormant, lagging a century behind in cultural development.

He also saw evidence of a society increasingly concerned with security as time went on. Everywhere he saw signs in the construction at Bonito that he interpreted as measures against marauders. For example, the original settlement had no door in its convex, or cliffward, wall. When the Late Bonitians came and built another tier of rooms along the outer edge of that wall they included doorways but later sealed them up. Each successive change closed up more doorways. Eventually, he said, they closed or partially closed all ventilators in the rear wall and barred the only gateway to the village.

When the Late Bonitians expanded the pueblo they closed up part of the main town gate, opening out of the southeast corner of the West Court. They left a smaller doorway but later sealed it with masonry. "From that time forward there was no gate, no open door, anywhere in the outside wall of the town. From that day every man going out to work in his field, every woman seeking water of fuel, went and returned by ladders that led up to and across the rooftops of one-story houses enclosing the two courts on the south." It was almost the portrayal of a society under siege, yet where the supposed threat came from, if in fact it was a serious one, we cannot say.

Judd felt certain that the Bonitians not only lived under the threat of aggressive outsiders but in fact had come under attack. He even concocted an imaginary battle scene: "Hand-to-hand struggles were waged in the very courts of the village; hafted stone axes and wooden war clubs bruised brown bodies and broke many a bone; flint-tipped arrows sought out crouching defenders of the terraced houses. Terrifying war cries echoed through the canyon. . . ."

He had to admit his scenario was only surmise. No proof of such battles existed; the case was only circumstantial.

Judd and his colleagues were constantly looking to the Pueblo Indian villages of New Mexico and Arizona for insights into lifestyles and ways practiced by their ancient ancestors at Chaco Canyon. His reports are sprinkled with photographs of and references to the people and architecture of these pueblos. He mentions, for instance, that the pueblo of Acoma ("Sky City"), on a mesa top a hundred miles south-southeast of Chaco, "contains several features closely paralleling those of Pueblo Bonito." Among these similarities are the arrangement of its houses in long rows, with a high wall on one side, unbroken except for small ventilators, and, on the opposite side, stepped houses overlooking the plazas. He noted that Acoma is considered to be the oldest continuously inhabited settlement in the United States. He reproduced one of his own photographs of a Zuni Indian boy framed in a window at Pueblo Bonito, and speculated that he might just be a descendant of the artisans who built it. He showed pictures of Zuni and Hopi pottery makers; Zuni bead drillers; Zuni girls grinding corn meal; young Zuni men carrying tree trunks cross country; a Hopi farmer in his sandy field of wide-spaced, squatty stalks of Indian corn; and a Pueblo woman cooking thin disks of *piki* on a hot stone slab, "just as the Bonitian housewives must have cooked them a thousand years ago."

Zuni boy photographed by Neil Judd in a doorway at Pueblo Bonito. "Who knows but what [this] Zuni boy . . . is a descendant of the aboriginal artisans who quarried stone and mixed the mud that went into the towering walls of Pueblo Bonito?" wrote Judd. © National Geographic Society.

Pueblo Bonito today, as seen from cliffs above and looking west.
Chaco Center, NPS.

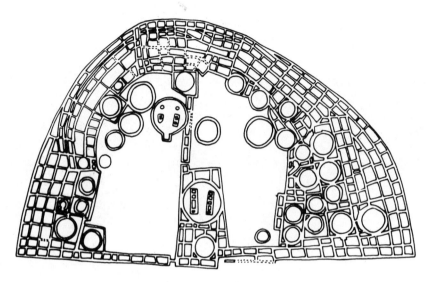

Floor plan of Pueblo Bonito. Chaco Center, NPS.

The archaeological work at Bonito continued four months each season for seven consecutive years from 1921 through 1927. The peak year, at least in numbers of Zuni and Navajo workmen on the excavation crews, was 1924. Twenty-eight of them, on average, were at work throughout that summer. A photograph of the camp at that time shows no fewer than eight canvas tents, each nearly the size of a small house, neatly arranged in a row down one side of the camp "street." External wooden frames lent some added stability to these canvas canyon homes. A flagstone sidewalk raised the walkpath up out of the worst of the dust and mud. A larger headquarters tent faced them from the other side of the street down near its end, the American flag and what appears to be the National Geographic Society flag flapping in the breeze. On down beyond the street's terminus, several more tents are anchored amidst the native brush. Parked at the left beside each other are the expedition's two open-sided, covered-top vehicles, looking surprisingly fit after their several years of archaeological logistics support among the wilds of northwestern New Mexico.

Judd joked that the expedition's corner grocery store was 106 miles away, "by happen-chance-road," in Gallup. Under good conditions the trip could be made one-way in seven hours. When the rains came, threatening to close the route, the drivers carried bedrolls and provisions for seven days. Even firewood had to be carried in from twenty miles away.

Even though no more than half a hundred men resided at the camp during the peak period of the summer, this made it, Judd delighted in noting, "the seventh largest settlement in San Juan County."

Ground-level view of Pueblo Bonito presents an almost endless series of rooms and kivas. Photo by author.

Series of doorways, Pueblo Bonito. *Photo by author.*

The work went well. "Delays and disappointments were but temporary." Every day, Judd said, "witnessed some definite progress toward the goal set when these expeditions were inaugurated. . . ." He reported in 1925 that "a hundred thousand tons of earth and stone and blown sand have been carted away." This peeling away of the covering of time revealed a maze of rooms "in which the former occupants unwittingly left the ineradicable thumbprints of their distinctive culture." Time hadn't dampened his enthusiasm for the ancient village whose history they were unraveling. ". . . Pueblo Bonito stands as a tribute to its unknown builders. It is one of the most remarkable achievements of all the varied Indian peoples who dwelt within the present United States in prehistoric times."

The abundance of kivas around Bonito's plaza attest to a society in which ritual is a primary force in daily life. Photo by author.

Pueblo del Arroyo rests in peaceful repose during a winter snowfall. Photo by author.

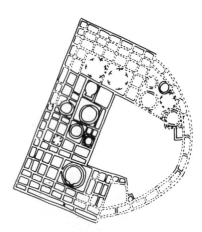

Floor plan of Pueblo del Arroyo.
Chaco Center, NPS.

Tri-walled structure at the rear of Pueblo del Arroyo hints of later influence or reoccupation from the northern San Juan region. Photo by author.

These were billed as the "Pueblo Bonito Expeditions." The neighboring ruin of Pueblo del Arroyo, which Judd had originally chosen to be excavated along with Bonito, definitely took second billing. Nevertheless work was carried out there as time permitted. Just 400 feet southwest of Pueblo Bonito on the edge of the Chaco arroyo, Pueblo del Arroyo was contemporaneous with Bonito. The expedition excavated 44 ground-floor rooms and 7 kivas in the pueblo, which Judd estimated contained 284 rooms and 14 kivas. Its masonry was of the later styles, Types 3 and 4, but was not as well done as at Bonito. Karl Ruppert, in charge of the digging at Pueblo del Arroyo, considered it to be the work of many individuals "each of whom built according to his personal preferences but with left-over materials, the choice building stones having been utilized elsewhere." As at Bonito most doorways had eventually been sealed and the single gateway into the courtroom had been blocked. Judd saw evidence of influence or occupation from the northern San Juan region to this pueblo, especially in the remains of a tri-walled tower structure near the back typical of ruins in southwestern Colorado. None of the several burials found showed signs of wealth. Most of the material recovered consisted of pottery.

Judd's heart was clearly with Pueblo Bonito, and he would forever be identified with the work there. His expedition not only excavated but took measures to preserve. Throughout the project, a repair crew was kept busy strengthening walls, patching broken masonry, replacing missing door lintels, and taking other steps to forestall further disintegration. He wished as much as possible to keep the excavated rooms on display, "let its empty rooms tell their own story." But some of the "ruder stonework" on the western side was protected by wholly or partially refilling these rooms, the refill cupped in the middle.

Pueblo Bonito, as Judd said, was not merely the largest and best-known ruin in Chaco Canyon, "but the very symbol of Pueblo civilization in full flower." His seven seasons of work there accomplished what he and the sponsors set out to do, to know more of this particular pueblo "in order to know more of this civilization."

In a summary of the insights into life there, he again expressed his admiration for the remarkable people of Chaco Canyon who created this magnificent pueblo: "Pueblo Bonito stands today a fitting memorial to its unknown and long-forgotten inhabitants. It stands a monument to their primitive genius, to their tenacity of purpose, to their ambition to erect a communal home in which each resident should find a deep and permanent interest."

Not all the suppositions of the 1920s stood the test of time. By the 1980s, for example, some archaeologists were even questioning whether Pueblo Bonito had been primarily a "colossal apartmenthouse," as Judd described it, or more of a structure for regional business and trade. Not all the mysteries Judd and his col-

The monumental but graceful elegance of Pueblo Bonito stands today, as Judd wrote, as a fitting memorial to the genius and tenacity of its long-forgotten inhabitants. Photo by author.

leagues had to leave to future generations to solve have been yet resolved. Judd lamented not being able to decipher the forces that hastened the eventual abandonment of the pueblo and its canyon, "problems which still await solution." The same could still be said today.

Judd returned to his duties at the National Museum in Washington. The press of this work over the next two decades delayed his writing a detailed synthesis of the scientific work until his retirement in 1949, published in two extensive volumes in 1954 and 1964. Neil Judd lived to the age of eighty-nine. He died in Silver Spring, Maryland, on December 26, 1976, nearly half a century after his major work, the scientific deciphering of Pueblo Bonito, a monument in itself, was completed.

3. The Secrets of Time

The next four decades saw the focus at Chaco Canyon broaden. Primary attention had been directed to Pueblo Bonito for so long that the public could be excused for assuming that Chaco was a one-site attraction. Judd, you recall, spoke only of "Bonitians," not "Chacoans." Regional maps often noted only one site of interest. Sometimes they failed even to show Chaco Canyon itself or the national monument that embraced it. Yet as Alden Hayes, an archaeologist in Chaco Canyon for many years, recently emphasized, the place teems with fascinating archaeological sites. "No place north of Mexico contains so spectacular an array of prehistoric ruins concentrated in so small an area as a ten-mile stretch of Chaco Canyon in northwestern New Mexico."

At last the other dramatic sites at Chaco were to get the archaeological attention they deserved. Several would be excavated in the decades following the completion of the Judd expeditions. Lesser ruins from earlier periods would be studied as well. Tree-ring dating would establish absolute dates for the ruins of Chaco, and a chronology of settlement and succession would begin to be established. Students by the droves would come to Chaco to learn and observe, and later to teach others. Comprehensive projects to preserve and stabilize the ruins would be set in motion. The full scope of life at Chaco began to be elucidated.

The next big ruin to come under the archaeologist's scrutiny was Chetro Ketl, the neighboring great village a half mile to the east of Pueblo Bonito. The man who led this work was Edgar L. Hewett. Hewett was Director of the School of American Research of the Archaeological Institute of North America in Santa Fe and was also associated with the University of New Mexico in Albuquerque. He had long had an interest in the prehistoric sites of New Mexico. In fact, it was he, while president of New Mexico Normal University, who in 1900 had pressed the complaint against the work of the Hyde Exploring Expedition in Chaco Canyon, claiming they were vandalizing the ruins and abusing public lands. He had pushed strongly for the legislation that had established Chaco Canyon as a national monument.

He was an educator with long experience directing students in the field. He loved to test them with near-impossible tasks. The archaeologist Alfred Vincent Kidder, who was to gain fame for his excavations of the Pecos pueblo, southeast of Santa Fe, once told of his first encounter with Hewett. It was in 1907, when Kidder was a student of anthropology at Harvard. A note sent by Hewett asking for volunteers for an archaeological expedition to the Indian lands of the Southwest and tacked on a bulletin board snared the interest of Kidder and two other students. All three applied; Hewett accepted them. They met him after a sixty-mile wagon ride from Mancos, Colorado, at a three-room ranch in McElmo canyon close to the Utah border. The next morning Hewett tramped them "miles down the blazing hot canyon." They panted after him to the top of a mesa. There all around them was a panorama of incredible canyon country. It extended from Mesa Verde and Ute Peak in Colorado to distant mountains way off in Utah; from the spectacular buttes of Monument Valley to the Lukachukai mountains in Arizona. "None of us had ever viewed so much of the world all at one time, nor so wild and barren and broken a country as lay about us," Kidder recalled.

"Dr. Hewett waved an arm. 'I want you boys,' he said, 'to make an archaeological survey of this region. I'll be back in six weeks. You'd better get some horses.' "

Hewett later wrote that he gave the three this incredible task—virtually impossible for such inexperienced young students—to try them out. It was a test, a trial, and Kidder would always remember and draw strength from the ordeal.

Hewett had begun some excavations at Chetro Ketl in 1920. He had cleared a few rooms and kivas, dug a trench into one large trash mound, and done some tests on the ruin's Great Kiva. When Judd's big expedition began work the next year, Hewett volunteered to suspend operations until that project was over. His work at Chetro Ketl resumed in 1927 and continued for the next eight seasons. He was assisted by several people who would later make names of their own, among them Paul Reiter, Gordon Vivian, and Florence M. Hawley.

Chetro Ketl, like Bonito, was a huge prehistoric settlement. These two together with Pueblo del Arroyo formed a trio of giant pueblos all within earshot

Chetro Ketl's four-story kiva presides over pueblo's massive ruins.
Photo by author.

of each other. This thousand-yard stretch of Chaco Canyon undoubtedly formed the densest concentration of population in the entire canyon during the heyday of life there.

When Lieutenant Simpson had examined Chetro Ketl in 1849 he estimated that no less than thirty million pieces of stone had been quarried, transported, shaped, and laid in the walls. Hewett found this estimate conservative. "We now know that he might more accurately have made his estimate fifty million." Hewett's higher total came only after years of work at Chetro Ketl. He found that much more of the town was buried than Simpson had supposed and also that in large sections of the walls there were 800 pieces to the square yard rather than merely the 450 counted by Simpson. Either way, it again recalls that wonderful phrase Simpson used to describe his first view of a Chacoan ruin, at Pueblo Pintado: ". . . a magnificent piece of mosaic work."

Hewett marveled at the effort implied by the construction of Chetro Ketl. It wasn't just the intricate stonework. "The thousands of logs, poles, and slabs that had to be cut in distant forests, transported by manpower, prepared with stone tools and built into structures; the tons upon tons of mortar that had to be made—altogether it represents a prodigious task for the rather small population of Chetro Ketl."

And Chetro Ketl was just one of many such structures, large and small. "This, it must be remembered, was repeated proportionately in each of the large

Thousands of poles and beams had to be cut in distant forests to build Chetro Ketl. Edgar Hewett estimated 50 million pieces of stone had gone into its walls. Photo by author.

With its long back wall and expansive walled plaza, Chetro Ketl measures more than 1,500 feet around. Chaco Center, NPS.

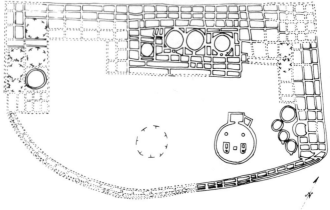

Floor plan of Chetro Ketl. Chaco Center, NPS.

communities of the Chaco Canyon, and an unknown number of small villages."
The ruins of Chaco have an extraordinary power to send all who observe them
into rhapsodies of delight and speculation, and Hewett was no exception. "It was
no unwilling work under the lash of priestly or kingly taskmasters," he proclaimed
in his *Ancient Life in the American Southwest;* "the American Indians were
never so ruled. It was the spontaneous impulse of a virile people, comparable to
the heaping up of great mounds far in excess of actual needs, by insect communities." Other examples of such "excessive activities" he said included the earth
mounds of the Mississippi Valley, the Egyptian Pyramids, the Great Wall of China,
and the European cathedrals of the Middle Ages.

Whether it was "excessive" or not, Chetro Ketl was certainly generous in
scale. The long, straight north wall, parallel to the canyon's north face, is more
than 450 feet long. Hewett pointed out that if one starts at the southeast corner of
the structure and follows its outer walls clear around to the starting point, he must
walk 1,540 feet—between a quarter and a third of a mile. "Here then was a com-
munity-residence (an ancient apartment house) which, if set down in a modern
American city, would pretty fully occupy two average blocks," he said. "As a
dwelling house, built by people for their own domestic purposes, I know of nothing to compare with it in the world—ancient or modern."

He also found Chetro Ketl especially beautiful. (He felt that Pueblo Bonito—
"Beautiful Village"—was surpassed in beauty by several of the other Chaco structures during their great days of occupation.) "Chetro Ketl is rich in the variety and
beauty of its walls. The striking banded effects, produced by courses of heavy
stone alternating with layers made up of fine laminated plates, are to be seen here
at their best."

Like many of the other great pueblos in Chaco Canyon, Chetro Ketl basically
took the shape of the capital letter E. Such a ground plan is ideal in many ways
for a large building. For one thing, the long section of the E can be built first and
the various stems easily added onto it later. This style of ground plan, Hewett
noted, is widely used today in American cities, "being dictated by economy and
efficiency as to light, air and space." He couldn't help adding that the Department
of Interior building in Washington, if it had its central stem shortened, "would be
in good Chaco-Canyon style." He thought, however, that the Chaquenos (as he
called the ancient residents here) would have spread the Washington building
over more space and made "a succession of terraces around the inner courts."

Chetro Ketl varied from the type, however, by having one of the stems of its
E, the eastern one, completely extended, and the western one only partially. There
was also a sweeping, curving front that tended to enclose the E, making it almost
more of a D. This curved front was not merely a wall as once supposed but a part
of the building two to three rooms wide and one to two stories high. It is 700 feet
long—well over two football fields. This wall is almost entirely buried—today as
well as in Hewett's time.

Chetro Ketl's back wall is more than 450 feet long. *Photo by author.*

Covered passageway, here outlined by a February snow-fall, connected Chetro Ketl's southwest and southeast corners, 750 feet apart. Photo by author.

Hewett began the excavation work at the southeast corner of the structure, laying out a ninety-square-foot area for attention. It wasn't long before he and his colleagues encountered some surprises. The curved front of the building, for one thing, was a massive structure, and it had no outside openings. But outside it was a trench eight feet deep and two feet wide, between heavy walls of masonry. Hewett found its floor to be hard and smooth, a sign of much use. "This trench, entirely unexpected, is without precedent in the ruins of the Southwest," said Hewett. He speculated that "it afforded a protected passage from the extreme southeast corner of the town to the southwestern quarter seven hundred feet away."

The southern extremity of the east wing of the building proved to have two stories buried. The excavation gave a good idea of some of the Chacoan construction knowledge and practices. Some of the partition walls were reinforced by imbedding timbers in the masonry "as we reinforce concrete walls with iron rods."

Before *its* excavation the plaza's "perfectly level" surface gave no sign of what was hidden in the dirt of centuries beneath. The extension of their digging a short way westward into the plaza revealed a labyrinth of kivas, shafts, and cists. Almost everywhere they dug they found kivas "crowding, cutting into and overlying one another." Each one was a variant from the conventional type of the San Juan cultural area. Their common characteristics were their circular shape and sturdily built masonry walls. Hewett was struck, however, by their diversity. "No two are alike in all respects." The features and structures they found likewise had little precedent in the San Juan area. Said Hewett, "There is something to keep the archaeologist guessing every day."

Just to the west of the area of excavated kivas was a large shallow depression. Some writers had guessed it was a reservoir; others, a huge kiva. "It proved to be one of the surprises that we look for in the Chaco," said Hewett, "an enormous circular ceremonial structure." Its average diameter is sixty-two and one-half feet. It was the largest structure of its kind excavated up to that time in the Southwest. (Casa Rinconada, a lone-standing Great Kiva on the southern side of Chaco Canyon excavated just shortly thereafter, would prove to be slightly larger.)

"We have uncovered here one of the most remarkable structures known in the Southwest," Hewett wrote. He suggested that probably three-fourths of its depth was subterranean. "The wall is the best Chaco Canyon masonry and averages about three feet thick." A bench of solid masonry about three and a half feet wide and four feet high extended around the inside of the bowl. This bench was interrupted by a two-and-a-half-foot-wide recess on the south and by a stairway on the north that ascended to a rectangular antechamber. The antechamber "has been finely plastered in what is now a good old ivory tint."

There were twenty-nine recessed niches each about a foot square at regular intervals around the circular chamber.

In the floor of the chamber were four pits twenty-six feet apart in the form of a perfect square. These masonry-lined holes had held the massive columns that supported the roof. The Chacoan civil engineers had provided the columns with a firm foundation: At the bottom of each hole they had inserted four enormous sandstone disks, one on top of the other, each weighing between one-half and three-quarters of a ton. Their effort paid off; more than 800 years later we see no sign of significant settling! The Chacoans had also placed into the pits, probably as a blessing, leather bags filled with bits of turquoise. The base of one of the upright timber columns still remained in place when Hewett's group uncovered it. It was a pine log twenty-six and one-half inches in diameter. "So far as I know," wrote Hewett, "this is the largest timber that has been found in the Chaco buildings." Think of the effort required to transport that monster log by hand from the distant forests to Chaco Canyon!

Giant kiva at Chetro Ketl. Edgar Hewett, who excavated it, called it "one of the most remarkable structures known in the Southwest." Stone disks at bottom of masonry-lined holes provided firm foundation for the massive columns that supported the roof. Wall niches were found to conceal necklaces having a total of 17,000 beads. *Photo by author.*

Snow outlines Chetro Ketl's giant kiva. View is outward to the south. The original floor of the kiva was discovered only after digging a total of twelve feet beneath the first floor. *Photo by author.*

For one more superlative about this extraordinary ceremonial chamber (for some reason he didn't seem to want to call it a Great Kiva), Hewett deferred to the ethnologist J. Walter Fewkes, "who expressed the opinion that this great bowl is the most important structure that has been excavated north of Aztec Mexico."

One reason for this kind of enthusiasm was that there was even more beneath this giant structure. Deciding to dig yet deeper, Hewett's crew of archaeologists laid off a forty-foot-long segment on the south side. They stripped the masonry from the bench around the interior. There, underneath, they found a more massive and far better built terrace. Extending the excavation down further, another and still another terrace was laid bare. The lower, or earlier, kiva wall also had niches built into them. There were ten of them, instead of the twenty-nine in the upper, newer kiva wall, and they had been sealed with masonry. When opened in 1932 each of the ten was found to contain a string of beads and turquoise pendants. Altogether there were 17,000 beads in the strands.

The original floor was not reached until they had dug a total of twelve feet below the first floor uncovered. Massive diagonal walls were found down there. "There is thus disclosed," wrote Hewett, "a vast structure in amphitheater form entirely new to southwestern archaeology, rivaling the temples of Mexico and Central America."

Another extraordinary feature of Chetro Ketl, Hewett made no point of, but later archaeologists certainly have. These are the walled-up colonnades along the wall at the end of the short stem of the E, facing the plaza. It was originally built as a row of masonry columns, which probably held up a roof over an open porch. Sometime later the Chacoans filled the spaces in between the columns with masonry to completely close the "porch." Many archaeologists take this to be a sign of Mexican influence at Chaco Canyon. Pillars and colonnades are well-known features of prehistoric architecture in central Mexico, but they were unknown in the American Southwest before the time of Chetro Ketl's construction. We will consider the controversial topic of Mexican influences at Chaco in a later chapter.

At about the same time the Great Kiva at Chetro Ketl was being unearthed to its lowermost terraces, archaeologist Gordon Vivian, Hewett's student, was also busy excavating Casa Rinconada. Rinconada nestles in a hillock across Chaco Wash to the southwest of Chetro Ketl. It is the largest Great Kiva in Chaco Canyon (sixty-three and one-half feet across at the floor level), and the only one that is not part of any community structure. Did it serve the ceremonial needs of people throughout a significant portion of the canyon or only those in the immediate vicinity, such as the three groups of small ruins within three hundred yards of its location? This is one of the mysteries we may never answer.

The kiva contains a bench around its circumference, like the one in Chetro Ketl, and four pits for the vertical roof supports. There is a stone firebox (some

Walled-up colonnades facing plaza at Chetro Ketl are seen by some as evidence of meso-American influence at Chaco. Photo by author.

have called it an altar) on the south-central floor and a subfloor vault on each of the east and west sides. One of its extraordinary features is its subterranean passageway. It is unique among the Great Kivas of Chaco. Leading from the northwest sector of the kiva floor, the passageway descends four steps and runs northeast in a fairly straight course. Then in a short curve, it passes under both the masonry bench and the main wall. Then it rises in a series of steps to the level of the first of two antechambers and by a second series of steps into the second antechamber. Whatever its ceremonial significance, this thirty-nine-foot-long passageway *would* have allowed the participants in rituals to appear on the kiva floor without the seated spectators seeing them entering from above or the side.

Indented into the masonry walls around the circumference of Casa Rinconada are twenty-eight regularly spaced niches, like those at Chetro Ketl's giant chamber, each about a foot wide, a foot deep, and a little more than a foot high. There are also six other irregularly distributed niches, lower in the wall than the others and asymmetrical in arrangement—four on the west side and two on the east side. The purpose of all these niches has been a source of speculation ever since their exposure.

No significant cultural material was ever found in the excavations at Casa Rinconada. Gordon Vivian later rechecked the records. He confirmed that no more than 385 decorated potsherds were recovered in the excavation of Rinconada.

Winter view of snow-covered Casa Rinconada, showing the bench and wall niches around its interior wall. Photo by author.

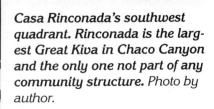

Casa Rinconada's southwest quadrant. Rinconada is the largest Great Kiva in Chaco Canyon and the only one not part of any community structure. Photo by author.

Subterranean passageway at Casa Rinconada could have allowed Chacoans participating in rituals to appear in center of chamber. Photo by author.

By this time, the School of American Research and the University of New Mexico had established a permanent scientific station in Chaco Canyon. Every summer, groups of university students came from far and wide to study problems in Southwestern archaeology. Hewett spoke with some pride of it as the training ground for graduate students who already had previous field experience in "the more elementary problems" elsewhere. Laboratories were set up to study the material gathered. A field museum was installed, together with library and photographic equipment. The research and education program covered not only archaeology but also geology, palaeontology, climatology, and desert life.

There is another story to mention before we proceed. It is of an amazing development that helped archaeologists to understand the cultural history not only of Chaco Canyon but also of the entire American Southwest. It is astronomer Andrew Ellicott Douglass's lifelong project which began as an effort to record the fingerprint of the sun in the growth rings of trees and ended instead in development of the science of dendochronology, or tree-ring dating.

Douglass had left the Harvard College Observatory at the age of twenty-seven to move to the Southwest and help Percival Lowell found the observatory that bears Lowell's name at Flagstaff, Arizona. Later he moved to the University of Arizona. In Arizona Douglass took up the study of tree rings as a hobby. It was clear that the width of the annual growth rings of trees varied from year to year and that these fluctuations reflected variations in annual growth conditions. He was interested in whether the roughly eleven-year cycle of sunspot activity on the surface of the sun had any influence on weather on the earth. If it did, he figured there should be some eleven-year repeating pattern in the width of tree rings. He worked very carefully and systematically on the problem. He invented optical instruments for identifying recurring width patterns. His effort to show an influ-

Wood beams from Pueblo del Arroyo, built A.D. 1053–1103. Wood specimens at various Chacoan ruins allowed archaeologists to trace the sequences of development in Chaco Canyon. Photo by author.

ence of solar activity on climate in the rings of trees never did prove persuasive, but what seemed at first to be merely a side effect of this work, tree-ring dating, had a profound impact throughout the word of archaeology.

Douglass's task was to compile a record of the patterns of annual tree-ring widths. By matching the pattern on the older end of a core of wood of known age with the pattern on the younger end of a core of wood of unknown older age, and repeating this process time and again, he was able to push farther back into time the record of tree-ring patterns. Then by counting back the total number of tree rings from the present to the outer ring on a particular piece of wood, he could ascertain the number of years elapsed between its death or cutting to the present. None of this was as easy as it sounds in the quick telling. It's a little like uniquely identifying one piece in a thousand-piece jigsaw puzzle in which each one is only slightly different from the rest. Many successions of patterns looked very similar to other successions. It is necessary to be extremely careful not to be fooled. Douglass was a careful man, and the technique proved successful. Its application to archaeology was inevitable.

How old was Pueblo Bonito? When were the various sections of the great ruins built? How long did the people stay? Everybody had asked these questions. Douglass and his tree-ring records were to provide the answer.

In 1922 Neil Judd had expressed a belief that Douglass's developing technique might provide an absolute date for Pueblo Bonito. With his cooperation and more National Geographic Society funding, three expeditions were sent into the field to collect the necessary beams that would provide a continuous record from the oldest trees then dated back to whenever the people of Chaco Canyon occupied the great structures there. One piece of wood eventually collected was a miserable-looking charred beam from an old ruin near Showlow, Arizona, whose outer, or youngest, rings overlapped perfectly with Douglass's previously oldest Arizona trees, which went back to A.D. 1380. There was no question whatsoever as to its dating. The innermost, or oldest, rings of the wood went back to before the middle of the thirteenth century. Said Douglass, "We learned that this charred old stick began its life as a promising upright pine A.D. 1237, just ten years after the Sixth Crusade moved eastward. . . ."

The problem now was to connect that unmistakable chronology, from the present back to A.D. 1237, with the beam records he had already obtained at Bonito and Aztec Ruin, north of Chaco Canyon and from other prehistoric ruins in the Southwest. That earlier work had allowed him to show the *relative* ages of those ruins. He had, for example, been able to send this little note to Earl Morris, the excavator of the Aztec Ruin: "I thought you might be interested to know that the latest beam in the ceiling of the Aztec Ruin was cut just exactly nine years before the latest beam from Bonito." He *thought* Morris might be interested? This precise knowledge had sent Morris into ecstasy. But Douglass had no way of knowing what the exact dates were. More ancient beams from ruins all over the

Southwest had been collected and a record of tree-ring variations in ancient times compiled. But this prehistoric chronology still did not connect with the standard chronology from modern times back to the fourteenth century. There was a tantalizing "gap," and nobody knew how long it was. This notorious gap remained unbridged for years.

Now, however, Douglass had before him the Showlow wood which extended the "modern" chronology all the way back to A.D. 1237. Was there a chance it would connect with the prehistoric chronology? He and his colleagues, he recalled, nervously tried to joke about the possibility, "but failed miserably." That night, like the characters in an Agatha Christie novel gathering in the drawing room to hear the solution to the crime, they met. Douglass described the scene:

"We gathered under the spluttering old gasoline torch in the village hotel, and beneath its flickering light, by the use of my skeleton plots of prehistoric tree rings, we began to determine whether our historical chronology . . . might not overlap the old chronology.

"As we studied these rings the answer came. There *was* a match. In fact, the overlap was considerable. "Our big surprise! We had not a gap to bridge, as we had thought, but one we had closed without knowing it!"

He explained. "Our two chronologies had covered an overlapping period. But those rings of the old series which overlapped the new . . . had been gathered from such small fragments that I had never been willing to accept their evidence as to this overlapping. . . . It was Beam HH39 [the Showlow beam] that cleared away all doubt."

Douglass couldn't get to sleep that night. Whatever the rest of us may count to try to get to sleep, he was counting, and visualizing, tree rings and their patterns. "Lying awake, I visualized all the individual rings concerned in this agreement and became completely satisfied that the relationship between our prehistoric and historic ring records had been definitely ascertained."

That poor decayed charred beam which had locked together the two chronologies of the Southwest had, by helping archaeologists to compile the cultural history of the region, ensured its own lasting place in history. ". . . Beam HH39. . . ," Douglass said, "in American archaeology is destined to hold a place comparable to Egypt's Rosetta Stone."

The rest was fun. The tree-ring calendar now extended all the way back to the end of the sixth century in the Southwest. "When I finally went to sleep," wrote Douglass, "it was with the consciousness that my old chronology had begun A.D. 700; that the earliest beam we had recovered from Pueblo Bonito had been cut A.D. 919 from a tree that was 219 years old when cut; that Pueblo Bonito had reached its golden age in 1067 and was still occupied in 1127."

A succession of definite dates of important events in the history of Pueblo Bonito and other major ruins in the region soon was at hand. For Pueblo Bonito various portions were under construction at different times: A.D. 919, 1017, 1033–92, 1102, and 1130. Pueblo del Arroyo, just across the way, was being built from 1053–1103. Up at Mesa Verde, Richard Wetherill's Cliff Palace dated at 1073; Oak Tree House, 1112; Spring House, 1115; Balcony House, 1190–1206; Square Tower House, 1204; and Spruce Tree House, 1216 and 1262. The age of Earl Morris's Aztec Ruin, geographically between Mesa Verde and Chaco Canyon, was now known absolutely, not just relatively. The beams Morris had sent Douglass for study now fit into the chronology at A.D. 1110–21. Over in Grand Gulch, Utah, some cliff dwellings came in at 1133–35. Out in the Chinle area on the Navajo Reservation in Arizona, Sliding Ruin yielded dates of 936–57. White House Ruin in Canyon de Chelley gave dates of 1060–96, 1219, and 1275; Mummy Cave, 1253–84.

The years of ambiguity were over; archaeologists could revel in the certainty of their newly established chronology of ancient settlement in the Southwest. I wonder if any archaeologist before the advent of dendrochronology even dared dream that one day he would have available a means to date thousand-year-old wood materials to the *exact year*. What an extraordinary discovery!

One of the first to take advantage of the new technique for understanding the full chronology of a site at Chaco Canyon was Florence M. Hawley, a student working there on her University of Chicago Ph.D. thesis. She would later join the faculty of the University of New Mexico and become one of the most respected scholars in Southwestern archaeology, ethnology, and dendrochronology.

She gathered wood specimens from Chetro Ketl and worked closely with Douglass in their analysis. Although any wood beam can be dated to the precise year it was cut, she realized one complicating problem had to be faced. The ancient people of Chaco Canyon, just as do their modern pueblo counterparts,

Tree-ring dating on the abundant wooden beams in Chetro Ketl enabled Florence Hawley Ellis to establish a detailed chronology of this Chacoan site. Photo by author.

frequently re-used old beams from demolished structures side by side with those freshly cut for new buildings. For that reason, she found it advisable to take a specimen of every piece of wood available in a room and date each one. The dates will vary some, but she should be able to tell the building date of a room from the clustering of the results. Older specimens would represent re-used materials. At some point the people of Chetro Ketl would have to use a new beam to replace some weakened old one, and the dates of all the other beams will cluster at some year prior to its age. By also checking masonry types and beam dates in adjoining rooms, the archaeologist can gain more and more confidence about the actual span of occupation of each room.

All this she did. She recorded all the dates from one room and charted the number of specimens from one room dating in any one year. Her work established a detailed chronology of the construction and occupation of Chetro Ketl. It became the best-dated ruin in Chaco Canyon.

She found that the history of Chetro Ketl could be organized into three rather natural periods. The first was the longest and least known. It lasted from A.D. 945 to 1030. No walls of this first period had yet been discovered at Chetro Ketl, since deep excavation had only begun. She knew of the existence of this period through discovery of timbers cut during this period but subsequently re-used in walls of later construction. But logs of these same dates had been found at other ruins in Chaco Canyon and were consistently associated with walls of crude masonry of Type I. Clearly this was the formative period of Chetro Ketl.

The second period was from 1030 to 1090. These six decades were marked by rapid growth of Chetro Ketl. The masonry was "excellent." Between 1030 and 1070 the masonry was of Type II. By 1062 masonry of Type III was already in use. From 1062 to 1070 both Types II and III were being used; after 1070 the masons of Chetro Ketl used Type III exclusively. During the period from 1060 to 1090 the people of Chetro Ketl were undertaking extensive remodeling and rebuilding of the pueblo. They built new additions that resulted in its growth on the ground plan still apparent today, except for a few additions made in the later period. Polished black on white pottery was widespread. This ware was the best pottery developed in Chaco Canyon. Some semipolished and unpolished ware was still being made. "The entire 60-year period," said Hawley, "appears to have been the most prosperous and flourishing of Chetro Ketl history."

The third and last main period was from 1099 to 1116. By now something had happened at Chetro Ketl. In this brief period the architecture degenerated. The stone masons used three types of masonry, but, Hawley found, "workmanship was not equal to that of the second period." It was, in fact, "crude." Polished black on white pottery remained prevalent; the other types were still being made too.

We can hardly help feeling a sense of sadness at having a window into this last period of disruption at Chetro Ketl, whatever its cause may have been. Chetro

Ketl, she found, was probably deserted about 1120. No beam dated after 1116 is found in its walls.

There seemed to be signs of reoccupation of this great abandoned village by some small migrating group. Some last stonework bears little resemblance to typical Chaco masonry types. It was conceivable that this masonry "may represent only the degenerate work of a small native group who lingered on in their old home," Hawley wrote, "but the fact that the Great Sanctuary [the Great Kiva Hewett's group had excavated] was finally relined in this style rather suggests the work of newcomers."

There was no evidence indicating that the abandonment of the great Chaco pueblos was the result of either a war of extermination or of pestilence. As others had noted, protective measures had been taken against possible increasing pressure from nomadic tribes during the second period—the village being enclosed by the curved outside wall—but there were no direct signs of warfare. Two long droughts during this period of Chaco history had made little impression on building activities at Chetro Ketl, she pointed out. Whatever the cause of the abandonment of Chetro Ketl, the tree-ring dates showed that "Chaco was the first of the large pueblo centers [in the Four Corners region] to fall," despite the influx of new residents from the north and northwest. "Its demise was followed by that of Mesa Verde, and considerably later by that of the Kayenta settlements."

Such a brief period of time Chetro Ketl remained at its peak! The history of its settlement, occupation, and abandonment had now been sketched in outline. Some questions had been answered; others, some of them disturbing, remained. We may never know all the whys; but at least we now know the whens.

For decades archaeologists had been busy throughout the Southwest compiling relative chronologies of the history of the people that settled, eventually built the great ruins of Chaco Canyon and elsewhere, and then moved on. Now they had absolute dates to anchor these general periods of time.

Several such chronologies, each with slightly different labels for the different periods of culture, had been established. Because each of them has certain advantages over the others and certain disadvantages as well, all of them remain in use today.

The first classification was established at a meeting of Southwestern archaeologists at A.V. Kidder's field camp at Pecos, New Mexico, in 1927. This was the first ordering of the cultural progress of the prehistoric inhabitants of Chaco Canyon and the Four Corners region. Later Frank H.H. Roberts, Jr., who had been in charge of Judd's trash-mound stratigraphy at Pueblo Bonito, proposed a somewhat different system of classification. In its final form, published in 1935, it offers large descriptive categories. Finally Harold S. Gladwin in 1945 offered still another classification system, designed to apply only to the "Chaco Branch."

AD	PECOS	ROBERTS	GLADWIN	EARLY ROBERTS
−100	Basketmaker I (Archaic)			Pre-Basketmaker
0				------------?------------
100				
200	Basketmaker II	Basketmaker		Basketmaker
300				
400				
500			------------?------------	------------?------------
600	Basketmaker III	Modified Basketmaker	La Plata Phase	Post-Basketmaker
700			------------?------------	
			White Mound Phase	------------?------------
800	Pueblo I	Developmental Pueblo	Kiatuthlanna Phase	Pre-Pueblo
900			Red Mesa Phase	------------?------------
	Early Pueblo II			Transitional
1000	Late Pueblo II		------------?------------	------------?------------
			Wingate Phase	Early Pueblo
1100	Early Pueblo III			------------?------------
1200		Great Pueblo	Hosta Butt Phase / Bonito Phase / McElmo Phase	Classic Pueblo
1300	Late Pueblo III			

Various classifications of Chacoan culture. *From Hayes, et al., 1981.*

The Pecos system is perhaps the most frequently used today. It suggests three periods of Basketmaker culture from before the time of Christ up to A.D. 750. Then followed the formative stage of Pueblo culture, Pueblo I (from 750 to 900); Pueblo II (from 900 to 1030); and Pueblo III (from about 1030 to the 1300s). What the Pecos system calls the Pueblo III period of pueblo culture, Roberts calls simply "Great Pueblo." Gladwin recognizes different cultural attributes in the same period. For instance, his system recognizes the Bonito phase (the great pueblos of Chaco, with their walls of fine-banded masonry) along with the Hosta Butte phase. These were small pueblos that were mostly contemporaneous with the Bonito phase but which architecturally differed little from Pueblo II structures. He also notes a McElmo phase, settlements apparently populated with Mesa Verde-type people.

Archaeologists today may use any one of these systems, depending upon the circumstances. The categories are the natural attempt of the archaeological sleuths to impose some kind of order on what we know about the trends in life and society of the ancient people of Chaco Canyon and the Southwest. They have, admittedly, no life to them. It is up to us not to lose sight of the living, breathing people who inhabited these vast canyon lands and these wonderful villages we now call ruins. We can envision the Indian men and women bringing about these changes over generations, erecting and living in the magnificent buildings whose wonders we observe today, and later gradually abandoning them to the ages. We can use our imaginations to populate the rooms, plazas, and fields with the people of Chaco.

Even though the excitment of the grand excavations of the 1920s and 1930s was now over, Chaco Canyon still occasionally bustled with archaeological activity, especially in the summers. The summer field schools at Chaco continued training some of the nation's outstanding young archaeologists each year. These lively and stimulating field schools remained a joint effort of the School of American Research and the University of New Mexico until 1937. That year the SAR pulled out and the University continued them singly until 1947, except for a hiatus during World War II. The University's work concentrated on a cluster of small pueblos across the canyon from Pueblo Bonito.

Beginning in 1947, the main archaeological work in Chaco Canyon was taken over by the National Park Service. The NPS's original mandate concerning Chaco was to preserve the ruins, and in that role it had been active to some degree all the way back to Judd's expeditions, when it provided some help in stabilizing the exposed walls of Pueblo Bonito. Gordon Vivian supervised the first sizeable stabilization project in the early 1930s at Bonito, Chetro Ketl, and Casa Rinconada. The NPS stationed a permanent ruins stabilization unit in the Canyon from 1937 to 1957. The excellent condition of many of the walls and rooms visitors see today in Chaco Canyon is a consequence of these preservation efforts begun back then. Such work continues today.

Kin Kletso
silhouetted by winter sun.
Photo by author.

Kin Kletso
from mesa wall.
Photo by author.

Gordon Vivian also carried out many of the NPS's *excavation* efforts. In 1939 he excavated an early Pueblo II community known as 3-C in the gap between Fajada Butte and Chacra Mesa. In 1950 he excavated the tri-walled complex abutting the rear of Pueblo del Arroyo, work the Judd expeditions had partially begun. In 1951 and 1953 Vivian and Tom Mathews excavated the ruins of Kin Kletso.

Kin Kletso, about half a mile west of Pueblo Bonito, is a compact, rectangular, medium-sized town having about fifty-five ground-floor rooms, four kivas, and a tower kiva. It is the only carefully excavated and reported Chaco site of what Gladwin's classification system called the McElmo phase of Pueblo III culture. All the evidence indicates that Kin Kletso was constructed and settled by people showing a northern (San Juan) influence. Here they erected their own residences; others of them probably moved into existing towns in Chaco Canyon, undoubtedly with the permission of the Chacoan residents at the time.

The Park Service also excavated two small ruins threatened by the erosion of widening arroyos. One was a late pueblo on the banks of Chaco Wash near Fajada Butte (dug in 1958); the other was Lizard House, a village contemporaneous with Chetro Ketl, located in a rincon just east of it. A survey of archaeologi-

Kin Kletso's simple masonry indicates it was built and settled by people showing a northern (San Juan) influence. *Photo by author.*

cal sites within the borders of the Chaco Canyon National Monument was carried out at intermittent intervals over the decades. The monument's archaeologists built on a record first begun by the University of New Mexico. By 1970 the total number of sites recorded had reached 395.

The focus of scientific interest in Chaco Canyon had long since ceased centering solely on the two or three major excavated ruins. The sites to explore were almost unlimited. More important, the questions about Chacoan culture had multiplied, not diminished. It was now time to turn the archaeological efforts toward understanding what had made the Chacoan culture so special. And that set the stage for the Chaco Project of the 1970s—the most intensive concentrated inquiry ever directed toward the ancient people of Chaco.

4. The Chaco Project

The enigmas of Chacoan culture had not been swept away by more than a century of discovery and exploration. The gulf of time that separated these mysterious prehistoric builders from the educated gaze of the probing archaeologists protected some of the Chacoans' most essential and tantalizing secrets. We now were able to *see* much of what had been sheathed in the dust of centuries, but we yearned to *understand*.

Thus was born the Chaco Project.

It was the vision of a man who had been one of the many university students trained in Southwestern archaeology during those summer field schools at Chaco Canyon back in the 1930s. His name was John M. Corbett. Three decades later he recognized Chaco's still-untapped archaeological richness. And, now as chief archaeologist for the U.S. National Park Service, he was in a position to do something about it. Corbett, according to friends, also retained a strong affection for the Southwest and for the legacy of its ancient prehistoric people. The open spaces and lonely vistas around Chaco seemed, as they do for so many others, to invigorate his thoughts. He was, in the best sense, a romantic. To a historian of the Chaco Project, a friend of Corbett fondly recalled some of their walks through Chaco. Corbett would slowly pronounce the names of the ruins—Kin Bineola, Kin Ya'a, Tsin Kletsin—"savoring the sound of each."

Corbett, said this friend Wilfred Logan, himself an archaeologist, was one of the last of the generalists in anthropology. "John never forgot that he was dealing with things human." He was "vibrantly aware" that the ruins, the potsherds, and the other visible remnants of Chacoan culture came from "people who lived, ate, starved, became angry, fought each other, loved, married, produced children, died, and were grieved for."

In 1968 he and his immediate supervisor, Ernest Allen Connally, made a trip to Chaco. They had for some time been discussing how the National Park Service could do "something big for Chaco," in Connally's recollection. They recognized the whole region's unparalleled archaeological significance. Connally hoped to raise the agency's archaeological research "to an undisputed place on the cutting edge of scientific inquiry."

The idea of a comprehensive fifteen-year (later reduced to ten-year) program of sophisticated research into every aspect of Chacoan culture took hold. These men and sympathetic archaeological allies escorted the proposal through the mazes and pitfalls of federal and local bureaucracies. After three years of some-times painful negotiations, a revised final memorandum of agreement establish-ing a joint National Park Service / University of New Mexico research center and scientific program to study the Chacoan culture was signed in September of 1971. Robert H. Lister, another one of the Southwestern archaeologists first trained at those summer field schools at Chaco Canyon, became its first director.

The Chaco Center eventually occupied quarters in Albuquerque on the sec-ond floor of the low Southwestern-style building housing the university's respected Department of Anthropology. Some of the center's archaeologists, all National Park Service employees, were given joint faculty appointments in the department. The Chaco Project was underway.

The scientific questions confronting the project's team of archaeologists were profound. They were also seemingly endless: What influenced the develop-ment and eventual downfall of town life in Chaco Canyon? How did Chacoan agriculture develop? What were its effects on the ecosystem and how did it relate to the culture itself? What were the relationships between the Chacoan's water-control systems and population size and political authority? What caused Chaco Canyon culture to advance so rapidly? What was going on with the several differ-ent types of communities in Chaco Canyon? What effects did the canyon's rapid population growth have on the culture itself and on the natural environment? How did resources, or the lack of them, cause the culture to adapt? What kinds of contacts did the Chacoans have with external cultures? What were the population movements into and out of Chaco? What insights into Chacoan social organiza-tion can be discerned? What implications might they have for past and present social problems? What motivated the abandonment of Chaco Canyon? How did it proceed and what were the people's destinations? . . . In other words, just about anything and everything anyone had wondered about this mysterious civilization.

One of the first projects began even before the Chaco Center was officially created. The University of New Mexico proposed to the center a reconnaissance of archaeological sites in Chaco based on systematic random sampling. W. James Judge, then in the university's anthropology department (and later to succeed Lister as director of the Chaco Center), supervised the fieldwork. He selected a rectangle 16 miles wide (east-west) by 8 miles (north-south) that was centered on the boundaries of the Chaco Canyon National Monument. The rectangle included all of the main part of the monument and a considerable portion of the land immediately around it. Most unconnected outlying areas of the monument, such as Kin Ya'a, Pueblo Pintado, and Kin Bineola, did not fall within the rectangle. Judge then divided the rectangle into eighty north-south strips. Each was 1,056 feet wide and 8 miles long. Twenty of these strips were then chosen for archaeological inspection.

During an eight-week period in June, July, and August 1971, four archaeologists (Dennis Stanford, John Beardsley, Leo Flynn, and Dan Witter) spaced 130 feet apart, walked along the length of these transect strips searching carefully for remnants of the prehistoric people who had lived there. They would survey half the width of one transect (528 feet) then double back on the other half.

Whenever anyone found an archaeological site, all four men converged on it, and they would all help carefully record everything found. They would spend up to an hour doing this at each site, before walking the transect again. The idea

Al Hayes at small site excavation in 1974. Hayes supervised an archaeological survey of Chaco Canyon during early years of the Chaco Project. *Photo by author.*

wasn't to collect artifacts but to record them, and to note their exact environmental setting. The whole process took longer than expected. When it was clear they would run out of time, they decided to survey only portions of the length of each transect strip. But the portion of each strip that passed through Chaco Canyon National Monument, including of course through the canyon itself, was surveyed.

This eight-week survey discovered evidence left by ancient people before any sedentary settlements and before any pottery making began in the Chaco region. At twenty different sites, most of them up on the mesas away from the canyon itself, they found ancient stone projectile points. These ranged in cultural age from the early Archaic Period through Basketmaker II—from all the way back to 5,000 B.C., when a few hunters roamed over an empty and lonely landscape, to shortly after the time of Christ. Archaeologists had long suspected that ancient followers of big game had hunted in the area, but these were the first definite sites identified or described.

A far more comprehensive archaeological survey began the next year. Its main goal was nothing less than a complete inventory of all the prehistoric archaeological sites within the boundaries of the monument—quite a task! The archaeologists also wanted to learn all they could about the distributions of populations and cultures from different periods and to determine why people located where they did.

The work began in the spring of 1972. Alden Hayes, another Hewett-trained archaeologist and old Chaco hand, supervised the survey. Twelve archaeologists went into the field. They divided into four three-man teams and walked abreast anywhere from 25 to 100 feet apart, depending on the terrain. They generally walked parallel to the crest of a ridge, or a wash, or a cliff face keeping a sharp eye out for any signs of prehistoric habitation.

A "site" might be a "lithic" area where some ancient hunter may have fashioned a projectile point, leaving a scattering of discarded chips of chert. It might be an area of potsherds, where residents of a thousand years ago had discarded their broken bowls. It might be the remains of an early Anasazi field house, the remnants of a single room probably erected for seasonal or specialized use by a few Indians. It might be a cliff emblazoned with prehistoric rock art, or an ancient stone cairn, or the remnant of an early Indian roadway or irrigation ditch. It might be a hearth, an isolated fireplace or baking pit or oven not part of any other structure. It might be the crumbled walls of a storage-room or a subsurface slab-lined cist. It might be an isolated kiva or a circle of stones, assumed to have had ceremonial purpose to its creators. Or it might be a pueblo, two or more rooms where an extended family or larger group had lived permanently.

Admittedly there is always some arbitrariness about what constitutes a separate archaeological site. Some archaeologists might consider "five sherds per five square meters" a site but not "three sherds and a stone chip." The Hayes survey decided simply that if "a recognizable stretch of sterile surface" lay between two areas of archaeological artifacts, then they would be considered two separate "sites." Most of the sites could be assigned to a cultural period, but not all. All in all, the accuracy of the field observations and the capabilities of the men making them always have to be assessed along with the information about the sites themselves.

Hayes put the matter this way: "Did he [the archaeologist], whether he brought dirty fingernails to the job, or a slipstick, know what he was looking at? A good deal of the time, I think we did. I know too that sometimes we did not."

By June of 1975 the crews of field archaeologists had systematically traipsed across forty-three square miles of Chaco mesa and canyon country, carefully recording every detail of ancient human habitation they could find. The area they examined included all the separated units of the then-Chaco Canyon National Monument (1,751 sites), plus nearly nine square miles outside the monument's boundaries, mainly to the south of the lower part of the canyon. They had identified 2,220 archaeological sites.

Seventy of them fell into the general span from Archaic times to Basketmaker II. Almost all of these were lithic areas where stone chips or an occasional knife, scraper, or spearpoint testified to the presence of early hunter-gatherers. Hearths were discovered at twenty-two of these areas.

These ancient sites were most commonly found in an exposed, south-facing position near the edge of a mesa or on a broad plateau or plain. Hardly any were in the bottomlands. But, as Hayes points out, that "does not necessarily indicate that mesas were favored locations, but rather that the mesas are where sites could be found." Many of the sites were found in areas scoured to bare rock by erosion and thus easily seen. Few were on the north sides of mesas. There is good reason for that, Hayes notes. The high ground trips the prevailing southwestern winds, making them drop their loads of spring sand on the north sides of mesas. Dunes are prevalent along these northeastern slopes, and there is no way of knowing how many Archaic sites rest buried beneath them.

The Basketmaker III period, beginning around A.D. 500, produced 188 sites. During this period the people took up the use of the bow and arrow instead of the atlatl (a device used by the ancient bison hunters to give added leverage and impetus to the throw of their spears), and so the projectile points changed tremendously. The houses of the Basketmaker III people were partly subterranean, basically circular pithouses, covered over with a roof of brush and mud. They built oval-shaped storage pits, or cists, lined with slabs of stone behind the houses. Pottery was rare. What there was of it was, by later Chaco standards, crude.

The archaeologists found 135 of these pithouse villages. A typical village might have anywhere from one to twelve pithouses and from zero to twelve cists. They also identified twenty-one Basketmaker III sherd areas, twenty-one isolated hearths or cists, and eleven field houses.

How many such sites are still undiscovered? Hayes believed the number found was "unquestionably much lower than their actual occurrence." He guessed that there are at least as many sites yet to be discovered as they found. Where are the others? Concealed under windblown sand on the mesa tops, buried beneath pueblos and other later structures built on top of them, and covered by deposition of silt in the arroyos. Fifteen Basketmaker III sites have been exposed by the erosional cutting of the sides of deep arroyos. One of them was nearly fifteen feet below the present surface. It was dated by the radiocarbon method to have an age of about A.D. 585. The watercourse seems to be about two feet lower than it was in the 1100s, so about thirteen feet of silt was deposited on top of the site in the first 500 years after its abandonment. Hayes guesses that there are at least 150 Basketmaker III sites still buried beneath the floodplain of Chaco Canyon.

The first period of permanent pueblo settlement, Pueblo I, began in the Chaco area around the middle of the eighth century. The people made their pit structures smaller and deeper. The external storage cists were fronted by open ramadas, and hearths were added. By about A.D. 800 in the areas around Chaco these ramadas were fully enclosed, and the houses became full pueblos. The pit-house had evolved into a kiva for the ceremonial life of the people. Apartments were formed by establishing the houses adjoining one another. There were three to six such units for each kiva. At first the people built them with poles and adobe, but as time went on they used more and more stone. Pottery painting styles underwent changes that help mark the occupations in distinctive periods.

The archaeologists found 457 of these Pueblo I sites. By now the occupation had begun to move into the canyon bottom, as a majority of the sites were found there and still more are believed to be buried in the silt.

Early Pueblo II builders most often used simple coursed masonry of selected stones. The houses were now built in straight lines, rather than the arcs of the earlier period. The builders of kivas were now usually lining them with masonry. The pottery was painted with narrow bands from the rim down to the shoulder, with the bases left plain. Four hundred ninety-eight Early Pueblo II sites were found.

Late Pueblo II was sometimes hard to distinguish from Early. The masonry was usually more substantial and kivas completely lined. The pottery was the main distinguishing feature. The archaeologists identified 449 sites as Late Pueblo II. The people had shifted their settlement locations rather dramatically by now. The mesas were virtually uninhabited. The canyon-bottom population was now nearly evenly strung out along the length of the canyon.

Something began to happen during the tenth century in Chaco Canyon. "Some new stimulus struck the slow, even progression of Anasazi culture in the Chaco," is the way Hayes describes it. This of course was the Early Pueblo III period, the time when the great, multistoried pueblos were constructed. Contemporaneous with them were many smaller, less remarkable pueblos, Gladwin's "Hosta Butte" phase. Their architecture was little different from that of Late Pueblo II. The dramatic "Bonito phase," however, which came at the same time, saw four-story-high structures rising up from the floor of Chaco Canyon, with massive walls, often banded masonry, numerous rooms, and giant kivas. The survey identified 400 sites as Early Pueblo III. Most of the pueblos were now in the canyon. This was the peak of population in Chaco Canyon.

By the time of the Late Pueblo III period in the late 1100s, the population had decreased. Some new construction was underway at New Alto, Kin Kletso, and Casa Chiquita, and Pueblo del Arroyo was expanded. The structures were made even more compact, and plazas were dispensed with. The masonry was now large blocks of stones, and the kiva design was in the Mesa Verde tradition. Hayes's survey identified 221 sites as Late Pueblo III.

The teams of archeologists also found water-control structures, quarries, and prehistoric roads, trails, and stairways (see later chapters). This detailed inventory survey of the material remnants of the prehistoric inhabitants over forty-three square miles of land in and around Chaco Canyon brought an enormous mass of new data to the study of Chaco culture. It would all contribute to the shifting ideas about who the Chaco people were and what they were doing.

This archaeological survey, detailed as it was, was just the beginning. The Chaco Project had as its mission a scientific examination of virtually every aspect

Distribution of early Pueblo III pueblos in area of Chaco Canyon. *From Hayes, et al., 1981.*

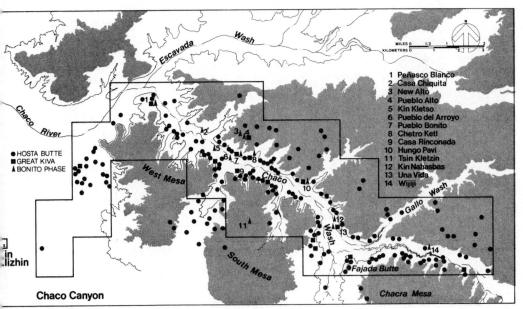

1 Peñasco Blanco
2 Casa Chiquita
3 New Alto
4 Pueblo Alto
5 Kin Kletso
6 Pueblo del Arroyo
7 Pueblo Bonito
8 Chetro Ketl
9 Casa Rinconada
10 Hungo Pavi
11 Tsin Kletzin
12 Kin Nahasbas
13 Una Vida
14 Wijiji

● HOSTA BUTTE
■ GREAT KIVA
▲ BONITO PHASE

Chaco Canyon

Chaco Project archaeologists at Chaco Canyon. L–R, front row: Peter McKenna, Tom Windes, Marcia Truell, and Jim Judge, Chaco Center director. Middle row: John Schelberg, Nancy Akins, LouAnn Jacobson, Cory Breternitz, Bob Powers, Wolky Toll, and Marcia Donaldson. Back: Steve Lekson, William Gillespie, Wirt Wills, and laborers. Chaco Center, NPS.

of the Chaco culture, and its archaeologists and other investigators into the prehistoric past would be kept busy for many more years.

Before the Chaco Project came to an end in 1981, 2,528 archaeological sites had been inventoried, and 27 sites had been excavated or tested. Putting aside for a moment the new understanding of Chaco culture that was being forged (the subject of our next five chapters), just the logistics of the project are impressive enough. More than 308,000 artifacts were recovered, including 255,000 ceramic sherds, 2,254 stone tools, 500 bone tools, 5,625 pieces of ground stone, 7,032 ornaments and pieces of minerals, and 1,000 miscellaneous stone artifacts. Nearly 120,000 other items were recovered, most of them animal bones but also egg shells, pollen samples, and plant specimens.

The records compiled were absolutely massive in number: 9,856 pages of field notes, forms, catalog sheets, and so on, 2,750 field maps and drawings, 15,987 black-and-white field photographs, and 2,257 color slides. Seventy-eight manuscripts and reports were on file. All this research was expected to lead eventually to at least twenty-one formal publications totaling more than 7,000 pages.

New Alto, on the mesa above Chaco Canyon. The Chaco Project excavated a portion of nearby Pueblo Alto in the late 1970s. Chaco Center, NPS.

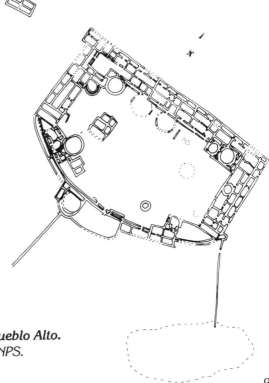

Floor plan of Pueblo Alto. Chaco Center, NPS.

93

This publication process itself was scheduled to go well into the mid-1980s. And that was if it could stay on schedule, a fervent hope but not a likely probability. Archaeology has never been very speedy in that regard. Judd's third and final report on his excavations in the 1920s was published in 1964. The Chaco Project, however, provided time to the archaeologists to analyze their results and write up their reports. For a while it seemed that the obstacles to writing and publication that have haunted so many other archaeological projects had in this case been averted. A number of reports were published, although with small printings. But in the end severe budget cutbacks in the mid-1980s eliminated government funding for those reports planned but not yet published. Their authors were forced to seek other ways to pay for their publication.

The intensity of the Chaco Project's research effort far outstripped anything done before at Chaco Canyon. One winter day in early 1983, after all the field-work was completed, I asked James Judge, the director of the Chaco Project from 1976 on, how it compared in magnitude to the early classic excavation expeditions at Chaco back in the twenties and thirties. There was no comparison, he said. "We have obtained more data and documentation from the excavation of the floor of just our sampled portion of Pueblo Alto than there had been from all the work done in all of Chaco Canyon previously."

5. Canals and Irrigation

For two days now the men of Chaco have anxiously watched the afternoon skies. Each day the puffs of white clouds that form off across the low mesas during the heat of the day have become greater in number. Some have turned the color of clay and grown into high pillars. But no rain has come.

It is the yearly time of great heat. The arroyo down below the great pueblos and below the neatly laid out fields of corn, beans, and squash lies empty. No water has been seen there since the last soft sprinkles of early spring, *Pus-chuts-otes* (the sticky ground, sowing month). The moon of *Sho-wats-otes* (ground soft like ashes, corn planting time) has passed, and so has *A-chin* (the month of the corn tassel). It is now *Hi-shin* (the moon of the first appearance of the corn ear)*, and the fertilizing powers of the rain are needed to bring the corn to fruition.

Ten days earlier the sun watcher had announced that the sun had reached its highest point in the sky. The days are long. The ancient fathers, the cloud spirits, must surely have heard their invocations, their rain-seeking prayers to the

---

*We cannot know the words the people of Chaco Canyon used for these months of April, May, June, and July. I have taken the liberty here of borrowing the Keresan-language names used by the Indians of Acoma and Laguna pueblos.

Thunderstorm from La Bajada. The Chacoans depended on rains from brief summer thunderstorms for much of the moisture for their crops. Photo by Laura Gilpin, 1946, courtesy University Art Museum, University of New Mexico, Albuquerque.

dead, whose ethereal presence in the clouds of summer will surely bring the life-giving rains and fertility:

> *Your little wind-blown clouds,*
> *Your thin wisps of clouds,*
> *Your great masses of clouds*
> *Replete with living waters,*
> *You will send forth to stay with us.*
> *Your fine rain caressing the earth. . . .*

This day the clouds have grown larger and darker. They have moved nearer, slowing over the mesas just behind the pueblos. Lightning flashes forth and the sharp crack of thunder echoes off the canyon walls.

The Chaco men who have patiently tended the crops recall again the prayers, the chants during the night, to the priests of the six directions. The deceased members of the priesthood and ultimately the clouds of the six directions have been sent an appeal:

> *Send forth your massed clouds to stay with us,*
> *Stretch out your water hands,*
> *Let us embrace!*
>
> *To Itiwana you will come*
> *With all your people,*
> *Hiding behind your watery shield*
> *With all your people;*
> *With your fine rain caressing the earth,*
> *With your heavy rain caressing the earth,*
> *(Come to us!)*
> *Raise the sound of your thunders!*

The farmers cast a glance at the stubby corn plants spaced carefully in the bordered rectangular gardens. The plants desperately need the water the clouds are holding.

> *All the different kinds of corn,*
> *Yonder all over their earth mother,*
> *They stand poor at the borders of our land.*
> *With their hands a little burnt,*
> *With their heads brown,*
> *They stand poor at the borders of our land.*
> *That these may be nourished with fresh water.*
> *Thus runs the thought of my prayer.* *

A few sprinkles of rain fall onto the ground and disappear in the dust. For a few minutes nothing more happens. Then the clouds open and the warm rain comes. It is not a soft, steady, drenching rain but a brief, violent one. The rain that falls directly on the tiny fields is welcome, but it is over too quickly to water the crops' thirst. The people of Chaco Canyon are counting on their engineering works to collect the runoff from the much greater area of the mesa tops and channel it to the fields.

They watch as the water begins to pour off the edges of the mesa and down the cliffs of the small side areas of the canyon, the rincons. Where the rincons open into the canyon proper, the Chacoans' diversion dams direct the water into

---

*These are prayers offered in modern times by the pueblo Indians of Zuni, where, as at Acoma and at other pueblos, some of the people of Chaco Canyon may eventually have settled. (From Bunzel, *Zuni Ritual Poetry*.)

a wide canal, part of its length lined by masonry. The canal takes the water 700 feet southeastward to the stone headgates, where it is directed a short distance south into a ditch along the north edge of the first of a series of bordered gardens.

There the men appointed the task that later agricultural society would call "ditchrider" temporarily open the side of the ditch and allow the precious water to course down the rows of beans and corn.

The first rain of the season is over, but the Chacoans' crops lie flooded with life-giving water.

The Chacoan irrigation system has done its job.

The specific details of the scene are imagined; the Chacoan irrigation system is not.

To societies in the Western part of the continent, prehistoric to present, water has always been a limiting resource. The Chaco Canyon region is not a desert, but it is semiarid. Precipitation is not especially bounteous. Except in the occasional instances when too much of it comes and causes local flooding or impassably thick mud, rain and snow here and in the rest of the Southwest are welcomed as a blessing, whether religious or secular.

People who live in lands of abundant rainfall find it hard to appreciate the importance residents of the Southwest give to rainfall and snowpack. The oven-hot days of June, the thermometer nudging the 100 mark on frequent occasions, are generally unbroken by any clouds. There is only the sun, the heat, the dry air, and that deep-blue high-altitude sky. More often than not this kind of a June follows a dry May. By July, when the two-month "rainy season" begins, the land is usually parched. The buildup of the snowy white afternoon cumulus clouds to the active dark boiling cumulonimbus of the thunderstorms raises hopes and spirits. The lightning flashes and the crackle of thunder go on into early evening most days. The rain may come with a force and primal noise of its own, but it seldom lasts long. Then the clouds break, and if the late afternoon sun has a path free to light up the moisture-laden air, a rainbow may arc across the entire eastern sky. The mesas are framed in that band of color and, glistening with their temporary cloak of moisture, reflect back a soft golden glow. Who cannot at such times rejoice?

Nearly half the eight and three-quarter-inches of precipitation Chaco Canyon receives on average each year falls during this all-too-brief late summer rainy season. (Winter snows account for about a quarter of the total; the rest is scattered modestly throughout the spring and fall.) The prehistoric Indians of the Southwest had to make the best of these short-lived cloudbursts and not let all the water rush off down the arroyos. This became especially true beginning around the eighth century, when climate patterns changed somewhat from a more equal winter-summer storm pattern to a predominately summer one.

Almost all Indian cultures of the Southwest developed some form of water control. The Hohokam of southern Arizona were indisputedly advanced in their water-control efforts. The Mogollon people of eastern Arizona and southwestern New Mexico were skilled in irrigation too. The Hisatsinom (Anasazi) in the Kayenta area of northeastern Arizona used a variety of water-control devices, most notably from A.D. 1150 to 1300. The people of Mesa Verde developed water systems as early as A.D. 900 and continued their use until abandonment about 1300. They had contour terraces, check dams, ditches, and reservoirs.

In most of these areas of the Four Corners region of the Southwest, the people usually opted for water-control systems that would not require managerial control. Chaco Canyon was a possible exception. Here they not only controlled the flow of runoff water, they may have been attempting to slow the erosion of topsoil and farmland as well.

A Chacoan using a digging stick to cultivate corn. Drawing by Jerry Livingston, National Park Service.

Watering corn by hand. Drawing by Jerry Livingston, National Park Service.

The man most noted for the study of the Chacoan's water-control systems is archaeologist R. Gwinn Vivian of the Arizona State Museum. Vivian is a second-generation Chaco archaeologist. He grew up in the canyon; he is the son of Gordon Vivian, who was the National Park Service's chief archaeologist in Chaco Canyon for many years and who was so active in the excavation and preservation efforts there all through the 1930s, 40s, and 50s. His father, along with Tom Mathews, first described the extent of the Chaco water control system, and Gwinn Vivian has carried the studies further.

In Vivian's view, the evidence at Chaco suggests that the people may have actively managed their water resources in a way that other diversion systems based on runoff at Gran Quivira and Mesa Verde did not. "It appears," he has said, "that the Chacoans, faced with problems of scheduling, control, and distribution as a result of increased runoff, opted for a strategy that involved greater individual system size as well as an increase in efficiency."

What exactly was the water-control and irrigation system used in Chaco Canyon? The major system made use of diversion dams, canals, ditches, headgates, and arrays of gardens bordered with mounds of earth. There probably also were reservoirs filled with water from the canals. All parts of the system depended upon the capture of runoff. The water was then transported to fields by canals.

The water-control system was developed to its greatest extent along the north side of the canyon, the side the major pueblos were located on. This probably was not coincidental. This was where the greatest population centers were, and therefore the greatest need. The great pueblos evidently provided a necessary social system for the construction and maintenance of the canals, ditches, and fields as well. Each pueblo seems to have its own water-control system; the systems were not interconnected. Also, the topography and the hard bedrock surface of the north-side mesas was more suited to water entrapment and channeling than that of the south side.

The canyon's south side is not totally devoid of water-control systems. There is a complex one in the vicinity of Casa Rinconada. The Rinconada system appears to have worked much the same way as those on the north side except that the water was carried a ways down canyon before its distribution to the fields. Signs of other south-side water systems may still be buried under the loads of sediment along the canyon's south edge. But this tendency for the waters to deposit more sediment on the south side may have limited the construction of irrigation works there.

Vivian used aerial photographs of the north side of the Chaco Canyon area to identify twenty-five separate drainage areas from where the water is channeled down to low spots and rincons indented into the side of the mesa. There are also three major side canyons that slash deep northward into the mesa and these drain their own, larger, areas. Manmade diversion systems were found in many of these drainage areas.

Vivian found an average of eight of the smaller drainage areas ranging from about 16 to 215 acres between each of the major side canyons. The side canyons themselves drained anywhere from 1,300 to 2,000 acres each. The total drainage on this north side of lower Chaco Canyon (the vicinity of the large pueblos) was about 10,500 acres. He estimated that there was no more than about 2,000 acres of farmland in this lower part of the canyon and that about half of that was on the north side and suitable for runoff diversion irrigation.

If somehow *all* the water that fell on these drainage areas could be collected and channeled to the farmland—hardly a likely hope—you would be multiplying the effect of the rainfall over the cultivated fields alone by more than 10.

The Chacoans' water diversion systems started at the points along the base of the mesa where the numerous small drainage areas were sending the runoff down the mesa edge. Here they built small diversion dams that channeled the water into canals. The canals took the water to a headgate where it was turned into ditches that entered the upper portions of the gridded fields.

The whole process started with the dams. They were built of earth and stone. Not all of them were small. Vivian excavated one of them in the summer of 1967. It dammed up the runoff from Cly Canyon, one of the major tributary side canyons in Chaco Canyon, and directed the water through a 3½-foot-wide gate near the center of the dam into a canal. The dam was more than 120 feet long, 20 feet thick, and stood at least 7 feet high.

Another massive masonry dam apparently impounded water from a small tributary of the Weritos Rincon just below the mesa top on South Mesa. It was 130 feet long, 5½ feet thick, and 8 feet high. Was it used for agriculture or for domestic water? Archaeologists Peter Lagasse, William Gillespie, and Kenneth Eggert suggest that the Weritos Dam may have been used primarily for domestic water for the inhabitants of the mesa-top pueblo Tsin Kletzin, about half a mile to the southwest. The water came from local runoff from the intense summer thunderstorms.

Lagasse and colleagues used computer modeling and other hydraulic analysis to study the prehistoric water-control systems at Chaco Canyon. One of the two systems they studied specifically was the one at Weritos Dam. They suggest that the dam adequately handled the water from small storms. Every couple years, however, a large thunderstorm probably caused the water to overtop the dam, damaging it. Eventually sediment would have filled the catchment area. The archaeologists conclude that the dam was either a shortlived project or the Chacoans had to do considerable rebuilding and sediment removal between large storms. Still the amount of labor necessary was not excessive.

The most impressive and to date most widespread remnants of the Chacoans' water control system are, in Vivian's view, the canals. Many of the town sites appear to have canals. They average about nine feet in width and were from two to five feet deep. Most of the canals were excavated and then lined with stone

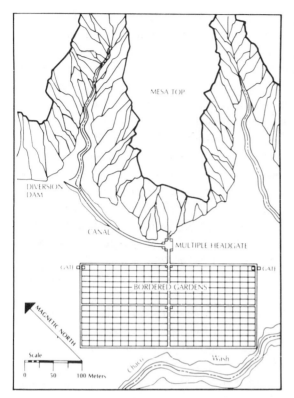

Rincon-4 North water-control system of Penasco Blanco group. This Chaco system used a diversion dam, canal, gate complex, and bordered gardens. Courtesy Gwinn Vivian.

slabs. Where they could not be excavated, they were formed by slab and masonry walls.

One of the best-described examples of the Chaco Canyon water-control systems is the so-called Rincon-4 North system of the Penasco Blanco group. The water collected off the mesa drainage area of Rincon-4 was diverted by a dam into a canal 15 feet wide and about 4½ feet deep. Part of this canal was lined with masonry. The canal ran in a gently curving arc in a generally southeast direction for 750 feet. There it entered a multiple headgate that also received water from another canal from the east and from a short ditch from the north. The gate slowed the water and directed it into one of the sets of bordered gardens, where it gave life to the Chacoans' corn, beans, and squash.

These gardens were probably something to behold during the great days of Chacoan occupation and agriculture. Their sizes would have varied greatly depending on topography and amount of drainage to serve them, but Vivian calculated that as many as 10,000 individual bordered gardens could have been farmed along the north side of the canyon.

The one we know best—because it still shows up well in aerial photographs—is near Chetro Ketl. Some twelve acres of bordered gardens are visible in the photos, but that may be no more than half what was originally cultivated. These twelve acres are divided into two adjacent rectangular plots with canals around their perimeter and down their center. Each plot contains eighty-four bordered gardens, each about seventy-five feet by forty-five feet, or about a thirteenth of an acre, in size.

Runoff at Chaco is greatest when the rain falls in a very short time. When the rains fall slowly and intermittently the water has time to soak in, and very little runoff may find its way down the mesa and into the water-collection system.

Most of the time, however, the summer rains in Chaco—when they occur—come down fast and furious, and this does produce copious amounts of runoff. One thunderstorm in July of 1967 when Vivian was there produced nearly an inch-and-a-quarter of rain in one hour. He calculated that this rainstorm would have yielded approximately 540,000 gallons of water to the twenty-four acres of farmland in the Rincon-4 North system—if only the Chacoans had still been around to ensure that the diversion dam and the canals, gates, and ditches were in good working order!

A representation of the original Chetro Ketl field. *Chaco Center, NPS.*

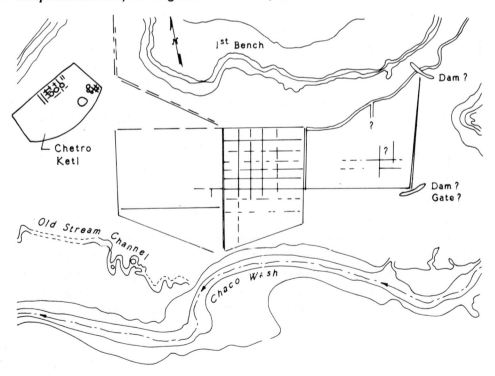

Even though its different parts were not physically linked by one master canal (topography didn't really allow that), the Chacoans had virtually a continuous water-control system along the north side of Chaco Canyon.

The Weritos, Chetro Ketl, and Penasco Blanco systems (Rincon-4 North is only one part of the latter) are just three of the systems that make up this whole water-engineering effort. Vivian identified a number of such systems in Chaco Canyon and at outlying Chaco settlements. His names for them are taken from the nearest major groups of ruins: Penasco Blanco, Cly Canyon, Rinconado, Pueblo Bonito, Chetro Ketl, Tsin Kletzin, Hungo Pavi, Una Vida, Vicente Wash, and Wijiji (all in the canyon); and Kin Bineola and Kin Klizhin (at the outlying sites). Constructions once attributed to water-control systems at Pueblo Alto, Pueblo Pintado, and Kin Ya'a turned out instead to be part of the Chacoan roadway system.

The computer models by Lagasse and his colleagues indicate that the Chacoans' small fields were just the right size to benefit from diverted water from local runoff. Their studies suggest that the structures operated in much the way Vivian proposed except they were probably not capable of handling runoff from the major lateral drainages. Instead the variety of ditch-and-gate structures at Penasco Blanco and the other irrigation complexes appear to be better suited to channeling runoff from the much smaller watersheds situated between the major tributary drainages.

The need for the water-control system may have helped shape the Chacoan society; the social system in turn helped maintain the engineering system and both benefited. "Once the importance of water control was established," said Vivian in an essay on prehistoric social organization in Chaco Canyon, "the construction and continued maintenance of canals, dams, and other works would have assumed special significance for the continuation of a social system that permitted more efficient and reliable utilization of a changing environment. Community investment in water control not only probably provided better crop assurance but reinforced an organization base designed for community undertakings."

In farm country where irrigation is the lifeblood of the economy, there is no harvest without a reliable system of irrigation. We feel an overriding sense of admiration for the Chacoans who planned, built, maintained, and used this elaborate water-control system in the heart of the San Juan basin's vast semiaridity. While their modern-day counterparts elsewhere can divert parts of nearby rivers into their fields, the people of Chaco had only the meager runoff from fleet-flying storms of summer. We feel their despair as canals and fields lay dry waiting for the first stirring signs of the seasonal rains. We feel their joy as the boiling dark clouds finally open and the canals run full into fields soaking up the bounty of the cloud-spirits.

6. Roadways
and Signal Towers

The setting sun silhouetted the Indian men and women walking along the plateau toward Chaco Canyon. Although traveling cross-country they moved quickly and surely. The broad roadway had been swept clear of even the tiniest stones. Its neatly edged borders marked the route even as the light began to fade. The last angled turn was a thousand paces back. Now the road shot ahead straight as an arrow for many miles. It disappeared down a small depression, then appeared again up the other side, and continued along the same line off into the distance.

As darkness descended across the San Juan basin, the light of the soon-to-set quarter moon reflected feebly off the earth-and-rock berm bordering this portion of the road. But ahead on a far-off promontory in line with the road the light of a small but unmistakable signal fire marked the course to follow. The people traveling this road to Chaco would arrive there safely long before the night was done.

One of the more remarkable discoveries in the 1970s about the Chacoan culture concerned the Chacoan roadway system. Archaeologists have discovered nothing like it anywhere else in prehistoric North America.

This network of broad, straight, well-engineered roads is more than just an archaeological curiosity. The extent of the roads across vast segments of the San

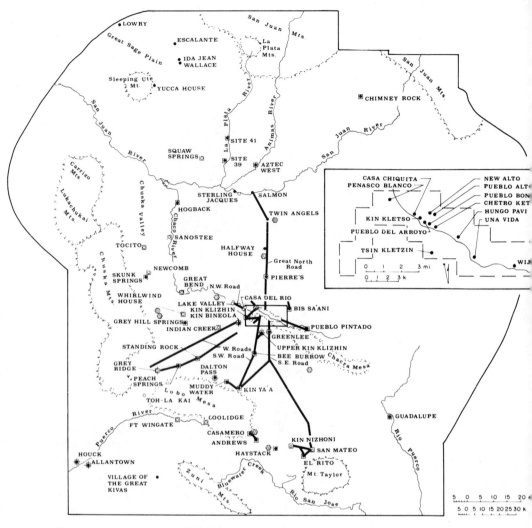

Chacoan roadway system and outliers. *Chaco Center, NPS.*

Juan basin has vividly demonstrated that Chacoan culture was not confined to Chaco Canyon itself but was spread over a large portion of what is now northwestern New Mexico. The effort and coordination that went into the building of these roads raises even more questions about the social organization of the society that built them.

Perhaps the most fundamental mystery about the roads is their width. They are far wider than necessary for ordinary foot traffic. The Chacoan people, like their contemporaries in Mesoamerica, had no carts or other wheeled vehicles. So a network of broad, engineered roadways is an enigma.

Many of the roads are thirty feet or more across. Others, sometimes considered spur roads, are about fifteen feet. Actually, a variety of figures are often quoted, partly because in places the original width is hard to determine with precision today. But most of the archaeologists investigating these roads during the past decade consistently report road widths of eight to twelve meters (twenty-six to forty feet) wherever the topography isn't a consideration, according to the most recent summary of the situation by Fred L. Nials. The roads tend to maintain their width consistently except in areas of steep terrain along the rims and walls of canyons and mesas.

Another extraordinary feature is their striking linearity and their "dog-leg" turns. Chacoan roads are laid out along straight lines. A road continues its bearing for miles. When it turns, it does so with a sudden, angular, jog. Then the new course continues in a straight line until the next dog-leg turn. Modern roads tend to have gentle curves and to avoid topographic obstacles. Chacoan roads go right over the top of low to medium hills instead of around them. In some places, such as along the South Road between Chaco Canyon and Kin Ya'a, roadcuts through such hills have been detected.

The roads are frequently bordered by broad, low, linear ridges of earth and rubble paralleling the roads at the margins. Nials calls these features berms. They are composed of the more-or-less unconsolidated materials that probably had been scraped or cleaned from the roadway and piled adjacent to it.

In many areas the roadway borders are formed mainly of numerous small stones. Some archaeologists have called these borders curbs. Nials prefers to reserve that description for low features of masonry construction paralleling a roadway, but so far no curb matching this description has been found along the Chacoan roads. The borders made of stone concentrations are common, however. They could have been formed by road maintenance activities, the Chacoans removing stones from the roadway surface (while not removing any of the soil) and piling them along the side. Or perhaps most of the earth in borders that were originally berms has eroded away, leaving only the stones.

In a few places, mainly near major ruins, the roads are bordered by walls of from one to six courses of unshaped blocks of stone. These walls can be from one to three feet high and from one-and-a-half to five feet thick. So far such walls have been found only near Pueblo Alto and Tsin Kletzin in Chaco Canyon.

Where the roads descend into the canyon the Chacoans cut broad stairways into the sandstone of the cliffs. Some of these stairways are nearly imperceptible today. Others remain quite spectacular. Most are in cliffs of Chaco Canyon itself. But others have been found elsewhere, notably at Ahshislepah Canyon west of Chaco Canyon, on a mesa south of Kin Ya'a, between Pueblo Pintado and Chaco Canyon, and on a bluff south of Farmington, New Mexico.

The Chacoans also sometimes built ramps, consisting of piles of stones, to provide access from one ledge to another. Several such ramps have been found in Chaco Canyon. It is not known whether the Chacoans had covered them with soil to make walking easier.

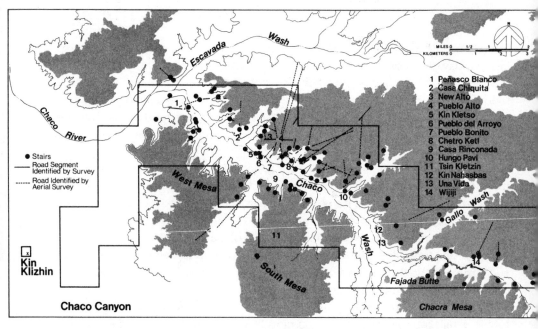

Map of roads and stairs in Chaco Canyon. From Hayes, et al., 1981.

In the map legend:

1 Peñasco Blanco
2 Casa Chiquita
3 New Alto
4 Pueblo Alto
5 Kin Kletso
6 Pueblo del Arroyo
7 Pueblo Bonito
8 Chetro Ketl
9 Casa Rinconada
10 Hungo Pavi
11 Tsin Kletzin
12 Kin Nahasbas
13 Una Vida
14 Wijiji

● Stairs
— Road Segment Identified by Survey
----- Road Identified by Aerial Survey

Kin Klizhin

Chaco Canyon

Chacra Mesa

In places they constructed causeways, places where both sides of the roadbed have been raised above the surrounding terrain. One such causeway is near Penasco Blanco. The Chacoans put in fill to raise the roadbed in two low areas. One of the areas has masonry borders two feet high and twelve feet long.

Many of the roadways are slightly depressed in comparison to the surrounding land. Those excavations that have been done across such roadways seem to indicate, according to archaeologist Margaret Senter (Gretchen) Obenauf, that "the depression was deliberately created by removing surface fill and rubble and piling it along the sides of the road. In some cases the soil was removed down to a shallow bedrock layer." In other cases it was removed down to a layer of harder soil.

It is not just the roads themselves that provoke scientific and popular interest. It is their extent and the network of transportation and communication implicit in their existence. More than 400 miles of Chacoan roads have been discovered. Only 100 miles of them are in Chaco Canyon and the immediate vicinity (within the bounds of the Chaco Culture National Historical Park). The other 300 miles radiate from Chaco to Chacoan sites elsewhere in the San Juan basin. It is a vast system. One road, now known as the Great North Road, runs more than 50 miles from Chaco Canyon to the San Juan River. Another, the South Road, runs 40 miles between Chaco Canyon and Kin Ya'a. In places there appear to be *two* parallel sets of roads. And in at least one place, the archaeologists have found evidence of a *double* set of parallel roads, four in all! The more the Chacoan roadway system has been investigated in the past few years, the more intriguing it has become.

In fact, the prehistoric Chacoan roads in the San Juan basin have become one of the central subjects of archaeological debate about the Chacoan culture. "The roadway system has become one of the more important aspects in the interpretation of Chaco Canyon," says Obenauf, who has mapped the road system in detail. "The very fact of their being wide, engineered roads, and not merely trails or paths, has important implications for their uses, and for the social complexity necessary for their construction and their utilization. This, together with the labor investment necessary for their construction and the extent of the system, has made archaeologists question many of the accepted ideas about the Chacoan occupation of the San Juan basin. The vastness of the system . . . has raised important questions about the nature of the past economic system in the San Juan Basin. Chaco Canyon can no longer be seen as an isolated phenomenon, but must be viewed as a part of a system which occupied much of the San Juan basin."

Discovery of the Chacoan roads was gradual. Although the full extent of the Chacoan roadway network was not identified until the 1970s, isolated segments had apparently been recognized throughout the preceding century.

A member of the Wheeler Survey, an Army geographic expedition to the Pueblo country of the Southwest in the mid-1870s, included this comment in his 1879 report: "Their trails are remarkable, extending as they do in a straight line from one pueblo to another, and even traced from ruin to ruin, These deeply worn paths, even on the rocks, passing without swerving to right or left, over valley, plain, or ascent of mesa—as though the trail was older than the mesas. . . ."

Archaeologist Alden Hayes comments that the author of these words was speaking in generalities of New Mexico, "although he might well have had Chaco Canyon specifically in mind." Another member of the Wheeler Survey referred to "traces of former road" between Pueblo Pintado, the easternmost Chacoan ruin, and Abiquiu, "sixty miles off, where ruins have also been found. . . ." This "road" may have been a historic Indian trail; no such prehistoric Chacoan road extending to the northeast has yet been identified.

The earliest mention of roads in Chaco Canyon itself is in the 1901 report by S.J. Holsinger. Holsinger, special agent from the General Land Office, had been sent by his Commissioner and the Secretary of Interior to investigate charges that Richard Wetherill and the Hyde Exploring Expedition were misusing federal land and plundering Chacoan antiquities (Chapter 1). His lengthy report on all the major archaeological features in Chaco Canyon included this reference:

"The remains of an ancient road-way . . . can be traced from Chettro Kettle stairway to Alto ruins. This road-way was 20 feet wide and walled up to a grade with loose rock and soil. It commenced near the top of the stairway referred to and followed a narrow shelving or terrace of the rock, westward, paralleling the canyon. It followed this ledge for about half a mile to a point where there are indistinct remains of a broad flight of steps, twenty-one in number."

Neil Judd was aware of signs of prehistoric Chacoan roadways in the 1920s. Archaeologists didn't have access to his brief written comments about them until his formal reports about the excavations were published by the Smithsonian Institution in 1954 and 1964. Yet the *New Mexico Highway Journal* had published a twelve-paragraph unbylined article about the roads and Judd's thoughts about them back in March of 1928. It was titled "Prehistoric Chaco Canyon 'Roads' Puzzle Scientists." It was clearly based on information provided by Judd.

The article began: "The Indian population of Chaco Canyon, New Mexico, a thousand years or more ago, built wide 'roads' extending many miles across the mesas and cut broad stone stairways out of the solid rock of the canyon wall. Why?"

Some of these "roads," it went on to say, are said by the Navajos to "extend 40 miles, up hill and down. . . . The roads, if that is what they were, vary in width from 15 to 20 feet, and are usually lined with boulders, which were rolled to one side in the clearing process. On sloping ground the lower side of the road was built up, and where the mesa changes levels abruptly, steps were cut in the rock." The article also described a series of terraces on the upper ledges braced with massive masonry walls. One of them, varying in width from 10 to 20 feet, was said to be traceable for more than a mile.

"Why the canyon dwellers built these things is not yet absolutely clear," said the article. It said Judd had traced the roads as far as he was able. "Mr. Judd found that they all seemed to lead back into the rincons, where pine trees formerly grew." It suggested that he felt the roads and stairs may have been built to help in the transport to Chaco of the thousands of pine logs needed for construction of the pueblos' roofs. "Of the 20 fragmentary beams excavated from Pueblo Bonito by the National Geographic Society's expedition in the last seven years," the article continued, "not one bears any evidence of scarring—a fact which indicates that the timbers were carried instead of being slid down the cliffs." (That any extensive pine forests existed in proximity to Chaco Canyon during this period is now seriously doubted. This means that the logs used in the Chacoan pueblos were transported even farther than Judd suspected.)

However intriguing they may have seemed at the time, Chacoan roadways were more or less forgotten by archaeologists in the succeeding decades. Edgar Hewett discussed them with students out at Chaco but never published anything about them.

Judd's 1954 report on the material culture of Pueblo Bonito contained his own first published references to them. Even then the subject arises somewhat obliquely. One autumn night in 1927 Judd talked for three hours with an elderly

Navajo man, Hosteen Beyal, as part of an effort to learn what "old timers" in the Chaco area remembered and knew about the canyon. Beyal had long ago been recommended to Judd for this purpose. Although now blind and, according to his son, about ninety-five years old, Beyal was said to have an especially keen memory. Judd asked him all manner of things. Beyal told him of cottonwoods and willows that had grown below Pueblo Bonito in the earlier years, the lack of any cut arroyo back then, the presence of old Chacoan irrigation ditches, and the condition of the ruins.

"When asked about the so-called 'roads' on both the north and south cliffs," Judd relates in his report, "Beyal remarked that they were not really roads, although they looked like them. He says they were built by the Chaco people. One road led from Pueblo Pintado to Pueblo Bonito and on to Penasco Blanco. Another led from Pueblo Bonito to Kin-yai; a third, from Kinbiniyol to Kin-yai; still another, from Kinbiniyol to, or through, Coyote Canyon and on to a point near Fort Defiance. On each of these 'roads' one could see, until recently, cuts where the road passed through small hills."

When Beyal tired of Judd's questions, Judd turned to his old Navajo friend named Padilla, who lived in a hogan about a mile downstream from Penasco Blanco. Asked about the "roads" (Judd always put the term in quotation marks) mentioned by Beyal as having been built and used by the Chacoans, Padilla replied that he had seen very few of them because they were washed out or covered with sand and silt. Cuts through low knolls, indicate their location, however. Padilla said a succession of these cuts could be seen as one rides over the country.

Judd had known Padilla for years and had even helped bury his daughter when she died in 1923. On the night of Judd's 1927 talk with Beyal and Padilla, Padilla was less communicative than he had been during an afternoon-long discussion about similar matters three years earlier. Recalling those discussions, Judd at one point mentions that Padilla told him that at the south end of The Gap, the opening in the Chacra Mesa across from Pueblo Bonito, "is a cut that some Navajo call a canal but it looks more like a wagon road to our informant." Then Judd adds this enigmatic parenthetical reference: "(It is, in fact, part of a 'ceremonial highway,' a type of construction to be described in a future publication.)" No such publication ever appeared. Whatever Judd may have based his conclusion on has been lost.

Judd did refer to the roads again in his 1964 report on the architecture of Pueblo Bonito. He mentioned that a stairway "is to be seen near every other major P III ruin in Chaco Canyon and broad pathways lead from one to another. The Navajo refer to these pathways as 'roads' and my guess is no better." Judd still had no solution to their mystery:

"Jackson's stairway [the spectacular carved stairway north of Chetro Ketl discovered by photographer William Henry Jackson in the 1870s] is one of the best, but what was its purpose? The diverse 'roads' are equally beyond convincing explanation. There is the broad pathway extending southeast from Pueblo Alto with 10- to 20-foot-wide hammer-battered steps at every ledge and a pecked groove throughout much of its length; there is the retaining wall edging a 30-foot cliff at the end of the trail. There is another step series across the canyon, irregular and cramped, and a cleared path from rimrock toward Tsin Kletsin. There is a magnificent stairway overlooking Hungo Pavie and a conspicuous 'road' dug through a sand ridge south of The Gap. Each was a prodigious undertaking of which the Late Bonitians or their contemporaries were thoroughly capable, but each remains a mystery."

Judd's impressions were of course all based on his work and conversations in Chaco Canyon in the 1920s. In 1948, Gordon Vivian interviewed Marietta Wetherill, the widow of Richard Wetherill, about the signs of prehistoric roads evident in the area when she and her husband had lived and worked before and after the turn of the century (Chapter 1). She described a wide roadway running from Pueblo Alto down to the Escavada Wash. "North of Alto in certain lights you can still see what appears to be a wide roadway running down to the Escavada," she told Vivian. "In the old days this was clearly defined in the spring or early summer because the vegetation on it was different from any other and it could be traced clear to the San Juan." (The San Juan River is about fifty miles to the north.)

Alden Hayes considers this conversation with Mrs. Wetherill a turning point in the conception of the Chacoan roads. He says her account of a prehistoric road crossing the Escavada "must have spurred him [Vivian] to get out on foot and find it, for a year after that interview he was pointing out the visible traces on the ground of the ancient track on both sides of the wash." (The surface evidence of the roads had apparently deteriorated markedly since the turn of the century as a result of the introduction of livestock and wheeled vehicles.)

In 1950 Vivian put together a mosaic of aerial photographs taken of the Chaco area in the 1930s by the Soil Conservation Service. The same roadway, as well as others, was traceable, in Vivian's words, as "wide, straight courses where minor alterations have been made to the natural terrain over a distance of several miles."

This was the first use of aerial photography, or "remote sensing," to study the prehistoric Chacoan roadways. The early 1970s brought the technique prominently to the fore in delineating the Chacoan road network. The Chaco Center, through its Remote Sensing Division, carried out the early work. It was the first large-scale research effort directed to the Chacoan roadways.

It was stimulated by "the rediscovery" of these prehistoric land routes by Gwinn Vivian, Gordon's son. The younger Vivian had begun his intensive investigation of the Chacoans' water-control systems. In fieldwork from August 1970 through May 1971 he and Robert Buettner, then a graduate student at the University of Arizona, excavated a section of Vivian's so-called "Canal 3," leading out of

Pueblo Alto toward Chetro Ketl. They found it unmistakably not a canal but a road. Vivian realized that at least some of his "canals" were roadways, and so he and Buettner began a pilot study of the roadway systems.

Vivian and Buettner identified and named six sets of roadways: Chaco East, Chaco North, Chaco South, Chaco West, Kin Ya'a, and Tsin Kletzin. The Chaco North Road system was the most complex. Pueblo Alto, atop the mesa, seems to have been a terminal point. They mapped three major roads converging on Pueblo Alto from the north and four spur roads linking Pueblo Alto with the large canyon-bottom pueblos Bonito, Chetro Ketl (with two spurs), and Pueblo del Arroyo. These spur roads had low masonry border walls and rock-cut and masonry stairways. The spur roads were about fifteen feet wide; the primary roads, about thirty feet. In places, the roads were indeed cut through low hills. The roads, as Vivian described them, were marked by "relatively straight courses showing occasional slightly alterations in degree of orientation."

One day in 1970, Thomas R. Lyons of the Chaco Center in Albuquerque was visiting Chaco Canyon. Gwinn Vivian was there, and he began pointing out to Lyons some of the roadway segments. He showed Lyons portions of roads visible on the ground and other lineations detectable on aerial photographs. In Gretchen Obenauf's phrase, "This was a case of the right person's being in the right place at the right time." Lyons was a geologist-archaeologist. He had been hired by John Corbett, then the chief archaeologist for the National Park Service, to experiment with the application of remote sensing to archaeology. Lyons had already used aerial photographs in his work as a geologist. Now was the perfect opportunity to apply them to a fascinating new subject in archaeology.

The use of aerial photography in archaeology was not new. Charles Lindbergh and his wife Anne had taken aerial photographs of Chaco Canyon and other ruins in the Southwest in 1929, only two years after Lindbergh's epochal solo flight over the Atlantic Ocean. Alfred Kidder and other archaeologists realized these perspectives could be useful to them. The photos could help locate new archaeological sites and better understand the relationships of sites to terrain.

Now Lyons began to apply aerial photography to the Chacoan roadways. He purchased existing black-and-white aerial photography of the region from the U.S. Geological Survey and the Soil Conservation Service. The SCS photographs had been taken in the 1930s; USGS's, in the 1960s. Roadways never suspected showed up in segments almost uniformly straight. At least one road was associated with almost every major pueblo site in the Chaco area.

Most of these ancient roadways are invisible, or almost invisible, from the ground, except where they cut through hillocks or where stone or dirt borders still exist. What is it about aerial photos that allows a scientist to detect a lineation not apparent when he may be standing right on it? Of course one reason is the scope of view the aerial perspective provides. We naturally find it very difficult to detect large-scale patterns and connections from our human-eye altitude of five feet.

The broader view from the air enables an observer to see connections not apparent from ground level.

But it is more than that. The slight depression of many of the prehistoric roadways in the sandy semiarid soil of northwestern New Mexico permits the former roads—even to this day—to accumulate and retain a slightly greater amount of moisture. The soil may stay just a little bit darker as a result. Also, the density of vegetation in the former roadways may be ever-so-subtly increased as a result of the greater moisture. Or the type of vegetation may be slightly altered. The changes in soil coloration are not easy to see or objectively evaluate from the ground. They show up better on the aerial photographs. The changes in vegetation density are usually not visible to the unaided eye. But two overlapping aerial photos can be placed in the stereoscope, giving a three-dimensional view. Such stereoscopic examination of aerial photos can detect the differential reflection of sunlight off the different densities and types of vegetation.

Over the next several years, Lyons and others such as Stephen Shure and graduate students Robert Hitchcock and James Ebert carried out research and photo interpretation on the Chacoan roadways. In 1972 and 1973 Lyons arranged to have aircraft take some new photos over Chaco Canyon in color and infrared and at various scales in black and white. The Remote Sensing Division researchers turned to this more sophisticated photography and also electronic enhancement to supplement their stereoscopic interpretations. The infrared film showed vegetation in bright pink and red patterns. It revealed several previously unsuspected roads. Multispectral imaging, photographs of the same scene at different wavelengths of light, provided more information. An electronic instrument known as a Digicol was used to enhance images. Ebert, who was the specialist in the electronic image enhancement, and Hitchcock described the machine as looking like "a cross between a television studio and an astronaut's instrument panel." It amplified faint images. Under electronic teasing, the sharp images of ramrod straight prehistoric roadways fairly leaped off the screen.

By the end of that summer the total number of miles of possible prehistoric Chacoan roadway mapped had increased from 80 miles to more than 200. The new photography helped as did the electronics. According to Ebert, about 20 percent of the total was discovered using the new electronic enhancing equipment.

Next came a difficult task. Archaeologists call it gathering "ground truth." They needed to check on the ground what the photography seemed to indicate were prehistoric roads. Until the roads could be confirmed in fieldwork, anyone was right to doubt that the lineations seen on the photos were indeed prehistoric roads. Besides, they wanted to better understand how the roads had been built.

The men transferred all the suspected roadway segments onto topographic maps. Then they went into the field, in two-man teams. They started at a spot most likely to be visible from the ground. If they could see signs of the road there, they noted it as verified and walked its length in both directions. They took measurements and photographs. They found, curiously, that the roads were more easily seen when one walked a few feet off their outer edges than on the roadbed itself.

This was a particularly wet summer, which hindered the visibility of the roads from the ground. But the Remote Sensing Project chartered a light plane to fly an infrared photography mission. This helped identify more road segments. It turned out that previously undiscernible parts of roadways now showed up clearly on the photos because of the lush growth of mustard weed and other plants in the prehistoric roadbeds.

One hundred miles of the prehistoric roads were verified by the ground-truth fieldwork that summer. As Ebert and Hitchcock later reported, in almost all cases the major highways were a precise nine meters—about thirty feet—wide, and all the roads proved to have a dish-shaped cross-section. They wondered if this resulted from the pressure of the feet of so many Chacoans walking over them over the decades the roads were in use.

The archaeologists' systematic walks over the lengths of prehistoric roads also revealed many of the other intriguing features of the Chacoan roads: retaining walls, cuts through hills, apparent wayhouses, even a footbridge to allow the Chacoans to cross an arroyo when it was filled with water.

Chaco Project archaeologists examine wall along a segment of roadway.
Chaco Center, NPS.

What were the roads for? The centuries that separate our time from the Chacoans' make it impossible to say. Ebert and Hitchcock's suggestion echoed the one heard earlier from Neil Judd. They pointed out that much of the food necessary to feed the people of Chaco must have come from the hinterlands. So must have the giant ponderosa pines, "as many as 100,000 of them," used in the construction of the pueblos in Chaco Canyon.

"One can imagine," wrote Ebert and Hitchcock, "crews of workmen carrying sixty-foot logs, some of them three feet in diameter, across mesas, down cliffs, and through arroyos in an ancient forewarning of the traffic on our own highways."

Another field project in the early 1970s was directed specifically to the prehistoric roads on the mesa around Pueblo Alto. The roads converging on Pueblo Alto indicated it must have had some special importance. To Lyons and Hitchcock these patterns of roads suggested that "this settlement served as a communication center of some importance." The walls that Gwinn Vivian had originally thought part of a water-diversion system were along a highpoint; channeling water was unlikely to be their purpose. "The configuration of the walls with flagstone paved surfaces in places and their direct alignment with road segments and stairways," Lyons and Hitchcock wrote, "suggest that they were part of the roadway system and served as causeways not unlike the Mayan *sacbeob*."

Middle of a road segment at Penasco Blanco. Chaco Center, NPS.

Curbing along west side of Alto-Bonito road. Chaco Center, NPS.

Lyons arranged to have an archaeologist named George Gumerman study Pueblo Alto's roads. Gumerman and his assistants used aerial photos, but the most important part of their project was the fieldwork. They did a series of test excavations. They found that formal preparation of the road surface was "the exception rather than the rule" in the prehistoric roads around Pueblo Alto. The Chacoans instead seem to have excavated the roads down to a hard, irregular surface of tan "calichified" sand a foot or so below the present surface. (Caliche is desert soil formed by the cementing together of sand, gravel, and other debris by porous calcium carbonate.) This caliche formed a hard, well-consolidated natural surface, an excellent road base.

The researchers also excavated the north wall near Pueblo Alto at a low point where the roads converged and found an opening or gate in it. For some reason it is only a little more than three feet wide. This is "surprisingly narrow considering the width and number of roads which apparently met at this section of the wall," reported Gumerman and John Ware.

Ware and Gumerman concluded that to understand the Chacoan roads better, more excavations would have to be done. And to understand them as a system, in their full cultural context, the roads would have to be mapped in as great a detail as possible.

This is where Gretchen Obenauf came in.

For her 1980 University of New Mexico master's thesis in anthropology, Obenauf in 1977 began a systematic search for prehistoric roadways connecting Chaco Canyon with the many outlying Chacoan ruins in the San Juan basin. Most of her effort was directed to sites outside the boundaries of the (then) Chaco Canyon National Monument; most of the studies up till then had focused mainly on roads near the canyon.

She did most of her photointerpretation of three different types of imagery. She used the U.S. Geological Survey photos, the old Soil Conservation Service photos, and recently taken large-scale photos of the national monument area and fifty outlying sites.

The actual photointerpretation was done in the lab on a mirror stereoscope mounted on a scanning track. She found this technique especially useful for her purposes. The stereoscopic method exaggerates the slight depressions of most of the roadways, and the three-dimensional image helped her better distinguish prehistoric roadways from historic tracks and geological lineations. She didn't use the electronic enhancement the Remote Sensing Project had used earlier. While that method was well-suited to look for all faint lineations in a given area, her technique was to look for extensions of known roads from the canyon to outlying towns. She looked for dark, straight lines connecting known Chacoan sites. Angled turns, their slight depressions, and their continuance over low obstacles also helped identify them as Chacoan roads.

She would use the mapped location of an outlying Chacoan community to find the ruin on the aerial photos. Then she would stereoscopically examine the area around the outlier for lineations, mark them directly on the photographs, and follow the alignments to see if she could find other segments. "In most cases in which a possible road could be detected near an outliner," she found, "it could be followed to a destination, usually another outlier."

She marked all roads detected this way on the photographs and then transferred them to U.S. Geological Survey topographic maps by placing the photo in a special overhead projection device made for working with maps and enlarging it to the scale of the topographic map. This technique, she found, was more accurate than the "eyeball" method used by the Remote Sensing Project.

In this way, Obenauf greatly enlarged the extent of the known Chacoan prehistoric roadway network. She notes that while about 200 miles of possible roadway had been mapped by earlier researchers, only about 100 miles were outside Chaco Culture National Historical Park. Her project delineated more than 200 miles of previously unmapped roadway, almost all of it outside the monument boundaries. In addition she remapped all the previously mapped roadways systems using her more accurate techniques for transferring the photos to maps.

She discovered possible roadways at almost all outliers that were anywhere where roads could be expected to be preserved. This is a strong indication that the Chacoans probably had roads at all the outliers. Some have undoubtedly since been obliterated by alluviation and erosion and by modern activity. Some sites have the misfortune of being located right in the center of modern-day activity. For instance, one of the largest Chacoan outliers is one known as the Newcomb site, some fifty miles west-northwest of Chaco Canyon. It was a major population center in Chacoan times. It could be expected to be an important part in a Chacoan roadway network. But the present-day town of Newcomb, New Mexico, on U.S. Highway 666 running between Gallup and Shiprock, and the area's modern agricultural fields are located just below and to the east of the site, obliterating any evidence of prehistoric roads there. Just southwest of there, where the terrain has not been disturbed, a possible roadway runs between Newcomb and the site known as Skunk Springs.

Before Obenauf's study, there were basically four known roadway systems, and they connected eight outlying sites with Chaco Canyon. The Great North Road started at Pueblo Alto and ran straight north past Chacoan communities known as Pierre's site, Halfway House, Twin Angels Pueblo, and then took a slight jog to the north-northwest to Salmon Ruins on the San Juan River. The South Road (it actually runs a bit south-southwest) connected Chaco Canyon with Upper Kin Klizhin, a site known as Bee Burrow, and Kin Ya'a, near Crownpoint. The East Road connected Pueblo Pintado and Chaco Canyon. The West Road ran from Chaco Canyon a fairly short distance northwest to Ahshislepah Canyon, and perhaps beyond. (The name "West Road" for this comparatively short route has now been dropped.)

Obenauf's study found several "new" roadway systems. Two of them connect Chaco Canyon with outlying areas far to the southwest. The first she calls the Coyote Canyon Road. Its most southwesterly visible point is near a distant outlier known as the Grey Ridge Community, north-northeast of Gallup, New Mexico. From there it travels to Peach Springs (a Chacoan outlier twenty-five miles southwest of Pueblo Bonito) and on toward Chaco Canyon's South Gap. The second is the Mexican Springs Road. Its trend is generally parallel to, and a few miles north of, the Coyote Canyon Road. It connects the Mexican Springs area, north of Gallup, with Kin Bineola and Chaco Canyon.

A third newly discovered road system she feels probably once linked the Casa del Rio outlier with Chaco Canyon and also with a line of sites to the west of the Lake Valley outlier.

A fourth road system is the Southeast Road. It seems to be a big one. It heads south out of Fajada Gap in Chaco Canyon to the Greenlee outlier. Ten miles farther south it divides into two, one part running southwest to Kin Ya'a (where it intersects the earlier delineated South Road), the other part running far southeast to the San Mateo area north of Grants, New Mexico. There in a series of angled jogs and cutbacks it links a complex of southerly Chacoan outlying sites known as San Mateo, El Rito, and Kin Nizhoni.

From the Greenlee site to the San Mateo outlier is a distance of forty-five miles with no known outlier in between. Obenauf feels this may be a sign that some outlying sites remain to be discovered along this route and along some of the other roads where considerable distances separate known sites.

This is an especially intriguing roadway system when one considers that, as Obenauf points out, "Nowhere else in North America has a similar system of prehistoric roadways been discovered."

"The eight roadway systems and numerous short roadways comprising the known Chacoan roadway network radiate from Chaco Canyon like the spokes of a wheel," she says. Yet she quickly acknowledges that the analogy is imperfect. "There are several directions containing no 'spokes.'"

For instance, no roadways are known in the quadrant northeast of Chaco Canyon. But much of this area has not been surveyed, nor was aerial imagery available. So far only two outliers are known in that direction, Bisa'ani, seven miles from Chaco, and Chimney Rock, eighty-seven miles from Chaco in Colorado. Are there really no roadways running northeast from Chaco or is it just that the area has not yet been examined carefully enough?

A similar question can be asked about a large area to the northwest of Chaco Canyon. Although the quadrant to the northwest of Chaco is circled by outliers, there are no outliers known in its interior. And part of that area has specifically been surveyed for them. No roadway has yet been found running far to the northwest of Chaco. If the outliers at the outer perimeter of this northwest quadrant had roads connecting them, would there be a separate spoke connecting them directly with Chaco, or would the connection be by way of other roads much farther to the south?

The extraordinary nature of the Chacoan roadway network was realized just as the United States government was strongly pushing a national policy that threatened the roads' preservation. Federal coal resources throughout the West, including the Chaco region, were to be aggressively developed. Strip-mineable coal is abundant immediately west, north, and east of Chaco Canyon. The U.S. Bureau of Land Management (BLM) was directed to begin competitive leasing of federal coal from the San Juan region in 1983.

The BLM recognized that the Chacoan roadways were invaluable in understanding the unique Chacoan culture. If coal was an energy resource, the Chacoan roadways are a cultural resource. To better prepare for managing both, the BLM in 1981 began a one-year-long Chaco Roads Project. Eight archaeologists and geologists led by BLM cultural resources specialist Chris Kincaid focused concentrated attention on nearly every aspect of the Chacoan roads.

Gretchen Obenauf joined the group and extended her analysis to new aerial photography of the roads. Other members of the team dug trenches across suspected roadways to confirm their prehistoric nature. Three of the roadway systems were examined in the field in detail. The study confirmed the existence and cultural value of the Chacoan's vast roadway network, which once linked Chacoan communities throughout a 60,000-square-mile area of northwestern New Mexico.

The new aerial imagery was a set of low-sun angle photographs of the North Road taken from an airplane in a mission flown especially for the project during early morning light in October 1981. Although the North Road had been seen and examined on all the earlier aerial photography, this was the best view so far. "On no other set was the road as consistently visible as on the low-sun-angle imagery," reported Obenauf. "Not only was the known route of the road clearly visible, but several previously unknown parallel segments were also visible. The

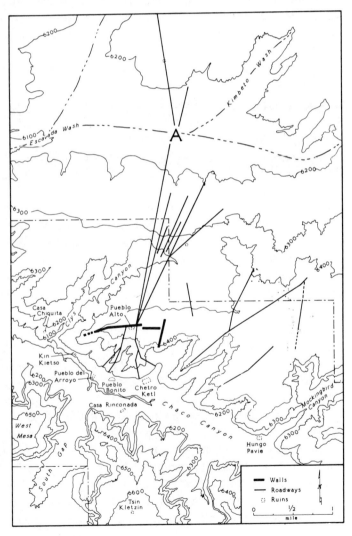

Map of roads in and north of Chaco Canyon. Note multiple parallel segments. Chaco Center, NPS.

shadows produced by the early morning sun greatly enhanced visibility of the road."

One of the more puzzling recent revelations about the Chacoan roads is the discovery of parallel segments in some locations. As Fred Nials reports, the North Road appears to have parallel segments for much of the distance from the Half-way House outlier ruin (about half way between Chaco Canyon and the San Juan River) and the point where it crosses the Ahshislepah Wash. Michael Marshall and colleagues reported parallel segments near the Muddy Water community and near Bee Burrow. The BLM's own 1981–82 investigations revealed parallel segments between Casa Patricio and Mesita de la Junta. Nials says examination of a site known as Haystack from a light airplane showed parallel road segments extending northwestward, and they were subsequently confirmed by ground observation. Obenauf plotted several possible parallel segments from the aerial imagery she examined. Nials says there are signs of parallel segments at several other locations on Chacoan roads.

There is even more. "One of the most intriguing of parallel segments," reports Nials, "is seen on aerial photographs of the area from approximately two to four kilometers north of Pierre's Ruin. In this area the North Road consists of not one set of parallel segments, but two. All the four segments appear to be almost perfectly parallel to one another."

He says the segments within each set are spaced less than 50 feet apart and the two sets are separated by roughly 100 to 130 feet. These "double parallels" have not been verified on the ground. "Although they are clearly visible on [aerial] photographs, all attempts to locate the roads on the ground were fruitless."

Why would the Chacoans have built roads parallel to each other? The archaeologists don't know. Nials suggests perhaps one replaced an older road-way, or that there were different roadways for different segments of society. "At the present time, however, no conclusive statement can be made as to relative ages or different functions of the segments."

The BLM archaeologists examined much of the North Road in detail on the ground. The Pierre's Ruin area, about twelve miles north of Chaco Canyon, pro-duced some other interesting discoveries. These finds confirmed the North Road's connection to a remarkable set of structures in the vicinity of Pierre's Ruin. The Pierre's Ruin complex is named after Pierre Morenon, an archaeologist work-ing at Salmon Ruins on the San Juan River in the 1970s who set about to identify roads extending southward. He is credited with the complex's "discovery."

In 1976 an archaeological survey crew from the Chaco Center in Albuquer-que led by Robert Powers inventoried the site. They described three massive con-structions built in the "classic Bonito" architectural style. Two faced one another atop a lofty mesa. The structures are collectively called "the Acropolis." Powers noted that every major elevation within a kilometer of the Acropolis supported at least one structure. Few sites were at the base of these badland pinnacles, but one of them was very special. It was the third and most massive of the Bonito-style constructions. BLM archaeologist John Stein calls it a unique architectural feature in the Eastern Anasazi world.

This structure apparently incorporated a lofty badlands pinnacle as a sort of tower. At the top of this natural tower the Chacoans had built a masonry "plat-form" or possibly a "housed" kiva. This masonry structure has now entirely col-lapsed into rubble. But remaining atop the spire is a hearth. Many large fires have been built on it. Visibility from it in all directions is excellent. And it so happened that this spire and its hearth aligned with the centerline of the North Road. The BLM archaeologists have named the badland cone and its apparent signal tower, El Faro, "The Lighthouse."

Yet the North Road itself in this area did not show up well on the aerial imagery, and that led to controversy about the association of the roads with the architectural complex and about the North Road itself. In August 1981 the BLM archaeologists began work in the Pierre's Ruin area.

To resolve the doubts, they tracked the path of the main branch of the North Road to within 300 meters of El Faro. They even identified a spur road that they believe ended in a formal "ramp" to the Acropolis's summit.

Pierre's ruin area. Nearly every pinnacle bears a Chacoan structure. A Chacoan road passes nearby. *Chaco Center, NPS.*

El Faro, "The Lighthouse." An apparent Chacoan signal tower.
Chaco Center, NPS.

They also found signs that the road alignment does indeed enter or abut El Faro from the north, but no evidence of the road skirting the structure either to the east or west. "It is more likely," reported Stein, "that the road passes or enters El Faro and continues up the narrow valley to the east."

Stein said the summit may also have been reachable from the north end of the mesa and also from a possible diagonal route that intersects the ramp. All this suggests that "the issue of road behavior in the Pierre's Ruin is a complex one."

A broad panorama of the San Juan basin north of Chaco Canyon can be seen from the Pierre's Ruin area. The structures atop the Acropolis and a fire atop El Faro would be visible from great distances in all directions, including from Pueblo Alto above the north face of Chaco Canyon and from a shrine described by Chaco Center archaeologist Thomas Windes on the south rim of Chaco Canyon.

"The placement of the ruin at so conspicuous a break in topography is consistent with other types of construction along the roads and almost certainly was no accident," wrote Stein in the 1983 BLM report on the Chaco Roads Project. "It is our judgment that the Pierre's complex represents a constellation of special-function architecture whose location was probably determined during the engineering process for the North Road." The site does not appear to be residential. It seems to have no relation to Chacoan agriculture either.

In 1976 archaeologist Dwight Drager described a possible Chacoan signaling and communication system in the San Juan basin. The signal-fire tower at Pierre's Ruin was just one of many high-elevation archaeological sites he considered to be a part of it. The previous year Alden Hayes and Tom Windes had reported several unusual archaeological features or shrines on mesa tops around Chaco Canyon that seemed to be in locations chosen specifically for high visibility. One site, for instance, has a direct view of Pueblo Alto, Pueblo Bonito, Chetro Ketl, Pueblo del Arroyo, Kin Kletso, Casa Chiquita, Penasco Blanco, Tsin Kletzin, and Kin Nahasbas. Other similar high-visibility sites were also found. Most of these sites also had in common similar constructions and types of artifacts found, in addition to highly visible locations.

Drager, building on these observations, suggested that "certain of the enigmatic structures" like the shrines and the tower kiva structures present at many major Chacoan pueblos "were the stations in a vast communication network which passed information of very specific types to other similar stations around the San Juan Basin." Drager identified twenty-three sites around the basin that were possibly part of the communication network. Each was visible to at least one of the other sites, but many were visible to half a dozen or more. "There is some degree of redundancy in the system," said Drager. "There is more than one path along which the message can flow."

Hayes and Windes had noticed a possible interrelationship between at least some of these line-of-sight signaling paths and the Chacoan road network. One such path aligned precisely over the prehistoric roadway to Kin Ya'a, for instance. Drager noticed other such correspondences.

So the Chacoans seemed to have had an extensive signal communication network. They could have made use of fires at night and smoke or mica mirrors during the day to link the Chacoan society with an integrated system of instant communications. The system might also have been used to mark the route of certain of the roads for travel at night.

What was it all for? Thirty-foot-wide engineered roads, radiating out across a vast basin and its surrounding mountain lands. A transportation network, not exactly like the spokes of a wheel centered on Chaco Canyon, but a series of interlinked geometrical linearities physically connecting all parts of the Chacoan culture. Parallel roads, or even double parallel roads, in some places. Signal stations at high points along the routes. And even more high-visibility sites allowing instantaneous communications among all the disparate communities.

The roads certainly made travel easier, no doubt about that. Pierre Morenon, mentioned earlier, conducted some interesting experiments in 1977. He carried out walking exercises on and just off what's left today of some Chacoan roads. His subjects walked on different slopes, with and without weights. He used a respirometer to measure the amount of work necessary in walking. He wanted to learn how much the prehistoric roads could have "minimized energy expenditure in travel and transportation into, within and out of Chaco Canyon." As expected, he found that using the roads—even in their condition today, some eight hundred to a thousand years after their construction—saves energy. Walking on the roads reduced calorie expenditures by up to 38 percent. It didn't matter whether the Chacoans were walking unburdened or carrying a load of goods. Either way, he found, the roads saved energy.

Fred Nials estimated the "efficiency" of Chacoan roads in comparison to modern roads. For comparison he chose the prehistoric North Road and the modern dirt road between Blanco Trading Post and Chaco Canyon. Both travel roughly the same route. Both trend north-south roughly perpendicular to the grain of the topography. "Somewhat surprisingly," Nials found, "the North Road, despite going straight over obstacles, would appear to be the more 'efficient' of the two roads, both in terms of elevation gain and ground distance to an objective."

The discovery of the extent of the Chacoan roadway network has shown that the Chacoan culture is more than just what we see at Chaco Canyon. It has become obvious, as Gretchen Obenauf emphasized, that "events in Chaco Canyon [can] no longer be viewed as isolated from the rest of the San Juan basin."

Most explanations for the existence of the roadway system have concentrated on practical economic matters—especially the transport of goods. Some Chaco Center archaeologists feel that surplus crops were probably carried on the roads to Chaco for storage. From there they could be redistributed to outlying sites in times of need. Corn and dried beans would have been the most profitable loads of crops to be transported the distances implied by the Chacoan road network, in Obenauf's view. Piñon nuts from the mountain outliers would be another easily transportable food. A large amount of broken pottery has been found on sections of the Great North Road, a sign of a high volume of traffic bearing ceramic containers. Obenauf feels it probable that, like Greek vases of the Mediterranean, Chacoan ceramics were only the containers for the actual product being transported.

Perishable food such as large game may also have been carried long distances over the roads from the mountains to Chacoan population centers. As Judd first speculated, the ponderosa pine trees used as roof beams were undoubtedly another commodity carried over the roads.

But as Gwinn Vivian points out, the transport of economic goods is not likely to be the only explanation for the Chacoan roads. Obenauf, in fact, favors a multiple explanation.

One such additional purpose of the roadway network may have been social integration of the Chacoan culture. "The roads would have provided an easily perceptible demonstration of the social, economic, and perhaps ceremonial links between Chaco Canyon and the outliers, and among the outliers," suggests Obenauf. The inter-community cooperation necessary in constructing and maintaining the roads would also have promoted social integration.

Religious integration may have been a third role of the roadway network. This, I feel, is a neglected topic. Obenauf points out that Chaco Canyon may have been the ceremonial as well as the political and administrative center of the Chacoan culture. If so, the roadways would have linked all the Chacoans culturally and provided easy transportation to Chaco Canyon for major ceremonies. Judd's intriguing label, "ceremonial highways," comes again to mind.

Perhaps it goes further than that. In illustrating how solely economic explanations for the road network may fall short, Vivian points to certain features about the roads that economics or other considerations of practical transport just don't explain: The great width of Chacoan roads, for instance, or the fact that some roads are exactly half the width of others, or the existence of parallel or even double-parallel roads in some areas.

I described some of these enigmatic features of Chacoan roads to a prominent Hopi Indian friend recently and asked if there was anything in his culture that could cast light on their width, their linearity, and the parallel segments. "Has anyone looked into whether they might be symbolic?" he asked. I asked him to explain. "What directions do they go from Chaco?" he asked. I told him there was a major road to the north and several to the south and southwest. "Are there any to the east?" he inquired. Not to my knowledge, I told him. He reminded me that his culture maintains extensive traditions about the migrations to the Hopi mesas of the Hopi clans. Many ceremonies and symbols recall the migration routes to Hopi. Perhaps, he suggested, the Chacoans did the same. In the case of the Hopis, traditions say that most of their clans came from the south, the southwest, and the north. None came from the east. Perhaps the same was true of the Chacoans. Perhaps, he suggested, the roads' directions symbolize the directions from which the clans that composed the Chacoan culture came.

The enigmatic existence of at least four parallel road segments for a considerable distance to the north of Chaco, might, he said, have symbolized the migration to Chaco of four clans from the north. The widths of Chacoan roads very likely also had religious or symbolic significance, he proposed.

I don't know if there would be any way to test these suggestions of the possible symbolic nature of the Chacoan roadway network. But they show how the Pueblo Indian world view can differ markedly from the interpretations our culture so readily puts on things. And it was Pueblo Indians who built the Chacoan roadway network.

The discovery over the past decade of the full extent and nature of the Chacoan roadway network has been a revelation. No doubt, as Obenauf says, "the roadway network contributed to the economic, social, and religious cohesion of the Chacoan system." It has opened our eyes to the need for a wider view of Chacoan culture than just the people in the great pueblos in the bottom of Chaco Canyon itself.

7. The Outliers

If the roadways were the first jolting
stimulus causing archaeologists to expand their view of Chacoan culture to the
entire San Juan basin, the outliers were the second. There was a bit of the
chicken-and-egg situation to it all, however. The roadways led to the discovery of
more outliers. The outliers led to the discovery of more roadways.

Although there was no comparable instrumental advance (unless you count
the remote-sensing technology), it was like the surge of astronomical discovery
that accompanies first use of any new observing device, such as a space telescope. In this case, the more the archaeologists looked, the more outlying communities they found. Chacoan outliers seemed nearly everywhere. Something
important was going on here.

New archaeological ground surveys supplemented by continuing remote-
sensing work was amassing the first good record of Chacoan outliers. Somewhere between thirty and sixty of these communities—most, but not all, of them
Chacoan—had by now been identified. And the numbers were rising all the time.

"The extent of the Chacoan cultural influence was known to a limited degree
for a long, long time," Thomas Lyons, who set up the Remote Sensory Division,
remarked in 1979. "But in the last year or so with more survey work going on in
the San Juan basin, many more of these outlier sites were identified and docu-

mented. So the concept of what that cultural sphere was has changed. It was much larger, much more complex than we realized." As a result, he believed that some of the most basic assumptions about the Chacoan culture should now at least be questioned.

"We have to be very careful now about considering Chaco Canyon as the center of the Chacoan universe. It's a natural thing for people working there to feel that way because that's where work has been going on—since the turn of the century, for heaven's sakes—and it is a national monument, and people have been working there intensively for several years." He paused for a moment.

"So there's a natural tendency to think of it as the center. It may be. I have reservations about that. I think what we need is to look at the whole sphere of influence and study it to really come up with a determination to see if there is such a thing as a Rome of the Chacoans—if all roads lead to Chaco Canyon."

The wider view of Chacoan culture he was talking about has definitely come to pass. The road network and the abundance of outliers have broadened the focus to the entire San Juan basin. As the Chaco Center's W. James Judge said, "We began to realize that we were dealing with the tip of the iceberg—much of Chaco lay far outside the Canyon." But it is probably fair to say that the idea of Chaco Canyon as the center of it all—politically, economically, culturally—has stood up rather well. Despite our newly expanded perception of the extent of the Chacoan culture, most archaeologists still consider the canyon to have been its regional hub.

That Chaco Canyon was more-or-less ringed by scores of Chacoan communities around the San Juan basin was a slowly accumulated realization. In archaeology, as in other sciences, insights don't usually burst suddenly upon the scene. Instead new evidence gradually builds upon old, views begin slowly to alter, and at no single time can anyone easily say when a new conception begins to be held favorably by a majority of the professionals in a field. The 1970s were undoubtedly the time when the basin-wide view of Chacoan culture was born. But it had been a long time gestating.

Several of the major Chacoan outliers had long been known. Take Aztec Ruin, for instance. This misleadingly named site (neither it nor the nearby town of Aztec, New Mexico, has anything to do with the Aztec culture) lies along the Animas River fifteen miles northeast of Farmington, New Mexico. This location happens to be about halfway between Chaco Canyon and the great cliff dwellings of Mesa Verde. Aztec is the largest of all Chacoan ruins outside Chaco Canyon itself. In fact, with an estimated 405 rooms and a 161,000-square-foot floor area, it is third in size only to the great Chaco Canyon ruins of Chetro Ketl and Pueblo Bonito among all Chacoan pueblos, in or outside the canyon.

A Spanish map made around 1777 refers to the "ruins of very old towns" at the location. Travelers mentioned them during the nineteenth century, nearby

Aztec ruin from the air. Aztec, northeast of Farmington, New Mexico, is the largest of all Chacoan ruins outside Chaco Canyon itself. Chaco Center, NPS.

residents dug in them in the 1880s, and Earl H. Morris systematically excavated them from 1916 to 1921, again in 1923, and again in 1933–34.

Morris is a legendary figure in Southwestern archaeology. He said he began his archaeological career at the age of three when his father gave him an old short-handled pick and told him to go out and dig. His first stroke uncovered the bowl of a black-and-white ceramic dipper, accompanied by a prehistoric skeleton. "Thus, at three and a half years of age there had happened the clinching event which was to make of me an ardent pot hunter, who later was to acquire the more creditable, and I hope earned, classification as an archaeologist."

Morris became identified with Aztec Ruin. His excavations there uncovered a D-shaped pueblo, a plaza enclosed by a low, curving wall, and a beautifully built circular Great Kiva. The Great Kiva is forty-one feet in diameter at floor level and forty-eight feet in diameter at waist level. In 1933 and 1934, Morris restored it to its original condition, where visitors to Aztec Ruins National Monument (yes, Morris was its first curator) can see it today.

The walls of Aztec are made of core-and-veneer Chaco-style masonry. The pueblo was three stories high in places. Today it is estimated that the structure had twenty-eight kivas in addition to the Great Kiva. We know through tree-ring dating beginning with the wood beam samples Morris sent A.E. Douglass (Chapter 3) that this main Aztec pueblo was constructed mainly between A.D. 1110 and 1120. In fact, the people built most of it from 1111 to 1115. This structure (sometimes called the Aztec West Ruin) is the largest of several prehistoric buildings in a tight aggregation of twelve sites collectively called the Aztec Ruins. This twenty-seven-acre site preserved as the national monument is in turn surrounded, according to one archaeologist's reckoning, by the remains of some ninety smaller pueblos within a mile and a half radius. Obviously the whole aggregation was quite a community in its heydey.

John Corbett, in his handbook on Aztec, brings life to this remarkable site:

"Aztec, at the height of the Chacoan occupation, must have been a fascinating sight. On a sunny summer day, the plaza and rooftops would have been a busy swarm of activity—mothers nursing and tending their young, grinding corn for tortillas, preparing meat for the stew pot, making baskets, and molding clay pots for later firing. Old men basked in the sun or instructed the young boys. Most of the men and older boys were busy tending the corn, beans, and squash in the fertile fields surrounding the pueblos. This was exacting work, since each plot, clan by clan, had to receive its carefully husbanded share of water from the irrigation ditch that ran along the slope of the high terrace just to the north of the pueblo. At times during the day, hunters would straggle in happily if burdened with game, sadly and slowly if empty-handed after a fruitless chase. Occasionally a wandering group of strangers would pass by with items to trade. They were made welcome and fed, and the whole plaza took on a festive air.

"At night the pueblo must have presented a vastly different appearance: dark, mysterious, and quiet. Here and there a small dying fire cast a flickering glow upon a brown adobe wall. In one or two of the kivas, a faint light through the hatchway in the roof indicated preparations under way for a ceremony, or perhaps a special highly secret meeting of one of the clan societies. If you looked closely you might make out one of the sentinels, silhouetted briefly against the night sky as he shifted position. But the pueblo was silent—a silence broken by an occasional dog's bark or baby's wail—until, shortly after the morning star appeared, the hunters crept quietly out of the pueblo, and as the star faded, the broadening morning light heralded the approach of another day in the life of Aztec pueblo."

This idyllic scene didn't apply for long. Aztec was occupied by its Chacoan-type people for only a few decades. By 1150 the pueblo was relatively empty.

Most of the people had left. It was apparently part of the vast movement out of Chaco Canyon itself by then. Abandonment may not have been total. Perhaps there was partial abandonment and a change in the culture reflecting closer ties with the Mesa Verde area. Probably some population was in residence until Aztec was resettled and remodeled (as is true of virtually all other Chacoan structures north of the San Juan River) by Mesa Verdean people in the thirteenth century.

Another example of a major Chacoan outlier was the Village of the Great Kivas far to the south of Chaco on Zuni Indian Reservation lands. This site, northeast of Zuni pueblo in Nutria Canyon, is about eighty air miles south-southwest of Chaco Canyon. Frank H. Roberts, Jr., who had worked with Neil Judd at Pueblo Bonito, excavated these Chaco-type ruins and published a detailed monograph about them in 1932.

Roberts uncovered a rectangular one-story Chacoan structure of about eighteen rooms encompassing two kivas. Adjacent to this structure, to the south, is an enormous Great Kiva that has been outlined but never fully excavated. Its average diameter is some seventy-eight feet. One of the "smaller" great kivas ("only" fifty-four feet across) Roberts did excavate. Partially subterranean and partially above

Village of the Great Kivas. This Chacoan site is eighty air miles south of Chaco Canyon on Zuni Indian land. *From* Powers, Outlier Survey.

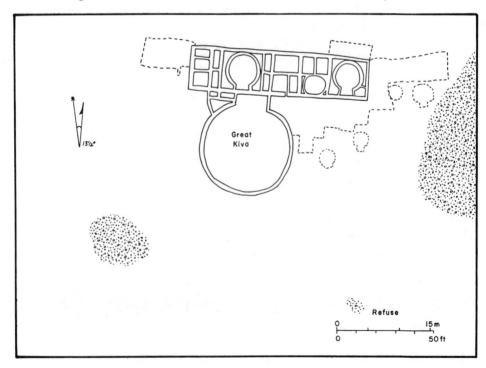

Salmon Ruin. Salmon, fifty miles north of Chaco on the San Juan River, is along the Great North Road. *Chaco Center, NPS.*

ground, it had four pillars supporting the roof. The builders had created the pillars from blocks of stone carefully laid in adobe mortar. Three of the pillars were about three feet square, the other close to two feet square.

The masonry at the Village of the Great Kivas is Chacoan style and so are some of the kiva features. Archaeologists working on the ground haven't discovered any signs of prehistoric roadways near the site. But roads aren't ruled out; no aerial photo imagery has been examined. Despite the large kivas and the impressive name, the Village of the Great Kivas rates as a relative "small" Chacoan structure, well down the roster of Chacoan outliers in size.

Not so the Salmon Ruin. Built in the shape of a square "C," its back side is 450 feet long and the arms of the "C" are each 200 feet long. Two to three stories high, with 175 rooms and a floor area of nearly 90,000 square feet, it is one of the larger of the "medium"-size Chacoan ruins, ranking in size just behind Pueblo del Arroyo and Una Vida in Chaco Canyon, and just ahead of Pueblo Alto on the mesa above Chaco Canyon.

Yet the Salmon site is some fifty miles north of Chaco Canyon on the San Juan River. About twelve miles east of the city of Farmington (and ten miles due south of Aztec), the Salmon site is joined to Chaco Canyon by the prehistoric

Great North Road out of Chaco. Salmon was constructed in the late eleventh century, some think by a group originating in Chaco.

Like Aztec, it appears to have been carefully preplanned and built as a well-organized effort in less than a decade. The stone masonry work is carefully done. Both the fine-banded masonry and the sophisticated architecture are reminiscent of the great pueblos in Chaco Canyon itself. The central plaza encloses a circular Great Kiva. It is one of the better preserved outlying Chacoan pueblos.

Yet until a short time ago, the Salmon site was in danger of destruction. The efforts of the people of San Juan County, New Mexico, prevented it. The episode is quite a story.

Unlike the Chacoan ruins in Chaco Canyon and at Aztec, the Salmon site was not under federal protection as a national monument. As was happening elsewhere to other ancient ruins around the San Juan basin, the Salmon site was slowly being destroyed by professional pot hunters. The local citizens of the county realized the danger to this extraordinary cultural resource. As the San Juan County Museum Association, they purchased the site, totally with local pledges. They later sold it to San Juan County.

In 1970 and 1971 members of the museum association contributed funds to do some initial testing and analysis necessary to begin archaeological research. Since there were no laboratory facilities nearby, the museum association campaigned for a county bond issue to construct an archaeological laboratory and museum next to the site. The Salmon Ruins Museum was built in 1973 and is now a major regional cultural center, with 35,000 visitors a year.

Out of this local involvement and concern in the site was also born an intensive archaeological research effort, the San Juan Valley Archaeological Program and its Salmon Ruin Project, headed by archaeologist Cynthia Irwin-Williams of Eastern New Mexico University. Hundreds of people participated in the effort throughout the 1970s. The goal was not only to excavate the Salmon ruins and describe them in detail but also to understand the Chacoan culture that built them.

A large field research effort was carried out from 1973 through 1978. The archaeologists concentrated their excavations on eleven areas, including the plaza, the back north wall, the Great Kiva and its antechamber, blocks of rooms in the southwest and northwest corners, the central sector (containing a Tower Kiva), and transects through a variety of other groups of rooms.

As summarized by Irwin-Williams, they completely or nearly completely excavated forty-two rooms in the original Chacoan structure. This is about 30 percent of the estimated 150 original ground-floor rooms. They also excavated some second-story deposits and structural portions still remaining. Eighty-three secondary rooms were wholly or partly excavated. They removed fill from an additional 26 primary rooms to preserve them by easing weight on exposed walls and to better exhibit them to the public. Trenching enabled them to map an additional 10 primary and 25 secondary rooms. They brought the existing surface down to the level of the final cultural deposits by the occupiers of Salmon in the plaza and along much of the back wall.

All this archaeological research into what Irwin-Williams calls "the structure of Chacoan society in the northern Southwest" was supported by an amazingly diverse variety of groups, from the federal government (National Science Foundation and National Endowment for the Humanities), to regional agencies (the Four Corners Regional Commission, San Juan County, the San Juan County Museum Association, the State of New Mexico), to other institutions (Eastern New Mexico University, Earthwatch, the Navajo Tribe, the Historic Sites Preservation Commission, the 1976 Bicentennial Commission, and the Friends of Salmon Ruin).

It was a very special collaboration. In the first of the series of reports on the investigations at the Salmon site, Irwin-Williams stated her feelings about it this way: "Our heartfelt gratitude also goes to the people of San Juan County, whose love of their land and its heritage and whose vision were responsible for the inception of this project. Their dedication and perseverance were examples for us and their warmth and kindness sustained us."

Most of the trees used in the main phase of construction at Salmon were cut in A.D. 1088 to 1090, with a few more in 1093. During this period, much of the structure's first story and possibly the second story around the Tower Kiva were built. From 1094 to 1104 some additional minor construction and finishing and maintenance work were carried out by the Chacoan occupants. There was only additional minor refurbishing until 1116, when a seventy-year hiatus in tree-ring dates begins. There is evidence of some continued Chacoan occupation until shortly after 1130. Sometime after this the last of the original Chacoan builders and their descendents moved out. Exactly when isn't totally clear. The exodus may have begun as early as 1116, however. In that year, says Rex Adams, one of the archaeological project's field directors, "rather dramatic internal modifications, such as the sealing of doors and the deposition of trash in the ground floor of many rooms began." He says the depositional history of the site indicates that final abandonment of the site by the Chacoan occupants "was rather abrupt."

As at Aztec, the site was then later reoccupied by people from the Mesa Verde area to the north. This reoccupation began around 1185 and continued through 1263. During that time the Mesa Verdeans used the structure extensively. But by A.D. 1285, Salmon no longer had any inhabitants, except for possibly a few Mesa Verdean stragglers.

Aztec . . . Salmon . . . the Village of the Great Kivas . . . Lowry Ruin in southwestern Colorado . . . Kin Ya'a south of Chaco. All are examples of ancient pueblo ruins long widely recognized as having Chacoan affinities. But they seemed not to fit into any pattern, and most archaeologists didn't know what to make of their Chacoan traits. But as archaeological investigation continued in the San Juan

Kin Ya'a, with remnant of its tower kiva, south of Chaco near Crown-point. Chaco Center, NPS.

basin, more and more Chacoan ruins were discovered. It became apparent that the major, well-known sites represented just a small fraction of the Chacoan communities around the basin. The people of Chaco were not confined to Chaco Canyon and a few major pueblos elsewhere. Chacoan communities or colonies— outliers—were scattered all over the vast lands of northwestern New Mexico and even into Colorado and Arizona.

In 1976, the Chaco Center began a systematic survey and reconnaissance of Chacoan outliers. Archaeologist Robert P. Powers, with the assistance of William Gillespie and Stephen Lekson, headed up the project. They studied three outliers—Bis sa'ani, Peach Springs, and Pierre's Ruin—intensively and a sample of thirty-three other outlier sites in somewhat lesser detail.

The men had originally intended to report on *all* known outlying communities. They soon realized that would be impossible. "The staggering number of communities that have been recorded since prevents such comprehensive treatment," said Powers. He estimated that the 36 outlier communities covered in their study "probably do not account for more than 20 to 30 percent of the postulated total." In other words, there may be anywhere from 120 to 180 outliers in the San Juan basin, a good share of that number still undiscovered.

Kin Bineola ("House in Which the Wind Whirls"), a massive house west of Chaco. This prehistoric community is, according to Marshall, the least "contaminated" and most "visible" of Chacoan communities, but it remains largely undocumented. Chaco Center, NPS.

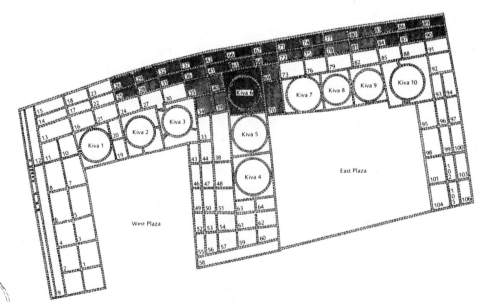

The E-shaped Kin Bineola contains ten kivas, two of them elevated or multi-story, and nearly two hundred rooms on three levels. From Marshall, et al., 1979.

In the same year, a related archaeological survey to locate and document Chacoan communities in the San Juan basin was begun by Richard Loose, soon joined by Michael Marshall and John Stein. This project was jointly funded by the Public Service Company of New Mexico (PNM) and the State of New Mexico's Historic Preservation Bureau. The impending conflict between large-scale energy development and the need to preserve important archaeological sites made such a survey of existing sites especially timely.

So suddenly Chacoan outliers, a topic neglected during the previous half century of investigations into the Chacoan culture, were being scrutinized in two archaeological studies. The two projects coordinated their activities with each other. The Chaco Center project (I'm going to call it the Powers survey from here on) generally concentrated on outliers on the Chaco Slope south of Chaco and the floor of the San Juan basin both north and south of Chaco. The PNM-State of New Mexico survey (I'll call it the Marshall survey, because Mike Marshall was the lead author of its report) concentrated on the southern periphery of the basin and studied ruins not previously visited by the Chaco Center. The Powers survey studied only Chacoan sites; the Marshall survey studied "Anasazi" communities generally, although in fact the majority of the communities they identified were distinctly Chacoan. The archaeologists in the two surveys freely traded their information and ideas. The two studies complemented, rather than competed with, each other.

In one sense the interaction was even more direct. In September 1978 Tom Lyons of the Chaco Center's Remote Sensing Division funded low-level aerial stereo-pair photography of forty-three "Anasazi" site locations (I mentioned these photos in talking about Gretchen Obenauf's roadway project in Chapter 6). Marshall and Stein put panels visible from the air on the sites before they were photographed, and then they made precise measurements of the panels' locations. With the photos and this information they were able to produce "engineering quality three-dimensional models" of the forty-three sites.

A question hangs. If the outliers are so numerous, why have they only recently been fully recognized? After all, the ruins of Chaco Canyon are quite dramatic in appearance, something you can hardly miss.

Most of the Chacoan ruins around the periphery of the San Juan basin are, to say the least, poorly preserved. What's visible of these structures is mostly rounded mounds of masonry almost entirely buried beneath the sand of the centuries since Chacoans last lived in them. Only an occasional segment of wall now stands above the rubble. Marshall and his colleagues point out that at first glance these mounds "bear no resemblance whatsoever to the well-known ruins of Chaco Canyon." In fact the archaeologists had to concoct ways to get useful architectural information about the original structure from these relatively pitiful surface remains. Remember that what we as visitors see of the great pueblos in Chaco Canyon today is the result of extensive excavations and stabilization and preservation work over many decades. Hardly any of the outliers have yet so benefited.

Yet to the trained archaeological eye, the mounds were clearly evident once the necessary surveys were begun over the vast basin. Many of the outliers are small in relation to the great pueblos of Chaco Canyon. Their masonry is usually not quite as good, and the sandstone their builders used was inferior to the dense sandstone used in Chaco Canyon. Yet their clearly Chacoan architectural features, uniform layout, and massive construction betray their Chacoan affiliation. The mounds with their partly protruding rubble usually rise somewhat unnaturally above the surrounding surface. More often as not the structures are in an open, elevated situation commanding a clear view of the surrounding landscape.

Closer inspection usually reveals the central mound enclosing the classic Bonito-phase Chacoan structure to be surrounded by lesser mounds containing the remains of small habitations. These smaller structures, according to the Marshall survey, generally have from three to ten single-story rooms and a small, fully subterranean kiva to the southeast. In other words, the outliers exhibit the same combination of massive apartment-style building and smaller habitations seen on the two sides of Chaco Canyon. We will consider this again later.

Let's now take a quick look at some of these outliers.

We begin with Peach Springs, one of three the Powers group examined intensively. Peach Springs lies in a shallow and broad northward-draining valley far to the southwest of Chaco Canyon. The Chacoan structure at Peach Springs

Peach Springs, unexcavated Chacoan outlier thirty-seven miles southwest of Chaco Canyon. It has a commanding view in all directions. *Chaco Center, NPS.*

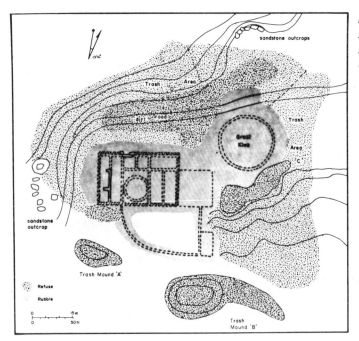

Peach Springs had several kivas and about thirty rooms. Chaco Center, NPS.

lies immediately adjacent to a prehistoric Chacoan road in this southwestern edge of the Chaco basin. Gretchen Obenauf called it the Coyote Canyon Road. Powers calls it the south branch of the West Road. (It is the more southerly of two generally parallel southwest-northeast trending Chacoan roads in this part of the basin. Powers's study calls them collectively the West Road, with north and south branches.) Peach Springs is thirty-seven miles from Pueblo Bonito in Chaco Canyon by this prehistoric road.

A series of drainages with colorful names such as Big Springs, Wild Berry, and Peach Spring Canyons have cut incisions through the Lobo Mesa to the south and deposited soil in the valley bottom. During the summer these canyons would bring considerable water out onto the flats, making the area a good location for agriculture. But the area also has, at least now, an artesian spring that supplies water continuously. Called Peach Springs, it has given its name to the prehistoric site. The spring is little more than a hundred yards south of the Chacoan structure. Powers and his colleagues point out that if the springs bubbled out a continuous flow of water in prehistoric times, they undoubtedly supplied the Chacoan residents with drinking and cooking water. In fact they may well have been the crucial variable in the location of the community here.

The Chacoan structure is at the south end of a densely settled ridge. It has a commanding view in all directions. But there is little left of the structure on the surface. Instead there is a broad mound of rubble and sand some 13 feet high.

Most of the structure is hidden. It appears to be a two-story, rectangular block of rooms fronted by a small plaza enclosed and tied to the house by a curved masonry wall. The house and plaza appear to be in the shape of a D. A low area in front of the structure appears to be a second-story kiva or possibly a tower kiva. Powers estimates that the structure contained thirty rooms and had a total floor area of 20,200 square feet.

The few wall segments that are open to view are of Chaco-type core-and-veneer compound masonry. An elderly Navajo woman who has lived nearby for most of the last half century told the archaeologists that one ceiling of the structure stood intact until the 1920s, but no wood or other ceiling parts are visible today. The site is surrounded by remains of smaller Anasazi houses from all archaeological time periods from Basketmaker III through Late Pueblo III. The prehistoric road at Peach Springs continues to the southwest and apparently terminates at another Chacoan outlier, the Grey Ridge community. Neither of the two outliers surveys examined it.

Bis sa'ani was the second outlier the Powers group studied intensively. (The third, Pierre's Ruin, we already described in the previous chapter, on the roadways.) The name of this site comes from Navajo words meaning "house on top of clay." It is a fitting name in a sense because the Chacoan structure at this site, only seven miles east-northeast of Chaco Canyon, "is rather precariously situated" in Powers's words. It rests at the top of a narrow and precipitous ridge of shale about sixty feet above the valley floor. The Escavada Wash flows through these bottomlands, bordered by desolate badlands of shale.

Bis sa'ani ("House on Top of Clay"), northeast of Chaco Canyon. *Chaco Center, NPS.*

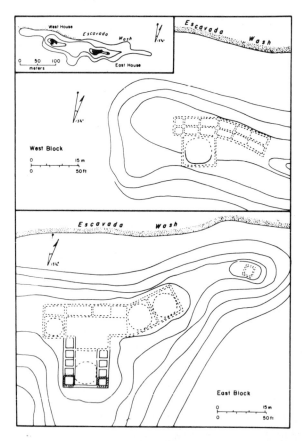

The Chacoans had to build Bis sa'ani in two segments to fit on its narrow and sinuous ridge. Chaco Center, NPS.

Bis sa'ani is precariously situated atop a high ridge of shale. It may have been a defensive outpost. Chaco Center, NPS.

The Chacoan structure atop the southern shale ridge is in two segments, separated by about a hundred yards. They could be considered two different sites, but the archaeologists consider them as one because the narrow and sinuous ridge presented the Chacoan builders with no other choice in locations. The ridge leaves no room for any substantial outside plazas. Each of the two blocks of rooms is roughly L-shaped. The west one has twelve rooms and a single kiva. The east one, twenty-five rooms and four kivas. Several of these rooms appear to be second-story. The total room area in the two blocks is more than 11,000 square feet.

The walls are mainly of core and veneer masonry, typical of many Chacoan structures. The Chacoan builders apparently carried the building materials to the site from a quarry near the crests of the southern badland more than half a mile away. Here there are extensive layers of hard, dark brown, and roughly tabular sandstone. The workmanship is fairly crude by general Chacoan standards. The masonry exhibits none of the craftsmanship or elaborate styles seen in Chaco Canyon. However, elements of most of the Chacoan masonry styles are at least recognizable.

The remarkable feature of the site is its location. "In their present condition, the Chacoan structure roomblocks, and particularly the eastern block, appear to contradict the principle of gravity," Powers and his colleagues reported. "The thick, outside walls of the latter structure, footed on shale, are now partially to almost completely undermined. Yet they stand unassisted for heights exceeding three meters [ten feet], supporting tons of rubble that fill the interior room spaces."

The Chacoan structure and almost all the other smaller habitations in this area of shale badlands are on prominences. The sites, especially the one the Chacoan structure is on, are almost inherently instable. The Powers study calls them "remarkably precarious."

Why did the Chacoans build a community here? "Access is difficult, the shale provides a poor architectural footing, and in general, the badland topography gives the impression of being rather undesirable," the Powers group points out. They suggest that a combination of "high visibility, availability of building material, and / or defense" may have been the key considerations for building in these wild badlands. It is hard to avoid the conclusion that the site may have been a kind of defensive outpost, especially when you consider that no other Chacoan outlier is yet known to lie out beyond this point to the northeast.

The Marshall study recorded data on scores of outlying settlements, most of them Chacoan. Most were already known. But in their fieldwork the archaeologists encountered at least four previously unrecorded sites where they had predicted outliers might be. These sites are now named Lake Valley, Indian Creek, Kin Nizhoni, and Blue Water Spring.

Kin Nizhoni is one of a cluster of Chacoan outliers far to the south of Chaco on the mesas north and west of Mount Taylor. Kin Nizhoni is on a nearly 7,000-

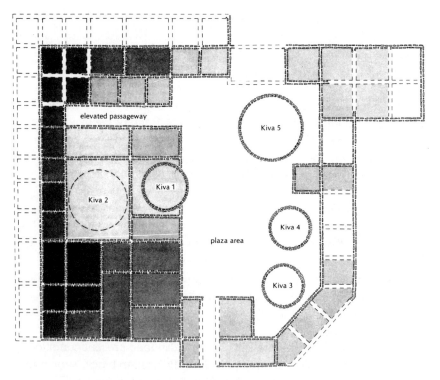

Floor plan of San Mateo, one of a cluster of three outliers on the north slopes of Mt. Taylor near the terminus of the great Southeast Road. From Marshall, et al., 1979.

foot-high mesa that the archaeologists describe as an "island surrounded by extensive marshlike bottomlands." It is at the terminus of the great Southeast Road that connects it, San Mateo, and El Rito to Chaco Canyon, some sixty miles to the north. The larger of two main Chacoan structures is moderate in size but occupies an imposing location on high ground. It is a multistory, double-terraced rectangular pueblo containing two inside kivas. It is exposed southeast to the winter sun and a panoramic view of the San Mateo Mountains and Mesa La Jara.

This is just one apparently public structure serving as the nucleus of a huge community. In addition to one other large masonry pueblo on somewhat lower ground, the archaeologists recorded sixty-one sites having eighty-six structural units containing an estimated total of 304 rooms. Most are within a one-mile-square area centered on the main Kin Nizhoni structure. The archaeologists expect that related settlements exist a mile and a half or more beyond.

Seven miles southeast of Kin Nizhoni is the El Rito outlier, originally rectangular, two to three stories high, with fifty-five rooms, four small kivas, and a great kiva. This is the southernmost Chaco-related community in this group in and around the Red Mesa Valley north of Mount Taylor. It is fifty-eight miles by the prehistoric Chacoan Southeast Road from here to Chaco Canyon.

The easternmost Chacoan outlier is Guadalupe Ruin, on an isolated mesa overlooking the Rio Puerco thirty-six miles to the northeast of El Rito and fifty-four miles southeast of Chaco Canyon. This location is only about forty-five miles northwest of Albuquerque. Guadalupe is a one-story, E-shaped structure with an estimated twenty-five Chacoan rooms and three kivas. It seems to have been built in the mid-to-late 900s and then remodeled and added to in Chacoan style at least three times between A.D. 1050 and 1125. There are many signs of a sizeable associated community in the vicinity. No signs of any prehistoric roadway connecting Guadalupe with Chaco Canyon or any other outlier have been found. This fact and its great distance from any other known outlier, makes Guadalupe one of the more isolated of all the Chacoan outposts.

Another southern outlier is the Casamero Community. This site is at the foot of erosion-sculpted sandstone cliffs forty-five miles south of Chaco Canyon. This makes it about nine miles northeast of Prewitt, New Mexico, a town on Interstate 40 west of Grants. The main Chacoan structure at Casamero is in the shape of an L and has about twenty-six rooms, two small kivas, and a great kiva. The great kiva, several hundred feet south of the unexcavated Casamero house mound, appears to be huge. Marshall and colleagues say a "conservative estimate" of its interior diameter would be twenty-one meters. That's sixty-eight feet.

Casamero, 45 miles south of Chaco, has 26 rooms, two small kivas, and a probably great kiva. From Marshall, et al., 1979.

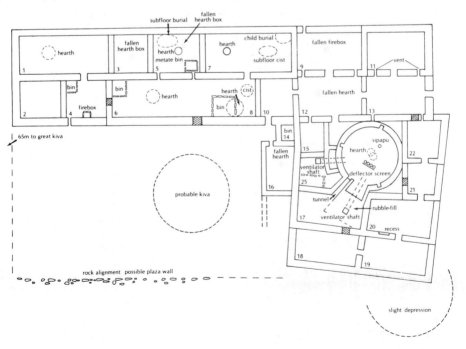

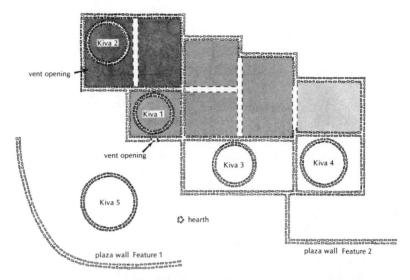

Andrews Ruin is almost all kivas. The isolated great kiva is south of the ruin and not shown in this drawing. A prehistoric road connects Andrews with Casamero, three miles away. From Marshall, et al., 1979.

Grey Hill Spring community, thirty miles southwest of Chaco. Two of its six unconnected structures are shown here. From Marshall, et al., 1979.

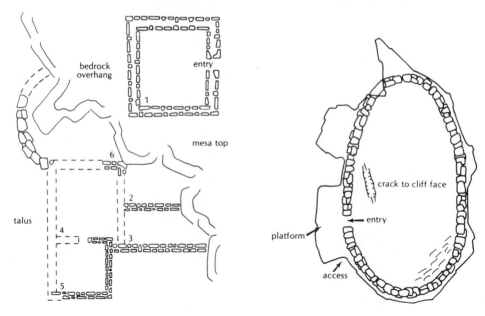

A prehistoric road connects Casamero with the Andrews outlier three miles to the southeast. The main pueblo at Andrews is almost all kivas. Five kivas and a single great kiva are evident. The great kiva is isolated from the rest of the pueblo. This kiva is defined at present by a massive depression in the ground. The Marshall study conservatively estimated its diameter at between twenty-three and twenty-four meters, or in excess of seventy-five feet. "This structure," they noted, "is among the largest of known great kivas."

So far to the southwest of Chaco that they are in Arizona lie the two Chacoan outliers of Allentown and Houck. Allentown is on a mesa southwest of Lupton, Arizona, nearly ninety straight-line miles from Chaco Canyon. The Chacoan structure there has two major rectangular roomblocks separated by a passageway. One was two stories high and contained about thirty rooms. The second may have originally stood three or even four stories high and contained sixty-five rooms, according to Frank H. H. Roberts, Jr., who examined the site in the late 1930s. No signs of any prehistoric roadway have been found.

Off to the west of Chaco toward the Chuska Mountains are many more outliers. The Grey Hill Spring community, thirty miles west-southwest of Chaco Canyon, has at least six different structures scattered on and around a barren mesa-canyon area. The largest pueblo has fourteen rooms. It appears to have been a single-story structure terraced down the slope of the mesa.

Whirlwind House is a small Chacoan pueblo on the end of a mesa a mile or two north of the Grey Hill Spring community. It is still in good condition, with standing walls. The house is in the shape of an L. It contains twelve ground-floor rooms, a small plaza, and a blocked-in kiva.

The Indian Creek community is about halfway between Grey Hill Spring and Chaco and a little further south. It includes two main pueblos, Casa Cielo, on an exposed mesa top, and Casa Abajo, on a ledge below and partially sheltered by the mesa. There are twenty mounds of house ruins scattered over a several-mile area down the Indian Creek drainage to the south and east.

Other sites lie farther to the north and west. Skunk Springs is about forty-five miles west-northwest of Chaco. This pueblo contains no fewer than three great kivas. They are enclosed by a walled-in plaza with gates opening to the exterior and backed by a partially multistory pueblo containing perhaps four smaller kivas. The wall enclosing the plaza is massive. In its southern part it is nearly six-and-a-half feet thick. There is a crescent-shaped apparent shrine made of masonry east of the pueblo.

Thirty miles to the north, nearly fifty miles northwest of Chaco Canyon, overlooking the Chaco River, is the Hogback outlier. It takes its name from a sharp, uplifted ridge, or hogback, of sandstone off to the west. The small Chacoan pueblo contains six large and nine smaller rooms and a plaza containing a circular kiva. More than a half mile to the southwest archaeologists have found the

Chimney Rock, a Chacoan outlier on a narrow mesa top in southwestern Colorado. Chaco Center, NPS.

Escalante, a Chacoan outlier overlooking the Dolores River Canyon west of Dolores, Colorado. It is 7,200 feet above sea level. The kiva in foreground was excavated by the University of Colorado. Courtesy Robert Powers.

well-defined depression of a Great Kiva more than fifty feet in diameter. Two other large clusters of structures containing a total of 300 rooms are scattered to the north and south of the main pueblo.

These are just a few of the Chacoan outliers distributed around the San Juan basin—just some representative examples. Not mentioned here are Chimney Rock, up on a narrow mesa in Colorado, or Las Ventanas, way south of Grants, or Haystack, or Dalton Pass, or Muddy Water. Other outliers include Kin Ya'a with its extraordinary four-story tower kiva, the Newcomb community scattered along a mile-long mesa top, Squaw Springs on the Ute Indian Reservation, Bee Burrow, Coolidge, Great Bend, Greenlee, Halfway House, Jacques, Raton Well, Sanostee, Tocito, Toh-la-kai, and Twin Angels. They are extraordinary cultural resources. (Recognizing the value and vulnerability of these Chacoan outliers, the federal legislation signed in December 1980 that renamed and expanded Chaco Culture National Historical Park also designated thirty-three of these outliers as Chaco Culture Archaeological Protection Sites. At least three more outliers are slated to be added to that total.)

Standing Rock outlier is adjacent to the prehistoric great road running southwest from Chaco. *Chaco Center, NPS.*

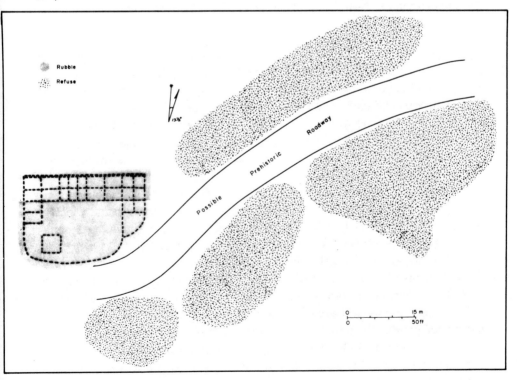

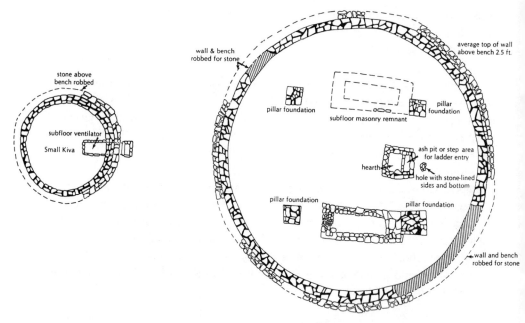

Fort Wingate Great Kiva. Between old U.S. 66 and Interstate 40, this enormous Bonito-phase Chacoan structure was excavated and then destroyed by the construction of I-40. From Marshall, et al., 1979, after Peckham.

Our view of Chacoan culture has expanded from a 10-mile-long canyon with a dozen major pueblos to a 33,000-square-mile basin with scores of Chacoan pueblos and their associated communities in a wide variety of environments. This is an enormous change from the days when Chacoan culture—at least our perception of it—was synonymous with Pueblo Bonito. What was happening in the San Juan basin at this time? Weren't the great settlements in Chaco enough? What was the relationship between them and all these outlying communities we now know about?

These questions dominate the next chapter. But for now some things can be said. One clue to the role of the outliers may be the great variability in their locations and environments. For the most part, the Chacoan outliers enjoyed greater average rainfall, better access to water, more productive soil, closer proximity to conifer forests, and in general a closer association with diverse environments than the settlements of Chaco Canyon. The canyon's alkaline soil is not very good for agriculture. It is remote from large sources of timber. There are no nearby mountains, where game would have been more plentiful. It seems highly likely that outliers helped provide the people in the canyon with some of their basic necessities. To Robert Powers, it all "suggests that the Chaco population was supported economically not only by the canyon environment, but as the center of a regional community and road system its economic range actually extended throughout the San Juan basin via intercommunity exchange." The Chacoan roads fan out from the canyon to widely separated peripheral areas. The known roads transect a diversity of environments. Powers points out that this pattern selects for maximum resource diversity and avoids reliance on a single resource area. This all seems to be an indication that, as Powers says, "canyon residents were attempting to maximize the variability present in the higher diversity outlying areas."

The Chacoans may have brought food crops, firewood, dried meat, hides, wild seeds, yucca fiber, basketry materials, pinyon nuts, and herbs from the outliers into the canyon. It is certain that ceramics from the outliers made their way into the canyon, and it is probable that salt, cotton, and turquoise (none of which occur anywhere near the canyon) did too. All these items could have been obtained in exchange transactions. The evidence indicates, according to Powers, that "outliers and road systems funneled goods to the central Chaco basin, and to Chaco Canyon specifically."

The big ponderosa pine timbers had to be brought in too, but Powers feels they were probably custom cut for specific canyon structures by groups of Chacoans sent out directly from the canyon.

What the residents of Chaco Canyon may have provided in return for all the inflowing goods is not totally certain. Powers notes the early architectural skills of the Chaco Canyon people. He suggests that the outlying Chacoan structures and their Great Kivas may have been constructed by crews from Chaco Canyon in exchange for foodstuffs and other necessary resources. If so, this could have been the start of the complex series of relationships between the canyon and the outliers. "The collected goods would have subsidized the parttime specialists [in Chaco Canyon], provided for canyon needs, and perhaps allowed some reinvestment to other areas affected by climatic perturbations." As the Chaco Center's Wolcott Toll has pointed out, once such relationships were established with several outlying areas, Chaco Canyon would have been on its way to becoming a regional trading center.

Of course there is no reason to consider economics as the sole link between canyon and outliers. There were undoubtedly important religious and ceremonial ties as well.

One other point about the outlying communities. The key word here is communities. Nearly every outlier, you may have noticed from those I briefly mentioned, consists of not just a large Chacoan structure but of many other smaller habitation sites surrounding it. In a sense this exists in Chaco Canyon itself, where there are large pueblos on the north side of the canyon and smaller structures on the south side. But in the canyon the number and size of the pueblos is such an overriding influence the smaller sites seem much less significant. Some archaeologists have felt that the presence of large pueblos and smaller ones were evidence of two different types of people living side by side in Chaco Canyon. But if that is true, would the same kind of dichotomy likely be evident at all the numerous outliers too? Probably not.

Yet in almost every case, an outlier's main Chacoan-style pueblo has many other smaller dwellings associated with it. The Chacoan structures are quite distinct from the small houses in both size and design. Prehistoric roads link some of the large structures; they bypass the smaller ones. The large structures frequently contain specialized features such as Great Kivas. Some Great Kivas are placed away from the large pueblos and near the smaller houses, but in no case are they located in the plazas of small-house sites or are they physically attached to them.

Clearly, with their Great Kivas, the large structures served the community's ceremonial functions. Powers suggests that they also were the community's administrative and economic centers. In this, Marshall and his colleagues are in agreement with Powers.

But they differ somewhat on the next step. The Marshall study suggests that the large Chacoan structures were *exclusively* public buildings. Powers considers them part public building but also part residential. He believes they may have housed a small number of an elite group of Chacoans, perhaps the community's administrators. Marshall sees no evidence of any such social elite.

"We believe that a socially complex, but basically nonstratified, populace lived in the small structures and used the larger structures for storage and for periodic sessions of special tasks related to public obligations and decision-making processes," state Marshall and his colleagues in their report. They say they noticed a gradual development and evolution of public architecture in the peripheral Chacoan communities. "The differences between the great houses and small houses are more likely functional than related to separate social units co-evolving throughout the San Juan basin." They suggest this also points to the type of relationship between the outliers and Chaco. This obvious evolution of large classic Chacoan structures in the periphery of the basin seems to demonstrate that the public buildings and their associated communities are "not the result of elitist colonization." "More likely," concludes the Marshall report, "productivity and alliance on the fringes of the Chacoan interaction sphere made the impressive developments at Chaco Canyon possible."

8. Population, Burials, and the Mexican Connection

Population

The image of a densely populated urbanized environment has been a part of public consciousness about Chaco Canyon for much of this century. A prehistoric city in the midst of the desolate Southwest . . . a center of Anasazi population . . . apartment buildings with hundreds of rooms. The phrases echo through the years.

When Neil Judd's Pueblo Bonito excavations were catching the public fancy back in the 1920s, the idea of an ancient metropolis in the desert was a romantic image. Judd wrote in one popular article that the 800-room structure remained the largest apartment building in the United States from the time of its construction by its Chacoan builders and residents until the 1880s, when a bigger one was erected in New York City.

Well into the 1970s, the official National Park Service brochure on Chaco Canyon said perhaps a thousand persons inhabited Pueblo Bonito alone. It estimated the peak population of Chaco at "about 7,000 individuals."

The public can easily be forgiven for extrapolating our ideas about modern cities onto impressions from the Chacoan past. Surely (so it seemed) many thousands, perhaps tens of thousands, of Indians must have been living and working in Chaco Canyon at its heyday. Figures of 6,000, 10,000, even 20,000 have been bandied about over the decades.

One of the first attempts to calculate the population of Chaco Canyon also produced one of the more extravagant estimates. It was made by Reginald Fisher and reported to Edgar Hewitt in his 1936 book *The Chaco Canyon and Its Monuments.* Fisher approached the problem from two directions. He calculated the amount of arable land available and estimated the capacity of the known ruins. During the classic period, the population between Pueblo Pintado and Kin Bineola was, said Fisher, "probably never greater than 25,000."

"One would have to agree with him," archaeologist Alden Hayes dryly commented in his 1981 report on archaeological surveys in Chaco Canyon.

In later decades the estimates dropped considerably. Most population figures proposed were between 4,400 and 6,000.

Two serious looks at the population problem were prepared in the early 1980s. The first was by Hayes, a veteran of archaeological work in Chaco and head of the archaeological survey in the early 1970s that began the Chaco Project.

Hayes began with two big assumptions. The first was that the average size of a Chacoan family was 4.5 persons. This figure came from ethnographic studies of modern pueblos. They show that such a figure is about right for the Zuni and the Rio Grande pueblos from 1880 to 1952, Cochiti pueblo from 1744 to 1952, and Jemez pueblo in the 1920s. Basically this works out to a family of two parents and a couple of living children plus a grandparent or stepchild living with every second family. Hayes felt that because infant mortality was very likely greater in the 1030s than in 1930 his estimate of average family size was conservative. But he said, "I would rather err on the generous side to make my low estimate more acceptable, because prehistoric populations have commonly been greatly exaggerated."

Second, he assumed that a basic housing unit was a suite or apartment of three rooms. This too was taken from ethnographic studies of pueblos such as Acoma, Zia, and Cochiti.

Hayes had to make a number of other assumptions too. For example, with early-site (Pueblo I) houses he figured that about 25 percent of the rooms were occupied at the same time. For the Pueblo II period, which lasted 150 years, he figured rooms lasted about 75 years and therefore about half the rooms constructed during this period were occupied contemporaneously. For the 125-year-long early Pueblo III period, he figured that about two-thirds of the rooms were occupied at any given time (the rest were abandoned or filled with trash). A few other such assumptions also had to be entered into the calculations. Hayes, whose humor and humility show through in his writing, at one point refers to the process as "devious shuffling."

When all was done, Hayes estimated that the population of Chaco Canyon reached maximums of 1,053 in the Basketmaker period, 1,674 in the Pueblo I period, 3,240 in the Pueblo II period, and 5,652 at its height in the Pueblo III period.

After that, followed the 125-year Late Pueblo III (post-classic) period during which over the decades people were gradually leaving Chaco. The population during this period fell to 1,022. This was even lower than during the Basketmaker period. After that, Chaco was occupied only for short times by small groups, with no permanent population.

Hayes's figure of just under 6,000 maximum population for Chaco at its height fit fairly well into the range of other, less systematic estimates.

"I'm aware that the convoluted reasoning and the juggling of figures is reminiscent of haruspicy or astrology," said Hayes, "but given the kinds of data available to us, I'm convinced the results are as close to the mark as the trajectories launched by more sophisticated, mathematical range-finders."

But what about the assumptions? How valid are they?

Most recent population estimates, such as Al Hayes's, had fallen into the range of 4,400 to 6,000. Although these kinds of figures were far more conservative than some of the earlier grandiose estimates—and they struck most archaeologists as reasonable—they still implied a substantial Chaco Canyon population. Given the marginal climate and scarcity of resources in the immediate area, a permanent population of this magnitude would fairly quickly strip the area of wood and other essentials. In fact it was this problem that led to models of a Chacoan society based on regional exchange and pooling of resources. They sought to show how such a relatively concentrated population could manage to cope.

Thomas Windes, supervisory archaeologist at the Chaco Center in Albuquerque, began to question some of the most basic assumptions about Chacoan population. One tacit assumption has been that Chaco was permanently inhabited for centuries. Another was that the large Chacoan pueblos (the towns), like the smaller structures (the villages), were more or less fully occupied. "A popular view of them" said Windes, "is of tenements packed with urbanites."

Windes began an analysis that questioned the twin assumptions of permanency and packing. Rather than focusing on mere numbers of rooms, he chose a more fundamental feature: the presence of firepits, or hearths. The firepit, he reasoned, is a universal necessity for permanent occupation. Absence of one suggests a lack, or a serious reduction, in the essential household activities of heating, cooking, lighting, and so on. Indoor firepits, he further reasoned, seem a necessity for cold weather and therefore permanent occupation in Chaco. (The mean low temperature in December and January over the past several decades at Chaco has been 12°F and the temperature has dropped to as low as -39°F.)

The room firepit appears to be a useful indicator of population, Windes decided. To keep things simple, he equated firepit rooms with single households. By his definition such a household firepit had to be large, constructed of adobe or slabs of rock, and it had to show evidence of intense burning. Firepits also often contain debris from cooking and other household uses. A firepit would be our equivalent of kitchen stove and furnace combined. Windes did not count mere "heating pits," unlined and poorly oxidized depressions scooped out of the floor. They usually reflect little use or only short-term use.

Next Windes confronted another issue: In the multistory pueblos, were the upper-floor rooms inhabited? Were they really separate living quarters, the eleventh-century version of walk-up apartments? Almost all population estimates assumed so. Yet Windes said there was little or no evidence for a pattern of upper-story habitation. The problem is that most upper-story floors had long ago collapsed. This naturally destroyed any evidence of upper-story habitation, proponents argued. But it could just as well be that there wasn't any evidence of habitation there in the first place, Windes countered.

He marshaled his argument around several key points:

If upper-story habitation had been widespread, said Windes, then investigators sooner or later should have stumbled on some evidence of it. Neil Judd had previously noted the scarcity of firepits at Pueblo Bonito. Work at a multistory non-Chacoan prehistoric ruin, Grasshopper, in Arizona, had readily identified features such as firepits and mealing bins after their collapse with rooftops and upper floors. The lack of such evidence at Bonito, therefore, may well be meaningful.

Second, there is considerable evidence of preference for ground-story rooms with direct access to the plaza. Most hearths, in fact, are found in just such rooms. This seems to hold for both Pueblo Bonito and a small sample of nearby contemporaneous Chacoan villages.

Third, Windes found few signs that the Chacoans were averse to using ground-floor firepits in multistory blocks in the large pueblos. About a third of those at Bonito and Pueblo del Arroyo were so situated. Almost all the rest at both sites were in single-story dwellings. At Una Vida, there were firepit rooms below upper stories and in single-story rooms facing the plaza. At Salmon Ruin, the large Chacoan pueblo forty miles to the north, the living rooms remained single story and plaza-facing despite the addition of upper stories. "While this does not prove that there was only lower-story occupation," said Windes, "it does suggest that residential locations may not have changed from village patterns."

Upper-story occupation may have been discouraged by the shallowness and light construction of the floors, Windes believed. These shortcomings would have made upper-story firepits difficult, and perhaps hazardous. He noted that Judd had remarked on the fire danger of a second-story heating pit at Bonito nestled into the roofing of a lower story.

What other features, not destroyed by time or excavation, might correlate with hearths or living rooms? The presence of wall niches might be one such feature. Although the evidence is not very certain, it is possible that room hearths and wall niches might for a time be highly associated. Ninety percent of the niches reported by Judd not in doors or vents occur in ground-story rooms. If Judd was consistent in his reporting of niches and if they correlate with hearths, Windes reasoned, "then again most domestic rooms would be assigned to the ground story."

If the upper floors of the large Chacoan pueblos weren't really separate apartments, housing additional families, then the estimates of maximum population in Chaco Canyon have to be revised drastically downward.

Furthermore, if you use one firepit as a sign that one household lived in the suite of connecting rooms, the population estimates for ground-floor rooms fall off too. In the earliest construction period at Bonito, from A.D. 920 to 925, there are seventeen rooms with hearths. From A.D. 1040 to about 1080, just 10 potential households—judging from the number of rooms with hearths—were built. And this was a period of great building in Chaco Canyon, often considered to be the height of the Bonito period. Whether the earlier-built households continued to be occupied into this period is doubtful. Most, Windes said, were abandoned and filled with trash and burials or built over by the end of this period. From A.D. 1085 to 1110, Windes concluded there were 18 households living in Pueblo Bonito. Windes considers the estimates for this period to be the most accurate. The Chacoans did little subsequent remodeling that could obscure the record. For this same period, Windes noted that Hayes's calculations would have yielded 179 Bonitian households.

"If upper story occupation is minimized at Pueblo Bonito," Windes pointed out, "then approximately 45 total households were noted for over a 200-year period. The count should be higher, of course, for rooms built over or torn down, but even doubling the number of households is a far cry from the hundreds predicted for peak population by other demographers."

Pueblo Del Arroyo likewise shows relatively small population at any one time in comparison with its size, judging from the number of rooms with hearths. Most hearths—and therefore households in this view—were in the plaza-fronting, first-story rooms. As at Bonito, Windes concluded, "the largest number of households might have been at the end of the site occupation, with the primary structure being practically devoid of population."

Some fresh perspective is available from Pueblo Alto, which Windes and colleagues partially excavated for the first time in the late 1970s. One advantage Alto offered is that it was a single-story pueblo. No assumptions about multistory habitation had to be made. The Chaco Center archaeologists led by Windes excavated eleven of the eighty-nine rooms at Alto. Four of the eleven excavated rooms, Windes felt, were potentially residences. One of them, however, seemed to have been designed for special, nonresidential use. Extrapolating from these three potential households, Windes found that "Alto conceivably could contain about twenty households in the late 1000s and early 1100s. This figure for various reasons may be too high—it certainly is maximum—and half may be more reasonable."

A number of shallow, temporary heating pits—in contrast to more permanent, constructed *firepits*—were found in Alto. Is it therefore possible that Pueblo Alto had only a small permanent population at best? Said Windes: "It is tempting to suggest that lack of firepits indicates, at times, a nonpermanent occupation. The expedient nature of the heating pits suggests an impermanent use suitable for long cold-weather occupancy. There is little labor investment in them. A shifting pattern of occupant duration is suspected, at least for the three households excavated. Intense occupation to be sure, but one that often did not require interior firepits. . . . It is logical to assume that interior firepits would be present if folks wintered in Chaco Canyon."

What does it all mean? How many people did live in Pueblo Bonito and the other large pueblos at Chaco, and what was the largest population in the canyon? Windes's analysis came up with almost shockingly low answers. In his words:

"If a high index of six persons per household is used, then Bonito might have contained roughly 100 people at its height." This, he agreed, is in "startling contrast" to earlier figures, such as the 1,200 suggested by Lloyd Pierson in 1949, the 1,100 suggested by Neil Judd, the 800 suggested by Hayes, or the 500 suggested by Dwight Drager. At Pueblo Alto, his analysis indicated a high population of about 100, in contrast to Pierson's estimate of 400, Drager's 320, and Hayes's 130.

"Extrapolating these figures to other towns, of course, would generate a considerably smaller canyon population, assuming occupation is contemporary and normal in the villages."

The debate of whether or not the upper stories were residences will continue. Windes noted that if upper-story residency is ever verified, it would change his calculations upward. Until then he said he would believe people in the large Chacoan pueblos ("towns") lived mainly in the single-story, or ground-floor rooms facing the plaza.

The maximum population of Chaco Canyon, by Windes's figuring, may have been no more than 2,000 people. The large pueblos weren't packed with apartment dwellers like New York City tenements. Most of the rear and upper rooms were apparently used for storage, or were empty, or had uses other than residential. The people lived mainly in the front, ground-floor rooms. The great size of the Chacoan pueblos may have misled us.

"In summary," Windes concluded in "A New Look at Population in Chaco Canyon," "a different perspective of town occupation is offered; one that suggests a relatively low population existed in towns, perhaps at times intermittently or seasonally.

"The obvious difference between village and town is in the amount of non-domestic space relative to living room space. This suggests that towns are not simply scaled-up villages inhabited by peasants but are occupied by all numbers of elite with differential access to resources and power.

"The effect of a greatly reduced population in the canyon, perhaps 2,000 or less will affect recent models that rely upon stresses induced by a large canyon population."

Burials

When I came to Chaco Canyon for the first time and encountered archaeologist Al Hayes and a group of students gently uncovering the newly unearthed skeleton of a Chacoan, I didn't realize how relatively rare such a discovery was.

For one of the fundamental mysteries about Chaco has been the small numbers of burials discovered. If, as always supposed, many thousands of people lived in Chaco, where were their remains? No large burial site has ever been located.

Neil Judd, writing a quarter of a century after the conclusion of his intensive excavations, said it bluntly: "The cemetery at Pueblo Bonito has never been found."

Archaeologist Al Hayes with newly unearthed skeleton of a Chacoan in 1974. Photo by author.

Judd said the inability to find a large Chacoan cemetery "adds to the mystery of the ruins" and lamented that it "limits our knowledge of its one-time occupants." He remained perplexed. "With an estimated peak population of over 1,000, and with one section inhabited perhaps 250 years, Pueblo Bonito should have experienced between 4,700 and 5,400 deaths. How the bodies were disposed of, and where, continue to be tantalizing puzzles."

The revised view of peak Chacoan population begins to hint that something may be awry with these expectations. But first, let's go back to some of the early discoveries.

The first report of a burial found in Chaco Canyon was by the expedition of William Henry Jackson in 1876. The men discovered a skull near Pueblo del Arroyo.

Col. D. K. B. Sellers of Albuquerque told Judd that in the late 1890s he (Sellers) and another man had broken into a large room on the west side of Bonito and there found part of what Sellers described as the "mummified" body of a woman and some turquoise, including two turquoise birds.

The Hyde Expeditions of George Pepper and Richard Wetherill exhumed perhaps twenty skeletons in Pueblo Bonito. Twelve of them were found in one six-foot-square area of one room (No. 33) in the northwest section of Bonito. These bodies had been buried in several feet of sand. The skeletons had been considerably scattered sometime after their interment. Pepper attributed the disarray to rainwater flooding through an open door and swirling about. Neil Judd favored a hostile plundering party as a far more likely explanation.

Beneath the floor of Room 33, however, Pepper's men found two additional skeletons. They had not been disturbed. They were lavishly bedecked with personal ornaments. The first of these two was accompanied by 10 turquoise pendants and 5,890 beads. With the second were 698 pendants and more than 9,000 turquoise beads.

Judd's National Geographic Expeditions discovered seventy-three skeletons, complete and incomplete. The first of the four burial chambers they encountered was, according to Judd, originally designed and used for storage. It had a flagstone floor, and a lone doorway in the middle of the east wall. "Despite its original purpose," wrote Judd, "Room 320 came finally to be used as a tomb, the sepulcher of eight women and two girls." The Chacoans had lain two of the adults side by side on a single rush mat. With them had been placed feather-cloth robes and cotton fabrics (only traces of these remained). No offering appeared to have been left with this double interment, although a few feet away were several baskets and pots. None of the other eight bodies remained intact.

The ten bodies had been lightly covered with earthy debris "including potsherds and pieces of adobe mortar and flooring." Windblown sand soon covered that. Eventually, part of the ceiling collapsed, and more windblown sand and debris dumped by the Chacoans accumulated.

Another room, No. 326, originally a family living quarters, became the common grave for a man, nine women, and an infant. Of these, the first to die was a woman, found upon a mat of selected and uniformly small bulrushes. No burial offerings were nearby, and her body had been covered with dried mud mortar from the nearby walls, six to eight inches of it. Upon that the Chacoans had placed a bulrush mat onto which they gently laid the body of another woman. She, in contrast to the other woman, was sent off to the Underworld with generous outfittings. Upon her left breast lay a turquoise pendant; on her left wrist, a three-coil string of turquoise beads. An oval basket tray was at her right shoulder. Fourteen earthenware pots had been neatly placed about her head and shoulders.

In this room also was found a dual burial. The two individuals had been lain side by side upon a layer of constructional waste and blown sand. A small bifur-

Dual burial and mortuary offerings in Pueblo Bonito, Room 326. *O. C. Havens, © National Geographic Society.*

cated basket, seven earthenware bowls, two pitchers, and a tray had been placed near their heads. Each person had a turquoise pendant around the neck, and one also had a pendant made of jet.

Over the time the Chacoans occupied Bonito, this room was gradually filled with layers of household rubbish and floor sweepings, including many potsherds, plus reconstruction debris. Then over a fairly short period of time, five more bodies were buried, three apparently together, each with pottery and other utensils placed about the head.

All the dead in this room had been placed on one or more sleeping mats. Most of the mats were made of carrizo or carefully selected bulrushes, uniform in size, carefully laid parallel and bound by twined threads every four or five inches. The bodies may have been placed in cloth bundles or sheets, as remnants of matting and cotton cloth were found.

Rooms 329 and 330 contained similar burials (twenty-three individuals in room 330 alone).

All of the human remains these expeditions found at Bonito had been buried within the house cluster itself. None was found in outdoor burial sites. "Thus of all the people who formerly dwelt there, young and old, we account for less than 100," Judd wrote in his 1954 report. He was genuinely mystified:

"Where did the Bonitians bury their 5,000 dead? The local cemetery is yet to be discovered. . . . If failure to locate the Pueblo Bonito cemetery has bothered me more than my predecessors it is because I have probably given more thought to the matter."

Judd considered two possibilities: cremation, and a burial site somewhat removed from the pueblo. The cremation idea was quickly abandoned. There was no evidence of burned spots or fragments of calcined bones anywhere. Besides archaeologists had concluded from other studies that cremation was rarely, if ever, practiced by the Anasazi. (In 1974, the Chaco Center again checked six large, sunken masonry fireboxes Judd had examined with this idea in mind. Their interiors had been fire-reddened from exposure to extreme heat. The Chaco Center re-excavated them and sifted for pieces of calcined bone that might have been missed. Nothing was found.)

Judd did look for burial sites beyond the immediate vicinity of Pueblo Bonito. Three feet of sediment has covered the canyon floor since the time of the Chacoans, and so he dug half a dozen test pits down through this overburden and into the ground below. All proved negative. "Therefore, unless we missed the cemetery completely, it lies more than a quarter mile from the ruin." He also examined the banks of the "greedy arroyo" after each summer rain. And they also found nothing to suggest burials in the talus at the base of the cliff immediately behind Pueblo Bonito.

"Thus," concluded Judd, "with every reasonable possibility exhausted, we could only leave to the future the mystery of the missing cemetery."

Before bringing the burial situation up to date, there is one more speculation which Judd obviously offered whimsically. It illustrates the delight he took not just in the formal scientific archaeology of Chaco Canyon but in the imaginative stories those who visited him and his colleagues at the site told (or concocted).

He may have given up and left the burial mystery unsolved for future generations, but "Our Chaco Canyon visitors," he recalled, "were not so easily discouraged." His defeat was their challenge. Everyone had a theory. These speculations may have been ludicrous, but then none of his had worked out. They did not lack for imagination. In Judd's words:

"One theorist, for example, had the dead of Pueblo Bonito floating down Chaco Wash, one by one, on log rafts. Here again . . . we have a single explanation that accounts for both our depleted forests and absence of a communal burial graveyard. Utterly innocent of the birch-bark canoe that carried Hiawatha on his final journey, these individual rafts floated westward down the Chaco and into the San Juan; thence, into the Colorado and Gulf of California. The alluvial fan at the mouth of the Rio Colorado is certainly one place I never thought to look for Bonitian burials."

In the early 1980s, Nancy Akins and John Schelberg of the Chaco Center reviewed the burial question. The most often mentioned figures for burials in Chaco were from 300 to 325, they noted. Al Hayes, in his 1981 survey report, said about 325 burials had been excavated in the canyon to date—only about a third of them from the great houses. These figures are indeed low, they said, but now they can legitimately be expanded.

"With the inclusion of isolated and unpublished materials, this number is now approximately 700. In addition, we are certain that many more burials were removed but were never systematically recorded or curated."

They point out that George Pepper said every "burial mound" investigated had already been explored by Richard Wetherill. No records of these informal excavations from that period have been located, but the number of bodies involved could be considerable. They note that the back of an old photo at the Western Archaeological Center in Tucson reads:

> Burial Mound Pueblo Bonito. In many places the ground is thickly strewn with human bones and pottery, the wind having blown the light material (sand and ashes) of the mounds away leaving hundreds of skulls and bones sometimes covering acres in extent. The mounds in places are yet 30 ft. high.

They believe this probably refers to sites across the canyon from Bonito and that the writing belonged to Richard or Marietta Wetherill. In an interview in 1948 with Gordon Vivian, Marietta Wetherill referred to the photo. She also said she was sure that a great deal of the early pot hunting, and therefore also destruction of burial sites, had been done by Navajos. She felt the lure of the turquoise and the money they could get for the pots more than made up for the taboos about the Anasazi dead.

The main purpose of the Akins/Schelberg study was not to settle the controversy over the supposed paucity of burials but to see if the details of the known burials could reveal something about social stratification in Chacoan society. Nevertheless the reexamination points up the possibility that far more burials may have been discovered (many of them dug up and destroyed) than appear in the formal archaeological records. Combine this with Windes's greatly lowered estimates of Chacoan population, especially in the large Chacoan pueblos. Then add Windes's idea that much of the Chaco population may have been seasonal. It begins to appear that the mystery of (too few) Chacoan burials is perhaps a little less mysterious.

The Mexican Connection

When Army Lieutenant James Simpson happened upon the ruins of Chaco Canyon in August 1849, he was sure they had been built by the Aztecs on their way south to Mexico. In fact, he was told they had been. Hosta, the expedition's Jemez Indian guide, said so.

"Hosta," wrote Simpson in his journal, "says this pueblo [Simpson was speaking here specifically of Pueblo Pintado] was built by Montezuma and his people when they were on their way from the north towards the south; that after living here and in the vicinity for a while, they dispersed, some of them going east and settling on the Rio Grande, and others south into Old Mexico."

Thus the stories about a Mexican-connection explanation of the ruins of Chaco Canyon civilization go back to at least the first day of their recorded "discovery" by a U.S. expedition.

Simpson described Hosta as "one of the most intelligent Pueblo Indians I have seen." Unfortunately, Hosta's history can't be trusted. Frank McNitt, Simpson's able biographer, describes Hosta, the civil governor of Jemez Pueblo in 1849, as a "friendly and imaginative fabricator of tall tales, which the usually perceptive Lieutenant Simpson was inclined to believe."

Earlier, when the expedition was in Jemez, Hosta told Simpson that two rectangular kivas there were "after the custom of Montezuma" and for that reason the Jemez people were not allowed to give them up. Hosta also called them the "churches of Montezuma."

Simpson was receptive to Hosta's imaginative stories about Montezuma because he had read the works of the American historian William H. Prescott (*History of the Conquest of Mexico*) and the German naturalist/explorer Alexander von Humboldt before the start of the expedition. These, says McNitt, led him to believe that the Aztec Indians had origins in the area of the Southwest he was now exploring. McNitt quotes a personal letter to him (McNitt) from a Franciscan priest at Jemez, Father Angelico Chavez, commenting on this matter: "The Montezuma legend is an importation into the pueblos, either by the Spanish colonists or the Mexican Indians brought along as servants. Early Americans heard the Pueblos talk of it, and accepted it as a genuine prehistoric tradition."

As for Hosta's reference to Pueblo Pintado as the work of Montezuma and his people, McNitt comments, "Hosta is romancing again." Tree-ring dates accurate to the exact year have of course now shown that Chaco's main ruins were built during the period A.D. 1000 to 1130. Montezuma I was born around 1390 and ruled from 1440–69; his grandson Montezuma II ruled from 1503 until his death in 1520 after being routed and taken hostage by Cortes in 1519.

Simpson sounded another theme heard time and again since: that the Chacoan ruins were of such superior design and workmanship they could not possibly have been built by the ancestors of today's Pueblo Indians without outside assistance. "This thing, however, is certain: the ruins I have described . . . discover in the materials of which they are composed, as well as in the grandeur of their design and superiority of the workmanship, a condition of architectural excellence beyond the power of the Indians or New Mexicans of the present day to exhibit."

Simpson felt the facts and evidence "do not with certainty *fix* an Aztec origin to the ruins of the Chaco; but they go to show that, as far as is known, there is nothing to invalidate the hypothesis, but, on the contrary, a great deal to make it probable."

The degree of Mesoamerican influence on Chaco Canyon has been debated ever since. Many of the nineteenth-century settlers took for granted that the great pueblos of Chaco Canyon were created by the Aztecs or other Mesoamericans or were built by a local culture dominated or strongly influenced by the ancient Mexicans to the south. This assumption is still reflected in the names given Aztec Ruin, the Chacoan pueblo northeast of Farmington, New Mexico, and Montezuma's Castle, in Arizona.

The Aztec *origination* view has been discarded. Archaeologists working in the early part of the twentieth century established a long developmental sequence in the Southwest. This demonstrated that many of the Anasazi ruins, including those at Chaco Canyon, predated the rise of the Aztec civilization.

Yet the idea of a Mesoamerican *influence* on Chaco Canyon remains. Some form of connection between Chaco Canyon and the cultures to the south is evident, but the importance of the link is disputed. Most scholars now believe the connection was fairly minimal and that Chacoan culture flowered more or less independently of events and cultures to the south. The general view is that although the Chacoan system may have been special, even unique, in the Southwest, influence from Mesoamerican cultures is not necessary to explain that fact.

Not everyone fully shares this view. In a 1978 paper Robert Lister, the first director of the Chaco Center, pointed to possible evidence of a significant Mesoamerican influence in Chaco Canyon. Lister, for the sake of discussion, listed thirty traits in Chaco Canyon that at least *could* be identified as, or presumed to be, Mesoamerican. These attributes are often referred to by parties to this controversy, and I will give a few of the main ones:

· The presence of square masonry columns used to front galleries or as colonnades, as at Chetro Ketl (where the spaces between columns were later filled in).

· The stone disks placed in the bottom of holes to serve as a foundation for the posts that hold up roof beams in several of the large kivas.

· Two conical-shaped objects found by Judd in Pueblo Bonito bearing incised designs on the flat surfaces. Lister called them stamps or seals.

· Water and plumed serpent motifs and other Mesoamerican design styles on pottery in Chaco.

· The presence of thirty-two small, cast copper bells in the ruins of Pueblo Bonito, and others in Pueblo del Arroyo and Pueblo Alto.

· Conch shells with their spires ground off and sometimes affixed with a mouthpiece, like a trumpet. Parts of nine such specimens were found in Bonito.

· The types and abundance of shell beads, suggesting Mesoamerican similarities.

· Discovery of twenty-nine macaw skeletons in Pueblo Bonito, and others in Pueblo del Arroyo and Kin Kletso.

· Remains of turkeys, including signs of ceremonial usage.

· Neatly polished, sharp-tipped bone pins.

Copper bells from Pueblo Bonito. *From Judd, Smithsonian Institution.*

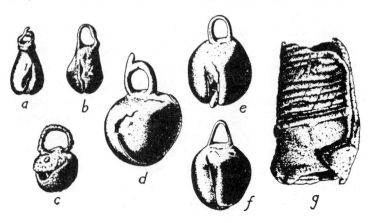

• Ceremonial canes.

• Large quantities of turquoise, native to New Mexico but assumed to serve as an important exchange item with Mexico.

• Cloisonne decoration on artifacts.

There are others, but these are the more interesting ones. Lister argued that the evidence appeared to support the concept that Mesoamerican influences somehow reached Chaco Canyon. "Such items as cloisonne, copper bells, and macaws appear as substantial evidence of contact with the south." Certain architectural features, decorative designs, and the water-control, roadway, and signaling systems constituted another set of less-strong relationships, in this view.

Another line of argument was made by anthropologist Jonathan Reyman. He reasoned that if traders from Mexico brought items such as copper bells and cloisonne-decorated items to Chaco Canyon in exchange for turquoise and other minerals or goods, evidence of the physical presence of such traders in Chaco Canyon might be found. The Mesoamericans had an exchange network organized and operated by the *pochteca,* Mexican trade guilds in the employ of ceremonial cults and/or cities. These people were both long-distance traders and agents of expansionist empires. They were a hereditary class, with their own rites, feats, courts, hierarchies, insignias, and so on.

Certainly in their widespread travels some of these people met with misfortune and had to be buried at the site of their demise. Had something similar ever happened at Chaco? Reyman acknowledged that archaeologists had virtually no evidence for the prehistoric presence of the *pochteca,* per se, in the Southwest. "That is, to date, no one has presented us with a body, warm or cold, at the sight of which we can raise the chorus, 'Aha! Here is a *pochteca* member in the flesh (or skeleton)!" But Reyman then proceeded to argue for the presence of just such "a *corpus delicti,* however fragmentary it may be after 600–800 years in the ground." He proposed that burials of *pochteca* members—long-distance traders of some sort, not Aztecs!—*have* been found at Anasazi sites, including Chaco Canyon.

Reyman examined what was known about certain burials excavated at three sites: Aztec Ruin, Pueblo Bonito, and Ridge Ruin (which he acknowledged might be classified as Sinagua rather than Anasazi). He argued that two burials found in Pueblo Bonito were in fact the graves and remains of *pochteca,* ceremonially put to rest by their host Chacoans. These were the two skeletons described earlier in this chapter, found beneath the floor of Room 33, accompanied by hundreds of turquoise pendants and thousands of turquoise beads. In addition, Reyman notes, there was a cylindrical basket covered with a turquoise mosaic, another basket decorated with a turquoise and shell mosaic, a conch shell trumpet, forty-one whole or fragmentary small bracelets, and hundreds of other artifacts. He quoted

George Pepper that these burials represent "people of great importance." Reyman called that, "A classic example of understatement."

Reyman concluded that these two skeletons from Pueblo Bonito and another burial from Ridge Ruin met his criteria for identification as *pochteca* members. He ended with a simple statement: "At Pueblo Bonito and Ridge Ruin, *pochteca* burials have been found."

In 1980, a University of Arizona anthropologist, Randall H. McGuire, considered the Lister and Reyman propositions in detail. In a lengthy critique, he found both seriously lacking.

He pointed out that the architectural features mentioned by Lister may replicate Mesoamerican forms but, as Gordon Vivian had said earlier, they function differently in Anasazi contexts. Furthermore, the suggested architectural parallels with Mesoamerica for tower kivas and tri-walled structures are based on little more than shape.

McGuire emphasized that there are pre-A.D. 1000 Anasazi precedents in the Southwest for many of the kinds of features that have been attributed to Mesoamerican influence in Chaco. T-shaped doorways, turkeys, and turquoise all are found in the Southwest earlier than in Mesoamerica. Shell beads occur in the Southwest at least as early as 6000 B.C. Macaws are found in the Southwest (in the Hohokam culture in Arizona) by A.D. 100. Incense burners are found in the Southwest (also in Hohokam) before A.D. 1, conch trumpets before A.D. 900, and so on.

"Of Lister's 30 traits of Mesoamerican origin which are supposed to appear suddenly at Chaco Canyon in the mid-1000s only eight are not of questionable Mesoamerican origin or do not appear in the Southwest before A.D. 1000," wrote McGuire. (To be fair, Lister knew this. He said *some* of the traits appeared after A.D. 1000; he did not say all.) McGuire felt Lister had overemphasized the extent and impact of the Mesoamerican influence at Chaco Canyon. More important, he said that none of the traits listed can be traced to specific Mesoamerican cultures.

As for Reyman's contention that *pochteca* burials have been found in Chaco Canyon, McGuire was unpersuaded. If the burials were of *pochteca*, there should have been artifacts of definite Mesoamerican origin associated with them. "In the burials identified by Reyman as *pochteca* all the associated goods are indigenous to the Southwest. "Furthermore *pochteca* burials are consistently associated with gold and jade. Neither of these materials was found at Chaco. The presence of large quantities of turquoise and other goods with a burial may indicate that the person was indeed important. But, as McGuire emphasized, it provides no information about a non-Chaco origin of the person.

"The case for the *pochteca* theory," McGuire concluded, "appears dubious. The *pochteca* theorists have overemphasized the extent and nature of Mesoamerican influence in the Southwest. The presence of such influence cannot be questioned, but it is not possible to connect Mesoamerican-derived traits with any specific Mesoamerican culture or sociopolitical group such as the *pochteca.*"

This doesn't mean that Mesoamerican influences on Chaco and the rest of the Southwest were nonexistent or even negligible. Trade between Mesoamerica and the Southwest may well have been an important force in Southwestern cultural evolution. But, in McGuire's view, trade wasn't the prime mover. Furthermore the whole subject of trade with Mesoamerica conveys an image of direct routes to central Mexico, with traders passing back and forth like the truckers on a modern interstate highway. This is certainly the wrong impression, and it has seriously muddled the issue. Says McGuire: "The evidence for contact between the Southwest and central Mexico is slight." He proposes an alternative view, not as glamorous but far more reasonable, that the trade and cultural exchange was with the nearby regions of northwestern Mexico. He says, ". . . The Mesoamerican influence in the Southwest resulted from interaction between northwest Mexican and Southwest societies rather than domination by a single social group such as *pochteca.* This interaction encompassed not only the exchange of goods but also of ideas, accounting for shared beliefs, symbols, and architectural forms in the two regions."

Frances Joan Mathien of the Chaco Center carried out a major evaluation of the long-distance trade model. Her studies likewise yielded little evidence that direct, long-distance trade with Mesoamerica explains the development of Chaco Canyon in any fundamental way.

She found it unlikely that most of the northern area of the Greater Southwest can be considered a part of a Mesoamerican world system. "The American Southwest would have been external to such a system. This does not preclude trade, but it does suggest that a different explanation must be offered for the evaluation of the evidence of social complexity in the American Southwest."

The volume of "exotic items" within Chaco Canyon does not suggest to Mathien the presence of specialized traders from the core of Mesoamerica. Only thirty-three copper bells and thirty-six macaws have been unearthed so far. And they occur in proveniences that span 300 years of time. "The low volume suggests very limited long-distance exchange, especially if one or more items were traded during one meeting."

What trade there was didn't require specialized traders traveling back and forth over vast distances between Chaco and Mesoamerica. The transcontinental trucker is not the right analogy. Mathien supports a model proposed earlier by Colin Renfrew for obsidian distribution in the Near East. Called down-the-line trade, it is a more natural and modest means of conducting exchange than the idea of trade emissaries traveling long distances. In down-the-line trade, there are a whole series of exchanges, like a bucket brigade, between adjoining regions. Each trades with its neighbors. Extensive travel is minimized, yet goods and information eventually can move considerable distances.

Such a system can explain similarities in cultural traits at either end of the line. It can also explain how such similarities become modified as they pass from group to group and become adapted to local requirements. "This would also account for the lack of identical items depicted in exact styles, since each group would evolve its own variation on a common theme...."

All in all, Mathien concluded that Mesoamerican influences on Chaco Canyon were minimal. "It is time to put aside the Mesoamerican-influence model and acknowledge the fact that the Chacoan Anasazi could well represent an indigenous cultural development, one of the few archaeologically documented examples of change from tribal to chiefdom level of organization."

The Chacoan culture, in this view, had indirect contacts with cultures elsewhere, including Mesoamerica, but it developed on its own. Its rise didn't require the beneficent help of outsiders. And neither did its eventual fall result from their departure.

Chaco Center Director James Judge put it rather pungently, when he suggested looking toward a variety of social and environmental factors—not the Mexican connection—for the major developments at Chaco, including its eventual demise. "At least that seems to fit better than the 'Mexican' alternative; i.e. that the resident pochteca simply got bored and tired of it all and moved back to Mexico, leaving the collapsed ruins of a noble venture behind him—plus 33 copper bells, 36 macaws, and from 2,000 to 6,000 relieved natives who quickly filled in the handfuls of colonnades he had used as a sun porch at Chetro Ketl."

9. The Chaco Phenomenon

Great pueblos. Multiple stories and hundreds of rooms. Graceful architecture. Giant circular kivas. Sandstone core-and-veneer masonry exquisite in order and design. Roof beams by the thousands brought in from ponderosa forests 50 miles away. Smaller village sites intermixed with the large towns. All this situated in a shallow, sandy-soiled canyon of meager resources and marginal moisture. Similar Chacoan settlements spread out across the 26,000-square-mile San Juan Basin. Broad, straight, engineered roadways linking many to each other and to the central canyon complex. Line-of-sight signal-tower communication links. Population possibly too small to account for the numbers of rooms in the canyon. Burial sites perplexingly few. Some evidence of trade with Mexico and the distant Pacific coast but persuasive indications of a unique indigenous culture.

What was going on at Chaco Canyon? The question forces itself on us. We yearn to know, to understand, to penetrate that black abyss of time and culture that separates us from the people and the culture of Chaco.

Yet even as we ask it we realize the effrontery of our inquiry, at least in part. What are the Hopi Indians of today doing out on their barren three mesas in northeastern Arizona? They live in hardly less challenging environments. The Zuni, the Acoma, the Laguna to the south and the Rio Grande pueblos to the east all manage to live life and retain a rich pueblo culture across the broad sweeps of

Kivas in eastern section of Pueblo Bonito. Ceremony and ritual have always been critical in Indian life. Chaco Canyon emerged as a ritual center of the Chacoan culture. Photo by author.

mountains, mesas, valleys and washes of northwestern New Mexico. The Navajo occupy lands almost aching in their vastness and rawboned beauty from the realm of Chaco west almost to the Grand Canyon.

The Chacoans, like the Indians of the Southwest today, were living their lives, building homes, having children, raising crops, tending animals, hunting for game, making pottery, fashioning jewelry, and seeking other necessities in trade with people down the road or across the mountains. They undoubtedly were doing all this in harmony with their own ritual needs and intentions, looking to the spirits of sun, sky, land, rain, animals, and plants for continuing guidance, help, and reinforcement. Attending to the essential material and spiritual needs occupied their lives, as it does their successors.

The Chaco Phenomenon, however, *was* something special.

The Chacoan pueblos, kivas, structures, sites, communities, roads, ceramics—whether in Chaco Canyon itself or at the outliers—are merely the material manifestation of the Chacoan culture's complex social-religious-economic system. This Chacoan system, or Chaco Phenomenon, may have been a cultural adaptation unique in North America. It was, in the words of W. James Judge,

Major features of Chacoan architecture. What were the labor requirements for Chacoan society and how might it have been organized to achieve its goals? Drawing from Lekson, Great Pueblo Architecture of Chaco Canyon, *Chaco Center.*

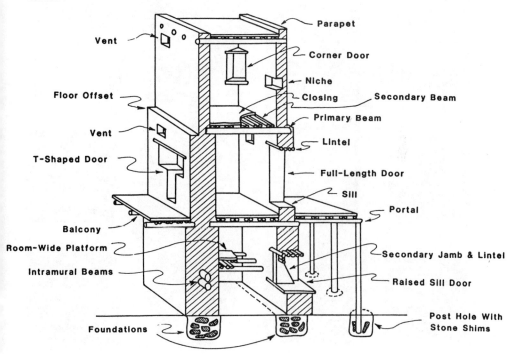

director of the Chaco Center during most of the Chaco Project, "a truly significant achievement."

How then to understand it? Before proceeding, let's take another excursion, courtesy of Chaco Center archaeologist Stephen H. Lekson. Lekson took on the task of reexamining the existing architecture at Chaco Canyon as a way of interpreting the culture's local and regional organization. Why Chacoan architecture? Shouldn't such an inquiry be redundant, considering a century of excavation and survey in Chaco Canyon before the Chaco Project? Not so. Lekson points out that the most extensive field studies of Chacoan building were the earliest, undertaken before tree-ring dating, while the most important dendrochronological studies (in the 1960s and early 1970s) were accomplished without the benefit of concurrent fieldwork.

Lekson divides Chacoan building into four periods: A.D. 900–40, 1020–50, 1050–75, and 1075–1130. Chacoans began construction in the early 900s at Penasco Blanco, Pueblo Bonito, and Una Vida. They made the three buildings large, multistoried, and arc-shaped (except for a dog-leg at Una Vida, mandated by topography). They gave them all remarkably similar floor plans. They created a

Examples of different styles of Chacoan masonry. Chaco Center, NPS.

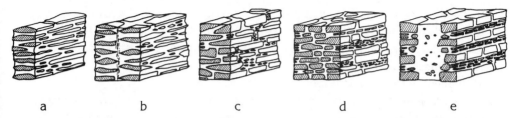

a b c d e

Different styles of wall sections used in Chacoan pueblos. *From Lekson, Chaco Center, NPS.*

line of large circular pit structures in the plaza. Behind them they built a row of large ramada-living rooms, a second row of large featureless rooms, and in the rear, a third row of smaller storage rooms. They formed above-ground rectangular rooms into suites, each of which consisted of a ramada-living room, a large room, and paired storage rooms. This pattern of rooms is remarkably similar to smaller sites built in Chaco and in the surrounding area at the same time.

The Chacoans situated the three large buildings at key locations where major side drainages enter the canyon: Una Vida, across from Fajada Butte and around the corner from Gallo Wash; Bonito, across from South Gap; and Penasco Blanco, on the bluffs overlooking the confluence of the Chaco and Escavada washes. These sites occupy strategic locations important to communities of smaller, contemporary buildings. "The simplest interpretation of early Chacoan

Part of the east wing of Pueblo Bonito. *Chaco Center, NPS.*

buildings," says Lekson, "is that they are scaled-up domestic structures, housing groups that are themselves of some strategic importance and centrality to their surrounding communities." He suggests that these three earliest Chacoan structures housed local (intracanyon) elites that together made up at most about 10 to 15 percent of the canyon population.

Following this early triad of construction the Chacoans may have taken an eighty-year hiatus. Generations came and went with little significant new construction.

The next major construction, from 1020 to 1050, was at Pueblo Alto, Chetro Ketl, and Pueblo Bonito (additions). The architectural forms begun in the 900s were continued.

Construction during the third period, 1050 to 1075, was mainly of additions to existing buildings. The Chacoan builders added wings, then less symmetrical additions, extensions, and modifications. They started only one new structure, Pueblo del Arroyo, again at South Gap near Bonito. The sequencing of these building programs steadily increased their labor requirements. In other words, more construction work was being done each year.

If one assumed that new rooms equal new population (a risky inference, as hinted in the previous chapter), the rate of growth at the large buildings was much higher than the rate for the canyon overall. "Something was going on at the large sites that cannot be attributed to internal population growth alone," says Lekson. "Perhaps the canyon population was aggregating in these structures, or perhaps rooms at larger sites equal something other than new population."

A winter view of Pueblo del Arroyo, with giant kiva in foreground. Photo by author.

Around A.D. 1075 the Chacoans began an unparalleled flurry of building activity that would last forty years. Lekson calls 1075 a watershed in Chacoan building. From then until 1115 the Chacoans carried out six major construction programs in Chaco Canyon. They built the east and west wings of Pueblo Bonito, added a three-story row of storage rooms to the rear of Penasco Blanco, built the north and south wings of Pueblo del Arroyo, and constructed Wijiji. "These six programs are truly massive," Lekson points out. "All are three to four times larger than building programs of the preceding periods. They seem to have been sequential—a program was completed about every 7 to 10 years with minimal overlap—but even so, yearly levels of labor were twice that of the A.D. 1050–1075 period." (Although Lekson focused only on large sites in Chaco Canyon itself, the study of outlying sites by Robert Powers and colleagues found that most of the construction activity there took place at this time also.)

How large a project was this, really? What were the requirements for labor? What does it mean for the organization of Chacoan society? Lekson has spent a lot of time and thought on these questions, asking:

"How are we to interpret this level of architectural labor at Chaco? I have heard some scholars (revisionists? reactionaries?) talk of Chacoan building as a quaint and antique form of the historic Pueblo, built by small kin groups. I have also listened to Chaco enthusiasts, unofficial members of the Chaco Chamber of Commerce, who are staggered by the labor expended on these buildings and see in them evidence for a regional corvee, almost like the Pyramids. These views on labor are polar, but I have never heard either supported by quantified estimates."

Lekson has tried to estimate the total labor represented by construction stages at large sites at Chaco. He has struggled with questions of scheduling. How was the labor sequence carried out? For the latter question, the main hints come from Chetro Ketl and Pueblo Alto. Remember that Chetro Ketl has produced extensive tree-ring samples. The Chacoans cut most or all of the wood used in one well-sampled room at Chetro Ketl over a very short period of time, perhaps a matter of weeks. They cut most of the wood for Chetro Ketl in the spring or early summer. For Pueblo Alto, evidence indicates that they took a minimum of three years to construct the north or central wing, with tree-cutting activities again mainly in the spring.

To illustrate a hypothetical analysis of labor scheduling, Lekson takes as an example a single large building program, construction of the east wing of Pueblo Bonito. This is the largest single construction event at Chaco.

He has determined that construction of the east wing of Pueblo Bonito required about 193,000 man-hours of Chacoan labor. Half of this labor was devoted to the cutting and transport of trees and the quarrying of stone. The other half was devoted to actual construction (masonry, mixing and carrying mortar, installing roofs). Only a small part of this half required skilled labor (shaping and laying stones).

**The Great Kiva
at Chetro Ketl.**
Photo by author.

**The tower kiva
at Kin Ya'a.**
Chaco Center, NPS.

He assumed for hypothetical purposes that the Chacoan builders worked a ten-hour day and a thirty-day work month. To cut and process all the timber used in the east wing of the Pueblo Bonito in a period of one month required about thirty men, or 30 man-months. Transporting the beams would have taken the Chacoans 180 man-months; quarrying and so on, 90 man-months; and construction, 324 man-months.

He further assumes that the Chacoans took about ten years to complete the east wing. This is a typical span to complete a project during the 1075–1115 building period. Based on the evidence at Alto, however, he estimates that actual construction was going on for only about three years during this ten-year period. Given all that, Lekson suggests a likely way that labor was apportioned over that span, "A crew of 30 could cut and transport beams for one month every year for seven years, and quarry and construct for four months every year for three years, and build the single largest construction program at Chaco."

Hardly a vast labor force! Yet construction was going on at more than one site at a time. How did that affect labor needs? Lekson divided the construction activity into five-year segments and found that the last five years of the eleventh century, A.D. 1095–1100, were the most labor intensive. During those five years, Chacoan construction programs took up an average of 55,645 man-hours, or 5,565 man-days, or 186 man-months, per year. Thus thirty-one men working six months a year or sixty-two men working three months a year could have carried out the most intensive single period of construction at Chaco Canyon.

"It is evident that Chacoan building did not require specialization of appreciable segments of the population, or corvee labor from outlier communities, or any of the other unlikely suggestions occasionally heard from enthusiasts of Chacoan architecture," notes Lekson. "These reasonable, plausible estimates can be doubled, tripled, or even quadrupled and there would *still* not be any rational cause to consider building a major problem for local, much less regional, labor organization."

There is no intention here to minimize the task the Chacoans accomplished in their wonderful building programs. The work was hard. The effort required organization and dedication. The achievements were grand. Most evidence points to construction taking place during the spring months, the same time as the planting season. The labor requirements, while not vast or mysteriously unfathomable, were considerable. The work spent building the large Chacoan pueblos was far greater than that devoted to small sites erected at the same time.

The numbers of trees required, and the distances from which they had to be brought, are astonishing. Especially so when we remember that the Chacoans had no metal tools or wheeled carts. Using a constant of beams per square meter of roof, Lekson estimates that the large sites in Chaco Canyon required more than 215,000 trees. (Others, using different assumptions, have estimated 200,000 trees, so we can be confident this number is generally reasonable.) The vast majority of these beams did not come from the area around Chaco. Most probably came from the forests behind Kin Ya'a, some thirty-five miles to the south, Pueblo Pintado, some twenty miles to the east, or perhaps Skunk Springs, some fifty miles to the west. These distances are incorporated into Lekson's labor estimates.

So what were these large buildings the Chacoans expended this effort on? Their form and the technology used offer clues to their functions. Lekson points out that the large structures at Chaco were clearly more "expensive" than the smaller sites and more "expensive" than those built by other prehistoric Indian cultures in the Southwest. They are more substantially built and consequently better preserved than other contemporaneous building. Some of the massiveness was necessary to carry out the multistory design. Some was perhaps for show, a symbol of power (human beings have always had a propensity to create large magnificent buildings for such reasons). Part was probably practical. The massive design definitely reduced maintenance requirements. "Perhaps the labor force available for upkeep was disproportionately small—'caretakers,' or perhaps the residents were above replastering and reroofing after every rainstorm—elites," suggests Lekson. "In any event, after seven centuries of nonmaintenance, the larger buildings were surprisingly intact while their smaller neighbors were reduced to low bumps on the landscape."

The forty-five-year building spurt beginning in A.D. 1075 created not just new structures but a surprisingly large number of interior rooms. As Lekson points out, the buildings were massive blocks. The east wing of Bonito is up to five rows deep and four stories tall. Few of the rooms created would have enjoyed any direct access to the exterior. What are these interior rooms? They wouldn't have made for pleasant living quarters.

Presumably, these interior rooms were not residential space. What were they for? It appears the Chacoans built them to be storage rooms. Notes Lekson: "From A.D. 1075 to 1115, a very great amount of potential storage space was created—much greater than would have been required by contemporaneously constructed domestic rooms (compared to earlier ratios of domestic to storage space). And these storage rooms were constructed in the most costly, planned building programs in the Chacoan sequence.

"These buildings, and the labor required to build them, suggest the nature of Chacoan building was changing from elite residence alone to large storage facilities with continued elite occupation."

After A.D. 1075, it appears, a great many of the rooms at the larger sites in Chaco Canyon were neither domestic residential units nor storage rooms associated with the residences. It appears that another public function had been added to the buildings in addition to the presumed function of an elite residence.

Somewhere in the mid-eleventh century, the larger Chacoan sites became central to a region that went beyond the limits of Chaco Canyon and its immediate surroundings. By the time of the massive construction programs of the last quarter of the century, some kind of regional system that required the addition of space for storage (or for something besides residential quarters) and supported the expansion of the large sites was already in full operation. The evidence indicates that Chaco had become central to the entire region, and the larger buildings played some role in that regional centrality. A regional system knit together by common bonds of religion, culture, and economics was flourishing.

There is little question that the influence of the Chacoan system was felt throughout the San Juan Basin. For a significant period of time, the great pueblos and smaller settlements in Chaco Canyon, the Chacoan outliers all across the basin, the roadways, and all other aspects of the culture functioned as a highly effective, well-integrated system. Nothing else like it has been seen in the Southwest before or since. What was this Chacoan system, or Chaco Phenomenon?

A general synthesis of our understanding of the Chaco Phenomenon calls on everything we have learned about the Chacoan culture. James Judge, director of the Chaco Center until after completion of its ten-year Chaco Project in 1985, offers a model to explain the origin, function, and demise of the Chaco Phenomenon. Other archaeologists proposed such explanations earlier, and Judge drew on many aspects of their ideas. His reconstruction, he emphasizes, differs from most not in its originality but in the fact that it is based largely on data retrieved and analyses completed in the past several years by the Chaco Center. This information was largely unavailable to other researchers until quite recently. What follows relies heavily on his synthesis.

Environmental conditions in the San Juan basin are one key to understanding the evolution of the Chaco Phenomenon. Almost always marginal, conditions were nevertheless not constant. To the Chacoans, who lived in a region where a difference of an inch or two of precipitation a year was the difference between just barely enough and too little, such fluctuations were crucial. Chacoan culture arose during the tenth century in an extremely variable environment. From A.D. 900–1050, precipitation was unpredictable. A few years of relatively abundant rainfall would be followed by a few years of markedly subnormal rainfall. Then from A.D. 1050–1130, the heydey of the Chacoan system, precipitation was generally above normal the whole time, except for a sharp but temporary dip in the early 1090s. The period A.D. 1130 to 1180, marked by absence of any more construction and a gradual depopulation of Chaco, was a time of prolonged below-normal rainfall. These fluctuations are most apparent in the record of the crucial summer rainfall as opposed to total annual precipitation.

These shifts in environmental constraints were important stimuli to the development of social complexity in the Chacoan system. They weren't the sole influence, but without them the Chaco Phenomenon may well have been something different. Judge views them as fundamental.

Judge refers to the first of Lekson's Chaco building periods, essentially the

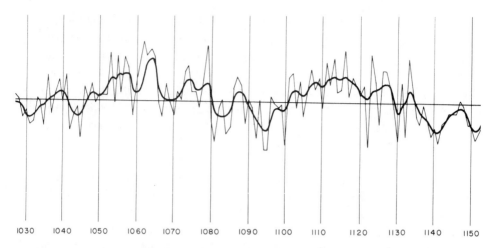

1030 1040 1050 1060 1070 1080 1090 1100 1110 1120 1130 1140 1150

Annual and summer precipitation charts New Mexico's Northwest Plateau,
A.D. *1030 to 1150. Chacoan culture arose during a period of variable rainfall,*
but during most of its peak years, A.D. *1050–1130, precipitation was gener-*
ally above normal. From Powers, Outlier Survey.

tenth century, as the time of Initialization. As already noted, the three pueblos
begun during the tenth century, Penasco Blanco, Pueblo Bonito, and Una Vida,
are all at sites strategically located at the confluence of major drainages and the
Chaco Wash. They may have functioned largely as storage sites to accommodate
the pooling and redistribution of resouces within the drainage systems they over-
looked. This is certainly consistent with what we now know about the extremely
variable precipitation of the time.

Most of the outlying Chacoan communities that existed during this early
phase of Chacoan culture were in the southern half of the San Juan basin (Skunk
Springs, Kin Bineoloa, Peach Springs, and El Rito). These communities presumably developed on their own in a manner analogous to the communities in the
canyon and for the same reasons, to carry out resource pooling and redistribution.

Chaco was not centrally located with respect to these sites. The influence of
the canyon on the other sites was probably minimal during this period. Chaco
Canyon was not serving as a central place, and very likely there was no such thing
as a "Chacoan system" yet in existence. The communities were undoubtedly
linked through reciprocity and trade, but they were probably relatively independent of each other for basic subsistence.

One thing did take place during this period that apparently set the stage for
formation of the Chacoan system. Chaco Canyon began to be an increasingly
important site of turquoise processing. Finished turquoise items were made there

in fairly large quantities. Tremendous quantities of turquoise have been found in the canyon. There is considerable evidence of bead manufacturing workshops, including turquoise, shale, and shell beads. Three small sites and Pueblo Alto, all excavated by the Chaco Center, have such workshops. Pueblo del Arroyo, Una Vida, Kin Kletso, Pueblo Bonito, and several others, excavated previously, do also. This work with turquoise began fairly early, in the tenth century. Other ornaments may well have been involved as well, but turquoise is the single type of ornament that has been documented as concentrated in Chaco Canyon.

Judge suggests that because Chaco was relatively poorer in resources at this time than the other communities in the basin, the Chacoans focused on the processing of turquoise as a buffer against shortages of resources during hard times. He proposes that by around A.D. 1000 or at latest 1020, Chaco Canyon was firmly established as the primary source of finished turquoise for at least the southern part of San Juan Basin, and perhaps for the basin as a whole. By now turquoise had become integrated into the area's exchange network as an item of economic value far surpassing its ritual role. It informally regulated the exchange of material items, both food and other supplies.

To dominate the processing of turquoise, Chaco would have had to control the source. Turquoise in the prehistoric Southwest came almost exclusively from the turquoise mine near the present town of Cerillos, New Mexico, in the hills south of Santa Fe, far to the east of Chaco. Thus it is probable that a strong link existed between Chaco Canyon and the easternmost outlier at Guadalupe. Guadalupe, situated high on a ridgetop overlooking the Rio Puerco of the East, would have served the canyon in controlling the source. As such, Guadalupe would be expected to manifest an early occupation as a Chacoan outlier. It does. We would expect also that it would have little evidence of turquoise processing since turquoise would pass through Guadalupe in bulk and be carefully conserved. That is the case.

From 1020 to 1050, Chaco's domination of turquoise production may have solidified and the role of turquoise as a ritual item may have become formalized. By now Chaco was assuming an increasing role as a site of ritual importance in the southern portion of the San Juan Basin. Rainfall continued to be highly variable. Chaco continued to rely on cultural subsidies to buffer its meager resources.

This period was the transition to the Chacoan system, and its gradual formalization. At this time the pottery known as Gallup Black & White became the dominant ceramic style. Judge suggests that Gallup was initially made locally in Chaco Canyon and became integrated with the emerging formalization of the turquoise exchange system. It thus also became a material symbol of the emergent system in addition to turquoise and the developing Chacoan style of architecture.

New construction at this time began to show the central portion of Chaco Canyon as highly significant. The beginning of Chetro Ketl and Pueblo Alto gave the central part of the canyon a dominance it did not hold previously. Pueblo

Guadalupe, the easternmost Chacoan outlier, overlooks the Rio Puerco East. It may have been in a strategic location for controlling Chaco's source of turquoise. Photo by Paul Logsdon.

Alto's position on the mesa behind Bonito, permitting visibility throughout the San Juan Basin, would have been beneficial if its function was initially related primarily to ritual.

During this time, development of outlying communities continued to focus on the southern part of the basin. Of eight new Chacoan outliers developed at this time, only one (Hogback) was not in the south. So the canyon, located on the northeastern periphery of established Chacoan communities, could still not yet be considered a central place geographically. Its influence, as exhibited by architecture and ceramics, was prominent throughout the southern part of the basin, yet its location was not central. For economic redistribution and exchange to be primary, a central location would seem necessary.

For these reasons, it seems probable that Chaco's emerging dominance was focused more on the nonmaterial realm. Chaco was becoming more and more a ritual center, with turquoise continuing as a beautiful, durable item of symbolic value. Judge explains it this way:

"I would suggest that during this period, the periodic visits to the Canyon to obtain turquoise became increasingly formalized under some kind of ritual metaphor. At the same time, alliance networks between the outlying communities would become more formalized as a means of integrating those communities through exchange of nonritual, material goods. As the system formalized, that is, as it began to develop into a true system, administration of the exchange networks would become necessary and could easily have fallen to those resident in Chaco Canyon, particularly if turquoise was the primary material symbol of the ritual and was controlled by the residents of Chaco."

This emergence of Chaco as a ritual center and the increasing formalization of exchange between Chacoan communities were no doubt influenced by the uncertain climatic conditions. The Chacoans would need to buffer their fragile base of subsistence. Trade of their turquoise for necessities would help. Ritualizing the exchange would reinforce and solidify their position. These ritual and exchange alliances would further integrate all the Chacoan communities and help all of them hedge a bit against the uncertain environmental conditions.

By A.D. 1050 the basic structure of the Chacoan system was in place. It developed during (and largely because of) a long period of variable conditions. Chaco was entering a long period of very favorable precipitation, but now the more abundant summer rainfall would make the system even more successful. This would particularly be so if the system were embedded in ritual whose purpose was to ensure continued favorable rains. The very fact that the summer rains continued to pour benevolently on the people and crops of Chaco would reinforce the perceived value and power of the system. It was a self-reinforcing situation. Nothing succeeds like success.

For the next thirty-five years, rainfall never once dropped below the long-term average. By 1075 the period of massive construction programs Lekson described got underway. Yet the population of the canyon was probably not very large. There were probably no more than 2,000 people living there year-round. There was little reason for more to live there, and if the canyon's primary function was indeed to serve as a center of ritual, only those necessary to that purpose would be needed.

Yet even if it is granted that large proportions of the rooms available in Chaco were for storage, it is still a fact that there was more residential space available than necessary for the people living there permanently. Why?

Judge suggests that the facilities in Chaco were constructed to accommodate periodic influxes of people in large numbers. He proposes that these people came to the canyon from the outlying areas on formal pilgrimages. Festivals at

Giant kivas such as Casa Rinconada could have been used for rituals not just by canyon residents but also by Chacoans from outlying communities during pilgrimages to the canyon. These ceremonies would have celebrated the Chacoan way and aided cultural unity. Photo by author.

Chaco Canyon would be periodically scheduled and announced throughout the basin. Goods would be brought in from the surrounding lands, and ceremonies would celebrate the general success of the Chacoan lifestyle and offer thanks and prayer for everyone's continued well being. In this way, widely dispersed Chacoan communities may have been integrated into a single social and economic system through periodic visits under a controlling ritual principle. All this might have served both the cultural cohesiveness of the Chacoan system and helped control and regulate the distribution of goods and services between outlying communities in the system. Says Judge:

"If the concept of pilgrimage festivals is reasonable, I would argue that the 'visits' to Chaco during prior periods developed into formal pilgrimages during this period of A.D. 1050–1115. By this I mean they became regularly scheduled ritual events at which goods were transported to Chaco Canyon from outlying locations, and were consumed and services performed there under a ritual metaphor. As the system expanded, these pilgrimages would be attended by increasingly large numbers of people, involve increasingly complex ritual, and thus would require increasingly larger degrees of control and administration by those in charge, presumably those resident in Chaco Canyon. Embedded in ritual,yet tied intimately to the continuation of a favorable environment, the system would also become increasingly vulnerable to environmental fluctuation."

During this time, more and more outlying communities sprang into being. In fact, the majority of Chacoan outliers are dated to this period. At least nineteen were built during this time, all but one (Haystack) in the northern part of the basin. Chaco Canyon had finally became a central place in a geographic as well as a metaphoric sense.

It was also apparently during this time that the roadway network was built. The roads are difficult to date, but presumably their construction began about A.D. 1050 and continued intermittently throughout the next sixty-five years. The roads south to Kin Ya'a were probably the earliest, the North Road probably the last. At any rate, the Chaco people, no matter where they lived, were linked to some degree now by a system of engineered roads, a strongly visible symbol as well as a practical manifestation of their social and cultural integration.

The proliferation of outlying communities and the creation of the roadway network meant that a great many more people had become formally integrated into the Chacoan economic and ritual system. They could share in the administered exchange-redistribution network between outlying locations and participate in a common religion—a religion that everyone could see had been very successful in attending to their continuing need for favorable rainfall. They were all obliged to participate in some way in the occasional pilgrimages into Chaco Canyon and to contribute goods and services for the common good there or elsewhere in the system.

"I suggest that the Chacoan system, now fully formalized as an economic and ritual entity, functioned well and expanded rapidly due primarily to the continuation of favorable environmental (climate) conditions in the San Juan Basin," says Judge. "This would be perceived indigenously as a result of adherence to an established, successful, and probably increasingly formalized, ritual system controlled by Chaco Canyon."

The Chaco Phenomenon *was* a phenomenon. For many decades, it was an enormous success, a peak of cultural integration and achievement we marvel at today. The people of Chaco had found a system of religion, social life, and economic matters that worked. In harmony with the beneficent rain spirits, who they no doubt revered and thanked, it allowed them to expand their culture, their unique architectural styles, and their principles of exchange throughout a large area. The Chacoan culture was on a high, broad plateau of triumph.

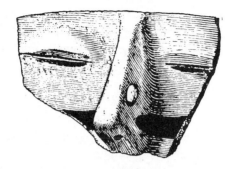

10. The Sky-Watchers of Chaco

The sky is an overwhelming presence in the Southwest. Few trees block the open vistas, and prolonged periods of overcast seldom shroud the deep blue high-altitude sky. Gentle billows of cumulus and ephemeral wisps of lofty cirrus decorate the daytime sky. The sun illuminates everything with a crystal clarity. Toward evening the western sky comes alive with a gentle play of pastels, and sandstone cliffs and granite mountains alike are awash with color seemingly drawn from interior hiding places within the rock. At night the stars and planets shine with piercing brilliance. All this lends an aura of openness and freedom and a sense of communion with natural truths.

For prehistoric people everywhere, including the Chacoans, the drive to know the rhythms of the sky was practical and symbolic as well as aesthetic. They needed to track and anticipate the seasonal progression of the sun through this vast dome of sky. For them, as for us, the sun was everything, life itself. In Zuni, the very word for life is *tekohanane,* "daylight."

The proper way of living depends on everything functioning in harmony with the natural order of things. The cycles of the seasons have spiritual and symbolic significance in addition to their overt effects on agriculture and daily life.

Knowing the course of the sun as it moved to its southernmost point at the winter solstice and back toward its northernmost point at summer solstice, and then south again, brought structure and a semblance of anticipation and control to ceremony and culture.

Imagine the concern early peoples must have felt as the chill of fall grew deeper and each day the sun appeared a little lower in the southern sky. With the lowering of the sun the day shortens and the sun's precious heat and light diminishes. What if it continued its southerly progression, and someday, disappeared altogether, never to return? Charting this cycle would help dispel these concerns and build confidence in the orderly rectitude of the heavens. Ceremonies could be correctly scheduled, and all of ritual-based life and culture could properly function. More modern cultures celebrate the annual turning of the sun back onto its homeward course at winter solstice as a symbol of the renewal of life; they celebrate the northernmost reach of the sun at summer solstice as a symbol of the completion and continuation of this natural cycle.

The people of Chaco were perceptive observers of the sun's seasonal course. Like their brethren elsewhere, they set up a variety of observing and recording stations and, no doubt, had specialist sun priests whose duty was to attend to these essential matters.

How this might work is known from historic practices in modern pueblos. Take this passage, for example, from the autobiographical book *Sun Chief,* the life story of a Hopi Indian, Don Talayesva, born in 1890. Here he recalls a memory as a child:

"Another important business was to keep track of the time or the seasons of the year by watching the points on the horizon where the sun rose and set each day. The point of sunrise on the shortest day of the year was called the sun's winter home and the point of sunrise on the longest day its summer home. Old Talasemptewa, who was almost blind, would sit out on the housetop of the special Sun Clan house and watch the sun's progress toward its summer home. He untied a knot in a string for each day. When the sun arose at certain mesa peaks, he passed the word around that it was time to plant sweet corn, ordinary corn, string beans, melons, squash, lima beans, and other seeds. On a certain date he would announce that it was too late for any more planting. The old people said that there were proper times for planting, harvesting, and hunting, for ceremonies, weddings, and many other activities. In order to know these dates it was necessary to keep close watch on the sun's movements."

Talayesva related that his great-great uncle Muute "was the Special Officer of the Sun Clan, and was called Tawamongwi (Sun Chief). He would sit at a certain place and watch the sun in order to know when it reached its summer home. It was the work of the Chief of the Flute society to guide the sun on its way."

When the sun arrived at its summer home, some of the Sun Clan men would go the next morning to the Sun Clan house "uniting their hearts in order to get their prayers through to the Six-Point-Cloud-people. They asked for rain, good crops, health, and long life."

Before sunrise the next day his uncle took the prayer offerings to the sun shrine on top of a high mesa two miles northeast of Oraibi. "He had to place the pahos on the shrine and pray for rain just as the Sun god peeped over the eastern horizon."

One day when Talayesva was in his twenties, his uncle Talasquaptewa, old and feeble, said to him: " 'My nephew, we have looked into your heart and chosen you to be the Sun Chief (Tawamongwi) instead of your brother Ira, who is older. You will succeed me shortly in this office. I want you to watch me closely when I make the offerings so that you will know how to do it when I pass away.' This meant that I was following in the line of succession—like a king—and would be Sun Chief of Moenkopi as well as Oraibi. He showed me the special place to stand or sit in guiding the rising sun in its journey to its summer house, and taught me all that I should know about the special office."

Ethnologist Frank H. Cushing lived with the Zuni Indians from 1879 to 1884. Among the valuable observations recorded in his *My Adventures in Zuni* is this passage about the Zuni sun-watching practices:

"Each morning, . . . just at dawn, the Sun Priest, followed by the Master Priest of the Bow, went along the eastern trail to the ruined city of Ma-tsa-ki, by the riverside, where, awaited at a distance by his companion, he slowly approached a square open tower and seated himself just inside upon a rude, ancient stone chair, and before a pillar sculptured with the face of the sun, the sacred hand, the morning star, and the new moon. There he awaited with prayer and sacred song the rising of the sun. Not many such pilgrimages are made ere the 'Suns look at each other,' and the shadows of the solar monolith, the monument of Thunder Mountain, and the pillar of the gardens of Zuni, 'lie along the same trail.' Then the priest blesses, thanks, and exhorts his father, while the warrior guardian responds as he cuts the last notch in his pine-wood calendar, and both hasten back to call from the house-tops the glad tidings of the return of spring. Nor may the Sun Priest err in his watch of Time's flight; for many are the houses in Zuni with scores on their walls or ancient plates embedded therein, while opposite, a convenient window or small port-hole lets in the light of the rising sun, which shines but two mornings in the three hundred and sixty-five on the same place. Wonderfully reliable and ingenious are these rude systems of orientation, by which the religion, the labors, and even the pastimes of the Zunis are regulated."

Note the two elements in these accounts of sun watching: A sun priest with special duties to watch and track the sun, from a certain location, and, in the Zuni account, a way of charting the sun's seasonal path available to nearly everyone by marking the changing position of the sunlight on an interior wall. These practices were followed into at least the middle of the present century. At Zuni, the last Zuni sun watcher, who died in 1953, plotted the seasons on a large, flat stone. A Hopi statesman and friend, Abbott Sekaquaptewa, who served eight years as chairman of the Hopi Tribal Council, once told me there are still houses at Hopi that mark the sun's seasonal procession with marks on an inside wall. At Oraibi, he said, one such location made use of a small recessed chamber on an interior west-facing wall. The time of solstice was when late-afternoon sunlight entering the room from an opening in the outer west wall illuminated this chamber.

An early observer of Hopi culture, Alexander M. Stephen, lived at the Hopi village of Walpi from 1891 until his death in 1894. He documented the horizon locations the Hopi sun watchers used to determine the beginning of Soyal, the ceremony associated with the winter solstice. Soyal was begun four days after the sun sets in a particular notch known as *Luhavwu Chochomon* (since identified as Schultz Pass) in the San Francisco Mountains, north of Flagstaff, Arizona. Just to the right of this pass are three volcanic cinder cones that are used as solar markers depending on which Hopi village the sightings are made from.

Similar horizon observations are to this day carried out not only at Walpi but also at the Hopi villages of Shongopovi and Mishongnovi.

Lunar and stellar observations are also used. The Hopi Powamu ceremony, for example, is regulated by observation of the new moon and involves determining a specific new moon following the winter solstice ceremony. While solar and lunar observations govern the date of ceremonies, stellar observations govern the timing of events within a ritual ceremony. On the final night of certain ceremonies, for example, the preparations and performances are timed to the hour by the progress of the stars across the sky.

Sekaquaptewa wrote about some of these matters. With his permission, I here relate several of them, in his words:

"The Hopi people have long known about and closely watched the sun. They annually observe the solstices with important ritual ceremonies. The dates of important economic, as well as ceremonial, events are based on phases of the moon. The timing of sacred ritual performances are determined on ceremonial nights by the position of the stars and constellations.

"Hopi sun watchers for centuries also used holes in the walls of clan houses through which shafts of sunlight entered to hit markings on opposite walls or ceiling beams to measure the progress of the sun, as well as horizon markers at sunrise and sunset for the same purpose. A good deal of this is still practiced today. Some of the wall and beam markings still exist in the older clan houses, unless they have been lost lately due to the efforts of the Home Improvement Program."

He admitted to several frustrations: the reluctance of some archaeologists to acknowledge that the people who occupied such places as Chaco Canyon and Mesa Verde "are the direct ancestors, at various stages of migration, of the Hopi clans," and the refusal of some scientists "to acknowledge that our ancients knew something about astronomy and its influence on life on Mother Earth."

Sky observations, he noted, are sometimes also necessary to make adjustments in the Hopi ceremonial calendar.

"Once in a while, the ceremonial schedule goes out of kilter when the phases of the moon do not coincide with the calendar, causing some people to fall out of step with others. There is a Hopi term to describe this situation, generally referring to the idea that there is a confusion over the moon. . . .

"There is a remedy for this in the Hopi system of doing things which involves not only monitoring the phase of the moon but the progress of the sun, so that an adjustment in the time consumed by the winter solstice ceremony is made to compensate when the sun and the moon *fall behind* each other.

"This adjustment is called Muy-Ko-Kon-To-Ta, and involves the elimination of one or a couple of the four-day cycles after the final rites of the winter solstice ceremony . . . Muy-Ko-Kon-To-Ta, literally *'breaking up the moon,'* . . . is the same as breaking up the month into a shorter period to adjust to the moon-sun lag."

This is a rather simple but elegant solution to a lunisolar calendric problem. Sekaquaptewa concludes with a note of restrained and understandable pride: "It gives an insight into one of the ways that the Hopis have been able to adjust to their natural environment, as opposed to some other cultures that attempt to control everything around them."

There are ample indications that the people of Chaco, like their Pueblo descendants, conducted a variety of sun-watching practices. Take the Wijiji sun-watching station, for instance. Wijiji is the easternmost Chacoan ruin in Chaco Canyon itself. More isolated than the others, it is little visited. Half a mile past Wijiji, along the northeast wall of the canyon, a rincon cuts into the canyon wall, and an ancient stairway leads up to a rock ledge. On the wall above the ledge is a white-painted symbol with rays emanating from the four sides. It is similar to a sun symbol at the Zuni sun-watching station described by Stevenson. From this ledge, a rock pillar to the southeast on the opposite side of the rincon reaches above the horizon. Astronomer Michael Zeilik has shown that from a spot on the ledge near the apparent sun symbol, the sun at winter solstice sunrise rises behind the top of the pillar, a clear marker of the sun's southernmost excursion. At sunset on the same day, an observer on the ledge stationed at a petroglyph-marked flat boulder sees the sun descend through a V-shaped notch on a cliff off to the southwest. So the Wijiji ledge-top site seems to serve as a marker of both sunrise and sunset at the time of winter solstice. Furthermore, a Chacoan sun priest could also have used the site to anticipate the coming of the solstice. From the exact spot on the ledge marked by the sun symbol, the sun rises over the rock pillar sixteen days before winter solstice. Modern pueblos announce the solstices several weeks *before* they arrive so that ceremonial planning can begin.

Or take the unusual corner windows at Pueblo Bonito. Two of them face the southeast, toward the winter-solstice sunrise. It appears that the Chacoans could have used at least one of them, the window to Room 228, both to anticipate the

Winter solstice sunrise from ledge near Wijiji. Sun rises directly over rock pillar on near horizon. Photo by Michael Zeilik.

Corner window at Pueblo Bonito. National Park Service.

coming of the solstice and mark its arrival. From inside the room, the rising sun will begin to appear in the late fall when sighting diagonally across the window jamb, from the opening's right interior across to its left exterior. This begins when the sun is still seven weeks (thirteen degrees) north of its solstice point. The morning light appears on the back wall as a thin beam that gradually increases in width as the sun moves toward the winter solstice. This beam widens and moves northward at a rate of more than one inch a day, easily enough to track the approaching solstice. On the morning of solstice, the sun's light at sunrise illumi-nates the north wall in a rectangle extending from the room's corner.

Casa Rinconada has also been examined for possible solstice markers. The largest kiva at Chaco Canyon and the only one off by itself, Casa Rinconada is also unusual at Chaco in that its upper portion extends above ground level. A horizontal row of twenty-eight regularly spaced rectangular niches extends around the interior circumference of this giant kiva. But there is also a second row, slightly lower, of six very irregularly spaced niches, two on the east side and four on the west. Just east of the north entrance of Casa Rinconada is a small window. On the morning of summer solstice, light from the sun about a half hour after sunrise comes through this window and shines on the opposite wall directly above one of the six irregularly spaced niches. As the sun moves higher in the sky, this beam of light sweeps downward and illuminates the niche. The effect is dramatic. Was this used by the Chacoans as a marker of the summer solstice? As with the other sites we cannot say for sure. It may have been accidental. The other irregular niches inside Casa Rinconada don't seem to have as special an astronomical orientation, and there are other problems, including the fact that the kiva was restored by the National Park Service in the 1930s and we don't know for sure the original size and placement of the opening.

Near the top of Fajada Butte in Chaco Canyon rests an entirely different type of solar marker. At some time in the past, three large slabs of rock fell away from the east-facing upper portion of the butte and came to rest in a vertical position on a ledge immediately below, their rear edges leaning against the rock wall. Behind them an unknown early Indian, presumably a Chacoan, carved a spiral petroglyph onto the cliff wall. This spiral pattern is about the size of a dinner plat-ter and is mostly obscured from view by the slabs.

This arrangement has some remarkable sun-marking properties. In the late 1970s, it was discovered and documented that sunlight at midday streams through the opening between the center and righthand slab and forms a narrow shaft of light on the cliff face behind. For about a twenty-minute period at midday on the solstice, this shaft, dubbed a "light dagger" by its discoverers, descends vertically through the spiral, its point passing right through the center of the spiral. This occurs for several days at the time of summer solstice. Although it cannot mark the *exact* day of the solstice, it nevertheless serves as a dramatic indication of the general time of this important astronomical event.

Fajada Butte, looking south. The midday solstice marker discovered there in the late 1970s is on the ledge just below the top of the butte, facing east-southeast. © *The Solstice Project.*

What is so unusual about the Fajada Butte site is that it makes use of the position of the sun during the middle of the day, not at sunrise and sunset as do most known prehistoric sun-watching sites. The seasonal movement of the mid-day position of the sun (from lowest in the sky at winter solstice to highest in the sky at summer solstice) is a somewhat more subtle matter to observe than are horizon positions. One could easily do it by, say, driving a vertical stake into the ground and then observing the changing maximum northward length of its shadow at midday. Or by observing the changing length of the shadow of an east-west wall at successive middays. But the Fajada site makes use of a play of sunlight not on the ground but on a vertical cliff face. The dynamic nature of the moving light beam at midday also appeals to our senses.

I accompanied the discoverers of this feature to the top of Fajada on two of their early excursions to photograph and measure these relationships and later wrote the first accounts of it. It was exciting to be there high above the rest of the canyon with a splendid view in all directions and try to imagine a Chacoan sun priest here 900 years ago tracking the changing location of the sun in the day-time sky.

The Fajada spiral also could be used to a certain extent to mark the location of the sun at the other key astronomical points, the spring and fall equinoxes (when the sun is midway between the solstice points) and the winter solstice. At winter solstice, for example, there is a time when the spiral appears to be

Stone slabs atop Fajada Butte. Sunlight passing down through opening between the middle slab and the right slab produces the sun-dagger effect through center of spiral petroglyph at summer solstice. The spiral is hidden behind the slabs. Karl Kernberger, © The Solstice Project.

"embraced" by two vertical light beams tangent to its right and left edges. The right beam at that time of the year is the same one that at solstice passes through the center of the spiral. The left beam is sunlight passing down through the opening between the center and *left* slab. After the winter solstice, the midday position of the rightmost beam begins moving slowly back toward the spiral's center. At the equinox, midday between the solstices, the beam is roughly midway between the edge and center of the spiral. These sunbeam locations, however, are less specific in indicating a seasonal demarcation than is the single bisecting beam at summer solstice, and it is not clear how useful they would be.

"Sun-dagger" passes down through center of spiral at time of summer solstice. Karl Kernberger, © The Solstice Project.

The discoverers of the Fajada Butte three-slab site also claim that other parts of its geometry were used to mark two key points—the northern minor and major standstills—in the 18.6-year north-south cycle of the moon. Discovery of this cycle is certainly not beyond the abilities of observant people with sufficient motivation, time, and the clear skies and clear view of the horizon available at Fajada. The idea that the Chacoans used the Fajada site to record the 18.6-year lunar cycle was initially greeted with puzzled silence by both archaeologists and astronomers. Since then, we have learned of major lunar standstill observations at Chimney Rock and Mesa Verde (see Chapter 12), and the case is advanced.

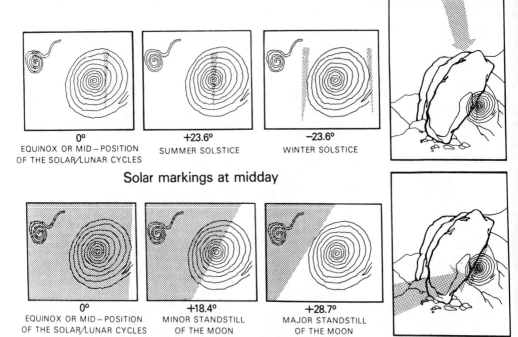

| 0°
EQUINOX OR MID−POSITION
OF THE SOLAR/LUNAR CYCLES | +23.6°
SUMMER SOLSTICE | −23.6°
WINTER SOLSTICE | |

Solar markings at midday

| 0°
EQUINOX OR MID−POSITION
OF THE SOLAR/LUNAR CYCLES | +18.4°
MINOR STANDSTILL
OF THE MOON | +28.7°
MAJOR STANDSTILL
OF THE MOON | |

Solar/lunar markings at rising

The patterns of midday light and shadow on the spiral on Fajada at the solstices and equinoxes and (lower) the shadow that the investigators say would be made by the rising moon at moon's minor and major northern standstills.
Anna Sofaer and Rolf Sinclair, © The Solstice Project.

The Fajada Butte solar marker is an aesthetically pleasing seasonal indicator. The thing that makes it so appealing is the interplay of light and shadow in a way that is different from most other known sun-charting sites. It is not more precise than the more common horizon markers used by prehistoric peoples at Chaco and elsewhere. It is therefore unlikely to be a kind of master solar calendar. Perhaps it served as a sun shrine, a dramatic location for paying homage to the source of all light, heat, and life. Its unusual features symbolized and marked the sun's journey in an interesting and fortuitous way. In any event, it does show us once again the concern Chacoans and other early Indians had with the sky and the sun's movements through it.

Two sites a short distance below the sun-dagger site on Fajada Butte may also exhibit intentional solar markings. Five petroglyphs are crossed by striking patterns of light and shadow close to solar noon in ways that, in most instances, indicate the solstices and equinoxes. These shadow transitions appear to form seven key markings of eleven key points in the daily and seasonal cycles of the sun. The glyphs involved are (at the east site) a rattlesnake, a rectangular shape, and a spiral and (at the west site) a double spiral and a second rectangular shape. The shadows that form these noon markings are cast by rock edges on the butte.

Examples: at the west site on the equinox, close to noon, a narrow daggerlike pattern of light moves upward through the center of the right whorl of the double spiral. At the same time, the rectangular shape below and to the right is also bisected by a vertical pattern, sunlight on the left, shadow on the right. At the east site, a shadow edge crosses the spiral glyph near noon year-round forming a seasonally changing pattern: a pie-shaped wedge at summer solstice, a quartering at equinox, and a bisecting at winter solstice.

All these markings of astronomical cycles at three sites on Fajada Butte have been discovered by artist Anna Sofaer and physicist Rolf Sinclair. Controversy continues over their intentionality and significance. The noon indicators, they feel, are a way of commemorating "a spatial and temporal halving of the day by recording when the sun was due south." They claim that a total of 17 astronomical points are recorded. "Many of these markings are unique in archaeoastronomy in combining simultaneous recordings of two key points in different cycles (such as noon and equinox or solstice)."

No doubt most kinds of sun-watching sites had no dramatic features that reveal themselves to us today. Charting the sun can be easily done from any location with a view of the horizon and some natural features that can serve as markers. And, as we have noted, man-made structures can easily incorporate a variety of ways to note the sun's seasonal path. There's no reason to believe that most of these arrangements meant anything more special and permanent to the Chacoans and their brethren than the calendars we hang on our walls mean to us. But a few sites in areas outside Chaco bear mentioning to show how universal the urge to chart the seasons must have been.

Prehistoric Indians related to the residents of Mesa Verde built a variety of stone buildings in the late 1100s and early 1200s at what is now Hovenweep National Monument, along the border between southern Colorado and Utah. The buildings include towerlike structures erected on rock outcrops. Most of these buildings have small ports, typically a few inches in diameter. Ports in one of these structures, Hovenweep Castle, have been shown to define a complete solar calendar. They permit narrow shafts of light to enter the apparent solar observing room, or sun room. At summer solstice sunset, light passes through a port and illuminates the north side of the lintel over a doorway on an east interior door. At winter solstice sunset, light from another port illuminates the east side of the lintel over a north interior door. At sunset on the spring and fall equinox, sunlight passes diagonally through an open external door to illuminate the center of the lintel on the east interior door. Furthermore, by charting the change in positions of these circles of light from day to day, all these key seasonal demarcations could easily have been anticipated, and preparations for appropriate ceremonies have been begun. The north interior wall may well have originally contained markings of the daily change of position of sunlight entering through the exterior door, but no such marks and no plaster remain intact today.

At another site at Hovenweep, a play of sunlight on normally shaded rock is reminiscent of the Fajada Butte marker. In a rock shelter near the Holly House ruins, a pair of spiral petroglyphs and a set of carved concentric rings are arranged in a horizontal panel. At summer solstice, these petroglyphs are split by two needles of sunlight that start at opposite ends of the panel and meet in the middle.

Many other special relationships between light and shadow on petroglyphs at the key astronomical demarcations of the seasons have also been found in the Southwest. Almost any surface on which shadows from the sun are cast can be used as a seasonal marker, with a little bit of observation and sufficient motivation, and the evidence is abundant that the Indians of the Southwest made use of many different types of them.

Apart from sun-marking functions, several of the large structures in Chaco have special astronomical / geometrical orientations. At Casa Rinconada, for instance, the major and minor axes of symmetry fall along lines of the four cardinal directions. The kiva itself is a carefully made circle. The four holes that served as sockets for the posts that held up the roof form a square that is oriented to the cardinal directions and whose center is the center of the kiva. Astronomer Ray Williamson believes Casa Rinconada was built in part as a metaphor of the cosmos, and for ethnological evidence refers to an Acoma emergence myth about the "first kiva." In this legend, the four roof-support pillars were from four different trees that were planted in the underworld for the people to climb up on. The walls of the first kiva represent the sky, its roof beams the Milky Way, and the kiva is made round because the sky looks like a circle.

The entire town of Pueblo Bonito is astronomically aligned. The wall that divides the Pueblo into western and eastern halves was constructed very nearly along a north-south line. The western half of the pueblo's south wall is nearly a precise east-west line. The eastern half of the wall is set at an angle three degrees north of the latitude line, however, a puzzling change that might have no significance at all or may have had some ritual meaning to the Chacoan builders.

Furthermore the D shape of Pueblo Bonito, its orientation so that its curved walls open to the south, and its stepped design so that the northernmost portions were four stories while much of the southern part was only one story all made it function efficiently as a solar collector. Its placement near the canyon's north wall and its great mass also served to collect solar heat and moderate internal temperature fluctuations. All these design factors would help to make it more comfortable for year-round occupation than a less well-planned structure would be.

It has been recently suggested that the North Road leading 30 miles or more out from Chaco Canyon may itself be an expression of the Chacoans' cosmography. The road is accurately oriented to within one degree of north for the first half and bears two degrees east of north for the second half. As we mentioned in ear-

Possible Crab Nebula supernova pictograph on an overhang beneath Penasco Blanco. Faintly visible at lower left are concentric circles that may mark site as sun-watching station. Photo by author.

lier chapters, in several long segments two and sometimes four wide roadways run in parallel, a puzzling feature. Sofaer and Sinclair have joined up with Michael Marshall to note that after traversing a featureless desert steppe, the road ends abruptly at the edge of a precipitous canyon, a panorama of mountains looming to the north. Here at the top of a pinnacle is a small structure that resembles prehistoric and historic Pueblo Indian shrines. "The significance of the North Road to the prehistoric Pueblo culture of Chaco," they propose, "may be reflected in the cosmologies of the descendant historic Pueblo groups who give north a primacy in ceremony and regard it as the place of their emergence to the earth as well as the place where the dead return to the world below." This interpretation of a cosmographic or symbolic significance to the Chacoan roads echoes in remarkable fashion the sentiments suggested by a Pueblo Indian friend that I mentioned at the end of Chapter 6.

Another site in Chaco Canyon may be the record of one of the more extraordinary astronomical events of the past one thousand years. We know from Chinese astronomical records that in the year A.D. 1054 there appeared in the sky a bright, but temporary, new "guest star" that suddenly flared into being and reached a magnitude about five times brighter than the brightest planet, Venus. It was so bright that it could be seen in daylight for twenty-three days. We now know that this event was the light reaching us from a supernova, or cataclysmic stellar explosion. The gas and debris emitted from this explosion has been expanding outward into space for more than 900 years, forming a diffuse nebula. This region in the constellation Taurus has been named the Crab Nebula for its somewhat crablike shape, and the event that created it is termed the Crab Nebula supernova.

On the underside of an overhanging rock in the western end of Chaco Canyon below Penasco Blanco are pictographs that some astronomers think may be a representation of this dramatic event. Painted on this overhang are a hand, a crescent-shaped symbol reminiscent of the moon, and an asterisk-like symbol that some think may represent the supernova. Nearby is a fourth pictograph, a sun-watching symbol used to mark the place where the rising sun could be lined up with features on the eastern horizon. The Chacoans were definitely living in Chaco Canyon at the time the supernova came into being. And given the usually cloudless skies, it seems likely they would have seen it. But what is the evidence that this arrangement of symbols represents the supernova? (The image of the hand, in Pueblo practice, marks a site as sacred.) We know that the supernova reached its brightest on July 4, 1054, a day or two after first being seen. From computer studies, astronomers have shown that on the morning of July 4 the supernova was located in the sky only two degrees from the waning crescent moon. The pictograph could therefore be a Chacoan observer's record of those two objects in their temporarily close proximity. With the supernova and the moon setting nearly together in the eastern sky, the sun still below the horizon, they would have presented a spectacular and memorable sight.

We don't know if this is in fact what the symbols represent. Some scholars are dubious. They point out that the symbolism there seems similar to that at the earlier-mentioned Zuni sun shrine. There a "great star" symbol certainly represents Venus, not the Crab Nebula supernova. Ethnographic studies also indicate that prehistoric Indians in the Southwest did not record unusual events. And anthropologists, whose business it is to understand human culture, point out that even if the Penasco Blanco pictographs do represent the supernova, that doesn't yield any further useful insights into the culture of the Chacoans.

All that is true. Yet we know the Chacoans were perceptive observers of the sky. We know that regular astronomically based cycles, and therefore seemingly any irregularities in the heavens, were important to them. And we know that the Crab Nebula supernova should have been visible to them.

Just as we can envision the Chacoan sun priests at work in their daily tasks of charting the sun's seasonal course, I like to think that one morning in the summer of 1054 they saw something in the brightening eastern sky that had never before existed. I am sure that, whether or not they recorded it on that rock overhang, they were struck by a sense of awe. We can share, over the centuries, that emotion of wonder, and, for just a moment at least, feel at one with the people of Chaco.

c

11. Destinies and Destinations

The Chacoan system remained a marvel of spiritual and economic organization well into the 1100s. From A.D. 1100–30, both summer rains and annual precipitation brought beneficent moisture in excess of the long-term average. The favorable summer rains were a vivid continuing reminder of the system's success in ordering the world.

But the seeds of change may already have been sown. This three-decade period had been preceded by a period of markedly dry summers in the 1090s, the worst drought of the eleventh century. That temporary return to harsher conditions may have served to warn the Chacoans that their world view might not always be successful in controlling the environment. This realization may have contributed to the establishment of competing outliers such as the Salmon site (much of the work completed in 1094), built way to the north on the San Juan River.

About A.D. 1115, signs of a significant reorganization of Chacoan culture began to appear. This reorganization took place over the next twenty-five years, until 1140. There was new construction in the canyon, but its nature had changed. Most of the new structures (Kin Kletso, Casa Chiquita, New Alto) were built in the so-called "McElmo Phase" masonry style rather than the classic Chacoan stonework. The Chacoans subdivided rooms in existing structures. They enclosed plazas with arc-shaped walls. They now deposited their trash in aban-

Restored kiva, Aztec Ruin. The focus of the Chacoan system shifted to the north, perhaps to either Aztec or Salmon. Photo by author.

doned kivas or rooms rather than in formal trash mounds. More of them were now living in small village sites. They ate fewer large mammals, especially deer; the meat in their diet shifted toward small mammals and turkeys.

A major change in function was underway. The change involved both the sites within Chaco Canyon and the relationship of the canyon to the rest of the San Juan Basin. "Basically, Chaco appears to become more residential (domestic) and less ritual in function," says Jim Judge. "Though pilgrimages may have continued, I doubt whether Chaco continued to function as the focus of such visits. Instead, I would argue that Chaco Canyon itself became the equivalent of an outlying area or perhaps a second-order center with primarily domestic, nonritual, functions."

Where was the new ritual-administrative focus of the Chacoan system? Judge says we must again look to the north, to the area of the San Juan River. The architecture and ceramics all show northern influences. Sites such as Salmon and Aztec would now be the more centrally located with respect to the newer additions to the outlier system in southwestern Colorado. Most construction activity during this period at outliers took place at sites in the northern half of the basin, at such places as Salmon and Aztec in far northern New Mexico and at Lowry, Escalante, and Ida Jean in Colorado. In contrast, there seems to have been little if any active construction at outliers in the southern part of the basin. In fact, only four of the twenty-five Chacoan outliers examined in the Marshall survey (Chapter 7) show ceramic evidence of occupation after A.D. 1125.

All in all, the Chacoan system was undergoing major shifts. Judge summarizes:

"I submit that there was a shift in the administrative and ritual locus from Chaco to the San Juan area, perhaps to either Aztec or Salmon, and that this shift was the outgrowth of a brief, but relatively severe, deterioration of climatic conditions circa A.D. 1090–1100.

"New sites in the southwest Colorado area were incorporated into the system, but the extent to which communities south of Chaco Canyon maintained active involvement in the system is unknown. Chaco itself, I suggest, shifted its primary function to that of a 'residential' outlying area—albeit a major one—with a supportive complement of village sites which contributed to the subsistence needs of the resident population."

Judge emphasizes that activity in Chaco Canyon did not decline. "If anything, it increased when viewed from the more permanent, rather than the periodic habitation perspective. There was, however, a fundamental change in function as Chaco lost its position of ritual dominance in the system."

In A.D. 1130 there began a severe drought that would last fifty years. It started with a sharp drop in annual precipitation, the effects moderated somewhat during 1133 by momentary recovery in summer rainfall. But then the summer rains declined too, and they would stay well below the long-term average for almost all the next half century.

By 1140 the drought had lasted a good part of the decade, and the collapse of the Chacoan system was underway.

The Chacoans did no more building after about 1130. The last known tree-cutting date on beams in the immediate vicinity of the canyon is 1132 at Pueblo Alto. The people continued to live in the buildings for a time, but the stratigraphic evidence indicates that by sometime in the middle of the twelfth century the area was no longer being used. (Mesa Verdeans would reoccupy parts of the canyon in the early 1200s.) The same thing happened at most of the outliers. There are no more building dates at Salmon following the end of the Chacoan construction there (1239) until the Mesa Verdeans moved in the 1260s, nearly a century and a quarter later.

Looking back to that time from the present we must be careful not to overly compress our perceptions and distort the record of events. Like a telephoto view of a distant scene that squeezes the farthest hills into one jumbled mountain, our view toward the past can yield an overdramatic picture of system collapse.

It undoubtedly was not a sudden "event" but a gradual trend over many years. The sites in the canyon seem to have been adandoned in an orderly fashion. The people took most of their useful material goods with them. There is little or no evidence of violence.

The Chacoan system was no longer the success it once had been. This realization would become gradually apparent, but I doubt if the Chacoans would have thought of their change of fortunes as a failure. Indeed there's no reason for them to have done so. They had had a workable system for many generations. But that does not mean they were locked into the same pattern forever. Part of the resiliency of Indian cultures is an ability to maintain tradition while adapting to changing conditions.

The realization that this might be a fortuitous time to change would, I think, very likely be accommodated into the Chacoan religious view. Just as ritual shapes life and provides permanence, the need to modify patterns of life would stimulate changes in the content of the ceremonial message. Now was the preordained time for the people of Chaco to alter their social system, move on, and try something a little different.

Pueblo Indian friends I've spoken to about the abandonment of Chaco find nothing surprising about it. It was clearly time to leave. Prophecies may have stated they were to stay only so long and then go elsewhere. The time was now appropriate.

It wouldn't be a mass exodus, any more than are migrations of people today. Families and clan groups would very likely just pick up and move on whenever the circumstances seemed right. They would join relatives or friends who preceded them. Others would eventually follow. Some of the Chacoans would move to communities in the most environmentally favorable situations within the San Juan basin. Others would probably leave the basin altogether. Many groups had been drawn into the basin during the eleventh century by the economic success and ritualistic attractiveness of the Chacoan system. It seems likely that some of these people returned to their places of origin, and reestablished preexisting social ties.

Many Chacoans would take up a more mobile, less centralized lifestyle, with somewhat more emphasis on hunting and gathering and a tendency to live in smaller, less formalized groups.

To summarize, climatic change and the diminishment of nearby resources were the overwhelming external influence in bringing about a change in the Chacoan system. Few cultures that live in a marginal environmental situation can long tolerate severe, long-term deteriorations in those conditions. But there's no reason to believe that the Chacoans had intentions of living forever in the formalized, integrated, interdependent system that had been evolved. They had had hints of its impermanence, they had probably long been prepared culturally and psychologically for a change in ways. The very success of the Chacoan system had drawn more people into it, and this saturation of population had made it more vulnerable to major environmental change. At first the system was so well integrated that the Chacoans couldn't revert to pre-system status, and so they merely reorganized. But when the long drought got underway and continued, the less-ritualized culture adapted to the new conditions and gradually dispersed.

The Chacoan experiment, effective for 150 years, was over.

Where did they go? They, and their cousins from Mesa Verde, Kayenta, and elsewhere around the region, became the Pueblo Indians of today.

Nothing is so nettlesome to those attuned to the connections between past and present in the Southwest than the idea, so often heard, that the Chacoans (or the Mesa Verdeans for that matter) "simply disappeared." It's often mentioned in tones of great mystery as though the people vanished into thin air, one of the great mass disappearances on record. Those who hold this view apparently assume there is no cultural continuity between the Ancient Ones of the past millennium and the Indians of today. This, despite the abundant similarities in life-styles, rituals, architecture, artwork, pottery, and farming methods.

Part of the trouble, I think, is unwittingly due to the anthropologists' use of the term "the Anasazi" for all those who occupied the now deserted great ruins and cliff houses of the Southwest. It has the flavor of a particular tribe of Indians, and since there are no "Anasazi" today their people must no longer exist. There may also be another reason for the misunderstanding: In addition to the similarities, there are also significant cultural differences between the builders of the ancient ruins and the modern Pueblo Indians. But that seems inexplicable only if one wrongly assumes that culture and conditions remain static. More than 800 years have elapsed since Chaco was last occupied. Their descendants have also been affected by 400 years of European influence. The introduction of diseases, livestock, Christianity, and modern transportation and communications has shaped Pueblo life just as it has transformed most cultures. "It is extremely naive to assume that the Pueblo people are living fossils," says Linda S. Cordell, now director of the University Museum and a professor of anthropology at the University of Colorado, Boulder. "They have had to be extremely resilient in the face of enormous forces." And that adaptability easily explains the differences between the Pueblo people of today and their ancient ancestors.

"I have been trying for a very long time to counteract the idea of disappeared folks," says Cordell. "The descendants of the Anasazi are indeed the modern Pueblo Indians of Arizona and New Mexico."

One doesn't have to go far along the Rio Grande in New Mexico or along the highways of western New Mexico or northeastern Arizona to find these descendants of the Chacoans and the other Ancient Ones. Their scattered villages dot

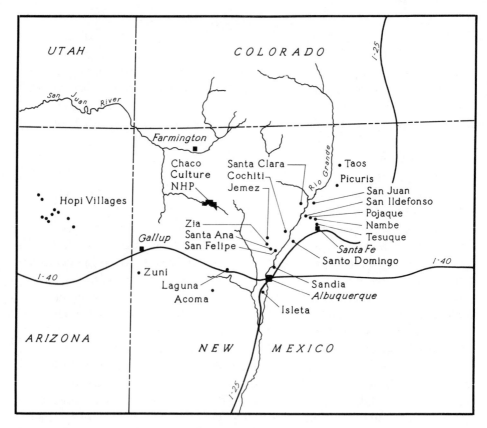

Map of the modern pueblos of New Mexico and Arizona.

the lowlands and plateaus. The names by which we know them include the Zuni, Hopi, Acoma, Santo Domingo, San Felipe, Zia, Jemez, and many more. Different villages and tribes, a variety of languages, a wonderful diversity of customs, but Pueblo Indians all, and cherished citizens of the land. They live in ancient-looking adobe structures sometimes hauntingly reminiscent of Chaco or in modern frame houses that would be at home in Suburbia, U.S.A. Some, like those at the Hopi village of Walpi, on First Mesa, Arizona, have, partly by choice, no electricity or running water. Some others, only a few miles away below in the valley, have satellite TV dishes. The Pueblo Indians draw strength from the ancient traditions, and, like the rest of us, seek to cope with all the challenges and opportunities of modern life.

Befitting their long and rich history, they have a refreshingly long-term view of things. While we struggle with exigencies of fiscal-year budgeting and the flow of daily events, they can bring true meaning to the phrase historical perspective. About the time the rest of the United States was celebrating its Bicentennial, a Hopi leader friend began working on plans for observance of the Hopi Millennium, the anniversary of a thousand years of Hopi culture culminating in the year

The face of the Pueblo Indian today. Antonio Sando, a former governor of Jemez Pueblo, is seen here in 1984 portrait. Photo by Susanne Page, courtesy of Futures for Children.

A Hopi Indian religious leader, Starlie Lomayaktewa, at Pueblo Bonito. The Hopis believe their ancestors include the Chacoans. Photo by author.

2000. A Jemez Indian friend one day told us of his hopes and plans for an erosion-control project that would, he said, benefit his people *two hundred years* from now.

I once took a small group of Zuni and Hopi Indians to Chaco Canyon to look over the ruins and talk about any connections they felt. They were fascinated by it all. Here and there they plunged into animated discussions among themselves about one or another attributes of a kiva that was slightly different from their own. The cultural memory of Chaco Canyon among these Pueblo Indians had long faded into the past, but they felt a strong affinity for the builders of Chaco and an admiration for their works. They were proud to consider them among their ancestors.

A few years back I had several long discussions with Andrew Napetcha, the Zuni Indian who until his death was the official historian of the Zuni tribe. A slight, scholarly man, he said the Zunis feel strong ties to Chaco. "A lot about the Chaco Canyon people fits in with the prayers and tradition of the people of Zuni," he said. "The influence of this Chaco Canyon culture has been felt among all the Pueblo Indians of the Southwest."

He told a long story from the Zuni oral traditions. It told of a religious order that, while on a migratory quest for the "center of the earth," lived for a time in Chaco Canyon. This medicine society was called the Sword Swallowers because they were considered to have special powers and carried out magic rituals or performances in which they put wooden swords down their throats. After living at Chaco, they eventually made their way to Zuni and petitioned to become a part of the tribe there. The Zuni priests put them to a test. To see "who had the strongest medicine," the Zuni priests arranged a competition. The Zuni priests performed their ceremonies. Four days and nights of continuous rain followed. It was then the Sword Swallowers' turn. They went through the same ceremonies. The storms came, but they turned into gray, winter storms. The cold drizzle turned to snow. Many feet of snow covered the whole valley. So the Zuni priests said, "We don't want you here, your medicine is too strong." But the Sword Swallowers argued that the snow was beneficial because it cools the earth off and prepares the soil and earth for the next planting season. "So" said Napetcha, "they were finally accepted in and became a part of the Zunis." He noted that until quite recently the sword-swallowing ceremony was performed by this order at Zuni

The late Zuni Indian historian Andrew Napetcha with Hopi religious leader Percy Lomaquhu at Chaco Canyon in 1982. "A lot about the Chaco Canyon people fits in with the prayers and tradition of the people of Zuni," said Napetcha. Photo by author.

every January. Napetcha said there were probably other groups from Chaco that had become part of Zuni also. He personally felt many of the Zuni religious and governmental traditions had come out of Chaco.

Napetcha also told of a time when his father, then in his seventies, went to Mesa Verde. "He saw it and said this was one of the places our ancestors lived. And in the museum there were some objects with a sign that said the anthropologists didn't know what they are. It was a little thing shaped like a cocoon and the size of a thumb." His father identified it for them. "Dad said, 'I've seen that in Zuni. It's one of the things that sorcerers use to cast spells on people.' "

Today's Pueblo Indians place strong emphasis on family and community. They understandably seek to protect the privacy and identity of essential tribal customs while at the same time expressing their generous and sharing spirit. After watching hundreds of costumed dancers perform for hours on the dusty plaza in one of the few open dances at Santo Domingo Pueblo, probably the most conservative and secretive of the Pueblo tribes, it was wonderful one day to be invited into a family home for a feast of chile and stew. Then we were led into the next room and proudly shown an antique cradleboard swing lovingly fashioned out of willow boughs and leather thongs and suspended from the ceiling beam *vigas* for the restful sleep of the newest member of the family. It was easy to imagine that same kind of cradleboard embracing a child at Chetro Ketl in Chaco Canyon 900 years ago.

Another friend, a Tewa-Hopi kachina maker, told once of his experience as a firefighter out on the slopes of Palomar Mountain in California. After the blaze had been extinguished, the grateful astronomers at the Mount Palomar observatory, the site of the 200-inch telescope that probes the most distant reaches of the universe, invited the men to look through the instrument at the heavens. Most of them declined, perhaps feeling unsettled at the thought of awesome mysteries of the heavens revealed. But our friend did look and found the vastness of the universe not at all alien to the Pueblo Indian mind and philosophy.

These descendants of the ancient ones have a sense of oneness with the natural world and of responsibility for its well-being that deserves our everlasting praise and appreciation. It is a feeling of community with the planet that many of us yearn for but few ever attain. When the Hopis go into all-night kiva sessions, as they frequently do, they pray not just for the Hopis or for Indians in general but for the welfare of the entire world and every single person and creature on it. And they mean this literally and seriously. They feel the responsibility is theirs.

So these, too, are the People of Chaco. They are very much with us now. God and the Pueblo deities willing, they will be always, for as long as there is a world and people on it.

12. Chaco in the Twenty-First Century

The power of Chaco Canyon and the Chaco Phenomenon to intrigue, challenge, and puzzle continues.

In August 1997 nearly 500 archaeologists who study the Southwest gathered at Chaco Canyon, meeting, talking, and socializing in a grand array of giant tents set up west of Fajada Butte. They camped out in long rows of temporary campsites strung out west of the south entry road. These Pecos Conferences of southwestern archaeology are annual affairs, but this was the fiftieth anniversary reunion of the last one in Chaco Canyon.

Old-timers from the 1930s and 1940s, veterans of the Chaco Project of the 1970s, and a host of new researchers entering the field in the 1980s and 1990s gathered to hear the latest reports and viewpoints. There amid the sun and the dust and the light glistening off the pale yellow sandstone cliffs, the power of the place, even for these people of science, was evident.

Many spoke of their sense of appreciation for and awe of not only the desolate beauty of the place but also the ancient people of Chaco, who erected the grand structures in and out of the canyon and created a culture that spread throughout the region and endured for several centuries before fading, leaving behind magnificent, enduring architecture and questions that we may never be able to answer.

The conference was a wonderful opportunity to renew acquaintances and to seek perspective on what was new and what had changed in the years since the Chaco Project was wrapped up as a field project. Most of the original Chaco Project researchers had scattered to other research sites and opportunities throughout the Southwest, but it was clear their curiosity and interest in Chaco has not waned.

Tom Windes is one who has remained. As the one Chaco Project archaeologist who has never ceased doing field work in and around Chaco, he put together this conference and was a central figure in all talks and discussions. Slender, wiry, mustached, he seems, whether in his archaeologist's jeans or his Park Service uniform, to be right for the place, timeless and ongoing, almost a part of the canyon itself. In speech he can seem iconoclastic and opinionated, but his words carry weight, wisdom, and common sense.

Archaeologist Tom Windes, here at Pueblo Bonito, continues active field work and study in and around Chaco.

Frustrated by the complicated messiness of the archaeology at the most famous and most studied Chaco site, Pueblo Bonito, the center of what he calls "downtown Chaco," Windes at one point commented, "I don't like dealing with the Bonito complex. We should just bulldoze that out of our life." Needless to say, he was speaking metaphorically. Bonito has been rich with information, but its multiple occupations and remodelings make it complex and difficult to decipher. He prefers cleaner sites capable of providing clear answers. Yet, says another researcher, the comment is "kind of like saying Rome is too complicated."

At the Pecos Conference, Windes chaired an informal evening moonlight session on research going on inside Chaco and the view from outside Chaco.

"We're still working on Chaco in the 1990s," he said. "These are a damn bunch of good folks." He noted that most of the field work at Chaco ended in the late 1970s. "But I've hung in there, twenty-five years now, every summer. I continue to do reports on it. Some are integrative. But also some are somewhat new."

One of Windes's many projects has been extraordinary—the documenting and tree-ring dating of thousands of pieces of wood used in the buildings at Chaco Canyon. The project dwarfs the original tree-ring dating efforts at Chaco in the 1920s and 1930s, as seminal as they were in establishing the first firm dates for construction and habitation at Chaco. In comparison to what has been done in the past ten years, he says, those early sample numbers for getting tree-ring dates from Bonito, were, as Windes says, "frankly pathetic."

"My crew [of volunteers] has documented every visible piece of wood in this monument," Windes told the Pecos gathering. "That has never been done before, anywhere—a complete mapping of wood resources. From Bonito alone we have 4,200 pieces. Our total count is 10,000 pieces. We've mapped every one, taken 3,500 samples. It's a whole new resource. We have 500 new dates at Pueblo [del] Arroyo. I know when those guys were doing their thing out there."

Why did he do it? (It was all accomplished without any government funding, by the way.) "I love dating," he said. "Why guess? We're going to guess anyway, but why not get the data?"

If Tom Windes is a down-in-the-dirt field archaeologist, Steve Lekson is a big-picture guy. (Yet he also does his share of field work. As he told me in June 1998 in the middle of a field project at Bluff, Utah, "Actually, I'm pretty dirty right now.")

Lekson also came out of the Chaco Project; he now works at the University of Colorado Museum in Boulder. (In Chapter 9 I describe his great-pueblo-architecture research results, carried out while a Chaco Project researcher at the University of New Mexico, into the scale of work necessary to build Pueblo Bonito.) Tall, blond-haired, and (like Tom Windes) adept at expressing his views in a refreshingly jargonless style, even in his formal reports, since the Pecos Conference he has been leading a grand synthesis of research at Chaco (see Chapter 15). In recent years he has championed the view that the Chaco geopolitical system was even more widespread than we'd thought only a decade or so ago. And he's the originator and proponent of a new view of a linear extension of Chaco Culture in both space and time. He and his bemused colleagues alike refer to it whimsically as "the geopolitical line dance." (More on that later.)

"If what I say is right," he told the gathering at the Pecos Conference, "it really does rewrite southwestern history. But it's big, and it bothers people," he says, and he admits it implies levels of political complexity that many of his colleagues are not quite ready to accept.

Others were invited to speak about their view of Chaco as outsiders, specialists in the archaeology of regional sites thought to have been just outside the periphery of the Chacoan influence. One from southwestern Colorado spoke of the need to mentally erase our view of state lines in the Four Corners region as some sort of separation relevant to the cultures a thousand years ago. "We think, this is Colorado, this is New Mexico. We've got to wipe that away. There has got to be a relationship."

Steve Lekson led that panel, and he asked participants to answer two questions: What is Chaco? What does Chaco have to do with where *you* work? The most revealing answers came to the second question.

It was interesting to see archaeologists who have investigated sites in southwestern Colorado, southeastern Utah, and northeastern Arizona strug-

Steve Lekson at Chaco in 1998, overlooking Chetro Ketl. Courtesy Ken Abbott/University of Colorado.

216

gle with the degree to which their sites were (or were not) part of or influenced by Chacoan culture.

Archaeologist Winston Hurst, for example, studies sites in southeastern Utah. As he said, that area is "definitely out beyond the 'burbs" of Chaco. Nevertheless, there is much at his sites that he describes as "Chacoesque." "There's Chacoesque stuff up here in southeastern Utah," he said. Some of the structures have the whole checklist of features of Chaco-style great houses, with great kivas, roads, and surrounding communities. There are roads to sacred places and roads to communities. "We have roads going every which way that can support almost any scenario."

But the research is in very early stages, far behind that at Chaco. "In Utah we don't have the dates yet. We don't have the research yet. We need a hell of a lot of work up there" before any firm conclusions can be made, Hurst said. Yet he was certain about one thing:

"There is no question in my mind that every human being on the Colorado Plateau knew about Chaco, . . . had names for them [the largest Chaco pueblos], and visited them."

Barbara Mills of the University of Arizona spoke from the viewpoint of her investigations at a site along the Mogollon Rim in northeastern Arizona that has a circular great kiva 30 meters in diameter and at sixteen to eighteen other sites with circular great kivas, all seeming to date in the first four decades of the 1100s. There are both similarities to and differences from Chaco. "We've come back from thinking we have Chacoan outliers proper, but believe there was some connection," she said.

Chris Downum thought a site he had studied between Winslow and Flagstaff, Arizona, "was safe, out of the clutches from Chaco," but then it began showing up on maps as a Chacoan outlier. It has turquoise, banded masonry showing some Chacoan influence, pottery styles having some Chacoan influence, but no roads yet discovered. "Chaco is an American Stonehenge," Downum said. It presents "many enigmas, many mysteries." But he suggested that many ideas proposed about the Chaco system "don't make sense." How, he asked, could one central point control everything? He suggested that seeing Chaco as the center may be right, or it may be just a concept we've invented.

Chaco Canyon and the mysteries of Chacoan culture continue their fascination and hold on archaeologists, as well as the rest of us. The Pecos conference, subsequent published and unpublished reports summarizing and commenting on research during the late 1990s and early 2000s, and my discussions and interviews with archaeologists make that clear. It is difficult to generalize, and controversies about every aspect abound, but this is my attempt to list in succinct summary form some of the major changes and developments in our understanding about Chaco in recent years. (I go on to explore some of the more interesting themes in more detail in the next two chapters.)

- The extent of Chacoan geopolitical system is seen by many archaeologists as even larger than had been thought in the 1980s. It covers parts of four states: New Mexico, Colorado, Utah, and Arizona. More Chacoan and "Chacoesque" sites have been documented in the latter three states. Other researchers, however, grumble about overly "Chaco-centric" contentions. A Chacoan Regional System, defined in the late 1980s by government and university archaeologists and, more recently, the Chacoan World reexamination of the late 1990s and early 2000s, now includes about 200 prehistoric communities and thousands of individual settlements over a 35,000-square-mile area in the four states. Each community has a great house (though much smaller than those in Chaco Canyon), and most have a great kiva and one or more short segments of road leading up to their major structures.
- Chacoan great-house architecture had its origin earlier than thought—in the A.D. 800s—and this early form of monumental architecture already existed beyond Chaco Canyon.
- That the Chacoan regional system existed is widely—although not unanimously—accepted. But what the Chaco Phenomenon or the Chaco Experience (to use a newer term some archeologists prefer) means—what the Chacoans were doing and why—is still hotly debated. Some think the mystery may never be completely resolved; others are more optimistic and suspect that it can all be—and in fact largely has been—sorted out.
- There is an ever greater acceptance of the viewpoint that explanations for the Chaco Phenomenon must embrace nonmaterialistic, noneconomic concepts involving Native American beliefs and spiritual thinking. The roads, for example, are now recognized by many archaeologists to be at least as much massive cosmographic symbols, commemorative monuments, or vast construction projects for the purpose of social cohesion as they are transportation paths. The large structures in Chaco are now seen more as monumental expressions of a major culture than as large apartment buildings and living quarters (although people did live there). In this view, the great-house architecture wedded topography and geometry and celebrated an underlying cosmology.
- The "decline" of Chaco in the early decades of the twelfth century is being viewed a little differently, with archaeologists Steve Lekson and Cathy Cameron seeing it as a time of a widening geographic extent of Chaco's exchange sphere, with increasing (not decreasing) regional interactions together with a general movement north of Chacoan influence and

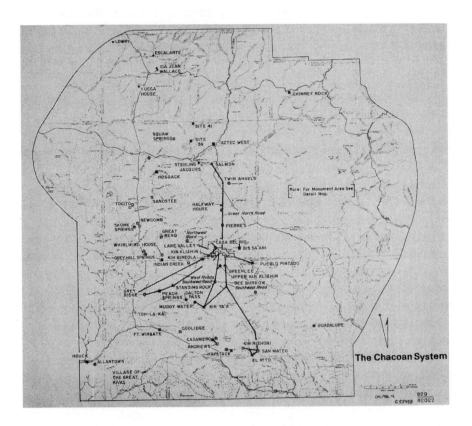

The Chacoan geopolitical system and settlement pattern extends into four states. This shows some of the better-known sites. From Doyel, 1992, 2001.

Chacoan-style grand construction. The Chacoan great houses remained fully functional monumental structures for many decades, even centuries.
- The Chaco Synthesis Project, funded by the National Park Service, the University of Colorado, and a variety of host institutions, was launched in the late 1990s in an attempt to synthesize the voluminous results of the Chaco Project. Steve Lekson organized a series of small, working conferences, each with both Chacoan and outside scholars, on specific topics. Many of the papers reworked after those discussions have now been published in special issues of archaeology journals or as reports published by archaeological societies. A single overall synthesis report was completed in late 2004. Chapter 15 is on the Chaco Synthesis Project and its insights.
- Pueblo Bonito's central place in the Chacoan world has been confirmed and reemphasized in a major reevaluation of a century of research at the monu-

mental structure. And three archaeologists who've studied the design of Bonito in great detail offer a startling suggestion: that the design may have been the work of one master Chacoan architect. I'll look at this project in Chapter 13.

- The small sites in Chaco Canyon—hundreds of habitation sites that line the canyon, particularly along the south cliffs, that fill in the spaces between the major great-house structures we see today—are being given far more emphasis as an essential component of Chacoan life. Many archaeologists now believe they are where many of the people lived. In this view the great houses like Pueblo Bonito and the others were occupied by relatively few families, perhaps several high-status groups (although this is hotly debated), while the people who made things work and who would represent much of what we would think of as the bustling daily life of the extended "city" of Chaco lived in the smaller sites. Most of these sites are not apparent to visitors to Chaco today, but some have been excavated. As archaeologists Steve Lekson and Karin Burd write, "New insights on planning, landscape architecture, and building sequences" create "a picture of a densely conceived and constructed Chaco Canyon, much different from the sparse, spaced ruins seen by visitors today."

- Likewise, large earthen mounds that used to be considered merely middens, or trash dumps, are being accorded greater significance. Some researchers now consider the mounds to be intentionally created landscape features. Most mounds are oval-shaped, sculpted accumulations of earth, construction debris, and trash, but a few had formal geometric shapes and were faced with masonry. Two such rectangular, masonry-walled platform mounds the size of basketball courts were in front of Pueblo Bonito, with steps leading to the top. Great-house sites outside of Chaco Canyon also frequently reveal similar "engineered" mounds.

- In the Chaco Wood Project, overseen by Tom Windes, every piece of wood in Chaco Culture National Historical Park has been documented. This had never been done before, anywhere. Subsequently, the same thing has now been done for Aztec Ruins National Monument. (Subsequent to this Chaco Wood Project, some sites at Mesa Verde have now been totally inventoried by the University of Arizona Laboratory for Tree-Ring Research and by Windes.) The total count at Chaco is 10,000 pieces. Thirty-five hundred pieces have been tree-ring dated, with 500 new dates in Pueblo Arroyo alone. This compares with the 135 dates for Pueblo Bonito, the largest ruin, known previously.

- Two separate studies have been published about the extraordinary amount of work and craftsmanship that went into obtaining and shaping the timbers used at Chaco and also identifying the sources of the trees that were cut for the timbers. Both studies were published in 2001 and address questions about the organization of that important work. The first, "Wood Production in Chacoan Society," was conducted by Tom Windes and Peter McKenna. The second, by a University of Arizona team, used strontium isotopes to pin down the two main sources of architectural timber used in Chaco Canyon—both on mountain ranges far away to the west and the south-southeast. A third, more recent study, by a team from Eastern New Mexico University and the U.S. Geological Survey, analyzed the whole suite of chemical elements in the wood to identify sources of the ponderosa pine used in Chaco. Because I find these three studies so interesting and impor-tant, I describe them in more detail in the next chapter.

• Strontium isotopes were also used to establish that much of the corn (maize) consumed in Chaco Canyon was also grown considerable distances away—50 miles to the west at the base of the Chuska Mountains (in the Newcomb/Skunk Springs area), or in some cases even farther away, on the San Juan or Animas river floodplains to the north. The researchers tested corncobs collected from Pueblo Bonito and a few other Chaco sites by the Hyde Exploring Expedition in 1886 and 1889 and now curated in museums. (Who could have imagined then what a lowly corncob might tell us now? No wonder archaeologists like to save everything.) The study, by Larry Benson of the U.S. Geological Survey in Boulder, Colorado, and six colleagues from the USGS, University of Colorado, and the Navajo Nation, was published in the October 28, 2003, *Proceedings of the National Academy of Sciences.* Say the authors: "We know of no previous study demonstrating that maize, a dietary staple of southwestern Native Americans, was imported from distant agricultural sites." And they add: "The finding supports the hypothesis that major construction events in Chaco Canyon were made possible because maize was brought in to support extra-local labor forces."

• Chaco, Aztec to the north (essentially a "new Chaco"), and Casas Grandes (also called Paquime) in far northern Mexico are on the same meridian line, and Steve Lekson argues strongly that this is intentional. Since the three sites were built and occupied at different times, with Chaco the earliest, the meridian alignment may have served to symbolize and commemorate cul-tural and historical continuity. (See Chapter 14.)

• The placement, layout, and interrelationships of the major structures of Chaco Canyon were much more organized and formalized than had been realized. The whole canyon layout—not just the structures themselves—appears to have been designed and planned. The orientations, internal geometry, and geographic interrelationships of the major Chacoan buildings were developed in relationship to the major cycles of the sun and moon. The identification of these forms of cosmographic expression in the archi-tecture and layout of Chaco has gained increasing acceptance and appreci-ation by archaeologists. I'll describe this more in subsequent chapters.

- The Fajada Butte solar (and lunar) marker was affected by erosion and human activity. In 1989 one of the three rock slabs was found to have shifted, so that the midday sunlight passing between the slabs no longer records the seasonal demarcations on the spiral petroglyph behind them with the same precision. A National Park Service stabilization project was carried out in 1990 to protect the slabs from further movement, but the decision was made not to try to restore the shifted slab to its previous position. Monitoring continues, and access to the site will remain highly restricted. An auto pullout for observing the site through a telescope has been constructed east of the Chaco Culture National Historical Park Visitor Center.

- Archaeoastronomy is more and more being integrated into archaeologists' models of a culture. Chacoans' cosmographic expression, displayed in their building orientations and layouts (see Chapter 14 for new material), is being accorded more and more respect. A specific subcomponent of that is the possibility that the Chacoans did indeed observe and record the moon's 18.6-year standstill cycle—the cycle between the moon's farthest north-south excursions. This idea has been given some added credence by discoveries at Chimney Rock Pueblo, a Chacoan outlier a hundred miles north of Chaco atop a double-spired mesa near Pagosa Springs, Colorado, and at Mesa Verde National Park, west of Chimney Rock. At Chimney Rock, University of Colorado astronomer J. McKim Malville has shown that for two years during each 18.6-year lunar excursion, the moon rises far enough to the north to appear between the two prominent natural rock towers on the mesa as seen from Chimney Rock Pueblo. Through tree-ring dating, Malville has found that the two episodes of construction at Chimney Rock coincided with the northern lunar standstills around A.D. 1076 and 1093. One possible explanation for this, he suggests, is that the Chacoans had noticed this effect at the earlier standstill in 1057 (just three years after the dramatic supernova of A.D. 1054 that may have sensitized people to unusual sky phenomena) and built the Chimney Rock site primarily for astronomical observation and related ceremonies. Also, he says, at Mesa Verde, the line connecting the four-story square tower of Cliff Palace and the center of the Sun Temple is oriented to the position of the setting moon at its southern major standstill. Pictographs in the Cliff Palace tower appear to mark out four lunar cycles, averaging 18.5 years in duration.

- A new Bonito-style great-house ruin—the East community—has been discovered (or rediscovered) 6 miles east of the national park boundary between Wijiji (at the eastern end of the park) and Pueblo Pintado (farther east, outside the park). Tom Windes and Rachel Anderson have been studying it, and they presented a paper on it in March 1998. Now shrouded under a large mound, the great house was nevertheless only one story high. The

Chimney Rock Pueblo near Pagosa Springs, Colorado, looking east, showing the prominent twin spires behind it that the Chacoans may have used to observe and record the moon's 18.6-year standstill cycle.
Courtesy J. McKim Malville.

Moon rising between the twin towers as seen from Chimney Rock Pueblo at the time of the major northern standstill of August 8, 1988. Only for a two-year period during the moon's maximum lunar excursion every 18.6 years is the moon far enough north to be viewed between these two chimneys from Chimney Rock Pueblo.
Courtesy J. McKim Malville.

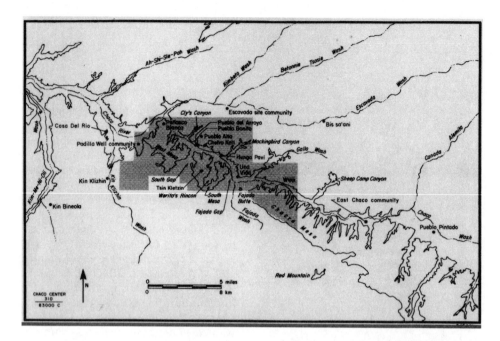

Important features in Chaco Canyon and its environs. The newly studied Chaco East community is halfway between Wijiji and Pueblo Pintado. From Windes and Ford, 1992.

great house and surrounding community were first occupied in the A.D. 900s. The canyon is narrower there than in the rest of Chaco, and the mesa tops are 500 meters above the canyon bottom. Shaded by the south canyon walls, most houses appear to have been used primarily for spring and summer, not winter, occupation. It was an integrated community. Virtually all of the forty-two Chacoan houses in the East community have a direct view of the great house, and this does not appear to be an accident. There are comunication shrines above the site with line-of-sight links to each other and to other Chacoan communication shrines. The area is higher in elevation and gets considerably more rainfall than central Chaco Canyon. Isolated pockets of large Ponderosa pine and Douglas fir trees dot the south side of the canyon. A side canyon to the south is well sited for run-off agriculture and was probably the breadbasket for local farming.

The official record of all this research, some of it protected behind lock and key, is kept in the Chaco Archives. The archives are part of the Chaco Museum Collection of the Chaco Culture National Historical Park, National Park Service, but are physically located in the Center for Southwest Research at the University of New Mexico General Library in Albuquerque.

By 2004, the archives contained 2,400 manuscripts, 70,000 black and white photos, 60,000 negatives, 7,000 slides, 2,400 maps, and approximately 300 linear feet of assorted project records, notes, site files, and published and unpublished papers.

The artifact collections from the Chaco Project (and earlier Chaco excavations too) are under the domain of the Chaco Culture National Historical Park Museum Collection, curated at the Maxwell Museum of Anthropology in Albuquerque by the National Park Service, under an agreement between these two institutions. In March 2004 its curator, Wendy Bustard, gave me a tour of the collection, then did some data searches for me and provided updated numbers for everything in it. It's amazing to contemplate. The total archaeological collection is estimated at 1 million items, of which she said 819,000 had been catalogued. These include 528,000 potsherds, 1,095 complete or partial ceramic vessels (bowls, jars, canteens, ollas, pitchers, and ladles), 150 stone or clay effigies, 1,500 projectile points, 4,650 ornaments, 1,875 bone tools, 530 wooden or vegetal artifacts (arrows, cordage, digging sticks, matting, sandals), 112,000 stone artifacts and tools (axes, abraders, knives, manos, metates, flakes, cores, paint

Curator Wendy Bustard with a small portion of Chacoan pottery in the National Park Service's Chaco Culture National Historical Park Museum Collection. Many of the large pots shown were found during the Chaco Project's excavation at Pueblo Alto in the 1980s. Photo by author.

palettes, pot covers), 11,750 mineral and shell specimens, 6,850 archaeological samples (carbon-14, pollen, soil, flotation) totaling 3.6 million grams
(that's 7,900 pounds), and 7,230 dendrochronological samples.

The new Hibben Center for Archaeological Research on the University
of New Mexico campus (named in honor of the legendary UNM archaeologist Frank C. Hibben, who died in 2002 at the age of ninety-one) is the
future home of the entire Chaco Culture National Historical Park Museum
Collection. The handsome new building, immediately south of the Maxwell
Museum, is built and partially occupied. Once the second and third floors
are completed, the Chaco collection will be moved into them. However,
congressional legislation authorizing and funding the Department of Inte-
rior/National Park Service share of the contruction ($1.75 million) and its
lease has to be passed first. In 2004, the Maxwell Museum began to move
its own Chaco artifact collections (mainly from the University of New
Mexico's program of summer student excavations during the 1930s and
1940s) into the Hibben Center. Whether to combine that collection with
the Chaco Culture National Historical Park Museum Collection was being
discussed.

Access to Chaco: The route into Chaco Culture National Historical Park

*David A. Phillips, Jr., Curator of Archaeology at the Maxwell Museum of Anthro-
pology, University of New Mexico, displays a Chaco bowl from the museum's
collection.* Photo by author.

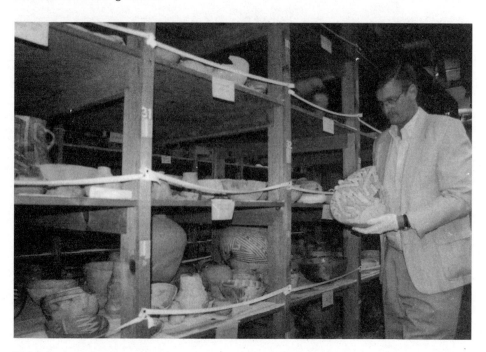

from the north has been redone. The old route entered the canyon from its western end and came past all the main sites. The new southbound route from off NM 44 near Nageezi, still mostly a gravel road but with a better surface, enters the eastern end of the developed part of the canyon, bringing the visitor first to the campground and National Park Service visitor center. The change provides for more control and reduces traffic past the major sites. One side benefit to the visitor of the new route that I appreciate is this: For miles while approaching Chaco, looming just beyond the end of the road to the south-southwest, is a magnificent view of Fajada Butte, a visual centerpiece of Chaco Canyon, drawing the eye toward it. The old route provided no such visual anticipation. Given the newfound appreciation of the Chacoans' sense of landscaping, especially the attention they gave to designing the approaches toward their major works of architecture (see next chapter), I find this wonderfully appropriate.

13. The Quest Continues

In an informal interview in his cramped second-floor office above the Maxwell Museum and the Department of Anthropology on the University of New Mexico campus in Albuquerque, Tom Windes leans back and elaborates on some of the points he and other archaeologists emphasized at the Pecos Conference in Chaco. It's a midwinter afternoon in January 1998, and Windes is between two of his frequent visits to Chaco—a 165-mile, three-hour drive to the northeast.

"Project focus-stuff isn't going on in the park, except for me—I think I'm the only one still working on the project level, actual field collection of data, in and around the park." He says he tries to resist talking too much about theory, the big picture, the meaning of it all. "In some ways I look at myself as sort of the inside guy," a researcher gathering data and looking at the small details. That's where Windes seeks the meaning. "I see myself as sort of the foundation builder. It's pretty hard to do all levels, and I'd rather work down at this level. We have a number of different players operating in different spheres."

There are a few exceptions. He looks up at a photo on his wall provided by colleague John Stein of a Chacoan outlier site far outside the boundaries of the national monument.

"Stein is still doing considerable work on the outlying communities. We're still doing work together."

Stein's photo is of the Navajo Springs Great House. Stein is working at

the site with Richard Friedman of McKinley County. The Navajo Springs
Great House, Windes tells me, is in Arizona 40 miles west of Gallup, New
Mexico, between Chambers and Navajo, Arizona. "It's right along the
interstate [I-40]," Windes says. "You can see it. When you drive down
the interstate, if you know where to look, about two miles off the highway."

He glances again at the photo. "Massive! I've worked at this site for two
years and it was the first time I've noticed—and now I've seen it at three
other places—where the small-site community around the great house is literally laid out in avenues, dual avenues like you might see in a street
in a major American city. Bang. Bang. Bang. Bang. Parallel avenues and
parallel rows of houses just *stuffed* against one another. There's an incredible amount of archaeology associated with these things. I've never seen
that before."

"And this is Chacoan?" I want reassurances.

"Oh, absolutely. Same era. Early 900s when they built the first houses.
In the 900s just like the rest of them.

"I've seen that also at Newcomb, where I've been working. And Skunk

The Chacoan Newcomb community at Newcomb, New Mexico, where there is
"solid archaeology" for 1.6 miles laid out in double avenues. From Windes and
Anderson, 1998.

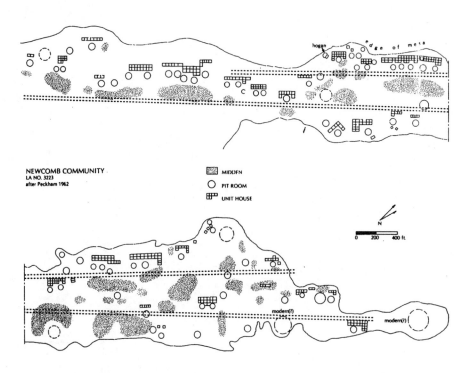

NEWCOMB COMMUNITY
LA NO. 3223
after Peckham 1962

▨ MIDDEN

○ PIT ROOM

⊞ UNIT HOUSE

N
0   200   400 ft.

Springs. To give you an idea of scale on some of these things, Newcomb not only is set out on a double avenue, with a house or something every twenty feet. Bang, bang, bang. It runs for one-point-six miles, and it's *solid* archaeology. There's not a single break that I know of. It's just mind-staggering."

(All three of these sites in the extended Chacoan region, Windes says, are more densely settled than any of the areas in Chaco Canyon. Navajo Springs is about 110 miles southwest of Chaco, as the eagle flies, and Skunk Springs and Newcomb, both near the present town of Newcomb, New Mexico, are about 50 miles west-northwest of Chaco.)

Wasn't this obvious earlier?

Windes says the site itself was long known. Earl Morris, who excavated Aztec ruin and other outliers early in the twentieth century (see Chapter 7, pages 130–31), explored the site, and there were rumors he took out numerous burials.

"I think Stein has known this avenue kind of thing, but you really have

The densely settled Skunk Springs Chacoan community near Newcomb also features parallel avenues. The same is true for Navajo Springs in northeastern Arizona. From Windes and Anderson, 1998.

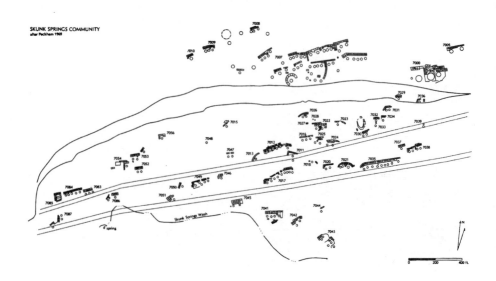

SKUNK SPRINGS COMMUNITY
after Peckham 1969

to spend some days and hours working up there before it comes to you, even though it'd be obvious once someone tells you. It's not so obvious unless you are spending time there. With me anyway, sometimes the most obvious thing can get by you, for decades actually. Unless you're really thinking along those lines. Which is what Stein started doing."

Windes says another far-flung site he now thinks is Chacoan is Lower White House in Canyon de Chelly, out in the middle of the Navajo Reservation in northeastern Arizona. He says Lower White House has the distinctive Chaco masonry, size, and architecture. The doorway lintels are uniform in size, length, and spacing like those at Chaco. "I think that it's Chacoan," he says.

I wanted to find out more about Windes's remarkable Chaco wood-dating project. (In the discussion at the Pecos Conference, one of the archaeologists had characterized Windes' dating project as "tremendous." Noted this discussant: "A lot of things [misinterpretations] are possible in the absence of solid data.")

Windes began with a tribute to the role of amateurs and volunteers in archaeology. He is absolutely dependent on them.

"Every year I have groups of Sierra Club folks come in here for ten days back to back, so I essentially run twenty straight days. I run anywhere from fifteen to thirty people. And it's cool. Because I couldn't possibly do it by myself. They do everything. Wood [helping take wood samples for the tree-ring dating], survey, mapping, backfilling, collecting ceramics. They're incredible. Without them I wouldn't have anything." These and other folks—some who have become quite experienced—take their vacations to help at his archaeology sites. "So those are my pool of volunteers. I don't think you could do archaeology without them."

This volunteer work is all the more necessary because beyond his own salary Windes has no National Park Service money for this work. "I have no budget. Never have. Everything I do, I scrounge for. But I'm not fighting for a diminishing pie each year—I can't operate that way. I raise my own money." Much of it has come from the Southwest Parks and Monuments Association and Maxwell Museum–sponsored tours.

When tree-ring dating was developed in the early 1920s (see Chapter 3), it proved a bonanza for southwestern archaeologists. Finally, they had a way to determine the date—the exact year—that a tree used for a roof beam had been cut down. Neil Judd quickly applied the technique to dating the major beams in Pueblo Bonito.

"When the tree-ring business started with a flurry back in the twenties, archaeologists kind of went nuts," Windes said. "It was like a land rush out there. In the early forties they went to the biggest beams because those were the ones most likely to date. They had the most rings. And frankly that's been about it. Almost nobody has done a systematic wood analysis since then—until the Tree-Ring Lab did one recently at Mesa Verde.

"What I have found is that big beams have high value and are most likely to get moved around and reused and therefore give erroneous dates. Some of those dates out of Chaco are unbelievable. We thought they were 900s occupation. That's dead wrong."

By dating the smaller pieces of wood used in lintels and latillas, Windes and his colleagues have recently been able to show that beams (vigas) used in the roofs consistently date four, five, or even six years older than the smaller pieces. (Windes and his colleagues take the core samples from the wood and analyze all the results. The actual dating is done at the Laboratory for Tree-Ring Research at the University of Arizona.)

Windes believes the Chacoans cut down many trees at once and let them cure (dry) at their location for several years before transporting them to Chaco for use as beams. The dryer, cured trees would be lighter and easier to carry. Smaller pieces of wood wouldn't have presented that same problem.

"I've got enough dates out of Bonito and Aztec to find that they must have been curing the big beams," he says. "They were stockpiling. Curing. Planning ahead.

"They cure those big guys. They have to carry them fifty miles. You're talking some weight there.

"I have five hundred dates from [Pueblo] del Arroyo all from the same brief period—A.D. 1101–1104. I don't think they were construction dates. They're harvesting the trees. After the last one is cut, they bring them in. Sometime after."

It is extraordinary the kind of detailed information it is possible to get by dating most everything.

"You take one of those rooms in Bonito or Aztec," says Windes. "The potential for the number of tree-ring dates, the number of trees that you can deal with, is literally around one hundred. In the past they'd sample at most one or two of the primaries in that room. So by any level, the sample is bad, two out of a potential hundred. That's not a very good shot."

"I've found some amazing things in these rooms when you do all of them. You see secondary doors going in, you see wood being moved around, you see repairs going on, you see choices of [wood] species being changed. You can learn a lot of history when you do a hundred of them.

"I've been trying to get people fired up about this. It's frightening. Nobody gave a damn about the wood. They didn't care." He said the emphasis used to be on the masonry and keeping the buildings stabilized.

"But the wood contains the data. The old philosophy at Chaco was, we already have enough dates. That was back in the forties."

It's not too hard to understand why more of the wood wasn't core-sampled and dated in those decades. The drilling to get the core samples had to be done by hand. It was hard work. "They were doing dates [core sampling] by hand. So you can be darn sure you're going to do beams that you can get dates from. That's the way it was up until the sixties. When you do it by hand, they were talking about their arms falling off."

What changed to make Windes's Chaco Wood Project possible was the advent of battery-operated drills. "With battery-operated drills it's much easier and I can go anywhere," Windes says. "I've got dozens of them. They have some torque to them." He also has portable generators to run them. Or battery-driven drills can be recharged off of car batteries.

"Only in the past twenty years has this been possible."

Have all these new dates changed any major conceptions?
"Oh, a lot of things," Windes says.
In 1996 Windes and Dabney Ford of Chaco Culture National Historical Park published a detailed paper in *American Antiquity* outlining a chrono-

Dabney Ford of Chaco Culture National Historical Park has collaborated with Tom Windes on the epic Chaco Wood Project and other studies.

metric reappraisal of Pueblo Bonito resulting from the Chaco Wood Project. Their results, based on inventory and analysis of 4,294 pieces of wood in Pueblo Bonito, reveal, as they say, "a fascinating history in the procurement, use, and reuse of wood through time."

Steve Lekson had derived the first refined schematic of construction at Bonito with 133 dates from 218 samples collected between 1895 and 1976 (see Chapter 9). Windes's Chaco Wood Project took 1,454 new samples from Pueblo Bonito since 1986, producing 390 new tree-ring dates. "The latest sample adds considerable refinement to Lekson's excellent work," Windes and Ford say in their paper.

A number of new interpretations have come from the new dates at Pueblo Bonito. For one thing, Bonito was started much earlier than had been thought. The new samples, Windes and Ford report, indicate that the earliest room construction at Pueblo Bonito occurred in the A.D. 850s or mid-860s, not in the A.D. 900s.

Another finding—this one even more surprising—is that major building events in great houses correlate with near-decade-long wet periods. Comparisons based on earlier data had indicated that these building events

The Chaco Wood Project's extensive new tree-ring dates have revealed that Pueblo Bonito was started much earlier than had been thought. Sections along the northern and northwestern part of Bonito (solid dark lines) were built in the A.D. 800s. From Windes and Ford, 1996.

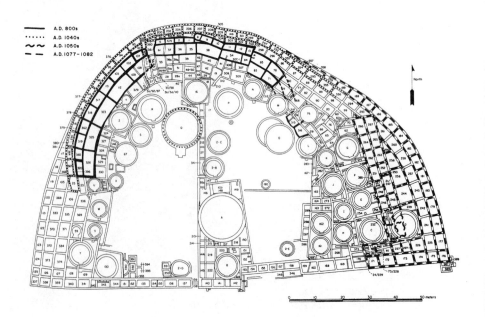

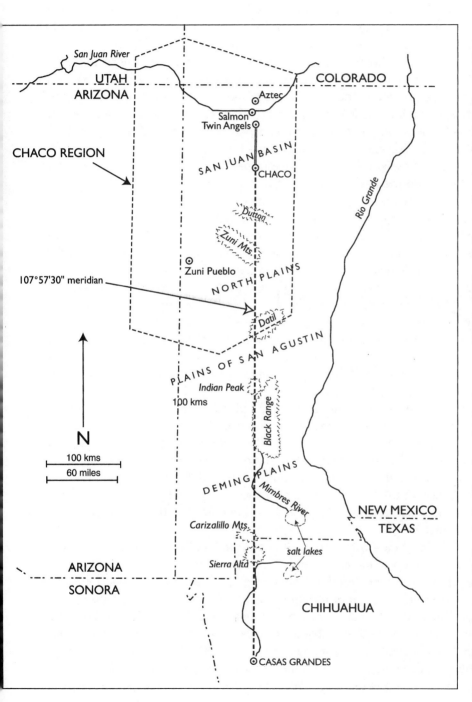

Chart of yearly precipitation in the San Juan basin from A.D. 902 to 1130 and times of major construction at Chaco Canyon shows that (except for the A.D. 1140s) decade-long wet periods are correlated with some construction episodes at Chacoan great houses. From Windes and Ford, 1996.

235

occurred during dry periods. The close correlation with wet periods starts with the very earliest construction, with the heart of Pueblo Bonito rising in the late 850s and very early 860s. The longest, wettest period during that entire century was from A.D. 850 to 864. Construction also took place at Una Vida and Peñasco Blanco during this same period.

The pattern holds throughout most of the period. Another example is a period of widespread building at Bonito between A.D. 1077 and 1081. During the decade preceding the start of this period, every year had seen above-normal precipitation. Windes and Ford suggest that the abundant precipitation led to food surpluses that encouraged building activities, including probably the construction of storerooms for food.

Here's how Windes and Ford summarize the major new interpretations resulting from the new tree-ring dates at Bonito:

"The initial construction of the site can be pushed back into the mid-ninth century; the work helps identify the earliest construction units as well as others during the site's major periods of use. The dramatic shifts in wood species mark the spread of procurement activities from local (in the immediate vicinity of Chaco Canyon or within about 20 or 30 km) to distant resources, with increasingly greater uniformity of wood selection through time. Most important, the data on wood use in conjunction with climatic reconstructions suggest that all but one of the major construction events were linked to periods of wetter than normal conditions."

After completing his massive Chaco wood project—documenting every piece of wood in Chaco Culture National Historical Park (9,400 pieces) and Aztec Ruins National Monument (8,700 pieces), and dating 3,000 of them—Tom Windes still wasn't done with wood. He next turned his attention to a series of even larger questions about the wood the Chacoans used to construct their massive buildings: Where did they get it? How did they cut the trees and finish the wood? What kinds of tools did they likely use? How did they transport the timbers? How much work was really involved—and how might the work have been organized—to accomplish this seemingly extraordinary task?

Windes joined with former Chaco Project colleague Peter McKenna, of the U.S. Bureau of Indian Affairs in Albuquerque, to consider the harvesting and use of structural wood in Chacoan great houses—scheduling, procurement, planning, and labor requirements. I think this topic is intrinsically interesting, but it is also a way to help better understand the Chacoan culture. As they say in their subsequent report on wood production in Chacoan society, published in *American Antiquity* in 2001, "Structural wood provides another approach to view the Chacoan social effort."

Ponderosa pines, spruces, and firs were the dominant species harvested.

As for where the timber came from, they note that "logistics, species, and oral history" suggest that the "downtown" Chaco sites received their timbers primarily from a limited number of sources in the Chuska Mountains 80 kilometers (50 miles) to the west near the New Mexico/Arizona border. "The mix of tree species found in the downtown sites in the A.D. 1000s closely matches present species within the Chuskas, specifically near the Chacoan great-house community of Skunk Springs, near Newcomb, New Mexico." Also Windes reports that ancient stone axes and ax heads have been found in abundance in the Chuskas near the most promising areas for wood harvesting.

I can't help pointing out that this means the linear, parallel-avenue Chacoan community sites of Newcomb and nearby Skunk Springs that Tom Windes was so excited about when we talked in his office apparently had far more importance to Chacoan life than their remoteness would indicate.

There's even some oral history about this. "In 1928, an era when there was little discussion among archaeologists about prehistoric roads, Navajos identified a road leading out of the Skunk Springs great house for transporting timbers to Pueblo Bonito," say Windes and McKenna, referencing an earlier report by Harold Gladwin. Gladwin did important archaeological work throughout the Southwest in the 1930s and 1940s. "This is," they say, "an oral history that certainly may have prehistoric roots."

As for the quantities of timber needed, the numbers seem staggering: "No matter how it is calculated," say Windes and McKenna, "tens of thousands of trees were procured for construction in Chaco Canyon. [Jeffrey] Dean and [R. L.] Warren estimated over 200,000 trees utilized for the great houses within Chaco Canyon, including 26,000 for Chetro Ketl, 50,000 for Pueblo Bonito, and 18,000 for Pueblo del Arroyo."

One tree might provide several wood elements needed for construction at Chaco. The biggest were the large, strong primary roof supports (vigas). These "primaries" were also stacked in an inward-progressive fashion to create the domes of the circular kivas, with the entire unit resting upon masonry and log pillars (pilasters). Other elements include the smaller-diameter wood poles (secondaries, or *latillas*) that are placed across the vigas, lintels used at the top of doors and windows (although stone was frequently substituted), sill rods at the bottom of window openings, platform poles, balcony polls, wall plate poles, shelf poles, wainscotting posts, and so on.

The vigas used in the great houses were about 9 inches in diameter and 10 to 15 feet long. Windes and McKenna estimate that at least two or three vigas could have been cut from the same tall tree. Indeed they say there's good evidence that multiple specimens were in fact cut from the same tree. They say most roof secondaries (the *latillas*) came from individual trees, usually juniper. Lintels came from saplings cut into individual pieces.

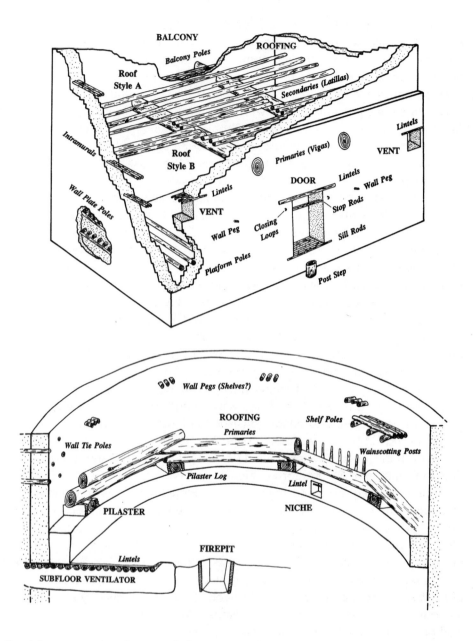

Great house construction wood element terminology. From Windes and McKenna, 2001.

As for *when* during the year, the tree-ring evidence shows that the majority of trees was cut down in the spring or early summer. (This is in contrast to many prehistoric puebloans, where summer or early fall harvesting seems more common.) The evidence also indicates that after about A.D. 1070—when construction in Chaco accelerated—tree cutting was carried out each spring/early summer for about four to five years, the wood was stockpiled, and then construction started during or after the last cutting episode.

Choppers, large hafted and unhafted cobble axes, small hand axes of petrified wood, and serrated saw axes, some made of chert found in the Chuskas, were among the tools apparently used. To cut down a single tree for roof vigas with a stone ax took about thirty minutes. The Chacoan loggers trimmed away the limbs (this might take five to fifteen minutes with a sharp stone ax) and then debarked the log almost immediately after cutting. This they apparently did very carefully, as no marks of bark removal have been found on timbers used at Chaco. (In contrast, at Mesa Verde National Park, where these later ruins were examined, 12 percent of ninety-five timbers sampled had ax marks from bark removal.) Windes and McKenna say the Chacoans could have used a tool like the European "bark spud," made of stone or hard wood, to remove bark shortly after cutting without leaving marks. It is similar to a spoon with a long handle, and the user "pops off" the bark, making it easy to peel.

The Chacoan loggers/craftsmen finished—carefully squared off—the ends of the logs. This too they did in the field, shortly after cutting—it would have been much more difficult once the wood had dried—and it is one of the more remarkable aspects of this whole process. When cutting down the tree, the Chacoan loggers would cut it until they could push it over, and this left a ragged projection much like a beaver's tail. At non-Chacoan sites, end finishing is rare, but for the Chacoan great houses, the crews whittled down the ragged ends of the beams until they were flat. Windes and McKenna say this must have been an intensive, time-consuming process. They note that many Chacoan beams reveal an incised groove around the circumference adjacent to the whittled end, perhaps to guide the whittling effort. The beams were apparently wrapped near their ends to prevent damage from errant strokes. Occasionally the ends could be ground flat, but, generally, except for totally dry wood, grinding the ends off is impractical because of the tree sap.

Why did they go to all this trouble? Flattened ends appear rarely in historic puebloan architecture, although they have been noted at some Hopi and Zuni sites. Windes and McKenna suggest that although there were some practical advantages, the major reason may have been aesthetic.

What Windes and McKenna call "the most intriguing aspect" of Chacoan wood production was the prefabrication of lintels used for the doors and ventilators. In Chaco Canyon and at Aztec to the north, yucca ties

BEAM END CONFIGURATION

PROBABLE TOOL TYPES USED

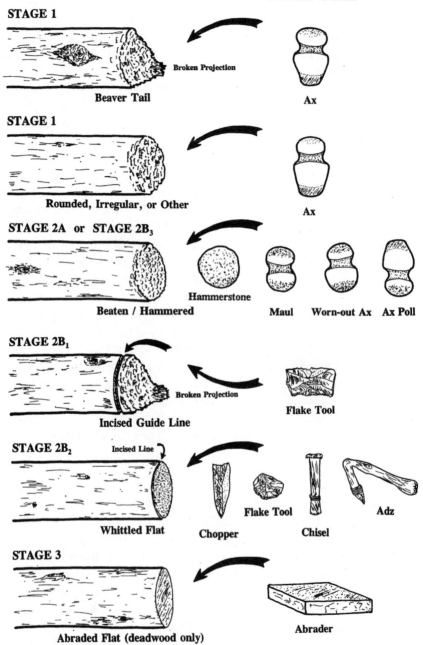

STAGE 1

Broken Projection

Beaver Tail

Ax

STAGE 1

Rounded, Irregular, or Other

Ax

STAGE 2A or STAGE 2B₃

Hammerstone

Beaten / Hammered

Maul   Worn-out Ax   Ax Poll

STAGE 2B₁

Broken Projection

Incised Guide Line

Flake Tool

STAGE 2B₂

Incised Line

Whittled Flat   Chopper

Flake Tool

Chisel

Adz

STAGE 3

Abraded Flat (deadwood only)

Abrader

Beam-end treatment types and the probable tools Chacoans used to create them. From Windes and McKenna, 2001.

bound the lintel elements together. These were preassembled before placement so that that the entire set could be placed in the wall at once. The two
archaeologists say this technique is not immediately evident because typically the ties were covered by mortar and masonry. The yucca used for
binding strips was not local to Chaco, and this suggests that the sets were
assembled in the harvest area and carried to Chaco.

What were the labor costs of all this? Some of their analysis is based on
experimental stone-ax cutting of ponderosa pine conducted by Kristine
Kunkel for her 1998 master's thesis, "Timber Harvesting Using Ground Stone
Axes," at Eastern New Mexico University. Her studies, and some earlier ones,
provide the figures I gave earlier of thirty minutes for cutting down a big tree
for primary beams and ten minutes for felling a smaller tree for secondaries.
Kunkel's work suggests that delimbing, debarking, and end finishing may
have taken seven times more effort than felling and topping the trees. The
biggest effort was the flattening of ends that I have described. Windes and
McKenna note that most construction projects were carried out over a number of years. This spread out the costs and reduced the impact on the people
involved. "These [facts] suggest that the efforts were not an extraordinary
commitment to those involved, although they were certainly not small-scale
projects."

When we look at the great houses in Chaco Canyon and contemplate
what was needed to construct them, the amount of work does "seem truly
astounding," Windes and McKenna note, but that may be an understandable
misperception. We're seeing the results of several centuries' worth of work
all at once. In his 1986 analysis of the total labor investment to build Chacoan great houses, which I describe in Chapter 9, Steve Lekson notes that
relatively small groups of workers—over periods of years—could have
accomplished the tasks required; the labor requirement was considerable but
not overwhelming or incomprehensible.

"Likewise," says Windes and McKenna, "our examination of one aspect
of that construction, wood production, could have been accomplished by
sustained efforts by small work groups." Windes and McKenna envisioned a
hypothetical crew of ten working ten-hour days, and based their analyses on
that—just to keep the examples simple. Windes tells me he wasn't suggesting the crews were actually that size. Of course, bigger crews could accomplish a given task in less time.

Let's take an example I culled from some of their published data: The
trees cut in the fall of A.D. 1100 and the late springs and early summers of
A.D. 1101–1104 were used for construction at Pueblo del Arroyo that began
in 1104 and lasted until about 1109. Two hundred fourteen rooms were built
during that phase. Here were the wood requirements: 561 vigas, 8,283 *latillas,* and 327 lintel sets (reflecting the actual numbers of doors and vents for

that construction phase). The estimated amount of labor required for harvesting and processing the trees into finished beams, adjusted for frequency of whittled-end beams at the site, totaled 8,658 hours. This means that a ten-man crew needed to work 86.6 days to accomplish that much work—a little less than three months—a completely possible scenario.

Given the heavy labor requirements and their traditional work with wood, it seems most likely that men did the tree cutting, preparation, and transport of the wood, Women, drawing on their skills in basketry, may have prepared the lintel sets.

Where did the workers live? Archaeologists used to assume the crews came out to the distant forests from Chaco. Windes and McKenna have another suggestion, which to me seems increasingly likely given the size of the community at Skunk Springs, in the Chuskas. More than likely, they say, the loggers and skilled craftsmen who procured the wood for Chaco did live at the base of the Chuskas, near the mountain forests. "If the labor force that procured the wood for great houses in downtown Chaco Canyon lived along the Chuskas, then many of the logistical problems for a similar force inhabiting the canyon would be greatly reduced."

They probably also served as caretakers of the dressed beams during the several years the beams were left to dry out before being transported to Chaco, 45 to 50 miles distant. In Windes and McKenna's view, also suggested by the noted British archaeologist Colin Refrew who took part in one of the Chaco synthesis conferences, the people did the timber work and brought the finished beams and other wood to Chaco Canyon as part of their periodic visits to Chaco, a place, to use Renfrew's phrase, of "high devotional expression."

(The transport distances were greater than Lekson had earlier estimated in his 1984 study. At that time, he assumed the source of timber would be an area to the south of Chaco called Lobo Mesa, beyond the Kin Ya'a Chacoan outlier. The distance from Pueblo Bonito to those stands of ponderosa pine, along the South Road, was 29 miles. But if a preponderance of the wood came from the Chuskas, about 50 miles distant, travel time would be increased proportionately.)

To estimate labor needed to transport that much wood to Chaco, the archaeologists figured two men could carry one viga, one man could carry six *latillas*—Windes says these would be full-length *latilla* poles, even though sometimes *latillas* were made shorter—and one person could carry four lintel sets. For that extensive multiyear effort to construct 214 rooms at Pueblo del Arroyo, they estimate all the wood could have been transported to Chaco from the Chuskas in 2,585 person-trips. A hundred people could transport all of it in about twenty-five trips.

Moving the huge posts for great kivas clearly involved "extraordinary efforts," they say. But they refer to numerous accounts in past history and modern times (Nepali porters in the Himalayas, South American log races, Mexican Tarahumaras, and historic puebloan people) moving heavy loads great distances, sometimes in rugged terrain. This, they say, indicates the effort was "not only possible, but relatively commonplace by non-Western standards."

"Labor costs for beam preparation, transport, and management of the harvest and construction sites were considerably greater than with other non-Chacoan construction but do not appear to be beyond the means of relatively small task group(s) given time and the probable cyclical nature of work and work groups," they say. "Given the consistent high level of finishing work and the timbering, transport, distribution and emplacement of wood elements, these work groups may well have been an established formal society within Chacoan culture, charged with the provisioning of construction timber from its cut to its placement."

Beyond that, how it was all organized we don't really know. This is part of the larger question of how Chaco society itself was organized. Chaco experts and outside scholars still hotly debate different aspects of this question. I'll discuss those theories in the final chapter.

In 2001, a group of scientists, using strontium isotope ratios, produced solid scientific evidence confirming that many of the trees used for the Chacoan great houses came from the Chuska Mountains to the west. Their evidence also showed that some other of the trees came from the slopes of Mount Taylor (at 13,301 feet the only dominant peak of the San Mateo Mountains), a similar or even greater distance south-southeast of Chaco. The study found that none came from another possible site a similar distance to the east of Chaco, the San Pedro Mountains, northeast of present-day Cuba, New Mexico. A wire-service news report claimed that this study "solved the mystery" of where the Chaco great-house timbers came from, but what it really did was just put our knowledge about the source of many of the trees on some solid scientific footing. The picture is not yet complete because the study did not sample the Zuni Mountains to the south-southwest of Chaco or any of the areas to the north in southwestern Colorado. Future studies will probably do those tests.

It turns out that the element strontium, which exists in local dust, water, and underlying bedrock, is incorporated into trees and that the ratio of the isotopes strontium-87 to strontium-86 in the trees is specific to the place where they are growing, making it a valid marker.

Nathan English from the School of Renewable Natural Resources, Jeffrey Dean from the Laboratory of Tree-Ring Research, and Jay Quade of the Department of Geosciences, all at the University of Arizona, and one researcher, Julio Betancourt, from the U.S. Geological Survey's Desert Laboratory in Tucson, carried out the testing, sponsored by the National Park Service and the Navajo Nation. In 2000 and 2001 the researchers measured the strontium isotopic ratios of bedrock, soil, and stream water and (via core samples they took) from spruce and fir growing at a variety of potential Chacoan logging sites in the San Juan basin. The strontium ratios were different and quite distinct for the San Pedro, Chuska, and San Mateo mountain ranges. They then obtained samples of wood from six of the twelve Chaco Canyon great houses—Pueblo Bonito, Chetro Ketl, Pueblo del Arroyo, Wijiji, Hungo Pavi, and Una Vida—and measured the strontium ratios in them. These dated samples were in the collections of the Laboratory of Tree-Ring Research. To give considerable time span to the study, the researchers tested wood samples cut over at least three human generations at each great house, from A.D. 970 to 1100.

The results were clear. The wood from the Chacoan great houses had isotopic ratios nearly identical to those at either the Chuska mountain sites (about two-thirds of the Chaco timbers they sampled) or the Mount Taylor site (the remaining third). None matched the ratios at the San Pedro Mountains site. The authors note that the crests of the Chuska and San Mateo mountains "would have been ideal sites for logging a great variety of conifer species and size classes."

The abundant Chacoan-related communities in these two areas—and the absence of any to the east in the San Pedro Mountains—may also be relevant. "There are huge communities at the base of these mountains," Betancourt told *Albuquerque Journal* science reporter John Fleck, echoing what Tom Windes had emphasized to me when we talked in his office. Betancourt speculated that resident planners in Chaco Canyon made elaborate architectural plans and then sent word out to the lumber towns in the foothills. "They were probably filling out orders," Betancourt said.

The authors put it a little more formally in their scientific paper: "Timber sources may have been determined by pre-existing sociopolitical ties between Chaco Canyon and outlying communities at the base of the Chuska and San Mateo mountains. . . . Alternatively, pre-existing ties to specific resources may have influenced the placement of certain outlying communities and the destinations of major Chacoan roads, putting a permanent stamp on the configuration, direction of growth, and extent of the Chacoan regional system. Chacoan outliers within a few hours' walk of the San Mateo or Chuska mountain forests were well positioned to regularly harvest, cure, and stockpile timbers."

All this, they say, "reflects the Chacoans' ability to organize large intercommunity labor forces to extract timbers from distant mountains or to motivate the inhabitants of the resource areas to acquire timbers for use in Chaco Canyon."

A newer study involving the chemical compositions of trees has since been completed by other investigators, confirming and expanding on the results of Nathan English and colleagues.

The project began with publication in 1999 of a feasibility study about

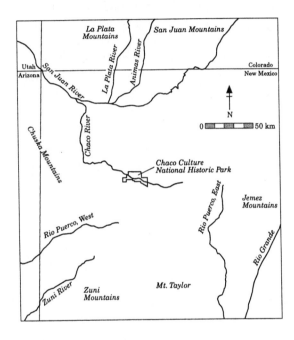

Northwest New Mexico showing the forested mountain ranges and the rivers that ring Chaco Canyon and the San Juan basin.
From Durand, et al., 1999.

the method by Stephen Durand of the Department of Anthropology and Applied Archaeology at Eastern New Mexico University, ENMU colleague Philip Shelley, and Ronald Antweiler and Howard Taylor of the U.S. Geological Survey in Boulder, Colorado. That paper was called "Trees, Chemistry, and Prehistory in the American Southwest." The Durand group's study technique samples the whole suite of chemical elements present in the wood. They used modern instrumentation (plasma atomic emission spectrometry and plasma mass spectrometry) to obtain element concentration values for twenty-nine major and minor chemical elements (barium, calcium, potassium, sodium, sulfur, nickel, and silica, to name just a few), from sixty-two trees on three bedrock types around the San Juan basin, Their analyses found that the main variation in the pattern of chemical elements was due to the bedrock—the substrate of rocks and soil where the trees were growing. They sampled substrates in three different canyons on the slopes of Mount

Taylor, three in the Chuska Mountains, and so on. Later they did the same kinds of chemical analyses on some samples of ancient wood from Chaco Canyon. They concluded, "Given the right problem and a sufficiently large sample, we feel that it is possible to determine the area(s) of prehistoric wood procurement." The method, they said, "should be broadly applicable for determining wood source areas [of Chacoan timbers]."

Since then they have done just that. The new Durand study focuses on ponderosa pine, which accounted for half of all the 200,000 estimated trees used in construction at Chaco Canyon. And the results, Durand told me in 2004, indicate that the majority of the ponderosa construction timbers (just as with the higher-elevation fir and spruce timbers studied by English, et al.) "came from the Chuska Mountains to the west and the San Mateo Mountains [Mount Taylor area] to the southeast of Chaco Canyon." He told me the study also eliminates the Lobo Mesa area directly south of Chaco as a source of the ponderosa timbers. Durand and his colleagues were writing a paper summarizing their results for submittal to a scientific journal. I find it interesting how there seems almost no end to the insights modern geo-chemistry can give archaeologists in unraveling some of the ancient secrets of Chaco.

Perspectives on the roads in the Chacoan system have changed in recent years to de-emphasize their importance as exclusively transportation corridors. They are now seen to have had multiple purposes, including travel, cosmographic expression, and as public construction projects that served to advance social integration and cohesion.

When I talked to Tom Windes in his office, he said Chaco archaeologist John Stein has been leading the new emphasis on what might be called the Chacoans' landscaping of the areas leading up to the great houses and mon-uments. Stein has shown that Chacoans spent considerable effort preparing landscapes prior to the construction of buildings. "Stein has started going to great lengths to try to tune into and learn about the landscaping, the manip-ulation of the earthworks around the great house, the creation of the avenues and approaches, the view of the traveler coming into these things."

Windes calls this the intentional creation of an "aura of magnificence. It's the same thing you might see at the Eiffel Tower. That kind of thinking."

He said John Roney of the Bureau of Land Management has been lead-ing the new take on the prehistoric road system.

Our view of the roads in the 1980s, as Windes puts it, was that "they seemed to run everywhere. The perspective was they [the Chacoans] had an interstate highway system out there, just running everywhere. Every site was connected. And that still may be true, but what John is saying—both Johns here—is you're seeing this kind of Eiffel Tower complex. You see prehistoric roads that are thirty feet wide and so forth, but once you get out into the hinterlands, those kinds of things disappear. They are not real formalized kinds of avenues or roads that go all the way across the landscape. A few of those do exist. But you used to just connect the dots, and this created this maze of roads that resembled an interstate system.

"But really the formal expression is that as you approach the last half mile to the site—you see this time and time against at the great houses—you have nice avenues, prehistoric roads anyone can follow. Roney's brought us around to that. Approaches were really important. They were landscaped in. They were formalized."

This new view was published in papers by John Stein and Steve Lekson on Anasazi ritual landscapes and by John Roney on prehistoric roads and the regional integration in the Chacoan system. Since then, it has been embraced by most archaeologists of Chaco.

Stein and Lekson introduce the concept of "ritual landscape." Such landscape features, they say, are "created by human hands but inextricably tied, physically and cognitively, to a broader sacred geography that embraces the natural landscape."

They and others talk about architecture—and they mean both buildings and landscape architecture—as a form of nonverbal communication. Even Chacoan trash mounds show uniform shape, proportions, orientation, and location relative to the associated structure and suggest, they say, "that the feature is intrinsically architectural." They point to examples of the earthen component at six widely separated landscapes located at considerable distances from Pueblo Bonito (Kin Hocho'i, Navajo Springs, Allentown, Tse Chizzi, Kin Cheops, and Chambers). "Note the character of the space defined by the earthwork and the dramatic increase in the scale and formality of the architectural composition beyond the great house. The setting for the great house is both intensively and extensively sculpted. The earthen component is the tissue that integrates the individual elements of the architectural composition."

What Lekson has described, referring to Pueblo Bonito, as overengineered, overbuilt, or scaled-up, is typical of monumental structures in the Chacoan and Anasazi world.

Stein and Lekson say this kind of architecture is best explained "as the outwardly visible manifestation of a shared ideational system (ritual)—one of several, and perhaps the most important, 'glues' that bound together a diverse Anasazi world in Chacoan times."

In his 1992 paper, Roney argues that the prehistoric roads "were not constructed in order to facilitate transportation and communication," that "the prevailing notions of the interconnectivity of the Chacoan road system are somewhat exaggerated," and that "their major cultural importance is the role that the activity of their construction played in reinforcing social organization." He points out that the North Road and the South Road are regional in scale and are clearly associated with the regional center at Chaco Canyon. However, he believes that it is entirely possible that many other Chacoan roads are purely local phenomena.

"The meaning the roads had for their makers, their precise emic function, is probably unknowable," says Roney. "They might have formalized preexisting routes of transportation and communication, but it is equally plausible that they were raceways, avenues for ceremonial processions, or even cosmographic expressions. I doubt that we can ever hope for more than plausible interpretations of this sort."

The important point, he says, is that the roads represent a "significant labor investment for nonutilitarian purposes related to social organization." The same thing, he says, is expressed in the stone carvings of Easter Island, the ziggurats of Babylon, the pyramids of Mesoamerica, and the megalithic monuments of Europe. The particular form they take and their explanations, he argues, are idiosyncratic. "Their importance is not their form and emic interpretation, but rather the role that the labor activity itself and the organization of the labor plays in reinforcing social cohesion and enhancing social unity.

"In the broader context of Southwestern prehistory," concludes Roney, "construction of the Bonito-style buildings and their associated features, including the prehistoric roads, represents an increasing labor investment in social organization, an intensifying emphasis upon the local and regional social networks that undoubtedly played a central role in the Anasazi adaptation to the Colorado plateau. We recognize the regional material correlates of this intensification as the 'Chaco Phenomenon.' "

Starting with the earliest archaeological expeditions to Chaco in the late 1800s, Pueblo Bonito has long been seen as the largest, most complex, and most magnificent "ruin" in the canyon. In his research in the 1920s sponsored by the National Geographic Society, Neil Judd spent seven consecutive seasons excavating at Pueblo Bonito (see Chapter 2). The Smithsonian Institution published his two volumes of reports on that important work, including his classic *The Material Culture of Pueblo Bonito*. (That didn't happen, however, until 1954, because Judd had to wait until he retired from the Smithsonian to write it. As I have earlier noted, in those times, especially, archaeology publication often proceeded at a stately pace.) The Chacoan pottery motifs used as chapter headings in my book are from the Judd volume.

In 2003, the Smithsonian Institution (specifically Smithsonian Books) published another volume about Pueblo Bonito, this one intended to sum up and reevaluate all that had been learned about the massive structure in the past century. It does that very well, and it validates and reemphasizes the centrality of Pueblo Bonito to the Chacoan world.

In fact it is called *Pueblo Bonito: Center of the Chacoan World*. Archaeologist Jill E. Neitzel, editor of the volume, says she got the idea for the book in 1995 when she realized that the following year was the one hundredth anniversary of the first full-scale excavations at Pueblo Bonito. Neitzel is a lecturer in the Department of Anthropology at the University of Delaware and author or editor of several earlier books about southwestern archaeology, including *Great Towns and Regional Politics in the Prehistoric American Southwest and Southeast.*

Neitzel says she originally thought she'd write the book herself but then realized the scope made that impractical. So she invited a number of Chacoan researchers and other scholars—Tom Windes, John Stein, Dabney Ford, Richard Friedman, Wendy Bustard, Nancy Akins, Frances Joan Mathien, Anne Lawrason Marshall, and James Farmer—to contribute chapters. She wrote three chapters herself, including the opening one titled "Three Questions about Pueblo Bonito" and the final one on organization, function, and population at Pueblo Bonito.

"It is the combination of all the individual chapters that creates an image of Pueblo Bonito as the powerful center of the Chacoan world," she says. "Furthermore, this combined research provides clear, redundant evidence that the society the inhabitants of Pueblo Bonito dominated was hierarchically organized."

Her point about hierarchy is one of continuing ardent controversy among Chaco researchers. I'll discuss that later but for now I want merely to give a sample of the more interesting and significant new developments and insights about Pueblo Bonito. Some reemphasize what we thought before; some modify or even negate aspects of our earlier understanding.

Neitzel, like so many others who have studied or explored Chaco, leaves no doubt about her awe about the Chacoan system in general and Pueblo Bonito specifically. She's unusually eloquent on this subject, and so I want to share with you some of her opening words:

"Approximately 1,000 years ago, there arose in the northern part of what is now the southwestern United States a place of unprecedented power. That place was Chaco Canyon, and at its center stood the structure known today as Pueblo Bonito. An enormous building, Pueblo Bonito rose four stories tall, held perhaps as many as 800 rooms, and encompassed almost three acres. Its occupants ruled not just the canyon in which they lived but also much of the surrounding region. Their power was political, economic, and perhaps most importantly, religious. It provided the unifying force for

New studies confirm that Pueblo Bonito, with its monumental scale, abundant blocked-in kivas, and evidence of elite occupants, exercised political, economic, and religious power and provided a unifying force over Chacoan society. Photo by Randy Montoya.

Chacoan society, one of the most complex societies ever to develop in the prehispanic Southwest. At its peak, Pueblo Bonito must have been a spectacular, awe-inspiring sight. Today, abandoned and in ruin, the structure continues to overwhelm all who see it."

One of the new studies at Pueblo Bonito published in Neitzel's book that I find particularly interesting is a cooperative project by John Stein, Dabney Ford, and Richard Friedman. They call it "Reconstructing Pueblo Bonito." They assembled a comprehensive plan view (overhead map) of the building, dismantled it into different construction periods, and modeled these

With as many as 800 rooms and walls four stories high in places, Pueblo Bonito was a massive symbol of Chacoan power. Photo by Randy Montoya.

periods in three dimensions. I've already sprinkled many references to Stein's prolific Chaco-related research throughout *People of Chaco*. Ford is an archaeologist with the Chaco Culture National Historical Park. I've described her work with Tom Windes on the Chaco Wood Project. Friedman is a computer and Geographic Information Services specialist and archaeologist who works closely with Stein.

These three researchers began by examining all previous maps (plan views) and cross-section views of Bonito from earlier research there. Such drawings are abundant, beginning with the first ones, prepared by Lt. James Simpson and the artist brothers Richard and Edward Kern during the very first visit by Americans to Chaco Canyon in 1849. (In Chapter 1, I show

Richard Kern's reconstruction of Pueblo Bonito. See page 33.) Stein and colleagues are complimentary about the work by Simpson and the Kerns, saying their mapping effort of Bonito and six other of the major ruins "was of very high quality." George Hubbard Pepper's work with the Hyde Exploring Expedition (see Chapter 1, page 38) from 1896 to 1899 and Neil Judd's work in the 1920s (see Chapter 2) also eventually resulted in publication of what Stein and colleagues call "exceptionally detailed" plan views and cross sections.

They then examine three popular visual reconstructions (artist's drawings) of Pueblo Bonito published over the years. These include the great western photographer William Henry Jackson's 1878 detailed drawing of a reconstructed Pueblo Bonito (Jackson's photographic plates were unfortunately ruined or we would have photos of Chaco from that time); Harvard architecture professor Kenneth Conant's reconstruction (actually four different views) prepared for Judd's National Geographic Society Expedition in the 1920s; and, most recently, artist Lloyd Townsend's aerial-view painting of a reconstructed Pueblo Bonito for the Reader's Digest Association 1986 book *Mysteries of the Ancient Americas*. (The current color brochure given out at the Visitors Center at Chaco Culture National Historical Park prominently features an illustration derived from the Townsend painting, but it includes digital revisions based on data furnished by Stein, Ford, and Friedman. The Townsend painting is also used, in black and white, on the cover of Neitzel's book.)

All these popular reconstructions have been influential. Stein and colleagues note the difficulties and compromises involved in making such drawings. The results, while visually dramatic, may not be entirely accurate. "Significant disparities exist . . . between popular reconstructions of Pueblo Bonito and the ground truth of the architectural remains," they say. All this they find quite natural, and they are sympathetic about it. "We note that an information gap often exists where, in the interest of science, an archaeologist is clear and insistent on details of archaeological interest but vague or noncommittal about details the artist needs in order to paint a picture."

The artist understandably has to find a way to fill in that gap. The drawings fulfill a larger purpose of dramatizing and giving a sense of the essence of Bonito as it may have appeared when the Chacoans were living in the canyon.

Stein and colleagues describe their approach to creating accurate three-dimensional reconstructions of how Pueblo Bonito appeared at different times as "reverse engineering." They first built actual three-dimensional models (mass concept models) out of Styrofoam. To do that they combined Judd's two-dimensional plans into one comprehensive plan; identified the boundaries and sequences of the primary construction episodes (based on tree-ring dates, masonry styles, and architectural relationships, most of that based on Lekson's work in the 1980s, the latest phase based on Windes's and Ford's more recent tree-ring-date analyses); dismantled the plan and filled in gaps; and modeled the construction episodes. They produced a separate model for each stage. They then took the models to Pueblo Bonito and checked all the relationships by direct observation. They also checked them against excavation notes and archival photos.

But that wasn't all. They next produced computer-generated models for each construction stage, making use of a Geographic Information System. This took a lot of time and effort, but Stein and colleagues say it was worth it to gain highly accurate spatial information useful for future research. They scanned and digitized Neal Judd's original published plans, then took a global positioning system (GPS) to Chaco and collected accurate position information from key references points at Pueblo Bonito. They then used that georeferencing data to translate Judd's published plan into real-world coordinates.

Their goal was to obtain standards of positional accuracy "equal to or better than the tolerances built into the structure by its original architect(s)." It wasn't easy. "This was no small challenge," say Stein, Ford, and Friedman, "considering that we were attempting to produce an as-built drawing of a large and complex building that was constructed of stone and adobe over a period of almost half a millennium, that was left open to the elements for another half millennium, and that has since been subjected to more than a century of treasure hunting, vandalism, 'scientific' excavation, park development, and preservation work."

But they feel they accomplished the task.

"We performed a number of tests for map accuracy, with the result that the maximum error in Pueblo Bonito proper was 0.5 meter." That's less than 20 inches. The areas around Pueblo Bonito itself may have introduced some additional small errors, but nothing to worry about. "Overall," they say, "a maximum position error of 1.0 meter (3%) in an area the length of three football fields is quite respectable and more than adequate for the purposes of this study."

Stein, Ford, and Friedman present a model of Pueblo Bonito that they say "differs in significant respects from popular reconstructions" and "is as accurate as we can make it given the time and quality of information available." In the Neitzel volume they present plan and perspective views of six different construction stages at Pueblo Bonito. For the actual timing of events they draw a lot on the analyses of dendrochronology dates by Steve Lekson in the 1980s and Tom Windes in the 1990s. (Windes also has a chapter in the Neitzel volume on the construction and abandonment of Pueblo Bonito, titled "This Old House.")

Their reconstruction view of Old Bonito (Stage I, A.D. 850–935) shows a much smaller, less dramatic semicircular-shaped structure than what we think of today as Pueblo Bonito. Stage II (A.D. 1040–1050) is when things really got interesting. It shows a massive new addition wrapped around Old Bonito's back wall. This new structure was one room deep, thirty-plus rooms in length, and up to four stories high. This was when the Chacoans introduced fully developed core-and-veneer masonry, providing strength for the additional stories and buttressing for the already aging walls of Old Bonito.

Stage III (A.D. 1050–1070) is when Pueblo Bonito's plan became very complex, The Chacoans built a growing labyrinth of foundation walls and numerous new kivas and great kivas. The authors say their Stage III generally agrees with reconstructions proposed earlier by Steve Lekson and by Windes and Ford but departs radically from Neal Judd's.

Stage IV (A.D. 1070–1115) involved major construction throughout Pueblo Bonito. The Chacoans razed the southern half of Old Bonito's east building and joined Old Bonito and the east block with new construction. They laid the northeast foundation complex, formalized the rectangular earthen mounds in front of Bonito, and completed the crescent shape of Bonito with additions on the east and west. They even razed one great kiva and constructed another. It all began with a major construction event dated A.D. 1077–1082 that the authors say is "possibly the single most ambitious undertaking in Pueblo Bonito's construction history." The Chacoans also built a northeast foundation complex consisting of low walls extending east

Perspective view of construction Stage IV (A.D. 1070–1115) of Pueblo Bonito proper, a period when Bonito underwent major expansion. Stein, Ford, and Friedman, 2003.

Friedman, Stein, Ford 2001

CONSTRUCTION STAGE IV
A.D. 1070 - 1115

PUEBLO BONITO
CONSTRUCTION STAGE IV
A.D. 1070 - 1115

Friedman, Stein, & Ford - 2001

Perspective view of construction Stage IV (A.D. 1070–1115) of all of Pueblo Bonito, including the northeast foundation complex. Stein, Ford, and Friedman, 2003.

from Pueblo Bonito either during this stage or in Stage V. Stein and colleagues follow Steve Lekson in interpreting the mounds in front of Bonito as architecture, not as trash dumps. "The 'mounds,' " they say, "are in fact paved platforms."

Stage V (A.D. 1115–1250) presents many puzzles. Between 1115 and 1130 the Chacoans remodeled two kivas, added some multiple-floor levels, and constructed Hillside Ruin immediately behind Pueblo Bonito. As Stein and colleagues say, there is no consensus among archaeologists about how long "downtown Chaco" remained in use after the last dated construction episodes in the early 1100s. And there is no consensus about the nature of its use. No newly cut, nonlocal timber was used after 1130. It's possible salvaged wood was used for some construction or remodeling after that period.

More interesting is evidence for the closure of Pueblo Bonito. They note, again drawing on Tom Windes's work, examples of intentional burning, erasure, burial, and concealment. This may suggest a period of "termination ritual." They suggest that closure of Pueblo Bonito might have been as early as 1130, "give or take a year or so," but say they are open to the possibility that it and other structures in downtown Chaco were used well into the thirteenth century and perhaps even the turn of the fourteenth.

Going back to the overall plan of Pueblo Bonito, Stein, Ford, and Friedman propose what I find to be one of their most startling conclusions—that the design may have been the work of one lone master Chacoan architect. This claim is based on considerable evidence of long-term planning and organization in creating Pueblo Bonito. They say the marked alignments and formalized foundations were all manifested prior to Stage II construction. Even prior to Old Bonito, they say Pueblo Bonito could have been conceived and calibrated, its major future outlines scratched out on the clay pavement the future foundations rest on and marked with sticks.

"Consequently," they say, "we argue that Pueblo Bonito's massive building episodes were not designed and implemented on an episode by episode basis by generations of individual architects following their interpretation of established rules. Rather, we propose that Pueblo Bonito may have had a single architect and that succeeding generations needed only to follow the instructions encoded in the tangible foundation alignments, as well as those carried forward by a few individuals as intangible esoteric knowledge. Perhaps Pueblo Bonito was the vision of one man, made tangible and set in motion in a single lifetime."

The other contributors to Jill Neitzel's volume take new looks at the siting of Pueblo Bonito, astronomy and ritual in Chaco Canyon, construction labor needed to build Pueblo Bonito, its architecture as the enclosure of space, burials, artifact distribution, and artifact interpretation. Drawing on all that and other recent research, Neitzel offers what seems to me a valuable summing up and synthesis of the latest insights about Pueblo Bonito. They're framed around three key questions: How were the people who built and used it organized? What was it used for? How many people lived there?

"Pueblo Bonito's architecture, artifacts, and burials all support the view that Chacoan society was hierarchically organized with an intermediate degree of complexity," she says.

She believes Pueblo Bonito had two major functions whose relative importance changed through time. Initially, it was primarily a residence. Later, although people continued to live there, it became primarily a ceremonial center.

She thinks that the early residents were probably "high-status members of Chaco society." Nancy Akins of the Office of Archaeological Studies of the Museum of New Mexico has dated Bonito's two paramount burials—men whose high status was inherited—to A.D. 1020. The older of these men was fifty years old at death, so one could reason that some sort of social hierarchy was in place when he was born in about A.D. 970.

Pueblo Bonito had been transformed into a major ceremonial center by A.D. 1050. The evidence includes its many kivas and great kivas, its astronomical alignments (see next chapter), its hidden stores of ritual artifacts, and its use as a mortuary for elite burials. Its astronomical alignments offer good evidence of scheduled rituals, probably conducted in conjunction with other sites at Chaco.

"The best answer to the question of what Pueblo Bonito was used for," says Neitzel, "is that the site had multiple functions whose relative importance changed through time. It was an elite residence, a ceremonial center, a mortuary, a storage facility, and a destination for trade goods." All these were probably interrelated, one aspect leading to another, she speculates.

As for the lengthy controversy over how many people lived there, and who they were, the numbers may have been small. In his "This Old House" chapter, Tom Windes says the chronological reproduction of Pueblo Bonito "suggests the site's resident population never exceeded 100 people." Neitzel offers this succinct view:

"Pueblo Bonito may not have housed many people itself, but it was the largest and most centrally located structure in what was the proto-urban-capital of Chacoan society. Pueblo Bonito was the focal point of Chacoan society, the center of the center. As such, although its residents were few in number, they were the most important and powerful people in the Chacoan world."

To what end was all that power exercised? Archaeologists still argue these points endlessly. Here, though, I'll share with you Neitzel's view of this crucial question:

"It appears that much of Pueblo Bonito's unifying power was religious, although the site apparently also exerted other kinds of power—economic, political, and perhaps military."

She notes that the large quantities of goods brought into Pueblo Bonito from throughout the San Juan basin—starting with those necessary to construct it—are the most obvious evidence of its economic power. The considerable labor necessary to build it speaks to its political power. Religion may well have motivated that effort, but political skills were necessary to direct and administer it.

Evidence that Pueblo Bonito may have exerted military power includes the violent death of one of the men in one of the site's two paramount burials, what some see as a defensive configuration of some great houses, and the signaling stations linking Pueblo Alto, on the mesa top directly above and behind Pueblo Bonito, with distant great houses. "Though it seems unlikely that armies marched Chacoan roads, the effect of force or the threat of it should not be ignored as a possible contributor to Pueblo Bonito's power."

All this power was probably "inextricably linked" to the site's ritual power. Neitzel wonders if this ritual power might not have been totally benign or benevolent. "Chacoan religion may have been stern, vigorous, and oppressive, not unlike the militant Catholicism of the Crusades or the Inquisition."

It's not necessarily the picture of a peaceful, communal society some would prefer, and many still argue for. The notions of power, social structure, and the like are difficult to ascribe with the same degree of certainty we can apply to the tree-ring dating of the exact year and season a tree used as a viga in a Chacoan great house was cut down. And different scholars' preconceived viewpoints often color how they come down on a variety of such issues. I leave discussion of these more abstract—although important—arguments until my final chapter.

Neitzel sums up what is so special about Pueblo Bonito with a welcome clarity of expression:

"Given all this, what was Pueblo Bonito? It was the most powerful place in its world. It was a sacred place—the place where the most important and elaborate ceremonies of the Chacoan religion were conducted. It was the home of a priestly elite composed of two families who, through their religious, political, economic, and perhaps military power were able to make Pueblo Bonito the preeminent Chacoan center.

"From there these families ruled a complex and far-flung society and influenced more distant areas as well. Pueblo Bonito was the center of the center—the most important structure in the most important settlement in the most powerful society ever to develop in the prehispanic northern Southwest."

"A millennium ago Pueblo Bonito must have inspired awe and a sense of mystery to all who visited it. Its ruins continue to do so today."

Chapter 14. Cosmography, Meridian, and Violence

Cosmographic Expression

When Anna Sofaer completed documenting the Fajada Butte three-slab-and-spiral-petroglyph solar and lunar calendar (see Chapter 10), she didn't stop there. She wondered if there was more evidence of the Chacoans' astronomical proclivities and cosmological interests in the orientations and interrelationships of the major Chacoan buildings.

The Solstice Project, which she had founded, investigated. She and a variety of archaeologists and volunteers, including professional geodesists from the National Geodetic Survey, carried out detailed surveys and measurements. They studied orientations, internal geometry, and interrelationships of the major Chacoan great houses for possible astronomical significance. The question she considered was whether the fourteen major buildings were oriented to the sun and moon at the extremes and midpositions of the solar and lunar cycles. The answer they found was yes.

The major buildings of the Chacoan culture contain solar and lunar cosmology in all three articulations: their orientations, their internal geometrical, and their geographic interrelationships were, reports Sofaer, developed in relationships to the cycles of the sun and moon. The work reveals an intricate astronomical system, evidence that Chaco was a center of ancestral puebloan cosmology.

The seasonal cycles of the sun are familiar to most of us, and of course they were of paramount importance to early peoples everywhere, the Chacoans included. Due to the tilt of the earth's axis, the sun's setting (and rising) positions along the horizon in the northern hemisphere range from a northern extreme (summer solstice), back to a midpoint (the equinox), on to a southern extreme (winter solstice), and then back again, completing one year. Early peoples everywhere found ways to observe and record the solar cycle.

Every latitude sees different angular positions of the solar extremes. From Chaco Canyon (latitude 36 degrees), the summer solstice sun rises and sets 60.4 degrees from north. The equinoxes are at 90 degrees, and the winter solstice is 60.4 degrees from due south.

The north-south lunar cycle is longer and more complicated. This is completely different from the lunar-phase cycle we're all familiar with. Documented cases of prehistoric indigenous peoples observing and recording it are fairly rare. In its excursions each month the moon shifts from rising roughly in the northeast to rising roughly in the southeast (and from setting roughly in the northwest to setting roughly in the southwest). But the envelope of these monthly "standstills" expands and contracts over an 18.6-year cycle. The extreme excursions are known as major and minor standstills. The time from one major standstill to the next major standstill is the 18.6-year lunar standstill cycle.

It happens due to the fact that the orbit of the moon around the earth is tilted by 5 degrees with respect to the apparent orbit of the sun (called the ecliptic) and this orbit as a whole completes a cycle in 18.6 years. The great Greek astronomer Hipparchus (ca. 190–120 B.C.) measured and explained the cycle.

At the year of the major standstill, as seen from Chaco, the moon rises and sets 6.1 degrees north and south of the positions of the rising and setting solstice suns. At the year of the minor standstill, 9.3 years later, the envelope is at its minimum width, and the moon rises and sets 6.7 degrees within the envelope of the rising and setting solstice suns.

The Solstice Project surveyed the orientations of the fourteen largest buildings of the Chacoan cultural region. Twelve are rectangular, two are crescent shaped. Ten are located in the canyon, four are located outside the canyon. They represent the Chacoans' most elaborate architecture. As Sofaer points out, they include "all the large buildings in the canyon and the outlying buildings that share the massive scale and impressive formality of the large buildings in the canyon."

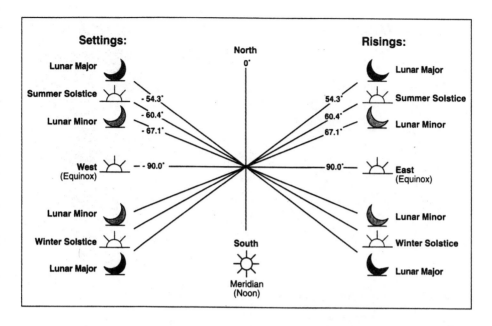

Azimuths of rising and setting of the sun and moon at the extremes and mid-positions of their cycles, at the latitude of Chaco Canyon (36° north). The meridian passage of the sun is also indicated. The lunar extremes are the northern and southern limits of rising or setting at the major and minor standstills. Fabian Schmid (David, Inc.) and Suzanne Samuels (By Design Graphics), © The Solstice Project, 1995.

The survey results show that the orientations of eleven of the fourteen major buildings are associated with one of the four solar or lunar azimuths on the sensible horizon.

As Sofaer summarizes them: Three buildings (Pueblo Bonito, Pueblo Alto, and Tsin Kletzin) are associated with the cardinal directions (meridian and equinox). One building (Aztec) is associated with the solstice azimuth. Five buildings (Chetro Ketl, Kin Kletso, Pueblo del Arroyo, Pueblo Pintado, and Salmon Ruin) are associated with the lunar minor standstill azimuth. Two buildings (Peñasco Blanco and Una Vida) are associated with the lunar major standstill. The illustration on the next page shows these relationships visually.

The Solstice Project Survey also found that of the eleven major rectangular Chacoan buildings there were strictly repeated internal diagonal angles and a correspondence between these angles and astronomy. At Chaco's latitude, the angles between the lunar standstill azimuths on the sensible horizon and the east-west cardinal axes are 22.9 degrees and 35.7 degrees. The project's measurements of internal angles show that sixteen angles in nine

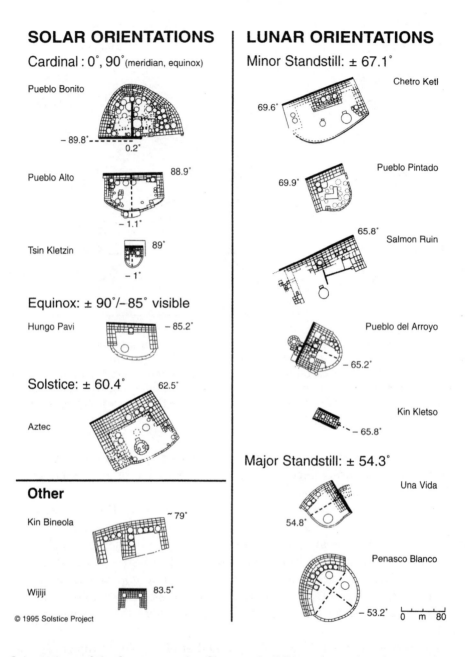

SOLAR ORIENTATIONS

Cardinal : 0°, 90° (meridian, equinox)

Pueblo Bonito

− 89.8°
0.2°

Pueblo Alto
88.9°

− 1.1°

Tsin Kletzin
89°

− 1°

Equinox: ± 90°/−85° visible

Hungo Pavi − 85.2°

Solstice: ± 60.4°
62.5°

Aztec

Other

Kin Bineola ~ 79°

Wijiji 83.5°

© 1995 Solstice Project

LUNAR ORIENTATIONS

Minor Standstill: ± 67.1°

Chetro Ketl

69.6°

Pueblo Pintado

69.9°

65.8°
Salmon Ruin

Pueblo del Arroyo

− 65.2°

Kin Kletso

− 65.8°

Major Standstill: ± 54.3°

Una Vida

54.8°

Penasco Blanco

− 53.2°   0   m   80

Orientations of the fourteen major Chacoan buildings shown in relation to the astronomical azimuths on the sensible horizon. For one building, Hungo Pavi, the orientation to the equinox sunrise on the visible horizon is also indicated.
Suzanne Samuels (By Design Graphics), © The Solstice Project, 1995.

buildings are between 23 and 28 degrees, six angles in four building are between 34 and 39 degrees. "The correspondence between these angles of the solar-lunar relationships and the internal diagonal angles is intriguing," says Sofaer. "It suggests that the Chacoans may have favored these particular angles in order to incorporate a geometry of the sun and moon in the internal organization of the buildings."

Three rectangular buildings (Pueblo Alto, Salmon Ruin, and Pueblo del Arroyo), appear to have both solar and lunar orientations. Writes Sofaer: "The Chacoans may have intended that the two phenomena—internal geometry and external orientation—be so integrated that these three rectangular buildings would have both solar and lunar orientation."

It gets more interesting still. The Solstice Project next asked if the geographical relationships between the major buildings likewise expressed astronomical significance. In 1978 John Fritz had observed that four key central buildings are organized in a cardinal pattern. The line between Pueblo Alto atop the north canyon wall and Tsin Kletzin on the south canyon

The locations and orientations of the buildings in Chaco Canyon. The diagram shows the inter-building bearings that the Solstice Project researchers say correlate with the orientations of individual buildings to the cardinal directions and to the lunar major standstill azimuths. Fabian Schmid (Davis, Inc.), © The Solstice Project, 1995.

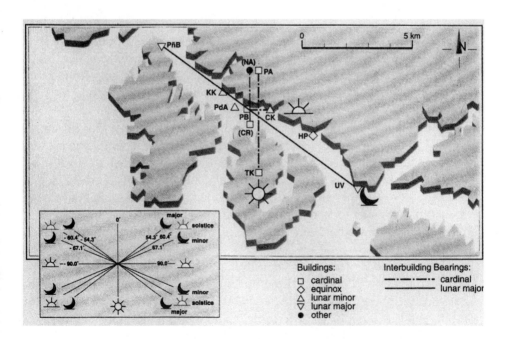

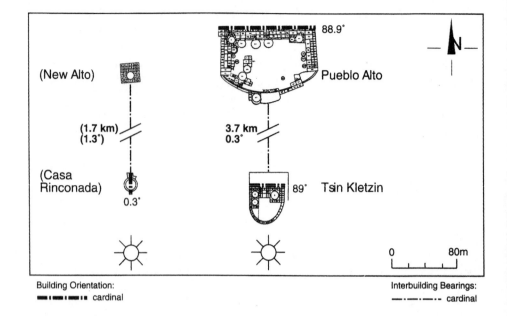

The relationships between two pairs of Chacoan buildings in the central complex that appear to be connected by north-south astronomical inter-building bearings. Fabian Schmid (Davis, Inc.), © The Solstice Project, 1995.

wall is north-south. In the canyon, the line between Pueblo Bonito and Chetro Ketl, the two largest Chacoan structures, is east-west. He also showed some symmetric patterning. The line south from Pueblo Bonito to Kin Kletzin evenly divides the east-west line between Pueblo Bonito and Chetro Ketl.

The Solstice Project's survey showed that three of these four buildings are also cardinal in their individual building orientations. Pueblo Bonito, Pueblo Alto, and Tsin Kletsin all have main walls aligned east-west with symmetrical orientations north-south. "These findings," says Sofaer, "suggested that the Chacoans coordinated the orientations and locations of several central buildings to form astronomical inter-building relationships."

But were there other such relationships between the major Chacoan buildings?

The Solstice Project found that thirteen of the fourteen major buildings have bearings to another one of the buildings that align with azimuths of the solar or lunar phenomena associated with the individual buildings. Pueblo Pintado and Kin Bineola, the two most isolated and remote buildings examined, are 27 and 18 kilometers respectively from the canyon center. The surveys found that the two buildings are on lines from the central complex that correspond to the bearings of the lunar minor standstill. "These lunar-based inter-building relationships are underscored by the fact that they involve buildings that also are oriented individually to the lunar standstills," says Sofaer. Specifically, the three major buildings in the central complex that are oriented to the lunar minor standstill—Chetro Ketl, Pueblo del Arroyo, and Kin Kletso—are also related to Pueblo Pintado and Kin Bineola on bearings oriented to the lunar minor standstill. Sofaer notes that Pueblo Pintado is also oriented to the lunar minor standstill, and two major buildings, Wijiji and Hungo Pavi, outside the major complex but within the canyon, are also on the bearing from the central complex to Pueblo Pintado and to the lunar minor standstill.

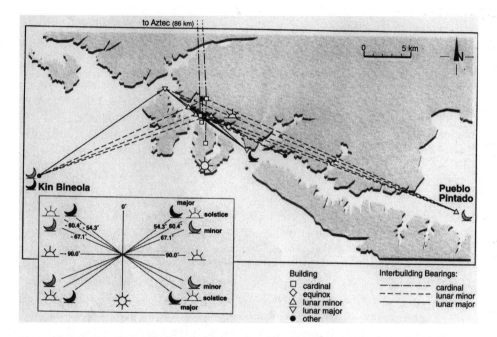

The locations and orientations of twelve of the major Chacoans buildings. The diagram shows inter-building bearings that the Solstice Project found correlate with the orientation of the individual buildings to the cardinal directions and the lunar major and minor standstill azimuths. Fabian Schmid (Davis, Inc.), © The Solstice Project, 1995.

Sofaer notes that the relationship of the central complex to Pueblo Pintado (southeast of the canyon) is to the rising of the southern minor standstill moon; the relationship of the central canyon complex to Kin Bineola (southwest of the canyon) is to the setting of the same moon. "The north-south axis of the central complex is the axis of symmetry of this moon's rising, meridian passage, and setting, as well as the axis of the ceremonial

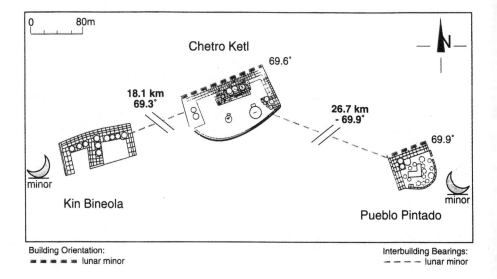

The relationships between three major Chacoan buildings connected by astro-nomical inter-building bearings aligned to the lunar minor standstill. Fabian Schmid (Davis, Inc.), © The Solstice Project, 1995.

center and of the relationships of these significant outlying structures to that center."

She notes that Pueblo Pintado and Kin Bineola are regarded as having particularly significant relationships with the buildings in the canyon. Chaco archaeologist Mike Marshall, who worked with the Solstice Project team, reports that these two buildings are more like the canyon buildings than like other outlying buildings. He suggests that their locations could make them "gateway communities."

There's more. From the central complex, bearings to the major stand-still moon are also the bearings to Una Vida and Peñasco Blanco, the only major Chacoan buildings that are oriented to the lunar major standstill. "Here it is also striking that the two buildings are equidistant from the north-south axis of the central complex. It is of further interest that the bearing from Peñasco Blanco to Kin Bineola also corresponds with the bearing to the lunar major standstill," says Sofaer.

Sofaer notes that each of the Chacoan expressions of solar and lunar cosmology contains within it an integration of the sun and moon. The Fajada Butte three-slab site she discovered clearly shows that integration. Chacoan architecture continues it. To summarize, she finds that five major buildings commemorate the solar cycles: three in their cardinal orientations, one in its equinox orientation, and one in its solstice orientation. Seven of the other nine major buildings commemorate the lunar standstills: five the minor standstill, and two the major standstill. And the overall patterning of the buildings joins the two sets of lunar-oriented buildings into relationships with the cardinal-solar center in a symmetrically organized design.

"Commemoration of these recurring cycles appears to have been a primary purpose of the Chaco phenomenon," says Sofaer. The planning, development, and maintenance of the massive Chacoan structures over generations would have "unified the Chacoan society with the recurring rhythms of the sun and moon in their movements about that central ceremonial place, Chaco Canyon."

She notes that in puebloan tradition time and space are integrated in the marking of directions that order the ceremonial structures and dances and in the timing of ceremonies to the cycle of the sun and the phases of the moon. Furthermore, the sun and moon are conceptually related to birth, life, and death. In many Pueblo traditions, the people emerged in the north from the worlds below (remember the Chacoans' Great North Road?) and traveled to the south in search of the sacred middle place.

"Chaco Canyon may have been such a center place and a place of mediation and transition between these cycles and between the worlds of the living and the death." Concludes Sofaer: "The solar and lunar cosmology encoded in the Chacoans' massive architecture—the buildings' orientations, internal geometry, and geographic relationships—unified the Chacoan people with each other and with the cosmos. This order is complex and stretches across vast reaches of the sky, the desert, and time. It is to be held in the mind's eye, the one that sees into and beyond natural phenomena to a sacred order. The Chacoans transformed an arid empty space into a reach of the mind."

What are we to make of all this? Solar alignments have vast historical precedents and antecedents in many parts of the prehistoric and historic world, but what about the lunar ones?

I asked University of Colorado astronomer J. McKim Malville for his thoughts on how and if these long-term lunar observations might have occurred. He's the researcher who has identified a probable observation site of the lunar standstill between the mountain spires behind the Chacoan community called Chimney Rock in southwestern Colorado (see Chapter 12) and also has found evidence that major lunar standstills were observed at Cliff Palace in Mesa Verde. He told me there are at least three ways to understand the Chacoans' interest in major lunar standstills:

> 1. Observations of the rising of the full moon would have easily led to a recognition of the changing position of the rising moon and its extremes. It

would have been natural to note that the moon's rising position could at times exceed that of the sun.

2. Traditional societies lead their ritual lives in sacred space and sacred time; sacred time is typically the nodes or critical times such as solstices, equinoxes, and extremes. Even though they may have no practical benefit, to perform a ritual at such a node in time often has great power, and it does appear that ceremony, ritual, and symbolism were very important for the Chacoans.

3. Sharp-eyed Chacoan astronomers may have noticed a relationship between eclipses of the moon and its standstill cycle. For example, at times of major and minor standstills, lunar eclipses can occur only on the equinoxes. A preferred date for major festivals in the canyon may have been at the time of full moon closest to winter solstice. An eclipse at that time would have been ominous. An ability to predict lunar eclipses would have increased the power and legitimacy, There were more than seventy lunar eclipses visible in Chaco Canyon between 1020 and 1100.

As for accepting Chacoans' astronomical observations and their applications, Chaco archaeologists may have been at first slow to incorporate them into their thinking, but Malville believes that they have now come around. Some even are enthusiastic about lunar standstills.

The lunar aspect of the Fajada Butte three-slab marker should no longer be disputed, in his view. "I don't think the major and minor standstills at the three-slab site are controversial at all," he told me. "There are pecked lines crossing the spiral at its center and upper lefthand side, which correspond to the position of the moon's shadow at those times. The angle of those lines is different from the orientation of the solar light-shadow events." He says some of the initial skepticism regarding Sofaer's work on lunar standstill observations on Fajada Butte was because there were no other known expressions of interest by ancestral puebloans in the lunar standstills, nor by the ancient cultures of Mesoamerica. But the jungles of the Yucatan did not have the sharp horizons that would have allowed detection of the standstill cycle. And at any rate, in the ancestral Puebloan culture area there is now evidence of observations of major lunar standstills at Chimney Rock and Mesa Verde that complement Sofaer's work at Chaco Chaco.

But does that mean he accepts every aspect of Sofaer's work with the Solstice Project? Not necessarily.

He says his own opinion of her work on cosmographic expression of the Chacoan structures is that "although her field work involved in measuring the geometries of the great houses is excellent, she has probably pushed her interpretation too far." For example, he says, the azimuths of lunar events corresponding to walls of great houses are sometimes not those observed from the site because the view would have been blocked by a canyon wall. The orientations Sofaer calculates correspond to a flat horizon. He suggests that the orientation of the great houses may have been influenced by a variety of issues involving the totality of the landscape and not exclusively the major or minor standstills of the moon. The position of the great house at Wijiji, for example, seems more influenced by nearby cliffs. In addition, the orientations of some irregular, partially fallen, or reconstructed walls of great houses are poorly defined. He says all of the proposed astronomical alignments need to be checked out with direct observations and photographed. Such confirmations in the field were becoming possible with the onset of major lunar standstills in 2004–2006. (The Solstice Project has done some of that work.)

The major work I've been describing—and the graphics I've used with Anna Sofaer's permission—are from a lengthy paper by Sofaer, "The Primary Architecture of the Chacoan Culture: A Cosmological Expression." Many Chaco archaeologists I've spoken to give high praise to Sofaer and her colleagues with the Solstice Project for their dedication, work, and perseverance in documenting a fascinating and significant aspect of the Chacoans' design and planning that previously had been given little attention.

A modern sign of that dedication is that Sofaer has also produced, directed, and cowritten a fifty-five-minute video, *The Mystery of Chaco Canyon,* narrated by Robert Redford and shown many times on PBS since the year 2000. It dramatically describes and shows all these aspects of the Chacoans' cosmographic expression. Beautiful on-site photography, sophisticated animation of many of the geometric interrelationships, time-lapse photography of solar and lunar risings and settings in line with wall alignments at times of solstices and lunar standstills, interviews with Native American ethnologists, and a background musical score make it a powerful presentation on the astronomical and cosmographic expressions of the Chacoans.

Meridian

Chaco archaeologists are used to endless discussions and debate about the size and extent of the Chacoan system. An area in excess of 50,000 square kilometers (about 20,000 square miles), and perhaps even greater than 100,000 square kilometers (about 40,000 square miles), is now thought to have been involved to various degrees in the evolution of the Chacoan phenomenon. But if Steve Lekson is right, one has to extend the Chacoan influence not only in spatial extent but also through time.

Lekson proposes that Chaco, Aztec ruin to the north, and Casas

Grandes (also called Paquime) in Chihuahua, Mexico, 630 kilometers (390 miles) to the south of Chaco, are intentionally linked along a meridian alignment that symbolizes the sequence and continuity of their dominance in Pueblo prehistory. The north-south line in question runs exactly parallel to the present Arizona–New Mexico border and about 60 miles east of it, down through all of New Mexico and into Mexico.

As he succinctly puts it: "The meridian alignment, at about longitude 107° 57' 30" of the Pueblo region's three most important sites—Chaco Canyon, Aztec Ruins, and Casas Grandes—was not coincidence. The three sites were sequential centers, spanning the peak of Pueblo prehistory from 900 to 1500. Each was the largest site of its time and place. Chaco emerged as the first regional center (900–1125); later centers (Aztec, 1110–1275) and Casas Grandes, 1250–1500) demonstrated their historical linkage to the first and greatest center by meridian symbolism—ideas of cardinality and monumental landscapes developed first at Chaco Canyon. . . . We now can define an overarching political geography for the ancient Southwest, from 900 to 1500, that requires rethinking and revising current models of Pueblo prehistory. "

It's a bit mind-blowing. Even Lekson agrees. The idea had its beginnings a quarter century earlier in the work of archaeologist Charles DiPeso (died 1982), who in 1974 noted intriguing similarities between Chaco Canyon and Casas Grandes. Huge stone disks set beneath structural posts, "bed platforms," colonnades, and platform mounts were found only at Casas and Chaco. Each was, at its time, the hub of long-distance trade in copper, shell, gems, and tropical birds—especially parrots and macaws. Chaco and Casas were the two most significant regional centers in the long history of the Pueblo Southwest. Yet the distances between them caused most archaeologists to reject any real link.

Tree-ring re-dating in 1993 showed Casas Grandes to be dated to the thirteenth through sixteenth centuries. No connection to Chaco there. But Lekson then noticed something peculiar. Chaco and Casas Grandes were on the same meridian. They were exactly north and south of each other. And Aztec was too. It was a third point on the same meridian. They were, says Lekson, "intriguingly sequential and alarmingly aligned."

As he puts it, the length and precision of the Chaco-Casas alignment are daunting and perhaps hard to believe. Over a length of 630 kilometers, or 390 miles, Casas is only about 1 kilometer east of the Great North Road that connects Chaco and Aztec. Lekson, like others, refers to the Great North Road as "the longest, most formal, and most elaborate of many Chacoan 'roads through time': roads that connected sequentially constructed buildings or communities." He suggests, as have others, that perhaps the

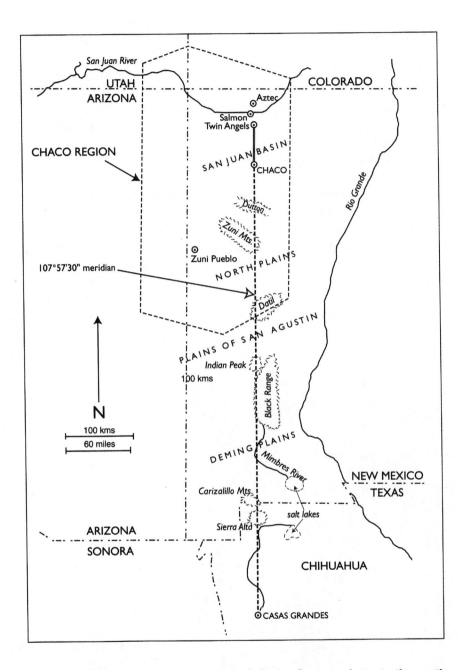

Meridian symbolism and cultural continuity? Chaco Canyon, Aztec to the north, and Casas Grandes, 390 miles to the south in Mexico, are all built on the same meridian line. Steve Lekson argues that this was intentional and that the meridian alignment symbolizes the continuity of the three sites' sequential dominance in Pueblo prehistory.

271

principal monumental function of the North Road was to commemorate the early twelfth-century shift in power from the old center at Chaco Canyon to the new center at Aztec.

States Lekson: "Aztec could have been built almost anywhere; its location was fixed by its meridian alignment with Chaco. The Chaco-Aztec transfer was legitimized by position. After Aztec, positional legitimization south along the same meridian led, literally, to the location of Casas Grandes, the third and final center."

Why would any of this have been done? From the viewpoint of our modern culture, the whole concept seemed a bit alien and difficult to understand. Then I remembered something my late friend Abbott Sekaquaptewa, former chairman of the Hopi Tribe, had told me when I was preparing the first edition of this book and discussing such questions with him. He urged me (and I suppose indirectly archaeologists as well) to consider the possibility that the major Chacoan roads, especially the Great North Road, in addition to whatever practical value they had, expressed something symbolic about the history of the Chacoans. In other words, he was trying to get me to think of them as possibly symbolic markers of the Chacoans' history and cosmography (see Chapter 6, page 127).

In regard to the Chaco roads, archaeologists have now mostly adopted

The late Abbott Sekaquaptewa, former chairman of the Hopi Tribe. He urged considering the Chacoan roads, at least in part, as symbolic expressions of Chacoan history. Photo by Susanne Page.

that kind of thinking. It doesn't seem much of a stretch to think that the pre-historic Pueblo peoples of the Southwest might well have considered a place such as Chaco so important to their world historically and symbolically that they would commemorate its meaning by building several subsequent sites—even vastly distant ones—on the same meridian.

Lekson puts his proposed explanation this way: "Position legitimization created landscape-scale references to mythical and historical pasts. Alignment between the new (Aztec, Casas) and the old (Chaco) demonstrated these connections both actively and passively. . . . The procedure of alignment must have been a major, memorable event. It required coordination of labor over large areas and considerable time—perhaps decades."

Steve Lekson is a professional archaeologist of good reputation. He realizes the whole topic of "alignments" is fraught with peril, that some people are prone to get carried away and see lines and links where justification is nonexistent. "I'm personally not interested in geomancy and New Age mumbo jumbo," he said in a talk at the Pecos Conference. "But they did align things."

He added, "The alignment is not a big deal to me." But it could well have been to the prehistoric Pueblo people. And there is a vast, legitimate archaeoastronomy literature about how early peoples often arranged major works along lines that express their sense of cultural connection to the natural world, including important positional and seasonal elements of the stars and sky.

North is important, Lekson points out. It's the only fixed point in the sky. And he reemphasizes that we know Chaco people paid attention to it—the Great North Road is not a misnomer. So, in a way, the Chaco–Aztec–Casas Grandes meridian connection is not surprising. "It's possible, it's practical, it's predictable."

"They were hooked up to the 'big line dance,' " he said. "The data are really solid."

Later, in a brief discussion at the Pecos Conference, Lekson told me, "I think it's real. But it's a hard sell. Few people are buying it. But they're listening." In 1999 he published a book, *The Chaco Meridian: Centers of Political Power in the Ancient Southwest,* that discusses candidly and thoughtfully (and in his typical lively, informal style) all the evidence, arguments, and objections. Will the hypothesis prevail? We don't yet know.

But as Lekson subsequently wrote to me: "I'm swimming upstream, of course; it's good exercise. I suspect that a few years of digestion and rumination will move the Chaco-Aztec-Paquime political history closer to the Southwest mainstream. Yesterday's bombshells become today's bromides. The 'alignment' business throws people off, because it's [seemingly] New Age archaeoastronomical ley-line scary, but that was part of the appeal of this research: How do we differentiate between fringe and fact?"

Violence

If you think the meridian alignment business is controversial, that's nothing compared to another, even more contentious issue that, so to speak, had been simmering on the far back burners of southwestern archaeology for years and came to a boil in late 1998: cannibalism.

It's a sensational and distasteful topic, but it must be faced. For thirty years physical anthropologist Christy G. Turner II of Arizona State University had been gradually amassing evidence from bones recovered from sites throughout the Four Corners region to support his argument that the ancestors of today's Pueblo Indians had engaged in cannibalism. His evidence comes from bones recovered at sites both from the prehistoric Anasazi cultures and from historic-era sites on Polacca Wash on the Hopi reservation in Arizona dated to A.D. 1580, plus or minus seventy years.

In his book *Man Corn: Cannibalism and Violence in the Prehistoric American Southwest,* published in 1999, Turner summarizes his life's work. He contends that the Anasazi and other Southwest Indians, far from being peaceful farmers and builders, engaged in warfare, violence, and the concomitant horrors of cannibalism. His argument is based on an assessment of human bone assemblages recovered from scattered floor deposits or charnel pits throughout the region. Turner and his coauthor, his wife, Jacqueline, who died in 1996, and other analysts claim to have identified a signature of burning, pot polishing, anvil abrasions, bone breaking, cut marks, and missing vertebrae that they say closely matches the signature of butchering animals. It is, they say, frequently associated with additional evidence of violence. They examined more than seventy-five archaeological sites containing several hundred individuals and contend that cannibalism probably took place at thirty-eight of them, and that extreme violence and mutilation was identifiable at most of the others.

And that's not all. Turner contends that the charnel deposits were often associated, both in time and place, with Chacoan great houses throughout the region. He further suggests that Chaco Canyon was the center of Anasazi cannibalism and that it was not an isolated practice but a purposeful policy to exert and reinforce social control. Whew!

The work puzzles many and angers some. For one thing cannibalism itself is a highly controversial topic in anthropology. This is not just because it is inflammatory and repugnant to many people's sensibilities but because many past claims and assertions about cannibalism have not stood the test of time. William Arens, an anthropologist at the State University of New York at Stony Brook, argues in his book *The Man-Eating Myth: Anthropology and*

Anthropophagy that while isolated cases of cannibalism undoubtedly occur, cannibalism as a common custom is a folk myth. One culture's greatest insult against a hated neighboring culture is to call them cannibals, and Arens argues that too many anthropologists have accepted stories about cannibalism as fact without the existence of any empirical evidence. Turner's arguments, however, arise not out of anecdotes and traditions but seemingly *are* based on empirical evidence. But how good is that evidence?

Many of Turner's critics have proposed alternative explanations to his evidence. Some of those points were included in a lengthy *New Yorker* article by Douglas Preston about Turner's work, titled "Cannibalism in the Canyon" and published November 30, 1998, just before Turner's book came out. Several investigators concede the grisly violence but suggest the destruction of the bones followed execution of people thought in Anasazi culture to be witches. The breaking up and crushing of their bones may have been a way of banishing the evil powers and proclaiming ultimate superiority. Others point to the lack of ethnographic record about cannibalism. Another criticism is that Turner lumps assemblages together and treats them all the same without enough distinction. The archaeologist for the Hopi tribe and the director of the Hopi Cultural Preservation office also criticized Turner for not producing evidence that anyone was actually eating human meat and for not considering alternative possibilities of unusual mortuary practices.

When I asked Steve Lekson in December 1998 what he thought about the claims, he said that with Turner's book and another coming out, the issue of cannibalism and warfare is not going to go away. "It's sensational," he granted. "Also, it may be correct, historically. My read on this is that Chaco had the use of legitimate political force—that is, institutional violence, but the jury is still out on institutionalized cannibalism. It was a different sort of place than Hopi or Acoma. But that view will not be popular in the Pueblos either."

Tom Windes was less accepting. "Almost everyone I know is skeptical about the claims—not so much that some treatment of human bodies has taken place but the extent of it and what it means. I am not a physical anthropologist type, so I don't know about that part of it. However, I am definitely against Turner's contention that this is a Chacoan-driven thing. All reports that I know of from digs in recent years have seen this evidence in sites late and north of the San Juan River (read 'Mesa Verdean'), when times were tough (A.D. 1100s and 1200s). Turner came out to Chaco to look at a couple of sites, but all his 'evidence' from Chaco comes from contexts that are very poorly controlled temporally (all were dug before 1930)—and I know that late occupation (Mesa Verdean) occurs in all of them, as well as earlier Chacoan occupation. Generally, bodies are common in late occupations in Chaco and rare otherwise."

One of the strongest critics of Turner's work is Peter Bullock, an archaeologist at the Museum of New Mexico in Santa Fe. In my 1998 interview with him, he first granted the possibility that at least some of the assertions may be valid. "I think this is one of those situations in which it [cannibalism] could exist at some level, but it would be very hard to prove. His [Turner's] work is so subjective. He ignores stuff that doesn't fit. The material—the bone evidence—is the kind of thing that can occur from a number of causes." He said Turner had been to their lab and looked at bones in which Turner had discerned breakage he felt was due to cannibalism, but in some of those cases, Bullock told me, "We know it's from other causes—back hoes, and so forth. A lot of us don't take it [the cannibalism claim] seriously."

A short book Bullock edited, *Deciphering Anasazi Violence,* had just been published by a Santa Fe publisher. "We're trying to get people to look at a wider range of possibilities, to shift the subject to the broader one of violence among the Anasazi." There's evidence of that, he said, without a need for "stretching the evidence" to imply cannibalism.

I remained a bit skeptical about claims of cannibalism in the prehistoric Southwest until a remarkable study was published in September 2000. The study went beyond evidence of smashed and processed bones to establish firm and—in my view and that of others—incontrovertible evidence of cannibalism.

The site in question is not at Chaco but at a place called Cowboy Wash in southwestern Colorado. The inhabitants lived not in any grand Chaco-style great house but in three pit houses. Nevertheless, they were Puebloan. Sometime around A.D. 1150, nearly two decades after the last construction at Chaco, the pithouses at this site (specifically termed 5MT10010) were suddenly abandoned. This exodus had been established during excavation as part of a larger archaeological study of seventeen Puebloan sites on the southern piedmont of Sleeping Ute Mountain. In contrast to other nearby sites, valuable items including cooking pots, serving wares, ornaments, and polished stone tools were left in place.

The most striking visual evidence indicated that during the abandonment or soon after, the bodies of seven people of various ages and both sexes were, according to the researchers in their report, "disarticulated, defleshed, and apparently cooked as if for consumption by other humans." The victims' incomplete and disarticulated remains were left directly on the floors of two of the pithouses. The body parts were scattered and piled. They hadn't been buried. More than a thousand human bones and fragments were found piled. Stone tools consistent with use in butchering were found and tested positive for human blood.

Even at this point the evidence of any cannibalism was circumstantial only. That was soon to change. The story now necessarily becomes a bit clinical—some might say gruesome, and so I hope you will forgive me in the name of archaeology. There is a biochemical test that can detect human tissue residues (as opposed to animal residues). Recovered shards from the cooking pot were subjected to this biochemical analysis. Myoglobin is a protein molecule that transports oxygen from the inner surfaces of membranes of skeletal and cardiac muscle cells to the energy-generating components within these cells. The shards from the cooking vessel tested positive for human myoglobin. Control tests were done on fourteen cooking vessel shards from a contemporaneous Pueblo site in southwestern Colorado. All control shards were negative for human myoglobin.

"The presence of human myoglobin only on cooking vessel shards from 5MT10010 is consistent with the hypothesis that human muscle tissue was cooked in that vessel," wrote researchers Richard Marlar, Banks Leonard, Brian Billman, Patricia Lambert, and Jennifer Marlar in "Biochemical Evidence of Cannibalism at a Prehistoric Puebloan Site in Southwestern Colorado," in the September 7, 2000, issue of the respected weekly scientific journal *Nature*. Marlar is with the Department of Pathology at the University of Colorado School of Medicine in Denver. The other authors are with scientific institutions in Colorado, Arizona, Utah, and North Carolina.

But, you might say, that only proves the human remains were cooked, not that they were eaten. Yes, that's true. That's where the next step of the study came in. In the ashes of the cooking hearth, the researchers found an unburned human fecal deposit, or coprolite. They point out that its unburned condition shows that it was deposited after the last use of the hearth. It was the only coprolite recovered and, say the researchers, "may be the only one identified from a structure hearth from anywhere in the American Southwest."

This discovery of a coprolite deposited during or shortly after butchering and cooking of human remains provided an opportunity to get direct evidence of cannibalism. There was no plant material in the fecal deposit, indicating that the meal was composed entirely of meat. To test the hypothesis of cannibalism, it was necessary to have a marker for human material passing through the digestive system. Myoglobin is found only in skeletal and cardiac muscle cells. It is not found in cells of the blood, skin, nor in the smooth muscle cells of the intestine. Therefore, the researchers reasoned, myoglobin should be present in fecal material only if it is consumed and passed through the digestive system of the person who deposited the feces. Furthermore, the chemical composition of myoglobin is different in humans and animals.

The researchers' analysis of the coprolite detected human myoglobin.

They carried out control tests on thirty-nine modern human fecal extracts, including samples from patients with blood in the stool samples, and twenty prehistoric coprolites from Salmon ruin in northwestern New Mexico with occupation contemporaneous with site 5MT10010. The results of all these control tests were negative—they contained no human myoglobin.

The case was made. "The analysis of the coprolite and associate remains from 5MT10010 at last provides definitive evidence for an episode of cannibalism involving ancient Puebloans," write Marlar et al. in their *Nature* report. "Results . . . are consistent with the archaeological and osteological evidence of cannibalism at 5MT10010. . . . These data demonstrate that humans both processed and consumed human flesh at the site."

Marlar and his colleagues finished by noting that cannibalism has occurred in a wide variety of societies for a wide variety of reasons, including starvation, ancestor worship, and political terrorism. "With the presentation of the first direct evidence of cannibalism in the American Southwest in the prehistoric era, we hope that the debate will shift from the question of whether or not cannibalism occurred to questions concerning the social context, causes, and consequences of these events."

In the same issue of *Nature,* the noted Pulitzer Prize–winning UCLA scientist, physiologist, and writer Jared Diamond provides a commentary calling the group's evidence "compelling." Diamond goes on to consider why there is such denial that cannibalism in various cultures takes place. One, of course, is that Westerners abhor cannibalism. But Diamond points out that friends of his among indigenous people of New Guinea, where he has studied (and where he is sure cannibalism is still practiced), find some Western practices that we accept abhorrent to essentially the same degree. These activities include circumcisions, U.S. treatment of the elderly, and U.S. funeral customs. Another reason is one of much concern to archaeologists studying in the Southwest—the perception among modern Pueblo people that the reports "slander" their ancestors. Archaeologists are increasingly sensitive to such concerns, and I think it's fair to say that NAGPRA, the Native American Graves Protection and Repatriation Act, which became law in 1990 and which gives Native Americans more control over the remains found in ancient burial sites—in some cases preventing their study—has made the situation even more awkward for archaeologists.

An example of the reaction to news of the *Nature* study was an op-ed piece by Roberto Rodriguez and Patricia Gonzales titled "Prehistoric Fecal Focus Serves No Valid Scientific Purpose," published in the *Albuquerque Journal.* "We're not contesting the findings," they wrote, "but rather facetiously wondering whether these specialists have nothing better to do than to sift through 850-year-old feces. . . . Archaeology should serve a purpose.

When it descends into providing fodder for a culture that likes to think of itself as superior or simply produces sensationalist material for a news-starved media, perhaps in this case, we've come to the 'end of archaeology.' "

So you can see why the whole topic makes some archaeologists uneasy.

In any event, at least one case of cannibalism among ancestral Puebloans in the Southwest, not that far from Chaco and taking place while Chaco was in decline, has been proven. Very likely there are others. What it all means—or doesn't mean—is still an open question.

In a *Scientific American* article "Once Were Cannibals," published a year after the Marlar group's study, Tim D. White, codirector of the Laboratory for Human Evolutionary Studies at the University of California, Berkeley, acknowledged that the topic "can shock, disgust, and fascinate in equal measure." He reviewed the evidence for cannibalism worldwide and called the Marlar study the most compelling evidence for it at Anasazi sites in the American Southwest. Concluded White: "It remains much more challenging to establish why cannibalism took place than to establish that it did. . . . Even in the case of the Anasazi, who have been well studied, it is impossible to determine whether cannibalism resulted from starvation, religious beliefs, or some combination of these and other things. What is becoming clear through the refinement of the science of archaeology, however, is that cannibalism is part of our collective past."

Maybe so, but is there any significant Chaco connection? Chaco archaeologists are fairly low-key about the topic. They may grant the possibility of occasional cannibalism in Chaco or its environs—perhaps as part of the more general and acceptable topic of warfare and violence (such as retribution against witches)—but it is difficult to integrate into previous views.

Nevertheless the evidence of the *Nature* study and Christy Turner's book is slowly being accommodated into Chacoan perspectives. "That cannibalism did occur [in the Southwest] is reinforced by the smoking gun of Cowboy Wash," writes David E. Doyel in the "Chaco Update" preface to the 2001 reprinting of the long-out-of-print volume he edited on Anasazi regional organization and the Chaco system, "but the temporal and regional implications of this finding have yet to be assessed." He refers to the understandable negative reaction from Native American groups and says, "Stay tuned for further developments."

In his freewheeling contribution to the same new preface, Steve Lekson chides his colleagues for wanting a peaceful, happy, violence-free Chaco. "The electorate [his colleagues in the Chaco Synthesis Project, see final chapter] seems intent on reestablishing a happy, peaceful Southwest, free of tyranny, taxation, and bad times. We want a *nice* Southwest (cannibals need not apply)."

Jill E. Neitzel, in her 2003 monograph on Pueblo Bonito published by the Smithsonian Institution (see Chapter 13), refers to formal mortuary rites conducted in Bonito and to the possibility that there was perhaps more to it than that: "Turner and Turner argued that Pueblo Bonito's burials exhibit evidence of cannibalism. If this is true, then some of Pueblo Bonito's mortuary rites, and perhaps other ceremonies as well, might have involved human sacrifice and even ritual cannibalism."

William D. Lipes, as part of his contribution to the Chaco Synthesis Project (see final chapter), has considered the question of whether coercive violence was involved in maintaining Chacoan control in the northern San Juan basin. The Turners and Steve Lekson have referred to what they call "extreme processing" (EP) incidents, in which human bodies have been mutilated, whether or not cannibalism was involved. They have suggested strongly that these cases might have been intended to make a political point, a terrifying way to exercise and maintain control.

Lipes points out that the best-documented cases of EP in the Southwest took place in the northern San Juan basin, and nearly all of them fall outside the period of construction of the Chaco-style great houses in the area. Even those whose time period may possibly have overlapped that of the Chaco great houses took place at the very end of the period and thus could not have been instrumental in the expansion and consolidation of the Chacoan system. Perhaps they were related to the social disruption during or following abandonment of the major sites, but that would have nothing to do with the golden age of Chaco.

Lipes also refers to what he calls good evidence that incidents of such extreme violence take place in conjunction with the execution of witches, a not-unheard-of act of intercommunity social control.

While Lipes doesn't say this, it is common knowledge among Pueblo people today that traditional lives steeped in spirituality and modes of conduct for daily living also contain the darker side—witchcraft and ways of eliminating witches, their rituals, their families.

Lekson, in a 2002 paper in *American Antiquity,* "War in the Southwest, War in the World," puts the subject in the wider context of violence and warfare in the ancient pueblos of the American Southwest. As Lekson writes, "A region conventionally considered peaceful is emerging as periodically violent." He notes that journalistic articles on these subjects have at times sensationalized the material and certainly exacerbated emotions on all sides, but he says that does not diminish their importance. This whole topic began to gain wider currency among southwestern scholars in the 1990s, particularly with the publication in 1999 not only of the Turners' book but also of Steven LeBlanc's *Prehistoric Warfare in the American Southwest.*

LeBlanc notes "ten generations of a virtual absence of war" in the period A.D. 900–1150. But in contrast to this extraordinary era of peace, he defines a limited but very specific form of violence during this same period: a series of group executions recognized over much of the northern Pueblo area between the late 900s and 1250 recognized by himself, the Turners, Tim White, K. A. Kuckelman, and others. These few incidents (perhaps about seventy-five instances) were few in number but exceptionally brutal. Small groups of people were executed, dismembered, mutilated, and, less certainly (in Lekson's view), cannibalized. The violence was certainly intended to do more than simply kill the victims.

Lekson told me in 2004, "I am no fan of cannibalism, particularly," but he nevertheless finds the evidence of these cases of extreme violence persuasive. In his paper on war in the Southwest, he clearly states his take on the matter: "I suggest that EP Events represent coercive force directed by and perhaps emanating first from Chaco and, later, from Aztec Ruins. Less than an army, but more effective than local villagers, forces from Chaco (and later) Aztec made brutal examples of families and households who, for whatever reasons, were deemed inimical to the Chacoan world order." As Lipes and others have suggested, it seems likely that those who weren't seen as living in the proper way—having offended against the ideological or ceremonial system—were deemed political foes or witches and eliminated.

Where most Chaco archaeologists decidedly part company from Christy Turner is with his suggestion that cannibalism was introduced into the Chaco region by Mesoamericans from the south as an instrument of terror and power. Consider this comment from veteran archaeologists Linda Cordell of the University of Colorado and Jim Judge (the former Chaco Project director, now at Fort Lewis College). It appears, with documenting references, in their paper from the Chaco Synthesis project conference on Chaco Society and Polity, published in 2001:

> The final, and most egregious, claim of Mesoamerican roots for Chaco is the Turners' assertion that Toltec cannibal psychopaths established Chaco in the wake of the fall of Tula. This interpretation is undone by any number of facts, not the least of which is that tree-ring dates for the early great house construction and Chaco predate the end of Tula by centuries.
>
> In our view, interpretations such as those offered by the Turners obscure the more enduring messages Chaco has to offer. Today many archaeologists

search the past for guidance to address the ills of modern society. As such, we must not allow ourselves to be distracted by ephemeral sensationalism designed to appeal to the prurient interests of an uninformed public. Even though depicting savagery, violence, and cannibalism seems to be currently in vogue, we feel that there are more meaningful messages to extract from the archaeological record.

15. The Chaco Synthesis Project

In the first decade of the twenty-first century, archaeologists took on an ambitious new challenge: to prepare and publish a synthesis of all that had been learned about Chaco. The emphasis was on lessons from the original Chaco Project of the 1970s and 1980s—probably the last major field project at Chaco in the lifetimes of today's southwestern archaeologists—but newer studies and findings would inform the synthesis as well.

By 2004 this Chaco Synthesis Project, led by Steve Lekson and funded by the National Park Service (primarily), the University of Colorado (secondarily), and a variety of host institutions, had already published a number of important journal articles and was nearing completion of a "final synthesis" report. Those partial quotes aren't mine, they're Lekson's. I think everyone who has conducted research at Chaco realizes that a full synthesis, while an admirable goal, may not be achievable, and that nothing about Chaco is ever really "final."

How do you summarize the largest field research project ever at Chaco? It isn't easy. Perhaps it takes a bit of audaciousness even to try. Lekson seems to have that quality. He also has the background and experience. He was a Chaco Project researcher from 1976 to 1986, got his Ph.D. in anthropology from the University of New Mexico in the process, produced several of the project's most cited research reports, and continues his very active research now from the Department of Anthropology and University Museum at the University of Colorado, in Boulder.

"The Chaco Project was almost certainly the last major archaeological research program at Chaco of our lifetimes," he says. It cost about six million dollars. That was the project's total budget over the years for fieldwork, analysis, and curation. That may or may not sound like much in these times, but it was a significant amount of government funding for a specific archaeological research project.

As I've described in earlier chapters, the Chaco Project's major fieldwork started in 1971 and ended in 1982. Minor projects have continued ever since. The Chaco Project archaeologists strived mightily to complete many specific reports in the 1980s, until their funding ran out in 1986, but even now that part of the project still proceeds on a smaller scale. All in all, they published about twenty technical monographs, in two major series, and an additional sixty or so journal articles, book chapters, theses, dissertations, and other shorter "official" Chaco Project contributions. Yet a synthesis evaluating and discussing all the Chaco Project's major findings eluded them.

Steve Lekson, with his archaeologist wife, Cathy Cameron (right), at a dig at Great Bluff House, a likely distant Chacoan outlier 125 miles from Chaco adjacent to Bluff, Utah. Lekson headed the Chaco Synthesis Project and edited its final report. University of Colorado at Boulder.

Lekson remembers that it was Chaco Project veteran Bob Powers who asked him to consider what a "final synthesis" effort might look like. The implication was that Lekson should lead it. Lekson's wicked, self-deprecating sense of humor colors his recollections about this. "My credentials," he says, were his ten-year association with the Chaco Project and "my famously poor judgment regarding foolish risks." He accepted Powers's challenge.

Joan Mathien was preparing an official history of the Chaco Project, detailing site excavations and what they produced, and it might have been natural for Lekson, or perhaps Lekson and Powers, to write the complementary "synthesis" volume. Lekson nixed that idea. "I felt strongly that I feel too strongly about Chaco," is how he puts it. "Lekson's Chaco—despite the fact that it is gospel truth—is not widely accepted," he says. "The Chaco Project's work was too important for me to control, intellectually, a 'final synthetic' effort."

So he proposed a series of small conferences, each devoted to a theme, and mixing Chaco Project "insiders" with interesting or influential "outsiders." And that's what was done. Over the next few years, archaeologists and other scholars met in small working conferences at Arizona State University, University of Arizona, University of New Mexico, Fort Lewis College, University of Colorado, the School of American Research (SAR) in Santa Fe, and Chaco Canyon. Bob Powers, Joan Mathien, Dabney Ford (and her National Park Service staff colleagues), and others helped in planning. The organization was, says Lekson, "somewhat complex and moderately elaborate."

The idea was that each of these mini-conferences would have no more than three or four insiders to Chacoan research and approximately three outsiders. Lekson considered the outsiders important to the process. "I wanted fresh eyes and fresh ideas to break us out of internal bickerings." Each small conference would produce half a dozen papers published in archaeological journals or books. And these conferences would lead to a final "Capstone" conference, and then on to the "synthesis" volume.

It seems to have worked pretty well. And, in contrast to the slow pace of Chaco archaeological publication in earlier decades, much of this Chaco synthesis work is published already. You almost get the idea that Chaco research is considered a hot topic! There has been, for example, an entire issue of *Archaeology Southwest* (the quarterly of the Center for Desert Archaeology, Tucson, Winter 2000); a special issue of the journal *American Antiquity* (Society of American Archaeology, January 2001); a special issue of *Kiva* (the journal of the Arizona Archaeological and Historical Society, Winter 2003), a special publication of the New Mexico Archeological Council (2001), and so on.

"The Chaco Synthesis was great fun and (I think) fruitful in its many activities and products," says Lekson in his draft introduction to the synthesis report, which was to be published by the School of American Research.

In the following pages I will be able to refer only to a fraction of this research, focusing on what (in my subjective judgment) are the key essentials. So I think it is important to credit all those who took part in the Chaco Synthesis Project conferences. Many are (whatever their age!) Chacoan old hands, familiar to you from earlier chapters; others are newcomers. Here's the lineup—with the theme of each conference, the organizers (in bold type), and then the other participants:

Ecology and Economy: **R. Gwinn Vivian, Carla VanWest, Jeffrey S. Dean**, Nancy Akins, Julio Betancourt, William Doolittle, Brian Fagan, Enrique Salmon, Mollie Toll, and "Butch" Wilson.

Organization of Production: **Catherine M. Cameron, H. Wolcott Toll**, Timothy Earle, Melissa Hagstrum, Peter J. McKenna, Peter Peregrine, and Lord Colin Renfrew.

Chaco World: **Nancy Mahoney, Keith Kintigh, John Kantner**, David Anderson, Roger Anyon, David Doyel, Dennis Gilpin, Sarah Herr, Winston Hurst, James Kendrick, Timothy Pauketat, Kathy Roler, Sarah Schlanger, and Ruth Van Dyke.

Society and Polity: **Linda S. Cordell, W. James Judge**, Nancy Mahoney, Mark Varien, John A. Ware, Henry T. Wright, and Norman Yoffee.

Architecture: **Stephen H. Lekson, Thomas C. Windes**, Wendy Ashmore, Taft Blackhorse, Patricia Fournier, Richard Friedman, Ben Nelson, John Schelberg, Anna Sofaer, John Stein, David Stuart, Phil Tuwalstiwa, Ruth Van Dyke, Michael Larkin.

Chaco, Mesa Verde, and the Confrontation with Time: **Patricia Limerick, Stephen H. Lekson**, Adriel Heisey, Roger Kennedy, Ann Fabian, Bob Greenlee, Enrique Salmon, Simon Ortiz, Peter Goin, Tessie Naranjo, Reg Saner, Leah Dilworth, Vine Deloria, Charles Scoggin, Kathy McKay, Terry Nichols, Russ Bodnar, Butch Wilson.

In addition, Karin Burd, Dabney Ford, Michael Larkin, Stephen H. Lekson, Frances Joan Mathien, Robert Powers, and Thomas C. Windes also attended most of the conferences.

The Capstone conference, inevitably, was not like the intimate workshops that preceded it. It was a full-fledged conference. ("It grew like Topsy," Lekson says.) Lynne Sebastian, then just elected president of the Society of American Archaeology (SAA), organized it. Still, the Chaco archaeologists and scholars weren't done. The School of American Research offered to host a small, conversational, post-Capstone mini-conference. The original Chaco Project had been planned at SAR in 1969, and it seemed appropriate to hold the final discussions there. So that mini-conference also was arranged, and it too proved successful. No one has ever said those who study the mysteries of Chacoan culture ever get tired of talking about them.

What the people of Chaco were up to remains a question tantalizingly just beyond our reach. Despite all the dedicated field study, despite all the discussion and theorizing, despite our most earnest efforts to try to peer back a millennium and more in order to understand the minds of these early Pueblo people, we cannot answer some of the most fundamental questions. We have huge amounts of data, but deep comprehension eludes us. We understand a lot, but not everything. Much mystery remains.

I don't find this surprising or distressing. We can study the material remains of past cultures—and the Chacoans left a wonderful legacy—but those remnants primarily help us answer the *what* kinds of questions. The *whys* are so much more difficult. Questions of motivation and purpose are difficult to satisfactorily answer even in regard to ourselves and our own

Participants in the Chaco Synthesis Project's small post-Capstone mini-conference at the School of American Research in Santa Fe in May 2003. Left to right, front row: Ruth Van Dyke, Timothy Pauketat, Steve Lekson, Ben Nelson, John Kantner, and Jim Judge. Back row: Richard Leventhal, Norm Yoffee, Lynne Sebastian, Tom Windes, Wolky Toll, and Linda Cordell. Not pictured: Gwinn Vivian. Photo by Katrina Lasko, ©2003, School for American Research, Santa Fe.

social groups and cultures today, so why should we think it would be easy to do so across the vast extent of time and cultural discontinuity that separate us from the people of Chaco? I find the attempt to gain that understanding ennobling, but I don't find falling short of fully doing so in any way unexpected or unsettling.

I'll try to give a flavor of the participants in the Chaco Synthesis Project struggling mightily in the first decade of the twenty-first century with all these kinds of questions. But first let's step back a bit.

In 1990, the SAA conducted a symposium at its annual meeting in Las Vegas, Nevada, focusing on Chacoan regional organization. Many of the most active researchers into the Chaco Phenomenon took part. The entire symposium was standing room only. Later, symposium organizer David E. Doyel edited and organized the revised papers—with a few new ones added afterward—into a conference volume that came out in 1992 but quickly went out of print. Copies of individual papers were kept, hoarded, and circulated like some underground publication. That's how I first got mine. Fortunately for others, in 2001 the Maxwell Museum of Anthropology reprinted the volume, with an added and very useful new multiauthor preface, "Chaco Update 2000." Looking back, editor David Doyel found the papers still relevant to Chaco research. Another contributor to the new preface, John Kantner, noted that research had been plentiful since 1992 but said many of the views stated in the 1992 volume have been confirmed, including (just to cite a few from his area of interest), "the scale of Chacoan expression, the importance of the ritual landscape, and the crucial role of exotic goods such as turquoise and Mesoamerican items."

Reviewing the papers in the Doyel volume, you can almost viscerally feel the researchers struggling with the uncertainties the Chaco system poses. Doyel himself contributed several elegant summaries attempting a synthesis of what had been discussed.

"Chaco retains an enigmatic, almost mystical character," he wrote. "Archaeologists agree that Chaco represented a new social order, but they disagree on specific interpretations of cause and the level of social complexity required."

Doyel makes a point that reaffirms my sense from listening to the archaeologists discuss these questions at the 1997 Pecos Conference at Chaco: "Current interpretation of the evolution and structure of the Chaco system is characterized by multiple models that have yet to be reconciled. . . . Numerous interpretations of Chacoan society exist. All of them cannot be correct. Currently the nature of Chacoan social organization is an empirical question in need of two future developments: the acquisition of additional archaeological evidence and the development of adequate measurement techniques. Meanwhile, the Chacoan mystery remains."

Windes, when we talked in early 1998, put this more bluntly: "It has gotten more confusing. The more we've learned, the more we don't know. The big picture has gotten more confused. The big picture is very difficult. It's too big and difficult to piecemeal out. We don't have that unity anymore."

Adds Steve Lekson: "We never did."

Windes, Lekson, and others encourage a look at archaeologist Lynne Sebastian's work. One of the newer models Doyel speaks of comes from Sebastian, who then was with the State Historic Preservation Division for the State of New Mexico and is now Director of Historic Preservation for the SRI Foundation. She spoke at the SAA conference and subsequently published a scholarly book on the subject, reprinted in 1996. Her work is based not only on her consideration of all the archaeological data; it also draws from a computer simulation she did of the relationship between variations in rainfall and probable abundance of corn production in the Chaco area.

Sebastian disputes explanations emphasizing that the rise of Chacoan sociopolitical complexity was an adaptive response to the difficulties of making a living raising sufficient food in the inhospitable environment of the San Juan basin. These explanations tended to emphasize the redistribution of foodstuffs as the central mechanism in this adaptation.

Instead, she argues that Chacoan sociopolitical complexity was a response to a slight amelioration of the San Juan basin environment—atypically abundant rainfall. In other words, the elaboration and expansion of Chacoan culture in the tenth and eleventh centuries, including the monumental construction programs, came about because at the time there was surplus production and little resource stress.

Sebastian believes groups in the 900s that had the best-watered farmlands extended that advantage into institutionalized positions of leadership. Then when rains came more frequently, as they did for several long periods in the ensuing century or so, the abundance led to expansion of control and expressions of success.

"In essence my argument," she writes, "is that a demonstrable minor improvement in the rainfall regime in the 1000s and early 1100s both enabled would-be leaders to legitimize their power and authority and provided the cultural system with sufficient capital in the form of excess production to permit the degree of cultural elaboration that is evident in the Chacoan archaeological record." (This seems to echo what Tom Windes told me about major building episodes correlating with near-decade-long wetter-than-normal periods.)

"The construction of great houses and great kivas, the acquisition of some of the trappings of power common at Chaco, and the construction of roads as visible ceremonial links to that center of power were all overlays on the basically local pattern of everyday life at these outlier sites.

"As the improved rainfall regime continued during the eleventh century, the power and influence of Chaco Canyon continued to expand, drawing more and more distant communities into the religious and sociopolitical system centered on the canyon."

Doyel says models like Lynne Sebastian's "point to productive and innovative directions and should be explored." He adds that separating out social, political, and economic factors will be important. And that's just one of the big issues with which the Chaco Synthesis Project archaeologists are still struggling.

Let's take some of their topics one at a time.

First, *The Chacoan World*. Was there really a Chaco regional system? How big was it and how did it operate? What were the Chacoan communities well outside Chaco Canyon itself like?

To help with these kinds of questions, Georgia State University archaeologist John Kantner and others assembled a database representing the state of knowledge on outlying great houses and the surrounding communities. Each great house was recorded using a standardized set of variables. The two seminal outlier surveys done in the 1970s and early 1980s by Mike Marshall and his colleagues and Bob Powers and his colleagues (the basis for my Chapter 7) were a starting point for the database, but, as Kantner says, "Much of that information has been updated in the last 20 years and many new great houses have been identified."

By the way, archaeologists are now downplaying the term *outliers* in favor of *great-house communities* or something similar. The idea is to avoid implying a secondary status for them in comparison to Chaco itself. This viewpoint is particularly important to archaeologists like Kantner and others who were brought into the Chaco Synthesis Project specifically to represent a more "outside" view, in an attempt to avoid any a priori assumptions about the relationship of great-house communities elsewhere with Chaco Canyon.

Few of the several hundred great houses outside of Chaco have been professionally excavated. For those that have, the information has been collected and put into the database. (It's at http://sipapu/gsu.edu/ chacoworld.html.) A total of 224 great houses in New Mexico, Arizona, Utah, and Colorado are listed and marked on an accompanying map according to whether the site consists of a great house only or a great house and a great kiva. Kantner notes that the database does not include any of the well-known great houses located in the heart of Chaco Canyon—"the area often referred to as 'downtown Chaco.' "

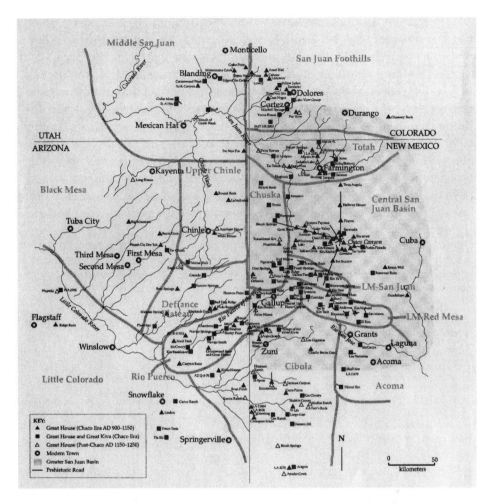

Distribution of great houses found in the Chaco World database. Courtesy John Kantner.

Are all of these great houses Chacoan? Well, obviously that raises a host of definition issues. Chaco Synthesis Project participant Keith Kintigh of Arizona State University tries to untangle the matter. The most common view is that "Chaco" refers to Chacoan archaeology wherever we might find it. But there isn't unanimous archaeological agreement about what that means. Kintigh uses the term "Chacoan architectural complex" to refer to a site that has a cluster of distinctive architectural features—including one or more great houses, great kivas, and associated earthworks and roads—that exhibit a strong affinity to the same features found in Chaco Canyon. He notes that originally, Chacoan great houses (Pueblo Bonito is, of course, the prime example) were described as unusually imposing pueblo structures with fine, often banded, core-and-veneer masonry, multiple stories or exceptional single-story height, and oversized rooms. They often have blocked-in or elevated kivas and frequently have great kivas and encircling berms and roads. Do the great house sites outside of Chaco have all these features? Well, no, but they have some. John Kantner points out that almost no single great house outside Chaco Canyon is known to have all these features. In Kintigh's view the presence of a great house "is a necessary but not sufficient condition" for a site to be considered part of the Chacoan architectural complex. It must have at least some of those other Chacoan features as well. So using this reasoning, he says the Chaco World database is a database of architectural complexes with great houses "that are *suspected* of being Chacoan" (my emphasis). He says that's exactly what was needed.

Number of Chacoan features identified at great houses for which complete data are available in the Chaco World database. Only those three features most often associated with Chacon architecture are considered: core-veneer masonry, multiple stories, and blocked-in kivas. Courtesy John Kantner.

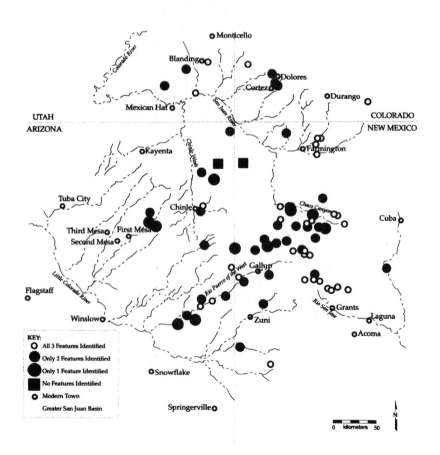

Kantner puts it in only a slightly different way: He, too, lists a variety of Chacoan features that distinguish Chacoan from unrelated sites—the large great houses, the core-veneer masonry, blocked-in kivas, formal great kivas, enclosed plaza areas, prehistoric roadways, Chacoan Dogoszhi-style ceramics, earthworks, and tower kivas. "The majority of great houses included in the database exhibit most of these features," he says, "although only a handful have all of them together."

What conclusions can we draw from this exercise?

"First, it may be that the Chaco world is bigger than we think it is," Kintigh says. "The Chaco world has expanded over the last 25 years, not so much because we have discovered new sites, but because people looked at old sites in new ways." He notes that for the last quarter century, "as archaeologists continued to look around the edges of the expanding Chacoan world, they have pushed the boundaries farther out. . . . I am not at all sure we have reached the end of that process."

Kintigh refers to "heroic efforts" by others to try to make sense of the data about these Chaco-like communities spread over what are now four states, but says despite that, in his view we still know very little about them. (Remember, almost none of these sites have been excavated; most archaeological inferences come from closely examining the mounds that betray their presence beneath.)

Did that expanded Chacoan world, however, function as a regularly interacting, interdependent, unified system? Chaco World database organizer John Kantner, in the 2003 special issue of *Kiva,* took on exactly that question. Kantner is one of the young breed of archaeologists Lekson brought into the Chaco Synthesis Project to bring a fresh, outside view of Chaco to the discussions. A professor in the Department of Anthropology and Geography at Georgia State University, he got his Ph.D. in 1999 from the University of California, Santa Barbara, with a dissertation on sociopolitical change and evolution of the Chaco Anasazi.

"Yes, Steve likes to refer to us as the 'Young Turks,' " Kantner told me in 2004. "I guess he includes me, Ruth Van Dyke, Jim Kendrick, Andrew Duff, Nancy Mahoney, and some others in that category. We're all in our thirties."

Kantner was born in 1967, just four years before Chaco Project fieldwork began. But age depends on how you look at it. Kantner noted that he was turning thirty-seven, "so 'young' is relative perhaps to the expectations of what professors should look like!"

Kantner has analyzed a variety of evidence noted by some of those "Young Turk" colleagues to reach some conclusions that the larger Chaco world outside of Chaco Canyon was not really an integrated system. In fact, he calls it a "non-system." He points to the fact that Chacoan roadways were

*John Kantner is one of the "Young Turk" archaeologists brought in to the Chaco
Synthesis Project to provide a new-generation, outside view of things.*

most elaborated near Chaco Canyon itself and around some of the outside
great-house communities but become far less distinct elsewhere. He says
the paucity of ceramics along the roads indicates they weren't very well
traveled. He points to evidence that the vast majority of ceramics in great-
house/Chacoan communities outside Chaco Canyon were locally
produced and that utilitarian material in Chaco was limited to having originated only along the inside edges of the San Juan basin (essentially just
northwestern New Mexico), not beyond. He believes the topographic
boundaries surrounding the San Juan basin substantially limited interaction
with the wider areas beyond. "I don't know whether those boundaries were
merely symbolic boundaries or were actually physically restricting," Kantner
told me.

He even tackles one of the cherished ideas of Chaco archaeologists,
that there was a widespread signal-fire communication system that
allowed information to be exchanged quickly throughout the whole Chaco-
dominated San Juan basin and beyond (see Chapter 6). He undermines one
aspect of such a proposed communications system, the idea that tower

kivas at various Chacoan sites could have been used for communication with other sites at some distance. The Chaco World database contains data on tower kivas, defined as elevated kivas that project one or more stories above the rest of the great-house structure. The database shows that nine of the ten tower kivas are approximately 25 miles apart, "indeed suggestive of their use as signaling stations," says Kantner. But here's the problem. Kantner and Georgia State University graduate student Ronald Hobgood conducted a study using a Geographic Information System of the tower kivas at two sites—Kin Ya'a and Haystack. This study, they say, shows that the tower kivas were not built to communicate with one another, even if intermediate relaying stations existed. "In fact," they report, "while their elevated positions greatly enhanced visibility of the immediate community area, their extra height did not increase long-distance visibility at all."

A whole variety of such evidence and arguments leads Kantner to suggest that "Chaco was not unified; the communities exhibiting Chacoan characteristics do not appear to have formed a single consolidated and integrated unit." He agrees that the great-house architectural tradition appears to have originated in the canyon, and says the Chaco World database confirms this. (The earliest great houses outside the canyon were nearest the canyon.) This may well have been true of landscape features such as roadways and the Dogoszhi style of pottery as well.

"The evidence indicates that whatever Chaco was, it was not 'a *regularly interacting or interdependent group of items forming a unified whole,*' " Kantner argues, referring to a dictionary definition of *system.* The extent to which stylistic similarities indicate a unified whole is unclear, he says. "Because the Chacoan features emerged in Chaco Canyon first, they were elaborated there sooner than in other areas and subsequently employed to the canyon's advantage."

He does concur with those who see the canyon as becoming increasingly important as a religious center. Kantner and colleague Keith Kintigh agree with others that members of outlying great-house communities must have occasionally visited Chaco Canyon bearing gifts or offering services such as labor. These ritualistic interactions could provide benefits to the outlying communities as well. Such large-scale social occasions might have bolstered social cohesiveness and perhaps marked and commemorated seasonal changes important to religion and farming. Kantner agrees with that view.

"However," Kantner argues, "it seems unlikely that Chaco ever became strongly hegemonic in the sense that it was able to directly influence activity in the distant Chacoan communities." (This, he and I both note, is in strong contrast to arguments Lekson and some others make.)

Kantner says the closer-in communities (in the San Juan basin itself, especially those to the south and west of Chaco) were naturally more closely linked to Chaco Canyon than those beyond. "These more distant communities appear to have acknowledged Chaco's reputation by adopting some of the Chacoan features to varying degrees and modifying them and presumably the associated ideology to fit into local sociopolitical dynamics." In other words, these more distant communities outside the San Juan basin had their own needs, outlooks, and resources. They could pick and choose what features of Chaco they wanted to adopt. Some of them, he suggests, did emulate at a much smaller scale what Chaco Canyon was doing across the San Juan basin, "as if they aspired to establish their own 'mini-Chacos.' "

Nevertheless, he says, "The main point is to emphasize the non-systemic nature of the group of communities exhibiting Chacoan features. . . . The evidence indicates that the group of Chacoan communities as a whole did not develop interdependence or regular networked interaction."

Architecture and Cityscapes. I've talked a lot previously about Chacoan architecture, and for good reason. It has a lot to tell us about the culture. But even within the canyon itself the view now is expanding from just the dozen monumental great houses—considered the central fact of Chaco—to what are increasingly being called "cityscapes." As Chaco Project veterans Steve Lekson, Tom Windes, and Peter McKenna say in their new review of Chacoan architecture for the synthesis project, "The Chacoan monumental landscape—we will say 'cityscape'—extended beyond Great Houses in a complex architectural composition. . . . The Chaco cityscape was unprecedented in Pueblo prehistory and unexpected in modern understandings of ancient Southwestern architecture."

Chaco Canyon was far more than just the twelve massive great houses known today. Earlier surveys show some three hundred smaller "pueblo" sites in the canyon, again most unexcavated. Generally these are called "small sites," but they are being given more and more significance. For one thing, most of the people who lived in the Chaco area lived at such sites.

"At a guess," Lekson, Windes, and McKenna say in their Chaco Synthesis Project paper, "95 percent of Anasazi people in Chaco's region resided in small 'unit pueblos' or 'Prudden units,' while 5 percent lived in great houses." They believe that such unit pueblo small sites were family residences—in some cases for large, extended families. Some small sites in the canyon aggregated together. Many—especially those built in the latter part of the eleventh century—exhibit a number of architectural techniques and features of the great houses. Some had elements of classic "Chaco-style" kivas. Some of the masonry was massive in the style of great houses, and several multistory small sites were built. Marcia Truell has noted more than forty small sites with the "core and veneer" masonry that was so typical of great-house construction.

These "great house–like" sites concentrate around South Gap in "downtown" Chaco. (South Gap is a break in the mesa forming the south edge of Chaco Canyon nearly directly opposite Pueblo Bonito. Scores of other small sites were concentrated around the other topographic break, Fajada Gap, where Fajada Butte is centered.) Lekson and colleagues say some of these sites are comparable in size to several named, smaller great houses such as Casa Chiquita, west of Pueblo Bonito.

"It is our opinion," they say, "that, if transported to other parts of the Anasazi region, many of the late, South Gap 'small sites' would receive serious consideration as 'outlying' great houses." Part of that may just be semantics, but the same thing, which they call increased "massing," is true of other small sites, especially in Chaco Canyon's core area. They call it a "Bonito-style" effect, subtly permeating the architecture of contemporary small sites.

All these small sites, emulating portions of the great houses to some degree, were a vital aspect of the Chacoan cityscape, Lekson and colleagues say. These residences would have brought life to the canyon. They were where most daily activity took place, in contrast to the monumental, walled, enclosed great houses such as Pueblo Bonito and Chetro Ketl. Roadways, earthern mounds, and waterworks would also have contributed to the designed, citylike feel of the canyon. Conventionally seen as "trash mounds," most mounds associated with great houses were in fact "earthen architecture," Lekson, John Stein, and many others now argue. Archaeologist Wirt Wills disagrees, saying they are middens, but Lekson, for one, thinks Wills is wrong. Windes believes that the mounds are at least in part middens but that they also fulfilled other architectural roles. The most obvious examples of the mounds are those in front of Pueblo Bonito, which stood six feet tall and had thick, repeated adobe upper surfaces and stairways to reach those surfaces. Other mounds, says Lekson, such as those at Chetro Ketl and Pueblo Alto, lacked the masonry facing, surfaces, and stairways but can likewise be seen as intentional architectural features. He says significant portions of the fill of these mounds was indeed trash, but the trash was often not the result of conventional daily living. Some sites (Hungo Pavi, Wijiji) have no mounds; others have mounds "wildly out of proportion to their size." Archaeologist Wolky Toll argues that much of Pueblo Alto's "trash mound" was ritual or ceremonial in nature.

These weren't the only earthen structures. Substantial berms also lined several roads within the canyon, and some other mounds appear to be free-standing, not associated within any great houses.

Lekson, Windes, and McKenna find the reluctance of some of their colleagues to accept the reality of earthen architecture at Chaco puzzling. They note that mounds—earthen architecture—were common among many corn-growing ancient societies in North America, from Mesoamerica and Mexico to the Hohokam in southern Arizona, to the Hopewell and Mississippian cultures. They ask why is it so hard to imagine the same kinds of structures at Chaco—especially since the evidence for them is so good.

Lekson argues that the Chacoan waterworks were also part of a designed landscape architecture, "a major visual theme in the cityscape." Chaco was a dry desert, but he says gardens, ponds, and canals apparently filled much of the space between great houses, small sites, mounds, and roads. There's even evidence that a large artificial pond or lake filled the lower canyon. He wonders—you have to admit it's an intriguing, even poignant thought in this mostly dry part of the continent—whether in some of their gardens the Chacoans raised flowers. He notes that flowers were, and still are, important to Pueblo cosmology. "Waterworks might become sparkling, dynamic, life-giving monuments, fringed with flowers," he says.

Much other work on the Chaco cityscape has been done by the Chaco Protection Sites group of John Stein and his colleagues (see Chapter 13) and the Solstice Project work of Anna Sofaer and her colleagues (see Chapter 14). Lekson notes that the work of both those groups is "unconventional" and "under-published" but says both groups have produced important conclusions and insights. "Whether or not their interpretations of the cityscape are completely correct, they are visionary in demonstrating that Chaco (like Mississippian and Mesoamerican cityscapes) was created *by design*: that is, shaped by cosmological, geomantic, aesthetic, and symbolic principles."

"The Chaco we present here is not Chaco as it is conventionally understood," say Lekson, Windes, and McKenna. "Chaco was not a valley with a half-dozen large pueblos. Chaco, we think, was a large, formal, designed settlement. . . .Chaco was monumental: A range of large, costly, permanent forms were employed to create a place unlike any other in its world. Chaco was multiethnic: conventional arguments for different cultural or ethnic groups within the canyon are buttressed by Chaco's place within its region, so large that many distinct groups and languages are implicated. Chaco was, for its time and place, cosmopolitan. . . .

"Chaco was far more than a rural village or a congerie of pueblos: Chaco was a city."

Hierarchy. And all that brings us back to one of the thorniest, most disputatious issues of all: What kind of social system was Chaco, and how did all that planning, work, and activity get organized? Some archaeologists argue that forms of hierarchical control were necessary; others prefer to see a more communal type of organization, much like that of today's Pueblo cultures. The arguments seem nearly endless. Some of the communalist, egalitarian thinking is aesthetic, it seems to me, perhaps even a tad romanticized, even though to its credit it is informed by an awareness of present-day Pueblo cultures. But which view does the evidence best support?

Lekson, Windes, and McKenna come firmly down on the side of hierarchy. "We believe that great house construction required centralized, hierarchical decision-making at Chaco," they say in their synthesis project draft paper. The labor requirements to build everything coupled with the view of a relatively small in-canyon population—perhaps several thousand people at most—seems to demand external labor. And this requires recruitment and coordination. And then there's the formal design of Chaco's structures and their interrelationships. The authors point out that communalism can account for "haphazard" pueblos of the type familiar all over the ancient Southwest. The Chacoan great houses, however "stand in stark, formal contrast" to those.

"We question 'self-organization' of form," Lekson, Windes, and McKenna say. "Great houses, the city of Chaco, and the region itself were designed, and their creation coordinated by planners and decision-makers. It is the scale and formality of Chacoan architecture, as much or more than the labor required to create it, that strongly suggest centralized authority and hierarchy. We may wish it were otherwise, but Chacoan construction, at least, very likely had bosses."

The Chaco Synthesis Project's mini-conference on Chaco society and polity spent a lot of time considering these issues. Linda Cordell of the University of Colorado and Jim Judge (the former Chaco Project director) of Fort Lewis College in Durango led that conference. They summarized its conclusions in papers in the newsletter *Archaeology Southwest,* in the conference volume itself, and in the final Chaco Synthesis Project draft volume. They report general agreement that Chacoan society was probably unique in the Southwest and perhaps among nonstate societies in general. "Chaco may represent a form of government that has no suitable analog in the historic, ethnographic, or modern worlds," they say.

They note that over the past fifteen years, different archaeologists have described Chaco society and polity "as ranging from egalitarian and resembling modern Pueblos to one of two kinds of rudimentary hierarchical societies, to a state capable of extracting tribute from outlier communities." They say the workshop narrowed the interpretive range of this spectrum of views "but perhaps not as much as some would like."

They do come down hard against one view: Was Chaco an outlier of some Mesoamerican state? "Here we would like to go on record, for ourselves and for the sentiment of the conference," write Cordell and Judge.

Ever since the work of Harold Gladwin in 1945 and with evidence constantly accumulating, "it has been abundantly clear that Chaco Canyon and all its monuments are ancestral Pueblo—conceived, made, and eventually no longer lived in by the ancestors of modern Pueblo Indians," they say.

Another thing the conference participants agreed on was the importance of ritual in shaping Chacoan society and culture. That Chaco was a ritual center is now widely accepted, and this religious or spiritual role contrasts to a degree with earlier practical, economic-based explanations. Rituality, they suggest, might voluntarily bring together people with diverse belief systems and backgrounds. Rituality can also be a political force in itself. It might even substitute to some degree for the need for central leadership.

"The importance of ritual does not mean there were not people with greater power and greater wealth," Cordell and Judge write. "Such 'elites' may have achieved their status through their ritual knowledge, but there is evidence that there were economic consequences." They point, for instance, to evidence that people of Pueblo Bonito were taller than people elsewhere in the canyon, presumably from eating better food than those elsewhere in the canyon. And better diets, all other things being equal, often indicate higher status and power.

They furthermore point out that the labor investment in Chaco great houses was "truly enormous." In their view, it was clearly beyond the capabilities of the resident population in Chaco Canyon, particularly if that population numbered only in the hundreds. "At the very least, some form of central leadership was needed to direct the construction efforts. But there is not compelling evidence for strong political leadership roles or an elite social stratum at Chaco." They say that in the end the conference participants were not comfortable with the use of the term *polity* to describe Chaco society. (The term refers to a center for a political organization of considerable regional size, and it implies a political coherence that not everyone sees at ancient Chaco.)

Conclude Cordell and Judge: "Chaco may have been a ritual entity, or something like the eastern Pueblos, but it appears to have been unique to itself, too: a society created in no image with which we are, today, familiar."

Nancy Mahoney, another participant in the Chaco Society and Polity conference, explored these questions through examination of Chaco's monumental architecture and what she calls "conspicuous display."

Chaco was, and still is, a splendid example of monumental architecture. The great houses were monumental in size and overengineered for any practical function they could have served, and this, she points out, is the very definition of monumental architecture. Monumental architecture plays a variety of roles in stimulating the human imagination, arousing a sense of awe, and creating a sense of unity.

Humans respond to monumentality in similar ways, whether the features are natural (mountains, canyons, oceans, and other dramatic settings) or manmade. "The quality of *magnitude* is awe-inspiring, and evokes, spiritual, religious, aesthetic, and even philosophical reactions," Mahoney writes. People also respond to monumental structures in a more rational sense as well. "Monuments convey a universal message of mass coordination of human labor. . . . It is clear that a society capable of building a monumental structure had the excess energy to alter the landscape above and beyond what was required for subsistence."

Another important aspect of monumental architecture is that it endures. She notes that it creates a "highly visible past" that survives across generations and shapes future actions and consciousness. Monumental architecture is also commemorative. The structures may commemorate important events and ideas, or important religious and cosmographic concepts; they certainly memorialize the process by which they came to be.

What does any of this mean for understanding Chacoan social and political organization? Well, Mahoney argues that it doesn't necessarily require or represent conspicuous consumption by elites. She feels it doesn't require strong political hierarchy. Looking at other societies, she finds that monumental architecture is frequently present even when independent evidence of elites is lacking. She argues that the great houses are the products of "conspicuous display behavior among groups—rather than conspicuous consumption by elites." This makes it possible to understand, she writes, "how and why such structures were built in societies that lacked institutionalized leaders."

"I still believe that the independent evidence for institutionalized leaders [at Chaco] is ambiguous at best. . . . To find leaders at Chaco we need to look at more than the architecture, and we need to accept the possibility that they may not be the kind of leaders that built monuments to legitimize their own authority."

Lekson will have none of it. Chaco had to have rulers, and strong ones, he believes, and he sees the evidence everywhere. He earlier wrote pungently about this in his part of the new multiauthor preface to the David Doyel volume's 2001 reprint by the Maxwell Museum. The Chaco synthesis project mini-conferences were over, although the overall "Capstone" conference was still to come. Lekson had done his best as organizer and host to stay out of the discussions, remain relatively neutral, and allow everyone their say. But he disagreed with many of the views he heard, and he couldn't hold off any longer.

"With the polls now closed, I move (temporarily) from grouchy host to crabby pundit," he writes. "I offer some post-election, pre-capstone observations. The electorate seems intent on reestablishing a happy, peaceful South-west, free of tyranny, taxation, and bad times. We want a *nice* Southwest (cannibals need not apply). We also want a *small* Southwest. Local auton-omy emerged as a strong theme in the sessions, and in recent literature: every site and site cluster is unique, postmodernly complicated, historically contingent, and happily local. And we want a *simple* Southwest. . . . And for the ancient Southwest, that's no boss at all."

"What about the high-status burials and elite residences?" he asks. "Chaco had both." He notes that conferee Nancy Akins had documented in considerable detail two high-status burials at Pueblo Bonito, in Lekson's words, "middle-aged men buried in log crypts with huge quantities of high-status goods, with other bodies piled on top."

Also, he asks, what about the elite housing? Chaco's magnificent build-ings, "strikingly different in scale and form from the homes of the other 95 percent of eleventh-century Pueblo people," yet inhabited by relatively few people, "suggest elite residences." Those who argue otherwise, he says, have to offer, argue, and believe "a number of remarkably strained alternate interpretations."

Lynne Sebastian takes a more cautious view of all these issues. In her concluding chapter in the Chaco Synthesis Project final report, she retreats a bit from Lekson's confidently stated conclusions to voice again archaeolo-gists' difficulties—once you go beyond the now-abundant knowledge of the Chacoans' tangible works—understanding the Chacoan culture at a deeper, more fundamental level.

"When we try to explain how and why all of this came about, how Cha-coan society was organized and functioned, it sometimes seems that we are no farther along now than we were when the Chaco project started more than 30 years ago," she writes. She laments that virtually every effort to explain Chaco gets bogged down in fruitless dichotomies—hierarchical vs. nonhierarchical, competitive vs. communal, egalitarian vs. nonegalitarian, and most recent, ritual vs. political control.

As I mentioned earlier in this chapter, these contradictions are hardly surprising. Material remains can provide good clues but not necessarily auto-matic answers about the deeper workings of a society, especially the motives and forces that drive it. Archaeologists just have to do the best they can in gaining understanding, sifting through all the evidence, debating among themselves, and presenting conclusions with whatever mixtures of semicer-tainty and humbling uncertainty seem to each appropriate.

With Chaco, the central unresolved question, at least to Sebastian and a number of others, is still this matter of were there institutionalized differ-ences in social, economic, and political power. At least the arguments have advanced a bit. As Sebastian says in her Chaco Synthesis chapter, "By the early years of the twenty-first century, the central issue in studies of Chacoan organization is no longer 'was it or wasn't it complex' but rather, 'how was it complex?' She acknowledges the strong evidence everywhere of rituality. She acknowledges the debate over evidence that certain Chacoans had greater personal wealth and power. But she argues that power differentials don't require powerful individuals. She points to many societies in the world—especially in sub-Saharan Africa—where power is vested in groups such as clans, lineages, fraternities, or councils. There she finds many examples of societies "in which complex relations of political and social power take a variety of nonhierarchical forms." Writes Sebastian: "Chiefs and kings are not the only route to organizational complexity and differential power." This, you will see, anticipates an argument made by Lekson.

Lekson came back in full form in 2004 in his draft introduction to the final Chaco Synthesis Project volume, of which he is the editor. It is vintage Lekson. "I have strong opinions about Chaco, and I felt honor bound [during the synthesis project conferences] to not load decks, rig juries, pull wires, self-fulfill prophecies. While I helped to shape form, I tried not to meddle with content. Consequently," he writes, "I disagree with many of the statements, conclusions, and interpretations" in the "excellent chapters" that follow his introduction. He adds that he nevertheless respects the authors of those opinions.

"Here's my chance at last," he says. "What I say can't bias the outcome." And he proceeds with what he sardonically calls "a few calm, dispassionate observations on a Chacoan matter which seems, to me, important."

(I asked Lekson in 2004 if he considers himself an iconoclast. He often seems to take an opposite view from many—but not all—his Chaco colleagues. "I only disagree with stuff I think is wrong and important," he told me. "Stuff that's wrong and unimportant isn't worth all the ensuing hassle." He added: "I've really tried to avoid the typical academic negative tactics, by using other people's research—and accepting their conclusions—in novel ways. That seems to scare people, too. Oh well.")

In his introduction, Lekson continues commenting on the issue of hierarchy at Chaco:

"What's important is this: Chaco had rulers, leaders, centralized hierarchical decision makers. Why flog that dead horse?" He notes that "many (most?) contemporary Southwesternists are not in sympathy with political hierarchy at Chaco. Many favor reconstructions of Chaco which are nonhierarchical, decentralized, pleasantly un-complex." He obviously disagrees: "Is it that great houses happened: happily, communally?" His answer: "No."

"Chaco was too big to just happen. It is the nature of leadership that is at issue, something political, permanent, and hierarchical; or something ritual and ceremonial, spiritual, situational, and evanescent?"

"Pueblos don't have political leaders, but Chaco did." And in support of that assertion he points to three lines of evidence: the high-status burials previously mentioned, the elite residences, and regional primacy.

"We have seen these rulers, archaeologically: the high-status burials from Pueblo Bonito and, particularly, the very rich crypt burials of two middle-aged men. I interpret scores of additional bodies piled above these burials as 'retainers.' These two men were buried in the mid-eleventh century (in my opinion), deep in the much earlier rooms of the original, early tenth-century 'Old Bonito.' Watch them closely: these burials tend to vanish in Chacoan debates. . . .

"Were there only two such rulers? Perhaps: Over a century span (Chaco's glory days from 1020 to 1125), two 'kings' might be all that were required. . . . These two men may well have been the rulers remembered as 'our kings'—a term used by a traditional Native American man from the Chaco area. . . . Found anywhere else in the world, the high-status burials of Pueblo Bonito would suggest political power. 'High-status' burials are strong evidence for elites and leaders."

Lekson talks about his synthesis project colleagues' discomfort, even annoyance, at his use of the word "kings." Says Lekson: "Europeans have kings, but Indians are allowed only chiefs." He notes that "chief" is not a Native American word. Nor, he notes, is "ruler," "leader," or "centralized hierarchical decision makers," or—for that matter—"shaman" or "priest." Asks Lekson: "Why not 'king'? If it looks like a duck, walks like a duck, and quacks like a duck . . ."

Lekson's second set of evidence is the Chacoan great houses. "Great houses themselves—elite residences—are monumentally obvious signs of hierarchy, hidden in plain sight. As long as we are getting into trouble, let's call them palaces, and see what happens. Outrage! 'Palaces' imply states. We don't allow (Native) states north of Mexico."

Lekson's third category for strong evidence of hierarchy is the regional system—Chaco's place in a large region of great houses. "Chaco sits at the center of a region of remarkable clarity," he says. "The Chacoan region is as clear an archaeological signature as we may hope to find in pre-state societies. Chacoan great houses are recognizable from Cedar Mesa in Utah to Quemado in New Mexico, from Hope in Arizona to Guadalupe in New Mexico. . . . The important thing is the reality of the empirical pattern of a region of hundreds of small great houses, with Chaco at the center."

Lekson reexamines at some length the debates about the Chacoan road system. He doesn't deny that the roads were "heavily, even primarily symbolic," but he argues strongly that they are real, that they went places (even the North Road continues far beyond where others have said it ends, he argues, down Kutz Canyon and toward Salmon Ruin), and that they are significant not just symbolically but as important parts of the regional network. Likewise, he doesn't find the variability among outlying great houses surprising or indicative of a weak, insubstantial system. "Why hold great houses to an undefined but apparently quite high standard of standardization? . . . I fear a return of provincialism to Chacoan studies, fracturing its region into small units, study areas perceived (as they must be) as wholly or largely independent."

He also suggests, seemingly contrary to Kantner, that the whole regional system could work in part due to "the large and complex line-of-sight communication system postulated throughout the Chacoan region." The communication system was proposed in the early 1970s (see Chapter 6), and Lekson says subsequent work has expanded knowledge of this system "to encompass most of the northern San Juan Basin and beyond." He told me that the line of site *does* work for most of the northern San Juan basin. "My point is this: the apparent absence of the line-of-sight system in Kantner's area [the southeast San Juan basin] does not negate the demonstrable system over much of the rest of the Chaco area."

"For example," he says, "Far View House, a great house on Mesa Verde [in southwestern Colorado] is aptly named; from Far View, they could see Chaco and Chaco could see them. Chimney Rock, at Pagosa Springs [also in Colorado, farther to the east] is another excellent example. We know that the line-of-sight system extends over much of the northern San Juan Basin; it is my firm belief that similar linkages will be found between Chaco and the most distant 'outlier' great houses in all directions."

Many things moved into Chaco, Lekson says. Communications moved out, and that, he suggests, is how the system worked. *What* the regional system did, and *why*, are questions for the next several generations of archaeologists, he says. "Still," he finds, "some things are clear, at least to me":

"Chaco was the central place in a large, well-defined region; moreover, it was a primary center, unmistakably larger, notably more elaborate, incomparably more monumental than any other place in its territory. The region was integrated by architectural monuments, (probably) roads, and (perhaps) constant contact via a complex communication system.

"Taken together, kingly burials, palatial great houses, and a large (if gossamer) region in which Chaco was a city among villages suggest Chaco was neither a Pueblo (in the 'ethnographic parallel' sense) nor an egalitarian commune. Chaco was the center of a complex polity, suffused with ritual and ceremony, but fundamentally political and hierarchical."

So if you want certainty, we can find much in Chaco's tangible remains and the insights that archaeologists have painstakingly teased from them over the past century, and especially in the past thirty-plus years beginning with the Chaco Project. As Lekson told me in 2004, "There are a few (many?) of us who think Chaco is remarkably clear in its evidence, that archaeology doesn't get any easier than this." But if you can embrace or at least tolerate uncertainty, some of the arguments continue. Despite the admirable efforts of the Chaco Synthesis Project participants and the extraordinary pace of publication since the late 1990s, Chaco provides abundant puzzles. Purpose and meaning, the whys and the hows, still prove elusive.

We can only, still, wonder and yearn to know and understand. In their grand architecture, their elegant masonry, their designed cityscape, their roadways and signal systems, and their networks of several hundred Chacoan great houses spread throughout parts of four modern states, the ancient people of Chaco left wondrous remnants of a creative, ebullient culture. They also left us with an equally priceless legacy: mystery and deep, unanswered—perhaps even unanswerable—questions.

Appendix

Chaco Place Names

Casa Chiquita   "Tiny House" in Spanish.

Casa Rinconada   *Rincon* & *rinconada* in Spanish mean "corner" in the sense of an inside corner only. (*Esquina* is an outside corner.) Thus, "House in a Corner" or "House in a Nook" is a good rendering. Properly in Spanish, *rinconada* is a noun, not an adjective, so obviously this is a gringo-produced word.

Chaco   All early Spanish sources show this as "Chaca." The -o ending is an error that began when the Spanish term was Anglicized. The Spanish may be derived (possibly second-hand through some Pueblo language), from the Navajo term *tsegai*—a contraction of *tse tigai*, "white rock"—currently used as a place name on Chacra Mesa. This would mean that application to the canyon is a secondary usage—which most likely took place in Spanish. This may help to explain why present-day Navajos can't figure out what we whites have done to come up with such a name!

Chetro Ketl   This name has gone through so many translations in so many languages that no one really knows its origin or meaning. Some suggested translations of the past have included "Rain Pueblo" and "Shining Pueblo."

Fajada Butte   (Pronounced Fa-HA-Da.) "Belted" in Spanish. So named because of the black band around it, which is a low grade of coal. This is where the "sun dagger" solstice marker is located.

Hungo Pavi   (Pronounced UN-Go PA-Vee.) Like Chetro Ketl, no one knows for sure where this name came from—much less what the original name may have meant. One suggestion is that it looks sort of similar to a Hopi Indian place name—perhaps. One suggested translation is "Crooked Nose"—but nobody knows!

*"Chaco Place Names" is provided courtesy of Chaco Culture National Historical Park. The information is a joint effort of National Park Service Curator and Historian David Brugge, who supplied the most specific definitions; former Chaco Park Archaeologist C. Randall Morrison; and Chaco Park Technician Ellen Boling.

Kin Bineola (Pronounced KIN BIN-E-OH-La.) This is definitely Navajo, from *Kin Binááyotí,* "House in the Wind" or "House the Wind Blows Around." This is one of the more than seventy separate Chacoan townsites scattered throughout the San Juan Basin and linked by over 400 miles of ancient roads.

Kin Kletso "Yellow House" in Navajo.

Kin Klizhin "Black House" in Navajo. Another outlier, to the south of Chaco Canyon, it can only be reached by crossing private land and is difficult to find.

Kin Ya'a "House Rising Up High" in Navajo. Another outlier, near Crownpoint, New Mexico.

Penasco Blanco (Pronounced Pen-YAS-Co.) In Spanish this means "Rocky White." This was, again, not quite correctly translated into English, but it currently seems to imply that the ruin is on a "rocky white" point of land.

Pueblo Alto "High Village" in Spanish. This site is on top of the mesa, due north of Pueblo Bonito, and is the terminus of many of the Chacoan roads—including the Great North Road that leads toward the Aztec and Salmon ruins—also Chacoan outliers.

Pueblo Bonito "Beautiful Village" in Spanish. This name goes back to Spanish-Mexican times and was written in the notes of the Washington Expedition of Topographical Engineers when they came through the canyon in 1849.

Pueblo del Arroyo "Village by the Wash" in Spanish. This structure shows many varieties of architecture and stonework, which support the idea that it was built, occupied, abandoned, then reoccupied.

Pueblo Pintado "Painted Village" in Spanish. This is another Chacoan outlier, almost as large as Pueblo Bonito. It was the first Chacoan ruin recorded by Lt. Simpson of the Washington Expedition in 1849. In early records, one of its names was "Pueblo de los Ratones," or "Village of the Rats"!

Talus Unit So called because it is built on the talus slope behind Chetro Ketl. The actual dates of its construction are unknown, but it is thought to be contemporary with Chetro Ketl.

Tsin Kletsin From the Navajo *tsin ttizhin,* "Black Wood". It is assumed to be derived from charred timbers once in the ruins—perhaps.

Una Vida "One Life" in Spanish. Also recorded by the Washington Expedition, this medium-sized pueblo near the visitor center has one of the best-preserved rock art panels in the park just a short distance up the slope behind it.

Wijiji (Pronounced Wee-GEE-gee.) Navajo for "Greasewood House"—possibly from the Navajo word for the greasewood plant, *díwóshiishzhiin.*

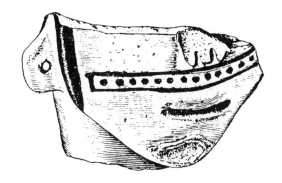

Selected Bibliography

Prologue. The Ancient Way

Astrov, Margot, ed. *American Indian Prose and Poetry.* New York: Capricorn Books, 1962.
Bunzel, Ruth. "Introduction to Zuni Ceremonialism.'" *47th Annual Report of the Bureau of American Ethnology,* Washington, 1932.
Bunzel, Ruth. "Zuni Ritual Poetry." *47th Annual Report of the Bureau of American Ethnology,* Washington, 1932.
Canby, Thomas Y. "The Anasazi: Riddles in the Ruins." *National Geographic,* November 1982.
Courlander, Harold. *Hopi Voices.* Albuquerque: University of New Mexico Press, 1982.
Eggan, Fred. *Social Organization of the Western Pueblos.* Chicago: University of Chicago Press, 1950.
Judd, Neil M. "Everyday Life in Pueblo Bonito." *National Geographic,* September 1925.
Keegan, Marcia. *Mother Earth, Father Sky.* New York: Grossman Publishers, 1974.
Muench, David, and Donald G. Pike. *Anasazi: Ancient People of the Rock.* Palo Alto: American West, 1974.
Page, Susanne and Jake. *Hopi.* New York: Harry N. Abrams, 1982.
Tyler, Hamilton A. *Pueblo Gods and Myths.* Norman: University of Oklahoma Press, 1964.
Vivian, R. Gwinn, Dulce N. Dodgen, and Gayle H. Hartmann. *Wooden Ritual Artifacts From Chaco Canyon, New Mexico: The Chetro Ketl Collection.* Anthropological Papers of the University of Arizona, No. 32. Tucson: University of Arizona Press, 1978.
Wormington, H. M. *Prehistoric Indians of the Southwest.* Popular Series No. 7. Denver: Colorado Museum of Natural History, 1947.

1. The Lieutenant and the Cowboy

McNitt, Frank. *Richard Wetherill: Anasazi.* Albuquerque: University of New Mexico Press, 1966.
Schmedding, Joseph. *Cowboy and Indian Trader.* Albuquerque: University of New Mexico Press, 1974.

Simpson, James H. *Navaho Expedition: Journal of a Military Reconnaissance from Santa Fe, New Mexico to the Navaho Country Made in 1849.* Edited and annotated by Frank McNitt. Norman: University of Oklahoma Press, 1964.

2. Judd and the Geo Excavations

Judd, Neil M. *The Architecture of Pueblo Bonito.* Smithsonian Miscellaneous Collections, Vol. 147, No. 1. Washington: Smithsonian Institution, 1964.
Judd, Neil M. "Everyday Life in Pueblo Bonito." *National Geographic,* September 1925.
Judd, Neil M. *The Material Culture of Pueblo Bonito.* Smithsonian Miscellaneous Collections, Vol. 124. Washington: Smithsonian Institution, 1954.
Judd, Neil M. "The Pueblo Bonito Expedition of the National Geographic Society." *National Geographic,* March 1922, pp. 323–31.
Judd, Neil M. *Pueblo del Arroyo, Chaco Canyon, New Mexico.* Smithsonian Miscellaneous Collections, Vol. 138, No. 1. Washington: Smithsonian Institution, 1959.
"A New National Geographic Expedition: Ruins of Chaco Canyon, New Mexico. . . . To be Excavated and Studied. . . ." *National Geographic,* June 1921, pp. 632–43.

3. The Secrets of Time

Douglass, Andrew Ellicott. "The Secret of the Southwest Solved by Talkative Tree Rings." *National Geographic,* December 1929.
Hawley, Florence M. *The Significance of the Dated Prehistory of Chetro Ketl, New Mexico,* University of New Mexico Bulletin Monograph Series, Vol. 1, No. 1. Albuquerque: University of New Mexico Press, 1934.
Hayes, Alden C., David M. Brugge, and W. James Judge. *Archeological Surveys of Chaco Canyon, New Mexico.* Publications in Archeology, 18A, Chaco Canyon Studies. Washington, D.C.: National Park Service, 1981.
Hewett, Edgar L. *Ancient Life in the American Southwest.* New York: Tudor Publishing Co., 1943.
Hewett, Edgar L. "The Excavation of Chetro Ketl, Chaco Canyon, 1932–33." *Art and Archaeology* 35(March-April 1934):51–68.
Lister, Robert H., and Florence C. *Chaco Canyon: Archaeology and Archaeologists.* Albuquerque: University of New Mexico Press, 1981.
Morris, Ann Axtell. *Digging in the Southwest.* New York: Doubleday, Doran and Co., Inc., 1940.

4. The Chaco Project

Hayes, Alden C. "A Survey of Chaco Canyon Archeology." In *Archeological Surveys of Chaco Canyon,* edited by Alden C. Hayes, David M. Brugge, and W. James Judge. Publications in Archeology 18A, Chaco Canyon Studies. Washington: National Park Service, 1981.
Judge, W. James. "Transect Sampling in Chaco Canyon—Evaluation of a Survey Technique." In *Archeological Surveys of Chaco Canyon,* edited by Alden C. Hayes, David M. Brugge, and W. James Judge. Publications in Archeology 18A, Chaco Canyon Studies. Washington: National Park Service, 1981.
Maruca, Mary. *An Administrative History of the Chaco Project.* Anthropology Division, National Park Service, Washington, 1982.

5. Canals and Irrigation

Bunzel, Ruth. "Zuni Ritual Poetry." *47th Annual Report of the Bureau of American Ethnology,* Washington, 1932.
Gunn, John M. *Schat-Chen: History, Traditions and Narratives of the Queres Indians of Laguna and Acoma.* Albuquerque: Albright and Anderson, 1917.
Holsinger, S. J. *Report on Prehistoric Ruins of Chaco Canyon National Monument.* Manuscript, General Land Office, National Archives, Washington, 1901. Facsimile copy on file at Chaco Center, Albuquerque.

Lagasse, Peter F., William B. Gillespie, and Kenneth G. Eggert. "Hydraulic Engineering Analysis of Prehistoric Water-Controlled Systems at Chaco Canyon." In *Recent Research on Chaco Prehistory,* edited by W. James Judge and John D. Schelberg. Reports of the Chaco Center, No. 8. Division of Cultural Research, National Park Service, Albuquerque, 1984.

Lyons, Thomas R., Robert K. Hitchcock, and Basil G. Pouls. "The Kin Bineoloa Irrigation Study: An Experiment in the Use of Aerial Remote Sensing Techniques in Archeology." In *Remote Sensing Experiments in Cultural Resource Studies,* edited by Thomas R. Lyons. Reports of the Chaco Center; No. 1. National Park Service and University of New Mexico, Albuquerque, 1976.

Tyler, Hamilton A. *Pueblo Gods and Myths.* Norman: University of Oklahoma Press, 1964.

Vivian, R. Gordon, and Tom W. Mathews. "Kin Kletso, a Pueblo III Community in Chaco Canyon, New Mexico." *Southwestern Monuments Association Technical Series,* Vol. 6, Part 1, 1965.

Vivian, R. Gwinn. "Conservation and Diversion: Water-Control Systems in the Anasazi Southwest." In *Irrigation's Impact on Society,* edited by T.E. Downing and M. Gibson. Tucson: University of Arizona Press, 1974. Reprint, Anthropological Papers of the University of Arizona, No. 25.

Vivian, R. Gwinn. "An Inquiry into Prehistoric Social Organization in Chaco Canyon." In *Reconstructing Prehistoric Pueblo Societies,* edited by William A. Longacre. Albuquerque: University of New Mexico Press, 1970.

Vivian, R. Gwinn. "Prehistoric Water Conservation in Chaco Canyon." Final Technical Letter Report to the National Science Foundation, Grant GS-3100. Manuscript, Chaco Center, Albuquerque, 1972.

6. Roadways and Signal Towers

Drager, Dwight L. "An Analysis of a Possible Communication System in the San Juan Basin of New Mexico." Manuscript, Chaco Center, Albuquerque, 1976.

Ebert, James I., and Robert K. Hitchcock. "Chaco Canyon's Mysterious Highways." *Horizon,* Fall 1975, pp. 49–53.

Ebert, James I., and Robert K. Hitchcock. "Spatial Inference and the Archaeology of Complex Societies." Manuscript, Chaco Center, Albuquerque, 1973.

Hayes, Alden C., and T.C. Windes. "An Anasazi Shrine in Chaco Canyon." In *Collected Papers in Honor of Florence Hawley Ellis,* edited by T.R. Frisbie. Papers of the Archeological Society of New Mexico 2:143–56, 1975.

Kincaid, Chris, ed. *Chaco Roads Project, Phase I: A Reappraisal of Prehistoric Roads in the San Juan Basin 1983.* Santa Fe and Albuquerque, N.M.: Bureau of Land Management, 1983. (Especially Chapters 3, "Identifying and Interpreting Chacoan Roads: An Historical Perspective" by R. Gwinn Vivian; 4, "Evaluation of Aerial Photography" by Gretchen Obenauf; 6, "Physical Characteristics of Chacoan Roads," by Fred L. Nials; and 8, "Road Analysis" by John R. Stein.)

Lyons, Thomas R. "Archaeological Research Strategies: The Chaco Canyon Road Survey." Manuscript, Chaco Center, Albuquerque, 1973.

Lyons, Thomas R., and Robert K. Hitchcock. "Remote Sensing Interpretation of an Anasazi Land Route System." In *Aerial Remote Sensing Techniques in Archeology,* edited by Thomas R. Lyons and Robert K. Hitchcock. Reports of the Chaco Center, No. 2. National Park Service and University of New Mexico, Albuquerque, 1977.

Obenauf, Margaret S. "The Chacoan Roadway System," Thesis, Department of Anthropology, University of New Mexico, 1980.

Obenauf, Margaret S. "A History of Research on the Chacoan Roadway System." In *Cultural Resources Remote Sensing,* edited by Thomas R. Lyons and Frances Joan Mathien. National Park Service, Washington, D.C., 1980.

"Prehistoric Chaco Canyon 'Roads' Puzzle Scientists." *New Mexico Highway Journal,* March 1928.

Vivian, R. Gwinn. "Prehistoric Water Conservation in Chaco Canyon." Final Technical Letter Report to the National Science Foundation, Grant GS-3100. Manuscript, Chaco Center, Albuquerque, 1972.

Ware, John A., and George J. Gumerman. "Remote Sensing Methodology and the Chaco Canyon Prehistoric Road System." In *Aerial Remote Sensing Techniques in Archeology,* edited by Thomas R. Lyons and Robert K. Hitchcock. Reports of the Chaco Center, No. 2. National Park Service and University of New Mexico, Albuquerque, 1977.

7. The Outliers

Ireland, Arthur K. "Chacoan Outliers / San Juan Basin Communities: Known and Unknown." Manuscript, Chaco Center, Albuquerque, 1979.

Irwin-Williams, Cynthia, and Phillip H. Shelly, eds. *Investigations at the Salmon Site: The Structure of Chacoan Society in the Northern Southwest.* Final Report to Funding Agencies, Volume 1. Eastern New Mexico University Printing Services, 1980.

Marshall, Michael P., John R. Stein, Richard W. Loose, and Judith E. Novotny. *Anasazi Communities of the San Juan Basin.* Public Service Co. of New Mexico and Historic Preservation Bureau, Department of Finance and Administration, State of New Mexico, 1979.

Powers, Robert P., William B. Gillespie, and Stephen H. Lekson. *The Outlier Survey: A Regional View of Settlement in the San Juan Basin.* Reports of the Chaco Center, No. 3. Division of Cultural Research, National Park Service, Albuquerque, N.M., 1983.

8. Population, Burials, and the Mexican Connection

Akins, Nancy J., and John D. Schelberg. "Evidence for Organizational Complexity as Seen from the Mortuary Practices at Chaco Canyon." In *Recent Research on Chaco Prehistory,* edited by W. James Judge and John D. Schelberg. Reports of the Chaco Center, No. 8. Division of Cultural Research, National Park Service, Albuquerque, 1984.

Hayes, Alden C. "A Survey of Chaco Canyon Archaeology." In *Archaeological Surveys of Chaco Canyon,* edited by Hayes, Alden C., David M. Brugge, and W. James Judge. Publications in Archaelogy 18A, Chaco Canyon Studies. Washington, D.C.: National Park Service, 1981.

Judd, Neil M. "VIII. Intramural Burials." In Neil M. Judd, *The Material Culture of Pueblo Bonito.* Washington: Smithsonian Institution, 1954.

Lister, Robert H. "Mesoamerican Influence at Chaco Canyon, New Mexico." In *Across the Chichimec Sea,* edited by Carroll L. Riley and Basil C. Hedrick. Carbondale: Southern Illinois University Press, 1978.

McNitt, Frank. *Richard Wetherill: Anasazi.* Albuquerque: University of New Mexico Press, 1966. (Especially Appendix F, "Chaco Burials.")

Mathien, Frances Joan. *Economic Exchange Systems in the San Juan Basin.* Ph.D. Dissertation, University of New Mexico. Manuscript, Chaco Center, Albuquerque, 1981.

Mathien, Frances Joan. "The Mobile Trader and the Chacoan Anasazi." Paper presented to the Anasazi Symposium, Mesa Verde National Park, Oct. 1–3, 1981. Manuscript, Chaco Center, Albuquerque, 1981.

McGuire, Randall H. "The Mesoamerican Connection in the American Southwest." *The Kiva* 46(1980):1–2.

Reyman, Jonathan E. "*Pochteca* Burials at Anasazi Sites?" In *Across the Chichimec Sea,* edited by Carroll L. Riley and Basil C. Hedrick. Carbondale: Southern Illinois University Press, 1978.

Windes, Thomas C. "A New Look at Population in Chaco Canyon." In *Recent Research on Chaco Prehistory,* edited by W. James Judge and John D. Schelberg. Reports of the Chaco Center No. 8. Division of Cultural Research, National Park Service, Albuquerque, 1984.

Windes, Thomas C. "A Second Look at Population in Chaco Canyon." Paper presented at the 47th Annual Meeting of the Society for American Archaeology, Minneapolis, Minn., April 16, 1982.

9. The Chaco Phenomenon

Judge, W. James. "Chaco Canyon-San Juan Basin." Paper presented at School of American Research Advanced Seminar, Dynamics of Southwestern Prehistory, Santa Fe, N.M., Sept. 25–30, 1983.

Judge, W. James. "New Light on Chaco Canyon." In *New Light on Chaco Canyon,* edited by David Grant Noble. Santa Fe: School of American Research Press, 1984.

Judge, W. J., W.B. Gillespie, S.H. Lekson, and H.W. Toll. "Tenth Century Developments in Chaco Canyon." Archaeological Society of New Mexico Anthropological Papers 6, 1981.

Lekson, Stephen H. *Great Pueblo Architecture of Chaco Canyon.* Albuquerque: University of New Mexico Press, 1986.

Lekson, Stephen H. "Standing Architecture at Chaco Canyon and the Interpretation of Local and Regional Organization." In *Recent Research on Chaco Prehistory,* edited by W. James Judge and John D. Schelberg, Division of Cultural Research, National Park Service, Albuquerque, 1984.

Lekson, Stephen H., ed. *The Architecture and Dendrochronology of Chetro Ketl, Chaco Canyon, New Mexico.* Reports of the Chaco Center, No. 6. Division of Cultural Research, National Park Service, Albuquerque, 1983.

10. The Sky-Watchers of Chaco

Aveni, Anthony F., ed. *Native American Astronomy.* Austin: University of Texas Press, 1977.

Cushing, Frank H. *My Adventures in Zuni.* Palmer Lake, Colo.: Filter Press, 1967.

Brandt, John C., and Ray A. Williamson. "Rock Art Representations of the A.D. 1054 Supernova: A Progress Report." In *Native American Astronomy,* Anthony F. Aveni, ed. Austin: University of Texas Pres, 1977.

Brecher, Kenneth, and Michael Feirtag, eds. *Astronomy of the Ancients.* Cambridge, Mass.: MIT Press, 1979.

Ellis, Florence H. "A Thousand Years of the Pueblo Sun-Moon-Star Calendar." In *Archaeoastronomy in Precolumbian America,* Anthony F. Aveni, ed., Austin: University of Texas Press, 1975.

Frazier, Kendrick. "The Anasazi Sun Dagger." *Science 80* 1(Nov.–Dec. 1979):1.

Frazier, Kendrick. "Solstice-Watchers of Chaco." *Science News* 114(August 26, 1978):148–51.

Frazier, Kendrick. "Western Horizons." In *Fire of Life,* Smithsonian Exposition Books, Washington, 1981.

Hadingham, Evan. *Early Man and the Cosmos.* Norman: University of Oklahoma Press, 1984.

Judge, W. James. "Archaeology and Archaeoastronomy: A View from the Southwest." In *Astronomy and Ceremony in the Prehistoric Southwest,* edited by John B. Carlson and W. James Judge (Maxwell Museum Technical Series), Maxwell Museum of Anthropology, University of New Mexico, 1986.

Krupp, E.C. *Echoes of the Ancient Skies.* New York: Harper & Row, 1983.

McCluskey, Stephen C. "The Astronomy of the Hopi Indians." *Journal for the History of Astronomy* 8(1977):174–95.

Newman, Evelyn R., Robert K. Mark, and R. Gwinn Vivian. "Anasazi Solar Marker: The Use of a Natural Rockfall." *Science,* 217:1036–1038, Sept. 10, 1982.

Reyman, Jonathan E. "Astronomy, Architecture, and Adaptation at Pueblo Bonito." *Science* 193(1976):957–62.

Sekaquaptewa, Abbott. "Kilroytewa Was Here" and "Out of Phase With the Moon Phase." *Qua'toqti* (Hopi Publishers, Kykotsmovi, Arizona), Jan. 13, 1983, and Feb. 3, 1983.

Simmons, Leo W., ed. *Sun Chief: The Autobiography of a Hopi Indian* (Don C. Talayesva). New Haven: Yale University Press, 1942.

Sofaer, Anna, and Rolf M. Sinclair. "Astronomical Markings at Three Sites on Fajada Butte." In *Astronomy and Ceremony in the Prehistoric Southwest,* edited by John B. Carlson and W. James Judge (Maxwell Museum, Technical Series), Maxwell Museum of Anthropology, University of New Mexico, 1986.

Sofaer, Anna, and Rolf. M. Sinclair. "The Astronomy of Prehistoric Chaco" (abstract). *Bulletin American Astronomical Society,* 16:924, 1984.

Sofaer, Anna, Michael Marshall, and Rolf M. Sinclair. "Cosmographic Expression in the Road System of the Chaco Culture of Northwestern New Mexico." Abstract submitted to Second Oxford Conference on Archaeoastronomy, Merida, Mexico, January 1986.

Sofaer, Anna, Volker Zinser, and Rolf M. Sinclair. "A Unique Solar Marking Construct." *Science* 206(1979):283–91.

Williamson, Ray A. *Living the Sky: The Cosmos of the American Indian.* Boston: Houghton Mifflin, 1984.

Williamson, Ray A. "Sky Symbolism in a Navajo Rock Art Site." *Archaeoastronomy* (1983) 659–65.

Williamson, Ray A., Howard J. Fisher, and Donnel O'Flynn. "Anasazi Solar Observatories." In *Native American Astronomy,* Anthony F. Aveni, ed. Austin: University of Texas Press, 1977.

Williamson, Ray A., H.J. Fisher, A.F. Williamson, and C. Cochran. "The Astronomical Record in Chaco Canyon, New Mexico." In *Archaeoastronomy in Precolumbian America,* edited by Anthony F. Avenie. Austin: University of Texas Press, 1975.

Zeilik, Michael. "Anticipation and Ceremony: The Readiness Is All." In *Astronomy and Ceremony in the Prehistoric Southwest,* edited by John B. Carlson and W. James Judge (Maxwell Museum Technical Series), Maxwell Museum of Anthropology, University of New Mexico, 1986.

Zeilik, Michael. "Archaeoastronomy at Chaco Canyon." In *New Light on Chaco Canyon,* edited by David Grant Noble. Santa Fe: School of American Research Press, 1984.

Zeilik, Michael. "An Astronomer's Guide to Chaco Canyon." Unpublished manuscript, 1981.

Zeilik, Michael. "The Fajada Butte Solar Marker: A Reevaluation." *Science,* 228(June 14, 1985):1311–13.

Zeilik, Michael. "Keeping a Seasonal Calendar at Pueblo Bonito." Manuscript, 1985.

Zeilik, Michael. "Summer Solstice at Casa Rinconada: Calendar, Hierophany or Nothing?" Manuscript, 1984.

Zeilik, Michael. "The Sunwatchers of Chaco Canyon." *Griffith Observer,* June 1983, pp. 2–12.

Zeilik, Michael, and Richard Elston. "Wijiji at Chaco Canyon: A Winter Solstice Sunrise and Sunset Station." *Archaeoastronomy* 8 (1983) : 67–73.

11. Destinies and Destinations

Jones, Dewitt, and Linda S. Cordell. *Anasazi World.* Portland, Ore.: Graphic Arts Publishing Co., 1985.

Judge, W. James. "Chaco Canyon-San Juan Basin." Paper presented at School of American Research Advanced Seminar, Dynamics of Southwestern Prehistory, Santa Fe, N.M., Sept. 25–30, 1983.

12. Chaco in the Twenty-First Century

Benson, Larry, Linda Cordell, Kirk Vincent, Howard Taylor, John Stein, G. Lang Farmer, and Kiyoto Futa. "Ancient Maize from Chacoan Great Houses: Where Was It Grown?" *Proceedings of the National Academy of Sciences,* 100(22) (Oct. 28, 2003):13111–15.

Lekson, Stephen H., and Karin Burd. Foreword in *Chaco Society and Polity: Papers from the 1999 Conference,* edited by Linda S. Cordell, W. James Judge, and June-el Piper. New Mexico Archeological Council, Special Publication 4, Albuquerque, 2001.

Malville, J. McKim, and Claudia Putnam. *Prehistoric Astronomy in the Southwest.* Boulder: Johnson Books, 1993.

Windes, Thomas C., with contributions by H. Wolcott Toll. *Investigations of the Pueblo Alto Complex, Chaco Canyon, New Mexico, 1975–1979.* Vol. II, Parts 1 and 2. Architecture and Stratigraphy. Publications in Archeology 18F. National Park Service, Santa Fe, 1987.

Windes, Thomas C., and Rachael Anderson. "Sunrise, Sunset: Sedentism and Mobility in the Chaco East Community." Paper presented in the symposium "The Chaco Anasazi Community: Inside Looking Out," Society for American Archaeology 63rd Annual Meeting, Seattle, Mar. 22, 1998.

13. The Quest Continues

Akins, Nancy J. *A Biocultural Approach to Human Burials from Chaco Canyon, New Mexico.* Reports of the Chaco Center, Number 9, Branch of Cultural Research, National Park Service, Santa Fe, 1986.

Akins, Nancy J. "The Burials of Pueblo Bonito." In *Pueblo Bonito: Center of the Chacoan World,* edited by Jill E. Neitzel. Washington: Smithsonian Books, 2003.

English, Nathan B., Julio L. Betancourt, Jeffrey S. Dean, and Jay Quade. "Strontium Isotopes Reveal Distant Sources of Architectural Timber in Chaco Canyon, New Mexico." *Proceedings of the National Academy of Sciences,* 98(21) (Oct. 9, 2001):11891–96.

Fleck, John. "Chaco Lumber Hints at Economy." *Albuquerque Journal,* Sept. 25, 2001, p. D3.

Flint, Richard, and Shirley Cushing Flint. *Chacoesque: Chaco-like Great Pueblo Architecture Outside Chaco Canyon.* Villanueva, N.M.: Richard and Shirley Flint, 1989.

Durand, Stephen R., Phillip H. Shelley, Ronald C. Antweiler, and Howard E. Taylor. "Trees, Chemistry, and Prehistory in the American Southwest." *Journal of Archaeological Science* 26:185–203, 1999.

Judd, Neil M. *The Material Culture of Pueblo Bonito.* Smithsonian Miscellaneous Collections. Vol. 124. Washington: Smithsonian Institution, 1954.

Bibliography

Lekson, Stephen, Thomas C. Windes, W. James Judge, and John Stein. "The Chaco Canyon Community." *Scientific American* 256(7):100–109, July 1988.

Mathien, Frances Joan, editor. *Ceramics, Lithics, and Ornaments of Chaco Canyon*. Vol. I. Ceramics. Publications in Archaeology 18G, Chaco Canyon Studies. National Park Service, Santa Fe, 1997.

Mathien, Frances Joan, editor. *Ceramics, Lithics, and Ornaments of Chaco Canyon*. Vol. II. Lithics. Publications in Archaeology 18G, Chaco Canyon Studies. National Park Service, Santa Fe, 1997.

Mathien, Frances Joan, editor. *Ceramics, Lithics, and Ornaments of Chaco Canyon*. Vol. III. Lithics and Ornaments. Publications in Archaeology 18G, Chaco Canyon Studies. National Park Service, Santa Fe, 1997.

Mathien, Frances Joan, and Thomas C. Windes, editors. *Investigations of the Pueblo Alto Complex, Chaco Canyon, New Mexico, 1975–1979*. Vol. III, Parts 1 and 2. Artifactual and Biological Analyses. Publications in Archeology 18F. National Park Service, Santa Fe, 1987.

Neitzel, Jill E. "The Organization, Function, and Population of Pueblo Bonito." In *Pueblo Bonito: Center of the Chacoan World*, edited by Jill E. Neitzel. Washington: Smithsonian Books, 2003.

Neitzel, Jill E. "Three Questions About Pueblo Bonito." In *Pueblo Bonito: Center of the Chacoan World*, edited by Jill E. Neitzel. Washington: Smithsonian Books, 2003.

Neitzel, Jill E., editor. *Pueblo Bonito: Center of the Chacoan World*. Washington: Smithsonian Books, 2003.

Refrew, Colin. "Production and Consumption in a Sacred Economy: The Material Correlates of High Devotional Expression at Chaco Canyon." *American Antiquity* 66(1):14–25, 2001.

Roney, John R. "Prehistoric Roads and Regional Integration in the Chacoan System." In *Anasazi Regional Organization and the Chaco System*, edited by David E. Doyel. Anthropological Papers No. 5, Maxwell Museum of Anthropology, University of New Mexico, Albuquerque, 1992 (reprinted 2001).

Stein, John R., and Stephen H. Lekson. "Anasazi Ritual Landscapes." In *Anasazi Regional Organization and the Chaco System*, edited by David E. Doyel. Anthropological Papers No. 5, Maxwell Museum of Anthropology, University of New Mexico, Albuquerque, 1992 (reprinted 2001).

Stein, John R., Dabney Ford, and Richard Friedman. "Reconstructing Pueblo Bonito." In *Pueblo Bonito: Center of the Chacoan World*, edited by Jill E. Neitzel. Washington: Smithsonian Books, 2003.

Vivian, R. Gwinn. *The Chacoan Prehistory of the San Juan Basin*. San Diego: Academic Press, 1990.

Vivian, R. Gwinn, and Bruce Hilpert. *The Chaco Handbook: An Encyclopedic Guide*. Salt Lake City: University of Utah Press, 2002.

Windes, Thomas C. *Investigations of the Pueblo Alto Complex, Chaco Canyon, New Mexico, 1975–1979*. Vol. I. Summary of Tests and Excavations. Publications in Archeology 18F. National Park Service, Santa Fe, 1987.

Windes, Thomas C. "This Old House: Construction and Abandonment at Pueblo Bonito." In *Pueblo Bonito: Center of the Chacoan World*, edited by Jill E. Neitzel. Washington: Smithsonian Books, 2003.

Windes, Thomas C., with contributions by S. Berger, D. Ford, and C. Stevenson. *The Spadefoot Toad Site: Investigations at 29SJ 629 in Marcia's Rincon*. Two volumes. Reports of the Chaco Center Number 12. Branch of Cultural Research, National Park Service, Santa Fe, 1993.

Windes, Thomas C., and Rachael Anderson. "Sunrise, Sunset: Sedentism and Mobility in the Chaco East Community." Paper presented in the symposium "The Chaco Anasazi Community: Inside Looking Out," Society for American Archaeology 63rd Annual Meeting, Seattle, Mar. 22, 1998.

Windes, Thomas C., and Dabney Ford. "The Nature of the Early Bonito Phase." In *Anasazi Regional Organization and the Chaco System*, edited by David E. Doyel. Anthropological Papers No. 5, Maxwell Museum of Anthropology, University of New Mexico, Albuquerque, 1992 (reprinted 2001).

Windes, Thomas C., and Dabney Ford. "The Chaco Wood Project: The Chronometric Reappraisal of Pueblo Bonito." *American Antiquity* 61(2):295–310, 1996.

Windes, Thomas C., and Peter J. McKenna. "Going Against the Grain: Wood Production in Chacoan Society." *American Antiquity* 66(1):119–40, 2001.

PEOPLE OF CHACO

14. Cosmography, Meridian, and Violence

Cosmographic Expression:

Brocious, Dan. "Looking for Answers in the Skies." *American Archaeology* 2(2):11–17, Summer 1998.

Sofaer, Anna. "The Primary Architecture of the Chacoan Culture: A Cosmological Expression." In *Anasazi Architecture and American Design*, edited by Baker H. Morrow and V. B. Price. Albuquerque: University of New Mexico Press, 1997.

Sofaer, Anna, producer. *The Mystery of Chaco Canyon*. Video narrated by Robert Redford. The Solstice Project, 1999.

Sofaer, Anna, Michel P. Marshall, and Rolf M. Sinclair. "The Great North Road: A Cosmographic Expression of the Chaco Culture of New Mexico." In *World Archaeoastronomy*, edited by A. F. Aveni. New York: Cambridge University Press, 1989.

Meridian:

DiPeso, Charles C. "A Comparison of Casas Grandes and Chacoan Architecture." In *Casas Grandes: A Fallen Trading Center of the Gran Chichimeca*. Vol. 4. Dragoon, Ariz.: Amerind Foundation, 1974.

Lekson, Stephen H. *The Chaco Meridian: Centers of Political Power in the American Southwest.* North Walnut Creek, Calif., AltaMira Press: 1999.

Lekson, Stephen H. "Chaco + Casas." Poster presentation, Oxford V, Santa Fe, Aug. 4, 1996.

Lekson, Stephen H. "Rewriting the History of the Ancient Southwest." Paper presented at New Horizons in Science, Council for the Advancement of Science Writing, University of Colorado, Boulder, Oct. 29, 1996.

Lekson, Stephen H. "Rewriting Southwestern Prehistory." *Archaeology* (Jan./Feb. 1997): 52–55.

Violence:

Arens, William. *The Man-Eating Myth: Anthropology and Anthropophagy*. New York: Oxford University Press, 1979.

Bullock, Peter, editor. *Deciphering Anasazi Violence*. Santa Fe: HRM Books, 1998.

Cordell, Linda S., and W. James Judge. "Perspectives on Chaco Society and Polity." In *Chaco Society and Polity: Papers from the 1999 Conference*, edited by Linda S. Cordell, W. James Judge, and June-el Piper. New Mexico Archeological Council Special Publication 4, Albuquerque, 2001.

Diamond, Jared M. "Talk of Cannibalism." *Nature* 407(Sept. 7, 2000):25–26.

Doyel, David E. "Chaco Update 2000." In *Anasazi Regional Organization and the Chaco System*, edited by David E. Doyel. Anthropology Papers No. 5, Maxwell Museum of Anthropology, University of New Mexico, Albuquerque, 2001.

LeBlanc, Steven. Prehistoric Warfare in the American Southwest. Salt Lake City: University of Utah Press, 1999.

Lekson, Stephen H. "War in the Southwest, War in the World." *American Antiquity* 67(4):607–24, 2002.

Marlar, Richard A., Banks I. Leonard, Brian R. Billman, Patricia M. Lambert, and Jennifer E. Marlar. "Biochemical Evidence of Cannibalism at a Prehistoric Puebloan Site in Southwestern Colorado." *Nature* 407(Sept. 7, 2000):74–78.

Neitzel, Jill E. "The Organization, Function, and Population of Pueblo Bonito." In *Pueblo Bonito: Center of the Chacoan World*, edited by Jill E. Neitzel. Washington: Smithsonian Books, 2003.

Preston, Douglas. "Cannibals of the Canyon." *The New Yorker*, Nov. 30, 1998, pp. 76–89.

Rodriguez, Roberto, and Patricia Gonzales, "Prehistoric Fecal Focus Serves No Valid Scientific Purpose." *Albuquerque Journal*, Sept. 27, 2000, p. A13.

Turner, Christy G., II, and Jacqueline A. Turner. *Man Corn: Cannibalism and Violence in the Prehistoric American Southwest*. Salt Lake City: University of Utah Press, 1999.

White, Tim D. "Once Were Cannibals." *Scientific American*, Aug. 2001, pp. 58–65.

15. The Chaco Synthesis Project

Akins, Nancy. "The Burials at Pueblo Bonito." In *Pueblo Bonito: Center of the Chacoan World*, edited by Jill E. Neitzel. Washington: Smithsonian Books, 2003.

Bibliography

Cameron, Catherine M., and H. Wolcott Toll. "Deciphering the Organization of Production in Chaco Canyon." *American Antiquity* 66(1):5–13, 2001.

Cordell, Linda S., and W. James Judge. "Perspectives on Chaco Society and Polity." In *Chaco Society and Polity: Papers from the 1999 Conference*, edited by Linda S. Cordell, W. James Judge, and June-el Piper. New Mexico Archeological Council, Special Publication 4, Albuquerque, 2001.

Cordell, Linda S., and W. James Judge. "Society and Polity." *Archaeology Southwest* 14(1):18–19, 2000

Cordell, Linda S., W. James Judge, and June-el Piper, editors. *Chaco Society and Polity: Papers from the 1999 Conference*. New Mexico Archeological Council, Special Publication 4, Albuquerque, 2001.

Doyel, David E. "Chaco Update 2000: Introduction." In *Anasazi Regional Organization and the Chaco System*, edited by David E. Doyel. Anthropological Papers No. 5, Maxwell Museum of Anthropology, University of New Mexico, Albuquerque, 2001.

Doyel, David E., editor. *Anasazi Regional Organization and the Chaco System*. Anthropological Papers No. 5, Maxwell Museum of Anthropology, Albuquerque, University of New Mexico, 1992 (reprinted 2001).

Kantner, John. "Preface: The Chaco World." *Kiva: The Journal of Southwestern Anthropology and History* 69(2):83–92, 2003.

Kantner, John "Rethinking Chaco as a System." *Kiva: The Journal of Southwestern Anthropology and History* 69(2):207–27, 2003.

Kantner, John, and Ronald Hobgood. "Digital Technologies and Prehistoric Landscapes in the American Southwest." In *The Reconstruction of Archaeological Landscapes through Digital Technologies*, edited by Maurizio Forte, P. Ryan Williams, and James Wiseman. Oxford, UK: Archaeopress, 2003.

Kintigh, Keith W. "Coming to Terms with the Chaco World." *Kiva: The Journal of Southwestern Anthropology and History* 69(2):93–116, 2003.

Lekson, Stephen H. "Ancient Chaco's New History." *Archaeology Southwest* 14(1):1–4, 2000.

Lekson, Stephen H. "Chaco Update 2000: The Chaco Synthesis Project." In *Anasazi Regional Organization and the Chaco System*, edited by David E. Doyel. Anthropological Papers No. 5, Maxwell Museum of Anthropology, University of New Mexico, Albuquerque, 2001.

Lekson, Stephen H. "Chaco Update 2000: Presidents, Precedents, and Pundits: Chaco Amid the 43rd Presidential Election." In *Anasazi Regional Organization and the Chaco System*, edited by David E. Doyel. Anthropological Papers No. 5, Maxwell Museum of Anthropology, University of New Mexico, Albuquerque, 2001.

Mahoney, Nancy. "Chaco World." *Archaeology Southwest* 14(1):15–17, 2000.

Mahoney, Nancy. "Monumental Architecture as Conspicuous Display in Chaco Canyon." In *Chaco Society and Polity: Papers from the 1999 Conference*, edited by Linda S. Cordell, W. James Judge, and June-el Piper. New Mexico Archeological Council, Special Publication 4, Albuquerque, 2001.

Sebastian, Lynne. *The Chaco Anasazi: Sociopolitical Evolution in the Prehistoric Southwest*. New York: Cambridge University Press, 1992 (reprinted 1996).

Sebastian, Lynne. "Chaco Canyon and the Anasazi Southwest: Changing Views of Sociopolitical Organization." In *Anasazi Regional Organization and the Chaco System*, edited by David E. Doyel. Anthropological Papers No. 5, Maxwell Museum of Anthropology, University of New Mexico, Albuquerque, 1992 (reprinted 2001).

Windes, Tom. "House Location Patterns in the Chaco Canyon Area." In *Chaco Society and Polity: Papers from the 1999 Conference*, edited by Linda S. Cordell, W. James Judge, and June-el Piper. New Mexico Archeological Council, Special Publication 4, Albuquerque, 2001.

Note: Much of the material in Chapter 15 is based on a draft version of the final report of the Chaco Synthesis Project, kindly provided me for background by Steve Lekson. It is tentatively titled *The Archaeology of Chaco Canyon, New Mexico* and is to be published by the School of American Research. Quoted material from the draft may or may not survive editing into the report's final version but was what the authors wrote at the time.

For information about visiting Chaco, contact: Superintendent, Chaco Culture National Historical Park, U.S. National Park Service, P.O. Box 220, Nageezi, NM 87037-0220. Telephone: 505-786-7014. Also check out its excellent Web site, www.nps.gov/chcu/.

Index

abandonment of Chaco, 78–79,
　131–32, 135, 205–7
Acoma people, 171
Acoma ("Sky City") pueblo, 55
"the Acropolis," 122–24
Adams, Rex, 135
aerial photography, 112, 113–14, 115,
　118, 120–22, 138
Akins, Nancy, 163, 249, 256, 302
Albuquerque Journal, 278–79
Allentown outlier, 147, 247
American Antiquity, 233, 236, 280,
　285
Amsdem, Monroe, 47
the Anasazi (Chacoan people), 13–14,
　252, 296, 298–306
　abandonment of Chaco, 78–79,
　　131–32, 135, 205–7, 280
　agriculture of, 14, 15, 102–3, 221,
　　239, 276
　cannibalism and violence,
　　276–82
　chronology of, 79, 80, 81, 89–91
　communications network, 125,
　　294–95, 305

construction of buildings, 174–77,
　179–80, 221, 236, 237–43, 246,
　254–55, 256, 299
daily life, 14–15, 50–51, 297
descendants, 207–8, 210–12
disappearance of, 207
family size, 154
matrilineal system, 15, 50
Mexican influences on, 26, 71,
　164–70
number of, 153–59
pottery of, 51–52, 183, 248, 295
rain invocation, 19–20, 95–97
space, concept of, 18–19, 267
see also burial sites; Chacoan sys-
　tem; outliers; religion of the
　Anasazi; roadway system; sky-
　watching; water control systems
*Ancient Life in the American South-
　west* (Hewett), 67
Anderson, Rachel, 222
Andrews outlier, 147
Antiquities Act of 1906, 42
Antweiler, Ronald, 245–46
archaeoastronomy, 222, 272–73

archaeological sites:
  definition of, 88–89
  lithic areas, 88, 89
  locations of, 89, 220
  surveys of, 87–91, 220
  undiscovered sites, 90
Archaeology Southwest, 285, 299
Arens, William, 274–75
Arizona, University of, 217, 221, 244
  Laboratory for Tree-Ring Research
    at, 220, 232, 244
Aztec people, 26, 164–65
Aztec Ruin outlier, 75, 77, 129–32,
  204–5, 221, 232, 261, 269–73
Aztec Ruins National Monument, 220,
  236

Balcony House, 77
Basketmaker people, 80, 81, 89
Beam HH39 (Showlow Beam),
  75–76
Beardsley, John, 87
beds, 51
Benson, Larry, 221
Betancourt, Julio, 244
Beyal, Hosteen, 111
Billman, Brian, 277, 278, 279
"Biochemical Evidence of Cannibalism
    at a Prehistoric Puebloan Site in
    Southwestern Colorado" (Marlar
    et al), 277, 278, 279
Bis sa'ani outlier, 141, 143
Buettner, Robert, 112–13
Burd, Karin, 220
Bureau of Land Management, U.S.
  (BLM), 20, 246
burial sites:
  absence of, 159–60, 162
  cremation and, 162
  destruction of, 163–64
  discoveries of, 39–40, 160–62,
    163–64, 255, 256
  at a distance from the pueblo, 162
  of the *pochteca*, 167–68
  raft burials, 163

turquoise beads in, 40, 160, 161,
    162, 167, 168
Bustard, Wendy, 225, 249

calendars, 191–92, 199, 259
Cameron, Cathy, 218, 284
canals, 101–2
cannibalism, 274–82
"Cannibalism in the Canyon" (Pre-
    ston), 275
Capstone Conference, 285–87, 301
Carravahal (Mexican guide), 25, 29,
    31, 32
Casa Chiquita, 91
Casamero Community outlier, 145,
    147
Casa Rinconada, 69, 71–72, 194
Casas Grandes, 221, 269–73
ceramics, *see* pottery
Chacoan people, *see* the Anasazi
Chacoan Regional System, 218
Chacoan system, 173–74, 249
  collapse of, 205–7, 218–19
  environmental conditions and, 181,
    185, 187, 205
  extent of, 216, 218–19, 244,
    269–73
  formalization period, 183–87
  influence of, 215–17
  initialization period, 181–83
  outliers and, 128–29, 182, 184,
    187, 204–5, 290–93, 295–300
  reorganization period, 203–5
  residential function, change to,
    204–5
  ritual center at Chaco, 185–87
  roadway system, role of, 109,
    126–27, 151, 187, 237, 246–48,
    293–94, 295, 304–5, 306
  time extent of, 216, 269–73
  turquoise processing and, 182–83,
    185
Chaco Archives, 224–25
*Chaco Canyon and Its Monuments,
    The* (Fisher), 154

Chaco Canyon National Monument, 42, 43, 64
    see also Chaco Culture National Historical Park
Chaco Center, 86
Chaco Culture National Historical Park, 220–21, 224–26, 233, 236, 252
    Museum Collection of, 224–25, 226
    see also Chaco Canyon National Monument
Chaco Meridian: Centers of Political Power in the Ancient Southwest (Lekson), 273
Chaco Phenomenon, see Chacoan system
Chaco Project, 213–15, 219, 225, 283–85, 286, 293, 306
    accomplishments of, 92, 94
    archaeological sites, surveys of, 87–91
    goals of, 86
    initiation of, 85–86
Chaco Roads Project, 120–24
Chaco Society and Polity conference, 300
Chaco Synthesis Project, 219, 280, 283–306
Chaco Wash, 31
Chaco Wood Project, 215, 220, 231–36, 251
Chambers outlier, 247
Chavez, Angelico, 165
Chetro Ketl, 244, 261, 264, 265, 297
    abandonment of, 78–79
    beauty of, 67
    central location, 183
    colonnades, 71
    construction of, 176, 177, 237
    dating of, 77–79
    discovery of, 32
    excavation by Hewett, 64–65, 67–69, 71
    ground plan, 67
    kivas, 69, 71
    masonry of, 35, 65
    ritual artifacts at, 16
    scale of, 67
    trench of, 68
"child presented to the sun" ritual, 17–18
Chimney Rock Pueblo, 222, 267, 268, 305
Chis-chilling-begay, 42
chronology of the Anasazi, 79, 80, 81, 89–91
Cliff Palace, 36, 77, 267
clothes racks, 50–51
Colorado, University of, 215, 219, 222, 283
Conant, Kenneth, 252
Connally, Ernest Allen, 86
construction of buildings:
    labor requirements, 177, 179, 239, 241–43, 244–45, 256, 257, 295, 299, 300
    material requirements, 179–80, 236, 237–43, 246
    periods of, 174–77, 234–36
Corbett, John M., 85–86, 113, 131
Cordell, Linda S., 207, 281–82, 299, 300
corn (maize), 221
cosmographic expression, 221, 259–69
Cowboy Wash, Colo., 276–77, 279
Coyote Canyon Road, 119, 140
cremation, 162
Cushing, Frank H., 190

dams, 101
dating of the outliers, 75, 77, 131, 135
dating of the pueblos, 75–79, 215, 222, 231, 232, 234–36, 254
Dean, Jeffrey, 237, 243–45
Deciphering Anasazi Violence (Bullock), 276
dendrochronology (tree-ring dating), 74–77, 215, 220–21, 231–36, 270
Department of the Interior, U.S., 44, 226
Diamond, Jared, 278

DiPeso, Charles, 270
discovery of Chaco Canyon, 28–29
Douglass, Andrew Ellicott, 74–76, 77, 131
down-the-line trade, 169
Downum, Chris, 217
Doyel, David E., 279, 288–89, 301
Drager, Dwight, 124, 125, 158
Duff, Andrew, 293
Durand, Stephen, 245–46

Earthwatch, 135
East community, 222–24
Eastern New Mexico University, 135, 221, 241
East Road, 113, 119
Ebert, James, 114, 115, 116
Eggert, Kenneth, 101
"E" ground plan, 67
El Faro ("The Lighthouse"), 123–24
El Rito outlier, 144, 182
English, Nathan, 243–45

Fajada Butte, 29–30, 213, 227, 259, 297
Fajada Butte solar marker, 194–98, 222, 266, 268
Farmer, James, 249
Fewkes, J. Walter, 71
field schools, 74, 81
firepits, 155–58
Fisher, Reginald, 154
Fleck, John, 244
Flynn, Leo, 87
Ford, Dabney, 233–36, 249, 250–56, 285
Friedman, Richard, 229, 249, 250–56
Friends of Salmon Ruin, 135
Fritz, John, 263
furniture, 51

gardens, 102–3
Geo (NGS) excavations:
    camp facilities, 57
    goals of, 44–45
    initiation of, 44
    Pueblo Bonito, 44–55, 57, 59, 61
    Pueblo del Arroyo, 61
    sandstorms, dealing with, 46
Geographic Information System, 253, 295
Geological Survey, U.S., 221
Gillespie, William, 101, 136
Gladwin, Harold S., 79, 81, 237, 300
Gonzales, Patricia, 278–79
Grasshopper ruin, 156
great-house architecture:
    construction and, 237–43, 244, 299
    dates of, 218
    geographic extent of, 217, 218, 297
    symbolic meanings of, 218, 246–48, 268–69, 304, 305
Great North Road, 113, 119, 121–22, 123–24, 126, 187, 200, 270–72, 273
Grey Hill spring outlier, 147
ground plans, 67
Guadalupe Ruin outlier, 145, 183
Gumerman, George, 117

Hawley, Florence M., 64, 77–79
Hayes, Alden, 63, 88–89, 90, 109, 112, 124–25, 154–55, 158, 159, 163
Haystack outlier, 187, 295
Hewett, Edgar L., 64–65, 67–69, 71, 74, 110, 154
Hibben, Frank C., 226
Hibben Center for Archaeological Research, 226
Hipparchus, 260
Hisatsinom, see the Anasazi
Historic Preservation Bureau (New Mexico), 138
Historic Sites Preservation Commission, 135
Hitchcock, Robert, 114, 115, 116
Hobgood, Ronald, 295

Hogback outlier, 147, 149, 184
Hohokam people, 99
Holsinger, S. J., 109–10
Hopi Cultural Preservation Office, 275
Hopi Millennium, 208, 210
Hopi people, 171, 272, 275
    children, rituals for, 18
    initiation ceremony, 20–21
    land system, 15
    matrilineal system, 15
    migration ceremonies, 127
    nature, unity with, 19
    ritual dances, 20
    sky-watching practices, 190–92
    space, concept of, 18–19
Hosta (Jemez guide), 26, 164, 165
Hovenweep Castle, 199
Humboldt, Alexander von, 164
Hungo Pavi, 31–32, 244, 265, 297
Hurst, Winston, 217
Hyde, Fred, 37
Hyde, Talbot, 37, 38
Hyde Exploring Expedition, 37–42,
    221, 252

Indian Creek outlier, 147
irrigation systems, *see* water control
    systems
Irwin-Williams, Cynthia, 134, 135

Jackson, William Henry, 33, 35, 111,
    160, 252
Judd, Neil M., 43–44, 62, 75, 231, 253
    on burial sites, 159–60, 162
    culture, interest in, 14, 49–55
    Geo (NGS) excavations, 44, 45–55,
        57, 59, 61, 248, 252
    on population of Chaco, 153, 156,
        157, 158
    on roadway system, 110–12
    turquoise beads, discovery of,
        52–53
Judge, W. James, 129, 170, 238,
    281–82, 300
    on Chacoan system, 173–74,

181–82, 183, 185–87, 204–5,
    299
    on Chaco project, 87, 94

Kantner, John, 288, 290, 292–96, 305
Kendrick, Jim, 293
Kern, Edward, 26, 28, 251–52
Kern, Richard, 26, 28, 31, 251–52
Kidder, Alfred Vincent, 36, 64, 113
Kin Bineoloa outlier, 182, 264,
    265–66
Kincaid, Chris, 120
Kin Cheops outlier, 247
Kin Hocho'i outlier, 247
Kin Kletso, 83, 91, 183, 261, 265
Kin Kletzin, 264
Kin Nizhoni outlier, 143–44
Kintigh, Keith, 291–92, 293, 295
Kin Ya'a outlier, 295
Kiva, 285
kivas, 16, 237
    Casa Rinconada, 69, 71–72, 194
    Chetro Ketl ceremonial structure,
        69, 71
    coordinate system and, 18
    at outliers, 130–31, 132–33, 145,
        147, 149, 152, 217, 218, 291,
        292, 293
    at Pueblo Bonito, 33, 254, 255,
        256
    at Pueblo Pintado, 28
    wall niches of, 69, 72
Kuckelman, K. A., 281
Kunkel, Kristine, 241

Lagasse, Peter, 101
Laguna people, 171
Lambert, Patricia, 277, 278, 279
LeBlanc, Steven, 281
Lekson, Stephen H., 136, 174–77,
    179–80, 215–16, 218, 219, 220,
    221, 234, 239, 241, 242, 253,
    254, 255, 269–73, 275, 279–80,
    281, 283–86, 289, 293, 295,
    296, 297–98, 299, 301–2, 303–6

Leonard, Banks, 277, 278, 279
Lindbergh, Charles and Anne, 113
Lipes, William D., 280, 281
Lister, Robert H., 86, 166, 167, 168
lithic areas, 88, 89
Lizard House, 83
Logan, Wilfred, 85–86
Loose, Richard, 138
Lowell, Percival, 74
Lower White House, 231
Lyons, Thomas R., 113, 114, 116–17, 128–29, 138

McGuire, Randall H., 168–69
McKenna, Peter, 221, 236, 237, 239, 242, 296, 298, 299
McNitt, Frank, 24, 25, 26, 32, 36, 164–65
Mahoney, Nancy, 293, 300, 301
Malville, J. McKim, 222, 267–69
Man Corn: Cannibalism and Violence in the Prehistoric American Southwest (Turner and Turner), 274–75
Man Eating Myth: Anthropology and Anthropophagy, The (Arens), 274–75
Marlar, Jennifer, 277, 278, 279
Marlar, Richard, 277, 278, 279
Marshall, Anne Lawrason, 249
Marshall, Michael, 122, 138, 200, 266, 290
Marshall survey, 138, 139, 143–44, 145, 147, 152, 290
masonry, 65, 220, 237, 241, 296–97, 306
    dating, use in, 78
    types of, 35, 48–49, 54, 217, 253, 254
Material Culture of Pueblo Bonito, The (Judd), 248
Mathews, Tom, 83, 100
Mathien, Frances Joan, 169–70, 249, 285
Maxwell Museum of Anthropology, 225–26, 231, 288, 301

meridian, 269–74
Mesa Verde people, 99, 132, 135, 267, 275
Mesa Verde ruins, 36, 220, 232, 268, 275, 305
Mexican influences on Chaco:
    Aztec origination legend, 26, 164–65
    colonnades, 71
    evidence for, 166–68
    limited extent of, 165, 170
    pochteca theory, 167–69
    trade model for, 169–70
Mexican Springs Road, 119
migration ceremonies, 127
Mills, Barbara, 217
Mindeleff, Victor, 50
Mogollon people, 99
Montezuma I, 26, 165
Montezuma II, 26, 165
moon-watching, 191–92, 197, 221, 222, 259–69
Morenon, Pierre, 122, 125–26
Morris, Earl H., 75, 130–31, 230
multispectral imaging, 114
Mummy Cave, 77
Muute (sun priest), 189
My Adventures in Zuni (Cushing), 190
Mysteries of the Ancient Americas (Reader's Digest Association), 252
Mystery of Chaco Canyon, The, 269

Napetcha, Andrew, 210–12
National Endowment for the Humanities, 135
National Geodetic Survey, 259
National Geographic, 44–45, 47
National Geographic Society, 43, 44, 248, 252
    see also Geo excavations
National Park Service (NPS), 81, 83, 86, 219, 222, 224, 225, 226, 231, 244, 283, 285
National Science Foundation, 135

Native American Graves Protection and Repatriation Act (NAGPRA), 278
Nature, 277, 278, 279
Navajo Nation, 221, 244
Navajo people, 46, 135, 173, 229–30
Navajo Springs Great House, 229–30, 247
Neitzel, Jill E., 249–58, 280
New Alto, 91
Newcomb outlier, 228–30
New Mexico, University of, 64, 74, 81, 86, 224, 226
New Mexico Archeological Council, 285
New Mexico Highway Journal, 110
New Yorker, 275
Nials, Fred L., 107, 122, 126
1976 Bicentennial Commission, 135
NPS, *see* National Park Service
Nusbaum, Jesse, 36

Oak Tree House, 77
Obenauf, Margaret Senter (Gretchen), 108, 109, 118–22, 126–27, 140
"Once Were Cannibals" (White), 279
outliers:
    abandonment of, 131–32, 135
    aerial photography of, 138
    architectural features, 139, 140–41, 143, 145, 147, 149, 291–93, 296–98, 300–301, 306
    Chacoan system and, 128–29, 182, 184, 187, 204–5, 228–30, 242, 290–93, 295–300
    as communities, 151–52, 290, 293, 295–98, 299
    daily life in, 131, 297
    dating of, 75, 77, 131, 135
    defensive function, 143
    discovery of, 128
    economic function, 150–51
    federal protection for, 149
    kivas at, 130–31, 132–33, 145, 147, 149, 152, 291, 292, 293

    location peculiarities, 143
    modern development and, 119
    number of, 128–29, 135–36
    roadways at, 118–20, 228–30, 293–94, 295, 304–5, 306
    ruins, condition of, 138
    survey projects of, 136, 138–41, 143–44, 145, 147, 152, 290, 296
    turquoise processing and, 183
    see also specific outliers

Padilla (Navajo man), 111
Palmer family, 37
Paquime, 221, 269–73
Peach Springs outlier, 139–41, 182
Pecos Conference (1997), 213–17, 228, 231, 241, 273, 288
Peñasco Blanco, 236, 261, 266
Pepper, George Hubbard, 38, 39, 47, 160, 163, 168, 252
petroglyphs, 198–99
photointerpretation, 118
Pierre's Ruin, 122–24, 141
Pierson, Lloyd, 158
pilgrimage festivals, 185–87
pine logs, transportation of, 110, 116
pithouse villages, 89
pochteca (Mexican trade guilds), 167–69
population of Chaco:
    family size and, 154
    firepits, relation to, 155–58
    housing patterns and, 156–57, 158
    popular conception of, 153–54
    research on, 154–58
    scientific estimates, 158–59
pottery, 14, 217, 295
    archaeological significance of, 46
    black-on-white pottery, 51–52, 183
    at Pueblo Bonito, 39, 46–47, 51–52, 248
Powamu (Bean Dance), 20
Powers, Robert P., 122, 136, 150–51, 152, 285, 290

Powers survey, 136, 138, 139–41, 143, 177

"Prehistoric Fecal Focus Serves No Valid Scientific Purpose" (Rodriguez and Gonzalez), 278–79

Prehistoric Warfare in the American Southwest (LeBlanc), 281

Prescott, William H., 164

Preston, Douglas, 275

"Primary Architecture of the Chacoan Culture, The: A Cosmological Expression" (Sofaer), 269

Proceedings of the National Academy of Sciences, 221

Public Service Company of New Mexico (PNM), 138

Pueblo I people, 80, 81, 90

Pueblo II people, 80, 81, 90

Pueblo III people, 80, 81, 90–91

Pueblo Alto, 261, 263–64, 297
    central location, 183–84, 249
    construction of, 176, 177
    population of, 157–58
    roadway termination point, 113, 116–17
    turquoise workshop, 183

Pueblo Bonito, 214–15, 221, 242, 244, 248–58, 297, 300
    apartments, 44
    astronomical alignment of, 200, 256–57, 261, 264
    attacks upon, 54
    burial sites, 39–40, 160–62, 167–68, 255, 256, 257, 280, 302, 304
    construction of, 174–76, 177, 179, 220, 234–36, 237, 250, 253, 254–55, 256, 257
    daily life in, 14, 50–51
    dating of, 75, 76–77, 215, 220, 231, 232, 234–36, 254
    design of, 219–20
    discovery of, 32–33, 35
    excavation by NGS group, 44–55, 57, 59, 61, 248
    excavation by Wetherill, 38–40, 249, 252
    kivas, 33, 254, 255, 256
    masonry of, 35, 48–49, 54
    modern villages, commonalities with, 55
    mysteries of, 61–62
    as over-engineered, 247
    peoples of, 54, 220, 249–50, 252, 256–58
    Pepper's notes on, 47, 252
    population of, 153, 156, 157, 249, 257
    pottery at, 39, 46–47, 51–52, 248
    rebuilding in, 49, 215, 255
    reconstruction of, 250–56
    security-oriented constructions, 54
    sun-watching windows, 192, 194
    trash dump mystery, 46–47, 220, 255, 297–98
    turquoise beads at, 40, 52–53
    turquoise workshop, 183
    water control system, 51
    as water storage site, 182

Pueblo Bonito: Center of the Chacoan World (Neitzel, ed.), 249–58

Pueblo del Arroyo, 35, 220, 244, 261, 263, 265
    construction of, 91, 176, 177, 237, 241, 242
    dating of, 77, 215, 220, 232
    excavation by NGS group, 61
    population of, 156, 157
    turquoise workshop, 183

Pueblo de Penasco Blanco:
    construction of, 174–76, 177
    masonry of, 35
    as water storage site, 182

Pueblo Indians, 13, 16–21, 207–8, 210
    see also specific peoples

Pueblo Pintado, 25–28, 222, 261, 264, 265–66

Pueblo Una Vida, 261, 266
    construction of, 174–76, 236
    discovery of, 31

firepits at, 156
turquoise workshop, 183
as water storage site, 182
Putnam, Frederic Ward, 38, 41

Quade, Jay, 243–45

raft burials, 163
rainfall in Chaco, 19–20, 98, 181, 185,
187, 234–36, 289–90
rain invocation, 19–20, 95–97
Reader's Digest Association, 252
"Reconstructing Pueblo Bonito" (Stein,
Ford, and Friedman), 250–56
Redford, Robert, 269
Refrew, Colin, 242
Reiter, Paul, 64
religion of the Anasazi:
abandonment of Chaco and, 206
great houses and, 218
nature, relation to, 19–20
ritual and ceremony in, 16–18,
20–21, 257, 265–66, 267, 268,
280, 281, 300, 301
roadway system and, 126–27, 218,
304–5
see also kivas
Remote Sensing Project, 112, 113–15,
118
Renfrew, Colin, 169
Reyman, Jonathan, 167–68
Rincon-4 North water control system,
102–3, 104
ritual artifacts, 16
ritual center, Chaco as, 185–87
roadway system, 105–6, 217, 218
aerial photography of, 112,
113–14, 115, 118, 120–22
berm borders, 105, 107
causeways, 108, 116
Chacoan system, role in, 109,
126–27, 151, 187, 237, 246–48,
293–94, 295, 304–5, 306
cosmological significance, 200,
246

depressed roads, 108, 114
discovery of, 109–10, 237
"dog leg" turns, 107
economic function, 126, 151
efficiency of, 126
energy saving with, 125–26
extent of, 108–9
fieldwork on, 114–15, 116
food transportation, 126
Indian accounts of, 111
labor and social organization in
construction of, 247–48
landscaping and, 246–48
linearity of, 107
mapping of, 118
outliers and, 118–20, 228–30
parallel segments, 122
photointerpretation of, 118
pine log transportation, 110, 116,
151, 237
ramps, 107
religious integration and, 126–27
sets of roadways, 113, 119–20
signal towers, 122–25
stairways, 107, 111–12
surface preparation for, 117
symbolic aspects, 127, 200,
270–72
termination point at Pueblo Alto,
113, 116–17
wall borders, 107
width of roads, 106–7
see also specific roads
Roberts, Frank H. H., Jr., 47, 79, 81,
132, 147
Rodriguez, Roberto, 278
Roney, John, 246–48
Roosevelt, Theodore, 42
Ruppert, Karl, 61
Sacred Space, coordinate system for,
18–19
Salmon Ruin outlier, 133–35, 156,
204–5, 261, 263, 305
Salmon Ruin Project, 134–35
sandstorms, 46

San Ildefonso pueblo, 20
San Juan County Museum Association, 134, 135
San Juan River, 275
San Juan Valley Archaeological Program, 134
Schelberg, John, 163
School of American Research, 64, 74, 81, 286
Scientific American, 279
Sebastian, Lynne, 286, 289–90, 302–3
security-oriented constructions, 54
Sekaquaptewa, Abbott, 190–92, 272
Sellers, D.K.B., 160
Shalako ceremony, 20
Shelley, Philip, 245–46
Shure, Stephen, 114
Sierra Club, 231
signal towers, 122–25
Simpson, James Hervey, 23–33, 35–36, 65, 164–65, 251
Sinclair, Rolf, 199, 200
sites, see archaeological sites
Skunk Springs outlier, 147, 182, 229–30
sky-watching:
    calendars and, 191–92, 199, 259
    Hopi practices, 190–92
    moon-watching, 191–92, 197, 221, 222, 259–69
    petroglyphs, use of, 198–99
    priests for, 189–90
    solstice demarcation, 192, 194–96
    star-watching, 191, 221
    sun-watching, 188–92, 194–96, 198–99, 259–69
    supernova, recording of, 200–202, 222
    Zuni practices, 190
Sliding Ruin, 77
Smithsonian Institution, 43–44, 248–49
Snake Dance, 20
Society for American Archaeology (SAA), 288–89
Sofaer, Anna, 199, 200, 259–60, 261, 264–67, 268–69, 298

solar collectors, 200
solstice demarcation, 192, 194–96
Solstice Project, 259, 260–65, 266, 268, 269, 298
Southeast Road, 119
South Road, 113, 119
Southwest Parks and Monuments Association, 231
Soyal (winter solstice ceremony), 191
Soyoko (ogre woman), 20
space, Anasazi concept of, 18–19
Spring House, 77
Spruce Tree House, 36, 77
Square Tower House, 36, 77
stabilization projects, 81
Stanford, Dennis, 87
star-watching, 191, 221
State Historic Preservation Division (New Mexico), 289
Stein, John, 123, 124, 138, 228–29, 246–47, 249, 250–56, 297, 298
Stephen, Alexander M., 191
Stevenson, Mathilde, 17
Sun Chief (Talayesva), 189
Sun Clan, 189
sun-watching, 188–92, 194–96, 198–99, 259–69
supernova, recording of, 200–202, 222
Sword Swallowers, 211

Talasemptewa (sun priest), 189, 190
Talayesva, Don, 189–90
Taylor, Howard, 245–46
Tewa people, 19
"Timber Harvesting Using Ground Stone Axes" (Kunkel), 241
Toll, Wolcott, 151, 297
Townsend, Lloyd, 252
tree-ring dating, 74–76, 215, 220–21, 231–46, 253, 255, 258, 270
"Trees, Chemistry, and Prehistory in the American Southwest" (Antweiler, Durand, Shelley and Taylor), 245–46

Truell, Marcia, 296–97
Tse Chizzi outlier, 247
Tsin Kletzin pueblo, 101, 261, 263–64
Turner, Christy G., II, 274–75, 279,
    280, 281
Turner, Jacqueline A., 274, 280, 281
turquoise beads, 71, 217
    in burial sites, 40, 160, 161, 162,
        167, 168
    Judd's discovery of, 52–53
turquoise processing, 182–83, 185

Van Dyke, Ruth, 293
Village of Great Kivas, 132–33
Vivian, R. Gordon, 16, 64, 71, 72, 81,
    83, 100, 112, 163
Vivian, R. Gwinn, 16, 100–101, 103,
    112–13, 126, 127

Ware, John, 117
warfare and violence, 274–82
Warren, R. L., 237
Washington, John M., 23
water control systems, 97–98
    canals, 101–2
    continuous systems, 104
    dams, 101
    drainage areas, 100–101
    erosion control through, 99
    floodwater method, 51
    north and south systems, 100
    rainfall patterns and, 98
    runoff, diversion of, 103
    social system and, 104
    storage sites, 182

West Road, 113, 119
Wetherill, Marietta Palmer, 40, 112,
    163
Wetherill, Richard, 36–42, 160, 163
Wheeler Survey, 109
Whirlwind House outlier, 147
White, Tim D., 279, 281
White House Ruin, 77
Wijiji, 222, 244, 265, 269, 297
    construction of, 177
    discovery of, 29
    masonry of, 35
    sun-watching station, 192
Wills, Wirt, 297
Windes, Thomas, 124–25, 155–59,
    214–15, 220–21, 222, 228–47,
    249, 251, 253, 254, 255, 257,
    275, 289, 296, 297–98, 299
Witter, Dan, 87
"Wood Production in Chacoan Society"
    (Windes and McKenna), 221
Wortman, Jacob L., 39
Wuwuchim (initiation ceremony),
    20–21

Zuni people, 171, 239
    Chaco, ties to, 210–12
    "child presented to the sun" ritual,
        17–18
    nature, unity with, 19
    Navajos, relations with, 46
    rain invocation prayers, 96–97
    Shalako ceremony, 20
    sky-watching practices, 190
    space, concept of, 19